IV. SYSTEMS

OPEN SYSTEM (OS)
Greater Openness,
Creativity, Autonomy
and Initiative

OPEN SYSTEM AND CLOSED SYSTEM

The Management Process in
 Business Organizations
 Educational Institutions
 Government Agencies
 Health–Care Organizations
 Military

CLOSED SYSTEM (CS)
Greater Routinization,
Less Flexibility,
Certainty

$13.15

FUNDAMENTALS OF MANAGEMENT
Functions, Behavior, Models

Fundamentals of Management

Functions, Behavior, Models

JAMES H. DONNELLY, JR.
Professor of Business Administration
University of Kentucky

JAMES L. GIBSON
Professor of Business Administration
University of Kentucky

JOHN M. IVANCEVICH
Professor of Organizational Behavior and Management
University of Houston

Revised Edition   1975

BUSINESS PUBLICATIONS, INC.   Dallas, Texas   75224
Irwin-Dorsey International   London, England   WC2H 9NJ
Irwin-Dorsey Limited   Georgetown, Ontario   L7G 4B3

Revised Edition

First Printing, February 1975
Second Printing, August 1975

ISBN 0-256-01689-5
Library of Congress Catalog Card No. 74–18714
Printed in the United States of America

Preface

The purpose of this revised edition remains the same as its predecessor, that is, to prepare students for managerial careers. More particularly, the concepts, theories, and analytical tools which comprise the discussion were selected for their usefulness to *future managers*. To achieve this end, the authors had to make difficult decisions regarding materials to be included. Accordingly, we selected material from the current literature which we believe will make lasting contributions to the practice of management.

The basic organization of the book has not been altered. Our belief remains strong that an introductory management course at either the undergraduate or graduate level should be structured around the contributions of three major schools of management thought in the context of the functions of management. Accordingly the text presents the contributions of the *Classical School*, the *Behavioral School*, and the *Management Science School* within the framework of the *planning, organizing*, and *controlling* functions. We believe that the theories and concepts found in each of these schools contribute positively to the total body of knowledge that comprises contemporary management thought.

The often used practice of using one school as a "strawman" in promoting another hinders the evolution of a science of management. The style and content of the book, however, does not preclude being critical about some of the theories, concepts, and models found in the various schools. If managers are to cope effectively with the changes occurring in their environments, they must have an understanding of the lasting

v

contributions of each of the schools. Hopefully, this book will show that the three schools of management are mutually supportive and not separate approaches.

This book is certainly not intended to be the "only way" that management knowledge can be classified. Rather, it is designed to show that a contemporary and realistic manager can benefit by integrating the approaches offered by the three schools of management. The manager who is able to use theories, concepts, and models from each of the three schools is designated as a reality-centered manager.

Like the first edition, this book is organized into four major parts, plus an opening chapter that serves as a concise introduction to the field. A significant addition to the revision is the inclusion of 16 incidents which we have titled "Practical Exercises." Each exercise stresses the "practical nature" of the material covered in the chapter by allowing the student to work through specific situations and decision problems. *Each and every incident* is essentially true and based upon the authors' consulting, training, and personal job experiences. The incidents are set in a variety of different types and sizes of organizations, and include problems of women and minorities and all levels of management. They were selected from a larger number which were classroom tested at the University of Kentucky and the University of Houston. The ones included in the revision received positive student response because of their relevance and ability to stimulate thinking about issues covered in the chapters.

The first section, "The Classical School of Management," has been revised in a substantial way, primarily by the reduction of some historical information and by combining Chapters 2 and 3 into a single chapter. The result is a discussion that is tighter and more congruent with the introductory chapters to the Behavioral and the Management Science Schools. The most significant change throughout this section was to make the material more relevant. An attempt was made to eliminate the possibility of any suggestion that the Classical School is simply a historical development in the management literature. The six exercises included in this section require students to use the contributions of the Classical School in actual settings. Finally, the framework of planning, organizing, and controlling as the basic management functions creates the thread of continuity that is woven into the following two sections.

Part Two presents "The Behavioral School of Management." Chapters 6–11 focus upon such areas as the behavioral sciences in general, motivation, work groups, leadership, organizational design, and organizational change and development. The authors decided to arrange this section in such a manner that "people factors" (motivation, for example) are discussed before organizational design. Some instructors may wish to begin with organizational design so that a macro view is provided first. Both approaches have merit and it is possible to realign the chapters in Part

Two to meet the particular teaching approach of the instructor. Ten exercises are included in this section which require the student to use the various contributions of the Behavioral School. Finally, introductory discussions of expectancy theory of motivation and contingency theory of organization design have been included in relevant chapters.

Much work has been done on Part Three, "The Management Science School," to bring it more in line with the needs of both students and instructors. The recommendations of adopters and nonadopters have been carefully considered and many have been used in this part of the book. First, it is shorter in this edition, with five chapters, one of which is the introductory chapter. Second, there is a great deal more discussion and less use of mathematical symbols and notation. For example, the algebraic solution to the linear programming problem is "set-up" but the two pages of mathematical manipulations to solve it have been eliminated since the solution is the same as the graphical method which is the only one discussed in detail. Also, the material in the Network Models on "computing the probability of achieving the project completion date" has been placed in a separate Appendix at the end of the book. A significant change in this section is that each of the chapters discussing management science models is now separated into two distinct parts. The first part of each chapter has been expanded and is completely narrative, discussing the nature of the model, its uses, advantages and disadvantages. The second part focuses on "Application" and contains an illustrative problem. What this means is that the instructor can now discuss each model and, depending upon the needs of his course, decide whether to spend time on the "Application" section.

Finally, the last chapter has been improved and expanded. The integration of the three schools of management has been reworked and a new diagram developed. A new section, "Management and the Changing Social Environment, has been added.

Numerous other changes and improvements have been made which need not be mentioned here, but taken in total they will, we hope, make this revision better organized and more relevant for the student and a better teaching aid for the instructor. While the book is not lengthy it is still doubtful that it can be used in its entirety, including each incident and management science application, in one semester. Sections of the book can be utilized, depending upon the orientation of the instructor, the objectives of the course, and the role of the introductory course in the curriculum. Some instructors will undoubtedly wish to utilize each "practical exercise" in Parts Two and Three and cover only the narrative parts of Part Four. Others will wish to spend more time on the "Application" sections in Part Four. The book has been developed with these multiple purposes in mind.

The authors are extremely grateful to the adopters of the first edition who provided many invaluable suggestions for this revision. Special thanks are also due those who read and commented on the revised manuscript: John Mee, Indiana University; M. Gene Newport, University of Alabama at Birmingham; A. Thomas Hollingsworth, University of South Carolina; Jan Muczyk, Cleveland State University; and Sonya Brett, Macomb County Community College.

We also wish to acknowledge William Ecton, Acting Dean of the College of Business and Economics at the University of Kentucky, for providing an atmosphere of positive support for our efforts. The typists who were an invaluable help in completing the manuscript were Patricia Scott, Teresa D'Arcy, Mary D. Varney, Kathleen Maur, Mary Heintze, and Joanne Fisher.

January 1975   JAMES H. DONNELLY, JR.
                                                    JAMES L. GIBSON
                                                    JOHN M. IVANCEVICH

Contents

Decision-Making Process: Certainty. Decision-Making Process: Risk. Decision-Making Process: Uncertainty. Summary.

Introduction. The Economic and Accounting Influence: *Fixed Costs. Variable Costs. Total Revenue. Marginal Costs and Marginal Revenues.* The Break-Even Model. Applications of the Break-Even Model: *Sales Problem. Distribution Problem. The Break-Even Model and Decision Theory.* Limitations of the Break-Even Model. The Inventory Model: *The Inventory Decision. Cost Factors in Inventory Control. Trial-and-Error Methodology. The EOQ Model.* Limitations of Inventory Control Models.

Introduction: *What is a Linear Programming Model?* Management's Use of Linear Programming: *The Value of Linear Programming. Some Specific Areas of Application.* An Application of Linear Programming: A Product-Mix Problem. The Graphical Method: *Finding the Optimal Solution.* The Algebraic Method. The Simplex Method. Summary.

Introduction. Network Models (PERT): *Fundamentals of PERT. Estimating Activity Time Requirements. Some Applications of PERT. The Value of Network Models. PERT and People. Other Popular Network Models (CPM and PERT/Cost).* An Application of PERT: Product Development: *Calculation of Earliest Expected Date. The Critical Path. Latest Allowable Date. Slack Time. PERT and Uncertainty.* Summary.

Introduction. Reality-Centered Managing. Integrating the Three Schools of Management: *A Graphical Representation. The Contemporary Manager.* Management and the Changing Social Environment: *Business Organizations and Social Responsibility. The Manager's Dilemma. The Future.* Information Technology and Organization Design. Management and the International Environment: Comparative Management. Introducing the External Environment. Summary.

Introduction

The Field of Management

1 The Field of Management

INTRODUCTION

Important work in our society is done by men and women who have such formal titles as president, executive, governor, administrator, chairman, dean, director, commissioner, foreman, superintendent, and officer. Less formal titles include "boss," "whip," and other, more imaginative and less flattering, ones. These people work in business firms, hospitals, colleges and universities, government and politics, voluntary associations, fraternities and sororities. These people are separated by distance, life style, and background, but are bound together by at least one commonality: They all engage in the practice of management. They each face situations and make decisions which differ along some important dimensions, but which are similar along other, equally important, dimensions. No doubt, a governor makes decisions which touch the lives of many more people than does a college president; and the chief executive of a major publishing firm commands more resources than does a production foreman. But despite these differences, a broad base of commonality exists.

The pervasiveness of the practice of management is widely recognized. Joseph McGuire states: "People who don't manage are either too young, too old, or are found in institutions for the incompetent."[1]

---

[1] Joseph W. McGuire, "Management and Method," in Joseph W. McGuire, ed., *Contemporary Management: Issues and Viewpoints* (Englewood Cliffs, N.J.: Prentice-Hall, Inc., 1974), p. 1.

An overstatement? We think not. If we consider the terms "management" and "manage" in a broad sense, then housewives "manage" their households, school children "manage" their allowances, and we all "manage" our time! These common usages of the terms reflect the practical fact that we all must engage in activities which are intended to allocate scarce means—whether our own or someone else's time, money, energy, or machines—toward numerous, competing, and insatiable ends. The student and housewife share this common problem—neither has enough of anything to accomplish everything. Each of these persons must make choices.

Since nearly everyone manages something, management can be viewed in an all-embracing context. However, this book will concentrate on the process of management as it relates only to a particular, though widespread, instance. We will develop our discussion of management as it arises when the scarce means include *the energies of other people.* For this book, management refers to *activities undertaken by one or more persons in order to coordinate the activities of others in the pursuit of ends which could not be achieved by any one person.* Heads of state, executives, administrators, commissioners, directors, foremen, office managers, superintendents, mayors, deans, and academic department chairmen all share the common problem of having to depend upon others to get the work done. Therefore, they all practice management as it is defined here.

Purpose of the Book

The purpose of this book is to prepare students for management careers by presenting those concepts and tools that we believe will be useful to the manager *in the future.* Our problem was, "What can we do in the present to prepare future managers for the future?" The result has been a book organized around the idea of what we believe tomorrow's managers should know. It was necessary for the authors to make decisions concerning the selection of material to be included. The authors' choice was based primarily upon the criterion of "general acceptability." Those topics are included which are regarded by most management scholars and practitioners as constituting the fundamentals of the field.

Accordingly the materials presented here include a variety of theories and opinions which attempt to describe what managers do and should do to be effective. Scholarly research and practical experience are the major sources which we have drawn upon in developing this presentation. Our belief is that one who aspires to become a manager can begin by reading, studying, and evaluating the fundamental concepts and tools of management.

Why Study Management?

Our definition of management highlights the *importance* and the *content* of management as a field of study. The *importance* of management is based upon the fact that modern society has developed through the creation of specialized institutions and organizations which provide the goods and services it desires. Moreover, these institutions are guided and directed by the decisions of one or more persons who are designated "managers." It is they who allocate scarce resources to alternative and competing ends. Managers, through their skill and judgment, determine the means-ends relationships; they have the authority (as granted by society) and the responsibility (as accepted by them) to build or destroy cities, to wage peace or war, to purify or pollute the environment. They establish the conditions for the provision of jobs, incomes, products, services, protection, health care, and knowledge. It is difficult to identify anyone in an advanced society who is neither a manager nor subject to the decisions of a manager.[2]

Our definition of management also directs attention to the *content* of the field. The formal study and systematic practice of management focuses on the nature of group effort, various forms of coordination, and the manner of setting, ordering, and measuring goals. The process of management is required whenever two or more persons combine their efforts and resources to accomplish a goal which neither can accomplish by acting alone. The necessity for coordination follows from the fact that the actions of group participants constitute parts of a total task. If one person acts alone to accomplish a task, no coordination is required, but once that person allocates a part of the task to others, the individual efforts must be coordinated in some manner.

To provide the background for understanding some basic management concepts, let us examine how the management process develops in the context of a business organization. In order to present management in a historical context, we will also briefly describe its evolution, with particular attention to the development of the literature which marked the early beginnings of the formal study of management.

THE EVOLUTION OF MANAGEMENT IN THE BUSINESS ORGANIZATION

As a business organization increases in size and complexity, the managerial process adapts by becoming more specialized. Most students are aware of the various modifying adjectives preceding the noun *management:* top management, middle management, first-line manage-

---

[2] Robert Presthus, *The Organizational Society* (New York: Alfred A. Knopf, Inc., 1962).

FIGURE 1–1

No Specialization of the Management Process

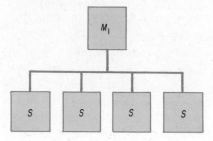

ment, general management, personnel management, production management, marketing management, and financial management. The history of most long-lived firms can be understood as a process by which the management has, in successive steps, moved from one manager with many subordinates to many managers with many subordinates.

The one-manager–many-subordinate firm is depicted in Figure 1–1. The manager, M_1, performs all the tasks necessary to coordinate the work of the subordinates, S's, toward the goals of the firm. If the firm is successful so that a larger volume of resources is available for allocation to more goals—more products, wider markets—the manager is confronted with the imperative of specialization. He may decide to specialize by assigning certain tasks, such as the marketing of the product, to another person (Figure 1–2), or may decide to assign the task of supervising subordinates to another person while continuing to be concerned with the marketing task (Figure 1–3). Whatever the decision, whether *hori-*

FIGURE 1–2

Horizontal Specialization of the Management Process

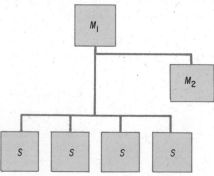

FIGURE 1–3

**Vertical Specialization of the
Management Process**

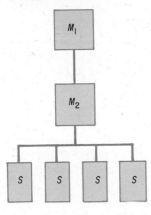

zontal specialization in the first or *vertical specialization* in the second
case, the managerial process is now shared, specialized, and more complex.

As the managerial structure of an organization evolves to a high degree of specialization, relationships among the members become more
complex. In Figure 1–4, it is clear that managers are concerned not only
with coordinating the efforts of groups (subordinates), but that they are
the object of coordinative efforts by *their* manager as well. It is also apparent that when the managerial process has been divided, the goals
must be divided; that is, each subtask of management must be accompanied by a subgoal.

FIGURE 1–4

Horizontal and Vertical Specialization of the Managerial Process

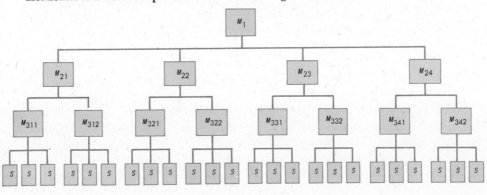

Vertical Specialization

The concept of specialized managerial tasks along the vertical dimension can be seen in Figure 1–4. The first digit of the subscript associated with each M refers to the position of that M in the scalar chain, that is, the chain of command and accountability. The resultant system of tasks in graded order is the *hierarchy*. Accordingly, the scalar chain is $M_1 \rightarrow M_{2x} \rightarrow M_{3xx}$. The second and third digits of the subscripts refer to horizontal specialization and are explained later.

In modern business parlance, M_1 is termed top management; M_{2x} are middle managers, and M_{3xx} are first-line managers, often referred to as supervisors or foremen. Each first-line manager derives authority from, and is accountable to, the appropriate middle manager who, in turn, derives authority from, and is accountable to, top management. Some obvious differences among the managerial tasks at each level can be noted.

First-line managers coordinate the work activity of others (S's), who are not themselves managers. The subordinates may be blue-collar workers, salesmen, clerks, or scientists, depending upon the particular tasks that the subunit must perform, for example, production, marketing, accounting, or research. Whatever the case, first-line managers coordinate the basic work of the organization according to plans and procedures provided by their superior, M_{2x}. They are in daily or near-daily contact with their subordinates. They are ordinarily assigned the task of first-line manager because of their ability to work with people—not only with their own subordinates but also with other first-line supervisors whose tasks are related to the tasks of their units. First-line supervisors in contemporary business firms engage in upward, downward, and lateral relationships. They communicate and interact with their own manager, with their subordinates, and with other first-line managers. The effectiveness of their coordinative efforts will depend as much, if not more, upon their communication skills as upon their technical ability.

Middle managers, unlike first-line managers, coordinate the activity of other managers; yet, like first-line managers, they are subject to the coordinative efforts of a superior. The middle manager coordinates the activity of a subunit of the firm. As shown in the following section, the important characteristics of middle managers are described in terms of horizontal specialization.

Top management of a business firm coordinates the activity of the entire organization through the immediate subordinates. Unlike other managers, the top manager is accountable to no other manager, but instead to the owners of the resources utilized in the business. The form of the enterprise determines the exact manner in which this accountability is exercised. If the enterprise is a corporation, top management reports to the board of directors, which represents the stockholders; top management will report to the partners if it is a partnership; and to the proprietor, and perhaps to himself, if it is a proprietorship. Whatever the business form, society grants ultimate authority to the owners of property (resources) utilized in the firm.

The vertical dimension of management is defined, then, as the process by which the right to act and to use resources within specified limits (authority) is delegated downward. As this is effectuated in practice, managers can be described in terms of the extent and limits of authority at their disposal. The delegation of authority also determines differences in the on-job relationships among managers at the same level, that is horizontal specialization.

Horizontal Specialization

The completion of a task requires the completion of a sequence of interrelated activities. As the sequence of activities is identified, and as the responsibility for completing each is assigned to a manager, the managerial process is horizontally specialized. Figure 1–4 illustrates horizontal specialization at two levels in the firm. The middle managers, M_{21}, M_{22}, M_{23}, and M_{24}, are responsible for the completion of major subtasks such as production, marketing, finance, and personnel. Each manager is at the same level in the hierarchy, as denoted by the first digit of the subscript, but each is responsible for completing a different part of the total objective, as denoted by the second digit of the subscript.

Similarly, the first-line managers are responsible for completing a subpart of the subpart. For example, M_{21}, the production manager, coordinates the activities of M_{311} and M_{312}, who may be the foreman of the fabrication department and the foreman of the finishing department. The successful completion of tasks assigned to the subordinates in these two departments, as coordinated by the foremen, results in the successful completion of the production manager's task. The manner in which the tasks are specialized horizontally is a problem of organizational design, as discussed in later chapters.

The managerial process in contemporary organizations is assigned to numerous persons in the firm who have had specialized training and competence to deal with the assigned task. Descriptive labels promote some degree of understanding of what these persons do and are expected to do. Thus the layman understands, partially, the assignment of production managers, marketing managers, and personnel managers. There is general understanding of the distinction between top management and first-line management. Yet the specific nature of each managerial task is idiosyncratic to the firm within which the task is performed, due to the diversity of business as a social institution and to the unique character and history of each individual firm.

THE EVOLUTION OF MANAGEMENT

The practice of management is as old as man's history. Throughout time, men have joined with others to accomplish a goal, first in families, later in tribes and other more sophisticated political units. Ancient people constructed pyramids, temples, and ships; they created systems of government, farming, commerce, and warfare. These social achievements were created through the use of management techniques. Professor Claude S. George, Jr. has provided an interesting survey of the management practices of Sumerian temple priests, Egyptian pharaohs, and other functionaries of ancient civilization.[3] He observes that management was quite widespread throughout these civilizations, and that the literature of the times refers to such managerial concepts as planning, staff assistance, division of labor, control, and leadership. But these societies made no effort to accumulate and synthesize knowledge of management practice; what knowledge did exist was passed along from generation to generation or was learned through experience.

Relatively sophisticated management practices emerged during the eras of the Greek and Roman empires. These ancient city-states created organizations to carry on political, commercial, and military activities. As Professor George reports,[4] the Greeks recognized the relationship between efficiency in manual work and standard motions. Through the use of musical accompaniment, the Greeks introduced tempo and rhythm into the work place. The significant writings on the subject were those of Plato, Socrates, Aristotle, Xenophon, and a host of other philosophers. These insightful thinkers espoused principles of logic, economics, government, and science which are the foundations of Western civilization. Roman thinkers also contributed to this early management literature as they documented and analyzed the problems of the Roman Republic and, later, the Roman Empire.

The administration of the far-flung Roman Empire required the application of managerial concepts. As James D. Mooney stated in his analysis of the historical development of management, "The real secret of the greatness of the Romans was their genius for organization."[5] Mooney's opinion is based upon his investigation of the Romans' use of

---

[3] Claude S. George, Jr., *The History of Management Thought* (Englewood Cliffs, N.J.: Prentice-Hall, Inc., 1968), pp. 3–26.

[4] Ibid., p. 15.

[5] James D. Mooney, *The Principles of Organization* (New York: Harper and Brothers, 1939), p. 63.

certain principles of organization to coordinate the diverse activities of the Empire. These principles stress the attainment of effective and efficient administration. Whether the fall of the Roman Empire was due to the eventual neglect of these principles is for the historian to decide.

The feudal system which evolved during the Medieval Period was an early experiment in decentralized government organization, and it is all the more interesting when compared to the centralized systems of Greece and Rome. The feudal system introduced the usual problems associated with the management of a decentralized organization, including delegation of authority, decision making, and accountability. The tenor of the times was not conducive to the literary arts; consequently, there is little written word to report the lessons in management to be learned from the feudal era. Niccolò Machiavelli did, of course, provide a treatise on the appropriate use of power. It is perhaps unfortunate that his ideas have been associated with despotism and the cynical use of power when, in fact, he may have provided the first codification of basic managerial thought.

The feudal system ultimately gave way to a recentralization of authority through mercantilism and, eventually, the industrial revolution. With the rise of the factory system and mass production, a need to rationalize the management process soon arose. Most students are well aware of the antecedents to modern manufacturing methods and institutions. It is sufficient to recall that the important developments were both technical and political. The development of steam power and the concept of interchangeable parts combined with a political philosophy of laissez-faire were the active ingredients of the industrialization of Western civilization. In an industrial society the management of business firms, *per se*, became the subject of specific analysis. It was during this period that practitioners began to evaluate the potential application of scientific thinking to the management process. They also began to share insights through common associations and writings. Thus, even though the practice of management was present throughout history, the literature of management is barely 200 years old, with the most significant writings appearing in the last 70 years. Historical hindsight permits us to classify this literature on the basis of its primary emphasis.

THREE SCHOOLS OF MANAGEMENT THOUGHT

The literature of management ranges over a wide variety of topics and has been produced by a wide variety of writers. The early writers were practitioners who described their own experiences, from which they generalized to broad principles. They were guided by pragmatic considerations; they wanted to share with others those practices which worked for them. A great deal of what is known about management comes from the autobiographies and memoirs of those who practiced management. On the other hand, there were other writers whose interest in management was (and is) solely scientific. Many social and behavioral scientists view the management of economic, political, military, and service institutions as an extremely important social phenomenon whose very existence justifies its study through scientific inquiry. As scientists using scientific methods, they make no value judgments regarding good or bad management practice; rather, their objective is to understand and to explain the practice of management.

Between the extremes of pragmatism and scientism there are a great number of other writers who have contributed to literature on management. Their professional identifications cover a wide spectrum of knowledge, including engineering, sociology, anthropology, psychology, economics, law, accounting, mathematics, political science, and philosophy. The different points of view represented by these disciplines have been the bases for numerous attempts to provide classification schemes. For example, Harold Koontz and Cyril O'Donnell identify seven schools of management thought: (1) the operational approach, (2) the empirical approach, (3) the human behavior approach, (4) the social system approach, (5) the decision theory approach, (6) the communications center approach, (7) and the mathematical approach.[6] Haynes and Massie label six approaches: (1) quantitative approaches, (2) managerial economics and managerial accounting, (3) universals of management, (4) scientific management, (5) human relations, and (6) behavioral sciences.[7] The student can get an intuitive grasp of the kinds of material and subject matter discussed in management literature from the labels which have been used.

Our purpose is not to complicate matters by proposing yet another classification scheme. However, we believe that the discussion of the field of management can proceed quite well by means of a classification scheme which identifies only three schools: the *Classical School,* the *Behavioral School,* and the *Management Science School.* We believe that the ideas and concepts found in *each* school contribute positively to the total body of knowledge which comprises modern management thought, and that a student of management need not, in fact should not, emphasize one school and ignore the others. All three are mutually supportive; each adds to the total store of management knowledge without detracting from the other two. Through these three schools we can see an evolution of what is known and what should be known about management. At the same time, we have not written a text on the evolution of manage-

---

[6] Harold Koontz and Cyril O'Donnell, *Principles of Management,* 5th ed. (New York: McGraw-Hill Book Co., 1972), p. 35.

[7] W. Warren Haynes and Joseph L. Massie, *Management,* 2d ed. (Englewood Cliffs, N.J.: Prentice-Hall, Inc., 1969), pp. 4–13.

ment thought, although the student of management should recognize and respect the fact that the field of management has historical origins and an extensive body of literature.

The *Classical School* of management is described in the literature which appeared primarily during the pre–World War II period. The writers of this era were seeking answers to quite basic questions. They were practitioners or scientists and engineers employed by business and government. At the most fundamental level these writers were concerned with questions of efficiency, that is, the maximization of output to input ratios. The technological insights of engineers were significant as business leaders sought to increase the productivity of workers. The efforts of these engineers led to the development of an extensive body of knowledge regarding plant and machinery design, work methods, materials flow, and the like. The basic orientation of this body of knowledge which was later termed "scientific management," was the application of scientific methods of inquiry to the problems of work and work management. Therefore the use of science to solve pragmatic problems placed management in the same category with engineering and medicine.

The emergence of the Classical School coincided with the creation of large, complex organizations. Persons who had practiced management within these organizations recognized that the management of organizations can be quite different from the management of work. Literature appeared which sought to explain management in terms of the functions of managers at every level of an organization. Thus the classical writers defined management as the process of coordinating group effort toward group goals. This is the definition used in this textbook. Moreover, through deductive reasoning the classicists identified (1) the *functions* which are necessary for coordination, namely, *planning, organizing,* and *controlling;* and (2) the *principles* of effective managerial action. The culmination of the Classical School is an elaborate conceptual framework which relates these three basic functions to logically identified subfunctions. The subsequent writers then added to and modified the work of the classicists.

The *Behavioral School* has used the concepts of psychology, sociology, anthropology, and other behavioral sciences to extend our knowledge of human behavior in the work environment. The classical writers did not provide in-depth insights into human behavior. This was not due to their ignorance of the importance of the human element, but to their lack of sophisticated training. The writers of the Behavioral School have brought their research skills to bear on the *organizing* and *controlling* functions, beginning with the Hawthorne Studies of the 1920s and continuing with vigorous attempts to evaluate, scientifically, the practical insights of the Classical School.

The literature which we classify as belonging to the Behavioral School has two common characteristics. First, the focal point of the school is human behavior, managerial as well as nonmanagerial, in the context of work organizations. Secondly, the method of inquiry is essentially the scientific method, with emphasis on the discovery of causal relationships. The findings of behavioral research can be blended with the insights of the Classical School to extend our understanding of the fundamentals of management.

The *Management Science School* in one sense is a modern version of scientific management. Its essential feature is sophistication in the use of mathematics and statistics to aid in resolving the operational problems of *planning* and *controlling*. The literature which we include in the Management Science School, then, focuses on technical (rather than behavioral) problems through the construction of quantitative techniques. The development of the computer has permitted analyses that were previously not possible because of their complexity. The computer has been of tremendous value to the growing importance of the Management Science School.

Our classification of management literature suggests the two main thrusts of management theory and practice since the Classical School. On the one hand there has been emphasis on behavioral problems; on the other hand, but coincidentally, there has been emphasis on technical problems. Rather than competing with the Classical School, this two-pronged attack is a natural extension of the earlier work.

CONTEMPORARY MANAGEMENT

The most powerful theoretical and practical insights into the nature and problems of management take into account the entire range of knowledge. The contemporary manager operates in an environment that is too complicated for easy, one-sided analyses. The manager must be able to blend the concepts, techniques, and models from each of the three schools. There are no easy solutions to managerial problems. To select naively the approach of one of the schools to the exclusion of the others can only compound the problems. The modern manager faces diverse and often conflicting demands. The sources of these demands are the many groups which have vested interests in any organization and include employees, customers, suppliers, creditors, owners, clients, patients, students, government officials, and the public at large. The demands of all these groups are seldom, if ever, completely satisfied by any management decision, a fact which results in the creation of dilemmas, situations requiring a choice between alternatives each of which may have unfavorable consequences. In recognition of this fact, managers must often accept "second-best" solutions which rely upon knowledge from all three schools.

Contemporary society is the product of many complex and interrelated forces. No doubt the basic force has been the ability of man to convert scientific discoveries to practical use. Technological innovations in production, distribution, and communication processes have wrought irrevocable changes. The concommitant changes in the nature and composition of society, including organizations and the concentration of power, are likewise irrevocable, at least in the short run. This means that managers, as the wielders of power, are called upon to answer to the grantors of that power.

In a traditional society consisting of many small and relatively insignificant firms, the legitimate function of business was to seek a profit through the production of goods and services. The rules of the game were only loosely drawn and seldom given force of law. The marketplace was counted on to provide the brake on the use of power. *Laissez-faire* and *caveat emptor* expressed the prevailing ideology of the times. Society granted considerable freedom to business in exchange for the creation of economic well-being. But, at the turn of the 20th century, the view of society as reflected by its laws was changing.

In the 1930s American society could be described more accurately in terms of large interdependent units than in terms of small independent units. Large firms confronted large unions, with the public interest represented by a large and expanding federal government. The "Great Depression" of the 1930s was a strong indication that all was not right with the way America did business. The stage was set for the enactment of reform and regulatory legislation that would permanently affect the function of the business manager.

The modern manager recognizes full well the legitimate necessity for complying with federal, state, and local legislation designed to regulate the use of economic power. The list of laws and acts will not be catalogued here. At a more subtle level, the manager is now being called upon to respond to a host of demands whose legitimacy is not so well established either in law or in practice. These demands find expression in the nebulous and ill-defined phrase, "management's social responsibilities."

That society should have expectations for business that go beyond the provision of goods and services within the framework of legal constraints reflects the ambivalence of society toward business. On the one hand it expects the traditional business function; yet it also desires such non-traditional functions as the location of plants in ghettos and in depressed regions. It desires training programs for the hard-core unemployed, yet asks for restraint on price increases in the face of inflation. In the midst of these developments, management must act or not act without the benefit of a clear-cut framework of values.

The resolution of the dilemmas which society imposes will ultimately depend upon managers' value systems. As they confront the conflicting demands in situations where some freedom of choice exists, their system of values will attach relative weights to these demands. That they will err in the minds of some is inevitable; that they must act is likewise inevitable.

SUMMARY AND INTRODUCTION

Thus far we have made a number of points concerning the field of management.

1. We have provided a basis for the importance of management to the workings of society: Society tends to organize its resources through specialized institutions.
2. The process of organizing necessitates some means for coordinating the organization's (group's) activities. This coordinating process is termed management.
3. The management process tends to become specialized as the organization becomes larger and more complex.
4. The literature of management has evolved as the importance of management as a field of study and analysis became more widely accepted.
5. A variety of perspectives and emphases has characterized management literature. We can introduce some clarity by identifying three mutually supportive schools—the Classical, Behavioral and Management Science Schools.
6. Finally, contemporary managers cannot ignore the contributions of any of the three schools if they are to deal effectively with their environment.

The identification of the three schools and our belief that the modern manager must recognize the contribution of each one have dictated the arrangement of subsequent materials in this text. Specifically, we have grouped the chapters in three parts, as follows: Chapters 2 through 5 comprise our discussion of the Classical School. In these chapters we present the ideas of the classical writers, with some discussion of the techniques and methods which implemented these ideas. Consistent with our understanding of the Classical School we suggest that classical management theory is the combination of concepts of (1) those who analyzed the management of work and (2) those who analyzed the management of organizations (Chapter 2). We then discuss the three management functions—planning (Chapter 3), organizing (Chapter 4), and controlling (Chapter 5). These three chapters stress the contributions of the Classical School, but also include descriptions of the more important techniques which implement the functions.

The Behavioral School concepts are presented in Chapters 6 through 11. An overview and introduction (Chapter 6) precedes the discussion of motivation (Chapter 7), work groups (Chapter 8), leadership (Chapter 9), organizational design (Chapter 10), and organizational change and development (Chapter 11). We believe that this outline of the school reflects the central concerns of its contributors. Throughout these chapters, the relationships between the classical and behavioral concepts are noted, with special attention to instances where the Behavioral School fills certain voids in the Classical School.

The next five chapters (12 through 16), present the basic materials of the Management Science School. An introductory chapter (Chapter 12) is followed by decision theory (Chapter 13), break-even and inventory models (Chapter 14), linear programming (Chapter 15), and, finally, network models (Chapter 16). We again make explicit the manner in which the Management Science School builds upon the Classical School. Our final chapter attempts to provide the reader with an approach to management which considers the contributions of each of the three schools and also suggests some future directions of management thought and practice.

DISCUSSION AND REVIEW QUESTIONS

1. Explain why management is required to coordinate group effort.
2. What is the significance of the fact that contemporary America is "an organizational society"?
3. Compare your school and a business firm that you know about with respect to the extent of horizontal specialization of management.
4. What are some of the problems you would anticipate as middle managers seek to coordinate the work of their units with the work of other units?
5. Evaluate the concept of management as "getting things done through people."
6. What might be the relevant factors bearing on a decision whether management should be horizontally or vertically specialized?
7. What, in your opinion, are society's legitimate demands of business firms?
8. What are the features of a value system which suggests that a manager should not fire an elderly employee with 20 years of service but who is no longer able to do his job?
9. What do you understand by the phrase "social responsibilities of management"?
10. What is meant by the statement: "Management is an applied science"?

ADDITIONAL REFERENCES

Cheit, E. F., ed. *The Business Establishment.* New York: John Wiley and Sons, Inc., 1964.

Cole, A. H. *Business Enterprise and Its Setting.* Cambridge, Mass.: Harvard University Press, 1959.

Drucker, P. *Management: Tasks, Responsibilities, Practices.* New York: Harper and Row, 1974.

Koontz, H. *Toward a Unified Theory of Management.* New York: McGraw-Hill Book Company, 1964.

Linowes, D. F. *Strategies for Survival.* New York: American Management Association, 1973.

McGregor, D. M. *The Professional Manager.* New York: McGraw-Hill Book Company, 1967.

Means, G. *The Corporate Revolution in America.* New York: Crowell-Collier Press, 1962.

Petit, T. *The Moral Crisis in Management.* New York: McGraw-Hill Book Company, 1967.

Stewart, R. *Managers and Their Jobs.* London: Macmillan and Company, 1967.

Walton, C. C. *Ethos and the Executive.* Englewood Cliffs, N.J.: Prentice-Hall, Inc., 1969.

SELECTED MANAGEMENT AND RELATED PERIODICALS

Academy of Management Journal
Academy of Management Review
Administrative Management
Administrative Science Quarterly
Advanced Management Journal
Business Management
California Management Review
Fortune
Harvard Business Review
Industrial and Labor Relations Review
Industrial Engineering
Industrial Management Review
Journal of Applied Behavioral Science
Journal of Applied Psychology
Journal of Business

Journal of Management Studies
Management of Personnel Quarterly
Management International Review
Management Review
Management Science
Organizational Behavior and Human Performance
Personnel
Personnel Journal
Personnel Psychology
Training and Development Journal

part one

The Classical School

$\mathscr{2}$ Foundations of the Classical School

INTRODUCTION

The development of any field of study requires pioneers who pursue answers to basic questions which define the field and its relationship to other fields. The literature produced by these efforts is typically termed "classical theory." The chapters which follow in this section concisely present the work of the classical writers in the field of management. The authors' intent is to provide the student with the perspective to understand contemporary management.

Classical management theory is a significant part of the contemporary theories in this field since it provides some important insights into the nature and scope of management. Certainly time and circumstances have changed since the pioneers first undertook their analysis, yet the essence of their work has endured. Contributions to management theory by behavioral scientists and management scientists during the past 40 years are compatible with the work of their predecessors. The classical theorists left many questions unanswered, but the student must not lose sight of the significant fact that they provided answers to many fundamental management questions.

Classical writers defined management in terms of the functions of a manager. Accordingly, the essential nature of management lies in the unique *functions* of managers. These *functions* should be the focus of the field. At the same time, the classical writers were interested in *prescriptive* management theory; that is, they sought to discover how managers *should* perform their functions. This prescriptive approach is readily seen in the area of scientific management where management's function is to discover the "one best way" to do manual tasks. This orientation toward the one best way is also found in the classicists' discussion of organization theory. According to their analyses, there is one form of organization that is appropriate for the firm, and one of the management functions is to discover that form.

These writers identified the *management process* which consists of three primary functions, namely, *planning, organizing,* and *controlling.* Each of these three can be broken down into smaller and smaller subfunctions. The classical analysis synthesizes the subfunctions and produces a grand scheme which describes the managerial process in detail.

The planning, organizing, and controlling functions can be understood by using an analogy from sailing. The captain of a sailing craft predetermines the ship's destination. He must also allow for any contingencies that will affect the success of the voyage—for example, weather and water conditions. In anticipation of the future the captain must prepare policies that will guide the ship through the waters. As part of, but separable from, the *planning* function, the captain must predetermine the duties of each member of the ship's company to assure that the necessary tasks of sailing a ship are performed in the right manner at the right time; that is, the captain must *organize* the crew. Finally, the captain must assure that the ship's passage conforms to the predetermined plan; he must *control* the actual ongoing activities of the ship and the ship's company. The fact that this process and these three functions go on continually and without obvious beginning and ending points complicates one's ready understanding of their significance.

In this section of the book, we present the foundations of classical management theory. The remainder of this chapter describes the contributions of the scientific management approach, with emphasis on men and methods. We next combine the ideas of the scientific management approach with those of a group of men who dealt with the problems of *top management* (as distinct from *shop management* which was the

FIGURE 2–1

Primary Contributors to the Classical School

Classical School of Management

Scientific Management (*the management of work*)	*Classical Organization Theory* (*the management of organizations*)
F. W. Taylor (1856–1915)	H. Fayol (1841–1925)
Frank (1868–1924) Lillian (1878–1972) Gilbreth	J. D. Mooney (1884–1957)
H. L. Gantt (1861–1919)	L. Urwick (1891–)
H. E. Emerson (1853–1931)	C. I. Barnard (1886–1961)

focus of scientific management). In Chapters 3, 4, and 5 the basic management functions—planning, organizing, and controlling—are discussed.

This presentation of material is based upon the authors' belief that classical management theory is the product of two distinct, but compatible perspectives in the literature, as shown in Figure 2–1. The first is the perspective which focused on the management of work—*shop management*. This body of literature has been labeled "scientific management," and the label is widely recognized and accepted. The second perspective focused on the management of organizations—*the total entity*. There is no generally accepted label for this literature; we have chosen to label it "classical organization theory."[1] *Therefore, Classical management theory is the blend of scientific management and classical organization theory.*

SCIENTIFIC MANAGEMENT:
THE MANAGEMENT OF WORK

In modern manufacturing the first-level manager is concerned with the day-to-day routine of coordinating the work of specialized labor. Each specialized worker does a job according to a set of rules and procedures designed to assure its completion. The rules and procedures result from analysis of the technical and human requirements of the job and of its relationship to other jobs. The state of the art dealing with 'work-doing is now highly developed, but this was not so at the turn of the 20th century. The breakthrough occurred when a group of engineers became interested in the techniques of work.

The body of literature which emerged from the efforts of these engineers provides the basis for scientific management, the dominant theme of which is that work-doing and the overseeing of work-doing are processes which can be analyzed from a "scientific" point of view. The engineers believed that objective analyses of facts and data collected in experiments should reveal the best way to do the work. Their analyses focused on tasks performed at lower levels in the organization—shovelling, pig-iron handling, and sheet-metal cutting, for example—yet such tasks were crucial to the industrial development of America.

Scientific management was based upon a definite ideology and, as is true of all ideologies, contained implicit assumptions. The ideology, simply put, stated that the cause of industrial conflict was inefficient use of scarce resources.[2] The claimants of the economic pie were continually

---

[1] This designation is consistent with the usage in Daniel A. Wren, *The Evolution of Management Thought* (New York: The Ronald Press Company, 1972), pp. 463–64.

[2] For a discussion of the historical setting and ideology of scientific management, see Samuel Haber, *Efficiency and Uplift* (Chicago: University of Chicago Press, 1964).

in conflict because one claimant's share could be increased only at the expense of another's. For example, wages could increase only at the expense of profit. But such is the case only if the total size of the economic pie is fixed. If the entire supply of economic goods and services is increased through more efficient use of resources, then the shares of the claimants can increase without impinging upon one another.

The proponents of scientific management believed that the economic causes of labor-management disagreements could be eliminated by applying certain physiological and engineering principles to the jobs of blue-collar workers. Thus, at a time of serious social concern for economic growth and resource conservation, scientific management became an important social and economic doctrine. Contained within the doctrine were certain implicit assumptions about the human element. Specifically, scientific management adopted the assumption of classical economic theory that man is basically motivated by his desire for economic betterment. Classical economists believed man is perfectly rational in his choice of means to the end of economic betterment.[3] Thus it followed (according to scientific management) that if managers and workers are taught new methods of work doing which enhance their chances for economic well-being, they would adopt them.

The implementation of scientific management entailed the adoption of certain methods which would change the ways in which workers and managers had traditionally done their jobs. The major and lasting changes were to be in the ways in which workers had historically done manual work. The suggested changes in the manager's job were minor in comparison.

MAJOR CONTRIBUTORS TO SCIENTIFIC MANAGEMENT

To appreciate fully the importance of scientific management as a philosophy and practice, one must understand the major contributors and the era in which they developed their ideas. We will discuss only four contributors to the scientific management literature, as noted on Figure 2–1. Of these four, the ideas of Frederick W. Taylor will receive most of our attention, since his place in the history of management theory development is well established.

Frederick W. Taylor: Principles of Work Management

At the turn of the 20th century, business was expanding, new products and new markets were being created, but labor was in short supply. To offset labor shortages, two solutions were available: (1) substitute

---

[3] William F. Whyte, *Money and Motivation* (New York: Harper and Brothers, 1955), pp. 2–3; and James L. Gibson, "Organization Theory and the Nature of Man," *Academy of Management Journal*, vol. 9 (September 1966), pp. 233–45.

capital for labor or (2) use labor more efficiently. Both approaches reduce labor cost per unit of output and, ordinarily, the average cost. During the last quarter of the 19th century, considerable efforts were made to solve the problem of labor efficiency. Most notable was the work done by the members of the American Society of Mechanical Engineers (A.S.M.E.).

Frederick W. Taylor joined the A.S.M.E. in 1886 and used the organization as a sounding board for his ideas which had started to take shape while he was employed in various steel firms. It was at the Midvale Steel Company that he had observed the phenomenon of "soldiering," men producing far less than their capacities would permit. Taylor believed that this great waste was due to ignorance of what constituted a "fair day's work." There were no systematic studies to determine expected daily output per man (work standards), and the relationship between work standards and the wage system. Taylor's personal dislike for waste caused him to rebel at what he interpreted as inefficient management practice which was based largely on hunch, rule of thumb, conventional wisdom, and ignorance. Taylor believed that ignorance on the part of both management and labor accounted for the great waste of resources.

As a foreman at the Midvale Steel Company, Taylor began an analysis of lathe work. Rather than accept soldiering and ignorance, he began the process of fact gathering and objective analysis which was to be typical of his entire career.[4] He studied the work of an individual lathe worker to discover exactly what the worker did as he performed his task. He identified each element of the worker's job and measured every element that was susceptible to measurement. In short, he was seeking a science of metal cutting. His aim was to provide the craftsman with an objective standard which would define a "fair day's" work.

Taylor sought means for combining the interests of both management and labor to avoid the necessity for "sweat shop" management. He believed that the key to harmony was to discover the "one best way" to perform a task, determine the optimum daily pace of the task, train workers to do the task in the prescribed way and at the prescribed pace, and reward successful completion of the task by using an incentive wage system. Thus, if workers and managers know what is expected and know the positive consequences of achieving mutual expectations, a close harmony between management and labor should result, since the interests of both parties are satisfied: Cooperation should replace conflict.

Consequently, Taylor undertook a series of studies to determine work standards. In some cases, he dealt with physical factors of work. He found, for example, that the optimum weight of a shovel load is 22

---

[4] Lyndall Urwick, *The Golden Book of Management* (London: Newman Neame Ltd., 1956), pp. 72–79, outlines Taylor's career and personal life. Also see Lyndall Urwick and E. F. L. Brech, *The Making of Scientific Management* (London: Sir Isaac Pitman and Sons, 1951).

pounds and that there is an appropriate shape for each kind of shoveling job. In other instances, he and his associates dealt with the human factor of work. He trained a pig-iron handler to increase his tonnage loaded from $12\frac{1}{2}$ to $47\frac{1}{2}$ long tons per day.

As described by Taylor, there is a science of carrying which relates load weight, load time, and fatigue. The physiological soundness of Taylor's work is not an issue here. The important point is that his analysis of the task of lifting and carrying a 92-pound pig of iron up an inclined plane onto a flatcar suggested the existence of a science that could be used to improve the task. Accordingly, his "law of heavy laboring" states that for each given exertion of energy under load, there must be recuperative time. Taylor applied the "law" to pig-iron handling and believed that a man moving 92-pound pigs can be under load only 43 percent of the time and must rest the remainder of the time. By closely supervising the work of a specially selected pig-iron handler, Taylor and his colleagues produced a remarkable 300 percent increase in production, and the workman's average daily wage increased from $1.15 to $1.85. The method was then learned by a number of workmen, all of whom increased their daily production and their daily wage.

The pig-iron episode illustrates the four principles of "scientific management" which, according to Taylor, are:[5]

First: Develop a science for each element of a man's work which replaces the old rule of-thumb method.

Second: Scientifically select and then train, teach, and develop the workman, whereas in the past he chose his own work and trained himself as best he could.

Third: Heartily cooperate with the men so as to insure all of the work being done in accordance with the principles of the science which has been developed.

Fourth: There is almost an equal division of the work and the responsibility between the management and the workmen. The management takes over all work for which they are better fitted than the workmen, while in the past, almost all of the work and the greater part of the responsibility were thrown upon the men.

These principles urged managers to take a more systematic approach in performing their coordinative task. Specialization of labor cannot be left to the "invisible hand," as Adam Smith would have it. Rather, the management process requires that initiative be seized by managers to rationalize the process.

The principles define the basic operating characteristics of scientific management as Taylor proposed it. But there was another aspect of scientific management—the essence, according to Taylor. He stated in his testimony before a Special Committee of The House of Representatives that ". . . scientific management involves a complete mental revolution on the part of the working man . . . and it involves the equally complete mental revolution on the part of those on the management's side. . . ."[6] Taylor went on to explain that the mental revolution of which he spoke would shift the emphasis of both management and labor away from the division of economic values and toward increasing the size of the available values.[7] We referred to this earlier in the chapter as the distribution of the economic pie. Taylor viewed scientific management as holding the promise for uplifting the economic well-being of society. But he believed that there could be no scientific management without the mental revolution.

Taylor also proposed that management itself could become more efficient through specialization. In his idea of *functional foremanship,* for example, he proposed that there should be at least eight foremen supervising each worker. Four would be in the planning room (consonant with Taylor's notion that planning and executing are separate processes) concerned with production routing, methods, time and cost, and discipline, while four would be on the shop floor where they would deal with the pace and quality of output and maintenance of machinery. According to Taylor, the economies of specialization could be realized through application to management as well as to labor. However, functional foremanship was never widely adopted in industry.

In the final analysis, Taylor's lasting contributions to management are to be found in the way work is done at the shop level. His experiments with stopwatch studies and work methods stimulated his contemporaries to undertake similar studies in other work contexts. Two important contemporaries were Lillian and Frank Gilbreth.

The Gilbreths: Principles of Work Simplification

The Gilbreths, a husband-and-wife team, made significant contributions to the emerging knowledge of scientific management. They combined their talents to produce important breakthroughs in motion study and job simplification. An untrained but insightful engineer, Frank Gilbreth was an apprentice bricklayer in his first job. His observations of skilled bricklayers' motions convinced him that many of the body movements could be combined or eliminated so that the procedure would be simplified and production increased.

---

[6] Frederick W. Taylor, "Taylor's Testimony before the Special House Committee," ibid., p. 27.

[7] Ibid., p. 30.

Gilbreth's analysis of the sequence and path of basic movements enabled him to reduce the number of motions required to lay exterior brick from 18 to 4½. Craftsmen who used Gilbreth's method were able to increase their production by 200 percent. Economy in the use of human energy, combined with technological improvements such as an adjustable stand to eliminate stooping for the brick and a mortar of proper consistency to eliminate "tapping," resulted in a science of the ancient and honorable craft of masonry.[8] Gilbreth's work was quite compatible and consistent with that of Taylor's as each sought the elusive "one best way" to do a job.

To add precision to his analysis of fundamental hand and arm motions, Gilbreth invented a number of devices. The microchronometer is a clock with a sweep hand which is placed in the field of work being studied. Gilbreth would use a camera to record the work being done against the backdrop of the sweep hand. By such methods, he was able to identify not only the basic motions, but also the time required for each hand and arm movement. The result of his efforts was the identification of numerous distinct movements which he labeled "Therbligs" (Gilbreth spelled backward with transposition of one letter).

Henry L. Gantt: Principles of Work Scheduling

A close associate of Taylor at Midvale and Bethlehem Steel was a young graduate engineer, Henry L. Gantt. Like Taylor and the Gilbreths, Gantt dealt with problems of efficiency at the shop floor level, but at the same time he recognized the human element of production work. Gantt's contributions to scientific management are most often recalled in terms of his development of a chart which shows the relationship between work planned and completed on one axis and time elapsed on the other. This chart, referred to as a *Gantt Chart*, is still used in industry. Yet Gantt's contributions go beyond this.

Unlike Taylor, Gantt believed that wage systems ought to provide a fair remuneration regardless of output. He devised a task-and-bonus system in which a workman received a bonus in addition to his day's wage upon completion of an assigned task. If the workman did not complete the task, he was not penalized, but received the day wage. Taylor's differential piecerate system, on the other hand, was a pure incentive plan whereby each worker received a wage based solely on his daily production. There was no guaranteed day wage. Should the worker produce more than the standard output, the piecerate was increased for all units produced.

In other respects, Gantt made unique contributions to the literature of

---

[8] Claude S. George, Jr., *The History of Management Thought* (Englewood Cliffs, N.J.: Prentice-Hall, Inc., 1968), p. 97.

management. He was among the first to recognize that nonmonetary factors such as job security are powerful incentives. His task and bonus plan with its assured daily wage implemented his belief. He argued strongly that a responsibility of management is to train workers to do their jobs. He also agitated for the acceptance of his concept of industrial responsibility whereby industry pursues a service objective rather than a profit objective. Such statements were premature for the times, though they are commonplace today.

In retrospect, Gantt can be understood as a valuable contributor to the literature of scientific management. He shared the skeptical orientation of Taylor and the Gilbreths: He, like they, believed that the accepted way of doing things was usually the wrong way. Gantt believed that the best sources of improved efficiency were the work methods of the manager, not of the laborer. He stated that expertise should be the sole criterion for the endowment of authority, and that managers, as the recipients of authority, have the moral obligation to make decisions by scientific methods, not by opinion. Thus Gantt broadened the scope of scientific management by including managerial responsibility as well as managerial methods as appropriate areas for analysis and change.

Harrington Emerson: Principles of Efficiency

The public became aware of Harrington Emerson in 1910, when he testified as an expert witness before the Interstate Commerce Commission that the railroads could save one million dollars per day through the use of the methods and philosophy of scientific management, and thus eliminate the necessity for a requested rate increase. Emerson's ideas are embodied in a set of principles that define the manner in which the efficient use of resources is to be accomplished. His 12 principles implement the basic elements of the scientific management approach. In summary form, they state that the manager should (1) use scientific, objective, and factually based analysis; (2) define the aims of the undertaking; (3) relate each part to the whole; (4) provide standardized procedures and methods; and (5) reward individuals for successful execution of the task.

Emerson's contributions go beyond his 12 principles of efficiency, though they and his testimony before the ICC would have assured his place in management history. In addition to these obvious contributions, Emerson also recognized the positive lessons to be learned from the military's use of formalized staff and advisory positions. In his capacity as one of the first management consultants, he proposed the creation of a strict organization whose activities would be defined by clear statements of goals and purposes. In this respect, Emerson moved away from the traditional scientific management concern for work doing and anticipated many developments of classical organization theory.

SCIENTIFIC MANAGEMENT IN RETROSPECT

If it were evaluated in terms of its impact on management practice at the time of its development, scientific management would receive a low grade. Its impact on contemporary management is more pronounced and significant. True, some firms adopted scientific management methods; yet the "mental revolution" which Taylor expected never occurred. Despite the fact that he, the Gilbreths, Gantt, Emerson, and others had provided a substantial, if unorganized, body of knowledge which offered to bring harmony to all participants in economic life, strife between management and labor continued and the methods of scientific management were largely ignored.

One cause of the seeming failure of scientific management is possibly found in the failure of its proponents to understand fully the psychological and sociological dimensions of work. Throughout Taylor's writing one finds the implicit assumption that man is motivated basically by economic considerations, and that when given adequate information, man is able to choose rationally the alternative which maximizes his well-being. This assumption was reinforced by classical economic theory which enjoyed its height of popular acceptance at that time. In the context of the times, such an assumption was credible. Factory workers were by and large first-generation immigrants, ignorant of their surroundings and eking out a living on subsistence wages. Granted the historical justification for the assumption, there was another movement competing with scientific management to bring about industrial harmony, namely, unionism.

The union leaders of the time viewed scientific management as a threat to labor. Taylor's concept of separation of work doing and work planning threatened the prerogatives of labor, particularly of craftsmen. Union leaders anticipated the erosion of the importance of labor as each individual worker's contribution diminished. Workers lose control as work becomes more specialized and as each worker is more or less substitutable for any other worker. A second source of threat to unionism was the proposal that wage systems be determined solely by management decision of what constitutes "fair wages" for standard output. This would undercut the attempts of unions to have wages determined through collective bargaining. The conflict between unions and Taylorism was most apparent in 1909, when the federal government introduced an incentive system at the Watertown Arsenal. The union struck and was supported by Samuel Gompers' American Federation of Labor. The period of active antagonism between unionism and Taylorism waned with the entry of America into World War I, when the concern for "efficiency at all cost" gave way to "production at any cost." The latter orientation prevailed throughout the 20s and ended in a crash with the Great Depression.

CLASSICAL ORGANIZATION THEORY:
THE MANAGEMENT OF ORGANIZATIONS

Scientific management raised questions, undertook analyses, and provided prescriptions which were narrow in scope yet concrete in reality. Issues related to the coordination of large organizations and the managerial roles in these entities are much more complex and abstract. A body of literature emerged simultaneously with that on scientific management, dealing specifically with these issues. The literature on classical organization theory was affected by the same environmental and cultural conditions which, in turn, affected scientific management. Indeed, as we shall see, the ideology and assumptions so apparent in the literature on scientific management are evident in the literature on classical organization theory.

The writers in this branch of the Classical School raised two questions: (1) What are the basic principles which should guide the design, creation, and maintenance of an organization structure? and (2) What are the basic functions of management within the organization? An overriding objective, similar to that of scientific management, was to provide *prescriptive* guidelines for effective and efficient management.

MAJOR CONTRIBUTORS TO CLASSICAL
ORGANIZATION THEORY

Practitioners of management were the major contributors to the literature on classical organization theory. They brought their pragmatic orientation to bear on the problem of coordinating large-scale organizations. In this respect, these writers share the action-oriented background common to writers of scientific management. In this chapter, the work of Henri Fayol, James Mooney, Lyndall Urwick, and Chester Barnard is presented. The reader should keep in mind that the concepts with which these writers dealt are considerably more abstract than those of scientific management.

Henri Fayol: Principles of Management

Work experience as the managing director of a large coal-mining company in France provided Henri Fayol with the background for his ideas about the managerial process. For 50 years, Fayol practiced and reflected upon the process of coordinating the diverse activities of the organization which he directed. His ideas were first committed to writing and became a part of the literature in 1916, when he contributed to the bulletin of a French industrial association. A more complete statement of his ideas appeared in 1925 with the publication of his book, but it was not until 1929 that the English translation appeared.[9]

Fayol sought to discover principles of management which determine the "soundness and good working order" of the firm. Such principles are flexible in the adaptation to circumstances and events. Fayol was not seeking fixed rules of conduct; rather, he sought guidelines to thinking. Deciding upon the appropriateness of a principle for a particular situation is the "art" of management. Fayol believed that any number of principles might exist, and described only those which he most frequently applied in his own experience.

Fayol's chief desire was to elevate the status of management practice by supplying a framework for analysis. His framework included a statement of *principles* and *functions*. We shall discuss them in that order.

Management Principles. Fayol proposed 14 principles which *should guide the thinking of managers in resolving concrete problems*. To reiterate, Fayol did not expound blind obedience to fixed courses of action; he relied upon managers' "experience and sense of proportion" to guide the degree of application of any principle in any situation. The principles are:[10]

1. Division of Work. Specialization of labor is the natural means by which institutions and societies have progressed and developed. It results in increased productivity through the reduction of job elements required of each worker.[11] Specialization of labor permits large-scale production at minimum cost. Additionally, the cost of training workers is considerably reduced since the content of each job has been greatly narrowed.

2. Authority and Responsibility. Much confusion exists in current discussions of authority and responsibility. The terms are highly abstract and difficult to define. Fayol recognized this difficulty; he defined *authority* as the "right to give orders and the power to exact obedience." But Fayol went on to distinguish between the *official* authority which derives from holding an office, and *personal* authority which derives from the office holder's own personality, experience, moral worth, and other personal characteristics that enable him to influence the efforts of subordinates. Fayol stated that authority and responsibility should be

---

[9] Henri Fayol, *General and Industrial Management*, trans. J. A. Conbrough (Geneva: International Management Institute, 1929). All subsequent references in this text are to the more widely available translation by Constance Storrs (London: Pitman Publishing Corp., 1949).

[10] This presentation of Fayol's principles is based upon his own discussion in ibid., pp. 19–42.

[11] Adam Smith, *The Wealth of Nations* (Chicago: Henry Regnery Company, 1962), pp. 9–10.

equal; yet he recognized that, as one moves up in the hierarchy, it becomes more and more difficult to fix exactly the responsibility of office holders. Fayol expected that the ultimate check on authority had to be the integrity and moral courage of administrators, and he fully recognized that such traits are "conferred neither by selection nor ownership."

3. *Discipline.* The essence of discipline, according to Fayol, is obedience to agreements reached between parties in the firm. He believed that clear statements of agreements are necessary, but not sufficient for discipline; he argued that the "state of discipline of any group of people depends essentially on the worthiness of its leaders," leaders who would judiciously apply sanctions in instances of breached discipline.

4. *Unity of Command.* Fayol believed that the existence of dual command (two supervisors, one subordinate) causes severe breakdowns in authority and discipline. Consequently he stated that an employee should receive orders from only one superior. He believed that recognition and observance of this principle would eliminate the causes of interdepartmental and interpersonal conflict arising out of jurisdictional issues. He also noted that the tendency of some superiors to bypass the chain of command and the difficulty of writing completely unambiguous job descriptions were major causes of disruptions in the unity-of-command principle.

5. *Unity of Direction.* Each group of activities having the same purpose should operate under one head and one plan. Fayol observed that this principle should not be confused with the unity-of-command principle. Unity of direction derives from a sound organizational structure which is departmentalized in an appropriate manner; the principle refers to the structure of the organization. Unity of command refers to the functioning of personnel within the structure. Unity of direction does not assure unity of command, but unity of command cannot exist without unity of direction.

6. *Subordination of Individual Interest to General Interest.* This principle states that the whole is greater than the sum of its parts, and that the overall objectives which the group seeks to achieve take precedence over the objectives of individuals.

7. *Remuneration of Personnel.* The remuneration of workers and managers for services rendered should be based on a systematic attempt to reward well-directed effort. Fayol regarded no particular wage system as a substitute for management competence. He discussed the advantages and disadvantages of various compensation plans, including piecerate, day rate, task rate, and profit-sharing plans.

8. *Centralization.* Fayol defined centralization as the degree to which the importance of subordinates' roles is reduced. He stated that the degree of centralization should be related to the character of the manager, the reliability of subordinates, and the conditions of the business.

Fayol recognized that these circumstances are quite varied and that they change over time. It is the responsibility of managers to determine the appropriate balance which will "give the best overall yield."

9. *Scalar Chain.* The graded chain of authority from top to bottom through which all communications flow is termed the scalar chain. This chain implements the unity-of-command principle and provides for the orderly transmission of information. Yet Fayol recognized that strict adherence to the scalar chain can result in delay and frustrated employees. Therefore he prescribed the use of "the gangplank principle," which authorizes persons at the same level to communicate directly, rather than through channels, so long as their superiors are aware of the situation and know in advance the kinds of issues to be resolved in this manner. Fayol introduced the problem of lateral communications and made explicit provision for carrying on such communications without threatening the integrity of the scalar chain.

10. *Order.* Fayol applied the principle of order to the material and human resources of the firm. This principle states that even as the material instruments of business must be arranged logically and neatly, so must the human instruments. To establish order in the human sphere, the manager must determine the exact nature and content of each job and demonstrate its relationship to the end product and to other jobs. These interrelationships appear in the form of an organization chart. All business concerns should have such a chart to guide the orderly arrangement of employees.

11. *Equity.* Fayol defined equity as the enforcement of established rules tempered by a sense of kindliness and justice. He believed that employees respond to equitable treatment by carrying out their duties in a sense of loyalty and devotion.

12. *Stability of Tenure of Personnel.* Fayol had observed that prosperous firms usually had a stable group of managerial personnel. He thus stated as a general principle that top management should implement practices which encourage the long-term commitment of employees, particularly of managers, to the firm.

13. *Initiative.* This principle states that employees must be encouraged to think through and implement a plan of action. Fayol believed that the opportunity to exercise initiative is a powerful motivator. The only limits on personal initiative should be the authority relationship defined by the scalar chain and by the employee's sense of discipline.

14. *Esprit de Corps.* Fayol defined *esprit de corps* as unity of effort through harmony of interests. In his view, the most effective means for achieving *esprit de corps* is through unity of command, and through oral rather than written communication. Many approaches to the creation of a sense of unity and harmony exist; Fayol suggested only those methods which seemed important to him.

Over the years, Fayol's principles were much discussed and much criticized in the literature on management. In any evaluation, the time and place in which they emerged should be kept in mind and should be an accurate reflection of Fayol's intent. He stated that the list of principles was not exhaustive, "This list has no precise limits"; the list of principles was not to endure regardless of time and place: "It [the list] seems *at the moment* especially useful . . . appropriate to concentrate general discussion." The principles do not answer questions of degree or specificity, but Fayol was not suggesting that the principles would absolve management from the responsibility for determining what he termed "the appropriate balance." Indeed, he emphasized time and again that the moral character of the manager would determine the ultimate outcome.

Management Functions. Fayol elaborated the managerial process by identifying five functions in which managers must engage, as follows:

1. *Planning* includes all those activities of a manager which result in a course of action. The manager should make the best possible forecast of future events that affect the firm and draw up an operating plan that guides future decisions.

2. *Organizing* includes all activities which result in a structure of tasks and authority. This managerial function determines the appropriate machines, material, and human mix which are necessary to accomplish the task.

3. *Commanding* is directing the activities of subordinates. To be successful, Fayol suggests, the manager should set a good example and know thoroughly the personnel and the agreements made between the personnel and the firm. The managers should have direct, two-way communication with subordinates. Furthermore, the manager should continually evaluate the organizational structure and subordinates, and he should not hesitate to change the structure if he considers it faulty, or to fire subordinates if they are incompetent.

4. *Coordinating* activities are those which bind together all individual efforts and direct them toward a common objective. Thus Fayol saw coordinating as simply another element of the total managerial process. The concept of management used in this textbook, on the other hand, suggests that coordination is the key element of the process.

5. *Controlling* activities are those which assure that actual activities are consistent with planned activities. Fayol did not expand the concept beyond stating that everything should be "subject to control."

Fayol's analysis provides a *means* (the five functions) for viewing the managerial process and *guides* (the principles) for implementing the process. The framework itself lacks logical clarity since it suggests nothing about the primacy of certain principles or the causality among these principles. It did, however, establish a basis for further elaboration by subsequent writers.

James Mooney: Principles of Organization

In 1931, James D. Mooney and Alan C. Reiley authored *Onward Industry,* which was revised in 1947 by Mooney and entitled *The Principles of Organization.*[12] This book is a most important part of the literature of classical management thought and, as will be seen, complements Fayol's work while also adding a new dimension.

Mooney viewed management as the technique, or art, of directing and inspiring other men. Organization, on the other hand, is the technique of relating specific duties or functions in a coordinated whole. The interrelationship between the two concepts is immediately apparent when we recognize that the duty of management is to devise an appropriate organization. Mooney's personal experience and his examination of organization in governmental, church, military, and industrial institutions were the bases for a framework of concepts which describes the essential nature of organizations.

The conceptual framework which Mooney used to analyze organizations is based upon logical reasoning. He believed that it is possible to deduce the underlying principles of organization which explain the existence of certain phenomenon in all organizations. From his own experience in business and government and his study of other organization types, Mooney observed that a structure of tasks and authority existed in every organization. Although the structure differed from one organization to another in terms of tasks to be done, its key features were the same, namely, a hierarchy of authority and specialized tasks.

These observations led Mooney to believe that natural laws of organizing existed, and it was these natural laws, or principles, which he sought to discover through logic. It is at this point in our discussion of classical organization theory that differences in the use of the term "principles" can be noted. Unlike Fayol who used the term to denote guidelines, Mooney used the term to denote fundamental law, or doctrine. Both usages are acceptable, but understanding classical organization theory is certainly made more difficult as a consequence. The reader should keep in mind the fact that Mooney was seeking to explain the rationale for organized activity; whereas, Fayol had the more modest intent of providing practical guidelines for managing.

Given this background, the principles of organization according to Mooney can be explained, in his terminology, as follows:

1. The first principle of organization is *coordination.* Note that Fayol defined coordination as one of the five functions of management. Mooney,

---

[12] James D. Mooney, *The Principles of Organization* (New York: Harper and Brothers, 1947).

however, viewed coordination as the primary law which dictates the necessity for organizations; coordination, or the coordinative principle, is *the reason* for organizing.

2. The necessity for organizing sets in motion other functions, or activities, which in turn are guided by other principles. *Scaling* the tasks to be performed involves the definition of each task in terms of its duties and responsibilities. That is, Mooney viewed the process of creating the hierarchy to be the natural outcome of the necessity for organizing. The scalar function implements the principle of *authority*, which is derived from, and legitimated by, higher authority—the people (in governments), God (in churches), and private property (in business firms).

3. The scalar process consists of two subfunctions: *delegating authority* and *defining tasks*. The delegation of authority is guided by the principle of *leadership*, which in Mooney's terms is the personification of authority. Through the delegation of authority, leaders confer authority on subordinates, and so on down the chain. Parallel to the process of delegating is that of defining tasks, termed functional definition. The principle of *specialization* underlies this function. Regardless of organizational type, the necessity exists for people to do different jobs at different times, as Fayol, Taylor, and other classical writers had observed.

Mooney's analysis provides a framework of concepts which he related through logical deduction. From the existence of organizations, he deduced the principles of coordination, authority, leadership, and specialization. Mooney believed that these principles explained the necessity for the organizing function and subfunctions. Yet though his analysis of the organizing function was complete to his satisfaction, there remained the task of synthesizing the totality of classical management theory. Lyndall Urwick undertook this task.

Lyndall Urwick: Synthesis of Classical Management Theory

A most important landmark in the literature of management is Lyndall Urwick's *The Elements of Administration*.[13] Urwick combined and synthesized the ideas of Fayol, Mooney, and Taylor into one conceptual framework. It is with Urwick's analysis that scientific management and classical organization theory blend and classical management theory begins to emerge. It provided practitioners and students of management with the basis for understanding the managerial process as it relates to the total enterprise. Its level of abstraction permits broad compre-

---

[13] Lyndall Urwick, *The Elements of Administration* (New York: Harper and Brothers, 1944).

hension, yet it is concrete enough to provide insights into specific managerial functions.

The synthesis of classical management theory is depicted in Figure 2–2. It is based upon Urwick's analysis, but it reflects the authors' interpretation of his work. It combines not only the ideas of Taylor, Fayol, Mooney, and other classical writers, but also Urwick's own analysis of the controlling function. From Taylor, Urwick took the idea that the management process is directed by the principle of scientific investigation. Urwick reemphasized that rigorous analysis, disciplined by the tenets of science, sets management work apart from nonmanagement work. Taylor and others of the scientific management approach had demonstrated that the management of work could be undertaken through the analysis of objective data gathered in the work place itself. Urwick generalized from Taylor's experience and stated the case for scientific analysis as the cardinal principle to govern all management functions.

The management process consists of three functions: planning, organizing, and controlling. These three functions have guiding principles—forecasting, coordination, and command. We have already discussed Mooney's analysis of the organizing function, Fayol's analysis of the planning function, and since Urwick adopted them intact, we need not elaborate them again.

The controlling function was analyzed by Urwick chiefly in terms of Fayol's principles. Urwick proposed that controlling entails the application of the principle of command—directing, or supervising, the activity of subordinates. Fayol had previously identified commanding as a single function, but Urwick elevated the concept to the status of a principle. Urwick also derived corollary functions and principles from the function of controlling and the principle of command.

The controlling subfunctions—*staffing, selecting and placing,* and *disciplining*—relate to the human elements of the organization. In simplest terms, Urwick believed that managers should consider the placement of people into the structure to be separate from the creation of the structure itself. Yet he recognized that if managers are to be effective, they must pay attention to the controlling function. It was with these concerns that he identified and defined the controlling function.

The staffing function involves the placement of managers into leadership positions and defining their authority and accountability in terms of their abilities. The principle of centralization, as Fayol defined it, requires the delegation of authority on the basis of individual abilities. Selecting and placing managers and nonmanagers alike are determined not only by job requirements but also by the principle of fair remuneration. Thus, a promotion should be awarded for performance, not for personality. The day-to-day supervision of subordinates involves dis-

FIGURE 2–2

Classical Management Theory

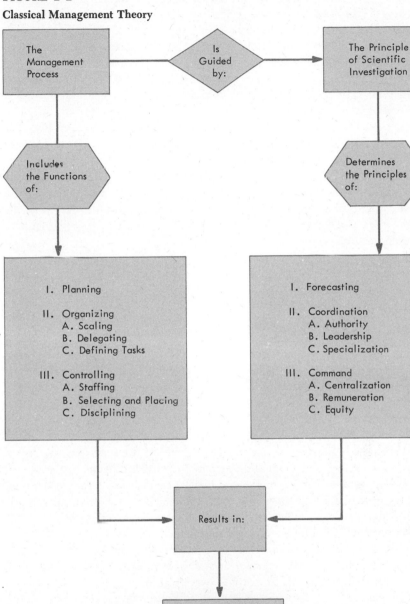

ciplinary activities which are, as Fayol stated, designed to assure compliance with prior agreements. The principle of equity, or fairness, is intended to underlie the disciplining function.

Finally, Urwick included in his synthesis of management theory the intermediate objectives of management: *order, stability, initiative,* and *esprit de corps.* He believed that to the extent that managers perform their functions with an awareness of appropriate principles, these four ends could be attained.

Urwick's synthesis and integration of scientific management and classical organization theory reflects the essence of classical management theory; it is "that all management principles fit together in a balanced and interrelated framework."[14] Yet, he also recognized that much remains to be done in the routine management of day-to-day operations. Even though the structure is defined and manned, there is room for managerial interpretation of appropriate styles and behavior. Thus, it is necessary to adapt the rather fixed concept of management to take into account the variable nature of human behavior. The first writer to undertake the task of interrelating the nature of organizations and the nature of man was Chester I. Barnard.

Chester I. Barnard: Organizations as Cooperative Efforts

The insights of Chester I. Barnard have influenced the development of management thought in significant ways. In fact, his ideas are so pervasive that our efforts to condense and summarize them will surely not do justice to them. Barnard had a background similar to those of Fayol, Mooney, and Urwick. He was a practicing manager, an executive with New Jersey Bell Telephone, where he was president. He also shared his colleagues' interest in analyzing the function he was performing; he wanted to make "sense" of his job and to provide others with the concepts that make sense of management. His ideas were widely circulated in the form of papers, speeches, and books. The most important source of his ideas is *The Functions of the Executive.*[15]

Barnard, who believed that the basic function of the executive is to provide the basis for *cooperative* effort, defined organization as a system of goal-directed cooperative activities. Barnard went on to analyze management's functions to include the formulation of objectives and the acquisition of resources and efforts required to meet the stated objectives. This point of view is quite compatible with those of Fayol, Mooney, and Urwick. The new dimension that Barnard introduced was

[14] Joseph L. Massie, "Management Theory," in James H. March, ed., *Handbook of Organizations* (Chicago: Rand McNally and Co., 1965), p. 413.

[15] Chester I. Barnard, *The Functions of the Executives* (Cambridge: Harvard University Press, 1938).

his emphasis on communications as the means for acquiring cooperation. He believed that the system of communication within the organization is the means by which persons are induced to cooperate.

According to Barnard, the degree of employee cooperation depends
upon the balance between inducements and contributions. Inducements
include the sum total of financial and nonfinancial rewards which accrue
to individuals in exchange for their efforts, that is, contributions. The
purpose of communication is to provide individuals with the necessary
information to evaluate the desired balance. At the same time, Barnard
recognized that the communication system is the active process by
which authority is implemented. Orders are transmitted downward as
superiors seek to acquire certain behavior from their subordinates. He
stated that the existence of the formal structure is no guarantee that
subordinates would in fact follow orders.

Barnard challenged the wisdom of relying solely upon the authority
structure to achieve compliance. Indeed, he stated a position that has
become known as the *acceptance theory* of authority. This theory
postulates that subordinates will determine whether an order is legitimate, and whether to accept or reject it. They will accept the order
only if they can understand it and are able to comply with it. Perhaps
more importantly, they will accept it (even if understood) only if the
required behavior is consistent with their view of the purposes of the
organization *and their own* personal interests.

The ideas of Barnard have been woven into the practice and theory
of modern management. It is now generally accepted that the manager
must know a great deal about human behavior. As we shall see in
subsequent chapters, the analysis of human behavior, singly and in
groups, by behavioral scientists has added significant insights; but we
must recognize the importance of Barnard as their forerunner.

CONTRIBUTIONS OF THE CLASSICAL SCHOOL
TO THE PRACTICE OF MANAGEMENT

The first and foremost contribution of the Classical School was
that of identifying management as a distinct element of organized
society. The classical writers believed that management, like law, medicine, and other occupations, should be practiced according to principles
which managers can learn. Moreover, these principles can be discovered
by the application of scientific methods. As Taylor pointed out, manual
tasks could be studied and subsequently managed by applying the basic
laws of physiology and physics. Mooney made a strong case that the
organizing function can be analyzed by applying the fundamentals of
deductive logic.

The identification of the planning, organizing, and controlling functions provided the basis for training managers. Many contemporary management textbooks and training courses are based upon these functions. The manner in which management functions are presented and explained often differs, depending upon the particular point of view of the writer or the trainer. Yet, the essence of any listing of management functions is the acknowledgement that managers are concerned with *what* the institution is to be doing, *how* it is to be done, and *whether* it was done.

Contemporary business firms, hospitals, universities, and government agencies have recognized the need to perform these functions. Planning offices, organizational analysis units, and quality control sections can be found in many large organizations. Smaller organizations implement these functions in more general, nonspecialized ways, primarily through the efforts of top management. The essential point is that the Classical School presented a strong case that either managers or their subordinates must perform these functions.

The manner in which planning, organizing, and controlling are implemented should, moreover, not proceed haphazardly. Rather, the manager should practice these functions according to defined principles, or guidelines. The classical writers, beginning with Taylor, identified these principles and argued that they were the bases for managerial work. These principles, according to the classicists, were universal in application; that is to say, they are valid regardless of the institutional setting in which management is practiced.

The contributions of the Classical School go beyond the important work of identifying the management field, its functions, and principles. Many modern management techniques are direct outgrowths of its endeavors. For example, time and motion analysis, work simplification, incentive wage systems, production scheduling, personnel testing, training, selection and placement procedures, cost accounting, and budgeting are modern management techniques which derive directly from the Classical School. These methods and others are topics of the next three chapters. Suffice to say at this point, the practical contributions of classical writers are many and varied because it was their primary intent to make such contributions.

DISCUSSION AND REVIEW QUESTIONS

1. What is the traditional role of classical theory in any field of study, and particularly in management?
2. Why should one study classical management theory? Of what relevance is scientific management to the problems of the 1970s?

3. What is your understanding of the term "ideology" as applied to scientific management?
4. Do you believe that there is "one best way" to perform any task, including the work of a scientist?
5. Compare the concept of the "average worker" to professors' concepts of the "average student."
6. What do the authors mean when they say that classical organization theory dealt with more complex and abstract problems than those which scientific management confronted?
7. Compare the ideologies of classical organization theory and scientific management.
8. What are "principles of management" as Fayol defined and explained them? Compare Fayol's and Mooney's ideas regarding principles.
9. What new dimensions did Barnard add to classical theory?
10. How would a scientist go about testing classical management theory? How would a manager go about applying classical management theory? Which is more important to you personally—testing or applying?

ADDITIONAL REFERENCES

Barnard, C. I. *Organization and Management.* Cambridge: Harvard University Press, 1952.

Brandeis, L. D. *Scientific Management and Railroads.* New York: The Engineering Magazine Co., 1911.

Church, A. H. *The Science and Practice of Management.* New York: The Engineering Magazine Co., 1916.

Davis, R. C. *The Principles of Factory Organization and Management.* New York: Harper and Brothers, 1928.

Drury, H. B. *Scientific Management: A History and Criticism.* New York: Longmans, Green and Co., 1922.

Emerson, H. *Efficiency as a Basis for Operations and Wages.* New York: The Engineering Magazine Co., 1900.

———. *The Twelve Principles of Efficiency.* New York: The Engineering Magazine Co., 1913.

Gantt, H. L. *Industrial Leadership.* New Haven: Yale University Press, 1916.

———. *Work, Wages and Profits.* New York: The Engineering Magazine Co., 1910.

Gilbreth, F. B. *Motion Study.* New York: D. Van Nostrand Co., 1911.

Gilbreth, L. M. *The Psychology of Management.* New York: Sturgis and Walton Co., 1914.

Hoxie, R. F. *Scientific Management and Labor.* New York: D. Appleton and Co., 1915.

Merrill, H. F., ed.   *Classics in Management.* New York: American Management Association, 1960.

Metcalf, H. C., and Urwick, L., eds.   *Dynamic Administration: The Collected Works of Mary Parker Follett.* New York: Harper and Brothers, 1942.

Munsterberg, H.   *Business Psychology.* Chicago: LaSalle Extension University, 1918.

Rowntree, B. S.   *The Human Factor in Business: Experiments in Industrial Democracy.* London: Longmans, Green and Co., 1921.

Urwick, L., ed.   *The Golden Book of Management.* London: Newman Neame Ltd., 1956.

3 The Planning Function

INTRODUCTION

The essential function of the management process is *planning.* Beginning with Taylor, the classical management writers recognized the difference between planning and executing, and they argued that managers should plan and that nonmanagers should execute. This theme was developed by Fayol and elaborated further by Urwick. Contemporary management literature no longer is concerned with making the case that managers should plan; rather the current focus of attention is on the techniques of planning.

The planning function includes all managerial activities which result in a definition of goals and the determination of appropriate means to achieve these goals. Yet more simply, planning is advance thinking as the basis for doing. In order to analyze the planning function in more specific terms, the function can be broken down into four distinct, yet interrelated, phases:

Phase 1—Establishing goals and fixing their priority.
Phase 2—Forecasting future events which can affect goal accomplishment.
Phase 3—Making the plans operational through budgeting.
Phase 4—Stating and implementing policies which direct activities toward the desired goals.

Each phase must be undertaken and related to other phases to complete the planning function. The end result is an overall plan which guides the organization toward the predetermined goals. In the remainder of this chapter each phase is discussed and some of the more useful managerial planning techniques are described.

GOAL SETTING AND ORDERING

The planning function begins with analyses of the goals which management seeks to accomplish, without which the organization would be an aimless entity. Goals have at least three dimensions: *priority, time,* and *structure.*

Priority of Goals

Priority of goals implies that at a given point in time, the accomplishment of one goal is relatively more important than others. For example, the goal of maintaining a minimum cash balance may be critically important to a firm having difficulty meeting payrolls and due dates on accounts. Priority of goals also says something about the relative importance of certain goals regardless of time. For example, survival of the organization is a necessary condition for the realization of all other goals.

The establishment of priorities is extremely important in that the resources of any organization must be allocated by rational means. At all points in time managers are confronted with alternative goals which must be evaluated and ranked. Managers of nonbusiness organizations are particularly concerned with the ranking of seemingly independent goals. For example, a university president must determine, implicitly or explicitly, the relative importance of teaching, research, and service goals. Of course the determination of goals and priorities is often a judgmental decision and therefore difficult.

Timing of Goals

The time dimension of goals implies that the organization's activities are guided by different objectives depending upon the duration of the action; it is traditional to speak of short-run, intermediate, and long-run goals. Short-run goals are those which extend for a period of less than a year; intermediate goals are those covering one to five years; and long-run goals are those extending beyond five years. The relationship between priority and timing of goals is quite close since the long-run goals tend to be stated in terms of "ultimates," that is, those objectives which must be accomplished in order to assure the long-run survival of the organization.

The timing dimension is reflected in the practice of many organizations to develop different plans for different periods of time. The long-run goal of a business firm could be stated in terms of a desired rate-of-return on capital, with intermediate and short-run plans stated in terms of objectives which must be accomplished to realize the ultimate goal. The management is then in a position to know the effectiveness of each year's activities in terms of achieving not only short-run but also long-run goals.

Structure of Goals

A third dimension of goals is structure. The process of breaking down the firm into units—for example, production, sales, and finance—requires that goals be assigned to each unit. Each unit is then given the responsibility for attaining an assigned goal. The process of allocating goals among various units creates the problem of potential goal conflict and suboptimization, wherein achieving the goals of one unit may jeopardize achieving the goals of another. For example, the production goal of low unit cost achieved through mass production of low-quality products may conflict with the sales goal of selling high-quality, high-markup products. The resolution of this problem is a careful balance of the goal for each unit, with the recognition that the goal of neither unit can be maximized. The result is a situation known as suboptimization of goals.

The problem of suboptimization of goals can be understood by recognizing a second aspect of goal structure.[1] If we view the business firm from the perspective of all those who have a stake in its operation, and if we recognize that the ends which each seeks in the firm's operation are potentially in conflict, we can readily understand the problem. Thus, at any point in time, stockholders (owners), employees (including unions), customers, suppliers, creditors, and governmental agencies are all concerned with the operation of the firm. The process of goal setting must recognize the relative importance of these interest groups, and the plans must incorporate and integrate their interests. The exact form and relative weight to be given to any particular interest group is precisely the nature of management's dilemma; yet it is precisely management's responsibility to make these kinds of judgments.

The management of the business firm must consider the expectations of these diverse groups because the firm's ultimate success depends upon them. For example, present and potential customers are the ultimate holders of power over the firm. If they are not happy with the price and quality of the firm's product, they withdraw their support (they stop buying), and the firm fails because of lack of funds. Suppliers have the

---

[1] See R. W. Morell, *Management: Ends and Means* (San Francisco, Calif.: Chandler Publishing Co., 1969), pp. 5–30, for a discussion of multiple goals and a suggested hierarchy of goals.

power to disrupt the flow of their materials to express disagreement with the firm's activities. Governmental agencies have power to enforce the firm's accommodation to regulations which, in modern times, are affecting nearly every aspect of the firm's operation.[2] The existence of these interest groups and the fact of their power to affect the goal structure of the firm express the reality that the business firm is a social invention; the firm will exist only so long as it satisfies the larger society.

Profit Seeking as a Goal

The widely recognized and understood fact that business firms, by their very nature, seek a wide range of goals has contributed to a generally blurred image of the role of profit seeking as a goal. There is a general acceptance that firms do not seek maximum profits as hypothesized in classical economic theory. Such an objective is impossible to achieve since it requires not only perfect knowledge of all future events which affect the firm's cost and revenue, but also perfectly rational decision-makers at all levels in the organization.[3] Yet, even though one may dismiss "profit maximization" as a goal, one cannot also dismiss "profit seeking." Indeed, we must not lose sight of the primary mission of the business firm—to make a profit in exchange for the production of goods and services deemed desirable by society. Unless the firm satisfies this objective, it cannot accomplish any other.

At the same time, to say that profit is a *necessary* condition for the firm's survival is not to say that it is a *sufficient* condition to insure it. A profitable firm earning a satisfactory return on stockholders' equity and paying a satisfactory dividend may not last long if it is not meeting the needs of employees for satisfactory working conditions, the demands of creditors for prompt payment of debt, or the insistence of governmental agencies for appropriate response to regulatory legislation. Society expects much from the contemporary business firm, but its fundamental expectation is that the management will use scarce resources in an efficient manner in the production of goods and services. Profit is a principal means by which the firm's management is assessed. All other goals are derivatives of the basic goal of profit seeking.

Figure 3–1 summarizes the discussion up to this point. It demonstrates that profit seeking is the ultimate objective of the firm and that all other objectives are derived from and must be compatible with it.

---

[2] For a complete analysis of the relationship between power and goal setting, see A. D. Newman and R. W. Rowbottom, *Organizational Analysis* (Carbondale, Ill.: Southern Illinois University Press, 1968), pp. 101–8.

[3] The realization that maximum profit is an unrealistic goal has led to the suggestion that satisfactory profit is a reasonable goal to seek. See James G. March and Herbert A. Simon, *Organizations* (New York: John Wiley and Sons, 1958), pp. 140–41; and Herbert A. Simon, "Theories of Decision Making in Economics and Behavioral Science," *American Economic Review*, vol. 19 (June 1959), pp. 262–65.

FIGURE 3–1

Goals of the Business Firm

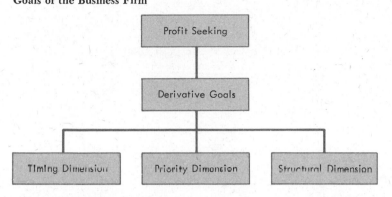

The various dimensions of goals which must be recognized in the goal-setting process are also shown. It should be pointed out that the final interpretation of the exact nature and mix of the firm's goals will depend in great measure upon the manager's personal goals as well as on his technical capacity to deal effectively with the problem. As Walton so neatly put it, "*What to make, what to charge,* and *how to market the wares* are questions that embrace moral as well as economic questions. The answers are conditioned by the personal value system of the decision maker and the institutional values which affect the relationships of the individual to the community."[4]

The fact that business firms pursue a relatively straightforward goal, profit seeking, implies that derivative goals can be logically linked to it. Yet, as Walton observed, logical linkages are affected by other, nonlogical considerations not the least of which is the personal value system of the manager. This important understanding has led researchers to try to discover the relative importance of goals as stated by practicing managers.

Studies of Actual Goals

A recent study sheds some light on the relative importance of goals, and at the same time reemphasizes the importance of profit seeking. George W. England[5] surveyed 1,072 American managers to obtain their judgments of the goals which they themselves viewed as important. The managers included in the survey considered profit and related goals of efficiency and productivity to be of supreme importance. The

---

[4] Clarence C. Walton, *Ethos and the Executive* (Englewood Cliffs, N.J.: Prentice-Hall, Inc., 1969), p. 192.

[5] George W. England, "Organizational Goals and Expected Behavior of American Managers," *Academy of Management Journal*, vol. 10 (June 1967), pp. 107–17.

respondents ranked as secondarily important certain goals pertaining to growth and stability. From the perspective of profitability, such goals can be viewed as directly related and even corollary to profitability. Ranked third in importance was a set of goals which concern employee welfare; ranked fourth were goals dealing with the general public, namely, social and community interests. England's survey findings support similar studies of management goals.[6] Furthermore, as Filley and House have observed,[7] the research to date suggests that goal structures which give first priority to customer-market-profitability oriented objectives are characteristic of successful firms. This is not to say that successful firms respond only to profit-oriented goals, but only that such goals are dominant. It also does not say that the dominant position of this goal is constant over time. Indeed, the tendency in recent years has been toward a reordering of priorities as the public's expectations have changed and as the public has implemented its power through governmental agencies. The responsibility of business to society beyond that of providing goods and services will not subside in the years to come.

The attitudes of business executives toward the growing demands for social responsibility were recently studied through a questionnaire sent to 1,400 subscribers to the *Harvard Business Review,* an important periodical in the field of management. The sample consisted of executives in 90 manufacturing firms employing 100 or more employees in a midwestern industrial area. The survey findings, based upon 209 returned questionnaires, indicated that executives as individuals believe that business firms must become more responsive to groups other than stockholders.[8] It is apparent that the managers of business firms are more and more being placed in the position of having to select and rank a number of derivative goals.

The discussion of goals to this point has emphasized their relatively abstract qualities. The implementation of goals requires that they be made concrete and specific, a requirement that raises two issues: (1) the clarity and unity of goals and (2) the measurement of goals.

Clarity and Unity of Goals

Goals should be defined in terms that are understandable and acceptable to those who must produce the effort required to achieve them. In

---

[6] See James K. Dent, "Organizational Correlates of the Goals of Business Management," *Personnel Psychology,* vol. 12 (August 1959), pp. 365–93; and J. H. Healey, *Executive Coordination and Control* (Columbus, Ohio: Bureau of Business Research, Ohio State University, 1956).

[7] Alan C. Filley and Robert J. House, *Managerial Process and Organizational Behavior* (Glenview, Ill.: Scott, Foresman and Company, 1969), p. 146.

[8] Rama Krishman, "Business Philosophy and Executive Responsibility," *Academy of Management Journal,* vol. 16 (December 1973), pp. 658–69.

practice, effective managerial action requires goal setting in every area which contributes to the overall goals. One writer on business management, Peter Drucker,[9] has stated that subgoals must be set in at least eight areas, namely, (1) market standing, (2) innovation, (3) productivity, (4) physical and financial resources, (5) profitability, (6) manager performance and responsibility, (7) worker performance and attitude, and (8) public responsibility. Drucker's classification in no way implies relative importance; he is simply pointing out the necessity for considering the entire range of subgoals. The priority of each subgoal will depend upon the conditions confronting the firm at the particular point in time.

The manner in which the subgoals are allocated to personnel in the firm depends in large part upon the organizational structure, particularly the degree of horizontal specialization. The next chapter develops the organizing function; therefore we need not go into its discussion at this point. It must be recognized here that it is important to assign goals in a clear and unambiguous way, and that the ultimate test of clarity is the recipient's understanding of the goal statement. At the same time, this statement must not be so detailed that it becomes a straightjacket which restricts the freedom of the subunit manager to exercise initiative.

The person assigned the responsibility for goal achievement enters into the process in a very important way. He himself is the final arbiter as to the appropriateness of the goal. As Barnard[10] pointed out, each participant in an organization determines for himself the range of acceptable behavior, and if the activities required of him are outside this range, he will not pursue the objective. A production-line foreman can find all kinds of legitimate means to foil a production schedule if the meeting of that plan requires behavior which he considers unacceptable. For example, if the schedule requires a heavy-handed approach to push his subordinates to levels of production beyond those which they themselves believe appropriate, the foreman can simply claim that it is impossible to meet. Thus, the necessity for clarity of goals includes not only clear and unambiguous communication, but also consistency with the individual goals of the person assigned the responsibility for goal achievement.

An important contribution of classical management theory was to analyze the means by which the goals of certain manual tasks could be clarified. The goal of such tasks according to Taylor and the Gilbreths is to produce a predetermined level of output during a specified period of time. By analyzing the basic elements of work doing—hand, eye, and

---

[9] Peter Drucker, *The Practice of Management* (New York: Harper and Brothers, 1954), and reemphasized in *Management: Tasks, Responsibilities, Practices* (New York: Harper and Row, 1974).

[10] Chester I. Barnard, *The Functions of the Executive* (Cambridge, Mass.: Harvard University Press, 1938).

body motions—Taylor and the Gilbreths were able to identify the "one best way" to perform tasks such as lathe turning, assembly work, and bricklaying. Their analyses, termed motion and time studies, provide the bases for modern day work-planning techniques.[11]

The subunit goals must be compatible with and contribute to the over-all goals. This is what is meant by "unity of direction." The relationship between each subgoal and the ultimate goal must be apparent to all concerned; otherwise the firm runs the danger of drift. The final test of the legitimacy and adequacy of each subgoal must be resolved in terms of the ultimate goal.

Measurement of Goals

As Drucker observed, "The real difficulty lies indeed not in determining what objectives we need, but in deciding how to set them."[12] The only approach, according to Drucker, is to determine *what* should be measured in each area, and *how* it should be measured. Immediately one can recognize the difficulty of measuring goals in certain areas. How, for example, does one measure employee development or public responsibility? The more abstract the goal, the more difficult it is to measure performance. Additionally, the measurement of abstract goals by quantitative means can lead to the problem of measurement orientation, that is, the tendency to focus attention on the measurement and away from the substance of the goal. Those in academic fields are familiar with the manifestation of this problem in universities and colleges which measure teaching and research accomplishment in terms of quantity of students graduated and articles published.

Nevertheless, effective planning requires goal measurement. A variety of measurements exist for each area.

Profitability measures include the ratios of profits to sales, total assets, and capital (net worth). The tendency in recent years has been to emphasize the profit/sales ratio as the important test of profitability,[13] perhaps because both quantities required to calculate this measure are taken directly from the income statement, which management generally regards as a better test of performance than the balance sheet. However, many managers believe that the true test of profitability must combine the income statement and the balance sheet. Accordingly, such managers

---

[11] Mitchell Fein, "Work Measurement: Concepts of Normal Pace," *Industrial Engineering*, vol. 4 (September 1972), pp. 34–39; and Mitchell Fein, "Work Measurement Today," *Industrial Engineering*, vol. 4 (August 1972), pp. 14–20.

[12] Drucker, *Practice of Management,* p. 64.

[13] Ibid., p. 79; and Neil W. Chamberlain, *The Firm: Micro-Economic Planning and Action* (New York: McGraw-Hill Book Co., 1962), p. 55.

would use the profit/net-worth ratio. The arguments for and against the use of either of these two are basically due to differences in point of view as to whether *source* of capital is an important consideration. The profit/total-asset ratio measures the efficiency of management's use of all resources regardless of origin (that is, creditors or owners), whereas the profit/net-worth ratio measures managerial efficiency only in terms of the use of the owners' contribution.

The resolution of the problem of which profitability measure to select lies in the recognition that the measures are not mutually exclusive. All three can be used to set and evaluate profitability objectives, since each measures a different, yet important aspect of the profit structure. However, the problem of the amount of profit remains to be solved, together with certain technical problems derived from the nature of accounting information. With respect to the amount of profit, we should recognize that the functions of profit are (1) to measure effectiveness, (2) to recover one cost element of being in business (return on invested capital), and (3) to provide funds for future expansion and innovation, either through retained earnings or through the capital market at rates made favorable because of the firm's history of profitability. Thus, the minimum profitability is that which assures the continuous stream of capital into the firm, given the inherent risks of the industry in which the firm operates.

A complete discussion of accounting theory as related to profitability measures is certainly beyond the scope of this book. However, it must be observed that the values assigned to balance sheet items are seldom true reflections of current or replacement cost values. The accounting convention of recording assets at original cost results in the understatement of assets at future points in time during periods of inflation, and overstatement during periods of deflation. Measures of profitability must be based on accounting data that are adjusted for this distortion if one is to obtain relevant measures.

Marketing measures must relate products, markets, distribution, and

FIGURE 3–2

Marketing Planning Matrix

	Existing Markets	*New Markets*
Existing Products	Target Volume Target Share Target Profit	Target Volume Target Share Target Profit
New Products	Target Volume Target Share Target Profit	Target Volume Target Share Target Profit

customer service objectives. Figure 3–2 shows the matrix of decisions required in the analysis of products and markets. In each existing and potential market and for each existing and potential product, a specified goal must be established for total volume, market share, and profit. Co-incidentally, management must develop an organization which will assure that resources are available to achieve the results.

Productivity measures are basically ratios of output to input. Other factors being equal, the higher the ratio, the more efficient is the use of inputs. In traditional terms, productivity measures have related the output for certain inputs, for example, labor; these have been referred to as ratios of labor productivity. Yet, when different inputs are used together, it is quite difficult to identify which output is due to a particular input. Moreover, since the firm exists as an aggregation of resources which must be directed and coordinated to specified ends, the productivity measure should evaluate precisely that which results from the total effort, not the efforts of each part.

Drucker proposes that the *ratio of value added to sales and to profit* is the superior measure of productivity.[14] Furthermore, he states that the firm's objective should be to increase these ratios, and that units should be evaluated on the basis of these increases. His argument for value added, which he calls *contributed value*, is that it measures the increase in value of the purchased materials due to the combined efforts of the firm, since value added is equal to the difference between market value and purchased price of materials and supplies. Thus the efficiency of the firm's efforts is measured directly. Furthermore, this measure of productivity could be used for internal comparisons of operating units.

Physical and financial measures reflect the firm's capacity to acquire resources sufficient for its larger objectives. The measurement of objectives in this area is comparatively easy due to the existence of quite a large number of accounting yardsticks which are appropriate for both physical and financial objectives. Rate-of-return measures are appropriate for setting objectives in decisions involving the acquisition of new plants and facilities. Liquidity and solvency measures are available for the measurement of financial objectives. Measures such as the current ratio, working capital turnover, the acid test, accounts receivable and inventory turnover, and debt to equity ratios can be used in setting objectives and evaluating results in the area of financial planning. These ratios are covered in greater detail in Chapter 5.

Subgoals in the areas of profitability, market standing, productivity, and physical and financial resources are amenable to measurement. Subgoals in areas such as innovation, employee development, and public responsibility are not so easily identifiable and measurable in concrete

---

[14] Drucker, *Practice of Management*, pp. 71–73.

terms. However, the important point to consider is that without measurement, subsequent evaluation is necessarily quite inconclusive.

The managers of business organizations are comparatively better able to measure progress toward goals than their counterparts in nonbusiness organizations. With the exception of subgoals such as innovation, employee development, and public responsibility, as noted above, business managers not only have straightforward goals, but also have information systems which produce fairly reliable measures of progress toward them. Managers of universities, hospitals, and government agencies are not so fortunate. For example, the dean of a college can measure the number of students enrolled in courses and the number of graduates, but not the *quality* of instruction. Moreover, a hospital administrator can chart patient-days, discharge rates, and cost per patient-day and yet know nothing about the quality of health care that patients are receiving. Unlike the business firm, nonbusiness organizations have no "bottom-line"—that is, profit—indicator of overall results. Yet the managers of these organizations are continually challenged by students, patients, taxpayers, clients, and other constituents to account for results.

FORECASTING

The setting of goals must be implemented. The critical step in the implementation of goals is that of forecasting the future, the second phase of the planning process.[15] The results of the forecasts are included in budgets which are the major planning documents of the firm. The two basic issues that must be resolved through forecasting are: (1) what level of activity can be expected during the planning period and (2) what level of resources will be available to support the projected activity. The critical forecast upon which all others depend is the sales forecast.

Sales Forecasts

The projected sales volume of the firm's product or service provides the basis for all other activities. The sales estimate sets the level of production and determines the level and timing of financial resources required to meet the sales volume. Because the sales forecast is so fundamental, we will discuss the methods for forecasting in the context of the sales forecast.

Forecasting is the process of using past and current information to predict future events. There are four widely used methods, each of which requires its own type of data. These methods range in degree of

---

[15] Refer to Harry D. Wolfe, *Business Forecasting Methods* (New York: Holt, Rinehart, and Winston, 1966) for a complete discussion of forecasting techniques.

sophistication from the hunches of experienced managers to econometric models.

Forecasting Approaches

Hunches are basically crude estimates of future events based upon
past sales data, comments by salesmen and customers, and visceral reaction to the "general state of affairs." The hunch approach is relatively
cheap and usually effective in firms whose market is stable or at least
changing at a predictable rate.

Market surveys of customer intentions provided by the customer or by
salesmen in the field can improve the accuracy of sales forecasts. At least,
through the means of statistical sampling techniques, the forecaster can
specify the range of projected sales and the degree of confidence that he
has in his estimates. Of course, one should be very careful to evaluate the
reliability of information that goes into the market survey.

Time-series analysis is a third technique of forecasting which, though
it is a fairly complex statistical device, is no more effective than the good
judgment of the analyst. Time series is nothing more than analysis of the
relationship between sales and time, as shown in Figure 3–3. The chart
shows points corresponding to the annual sales for each of the years.
A straight line is drawn through the points to show that there has been
an upward pattern in the sales of the firm during the period.

FIGURE 3–3

Hypothetical Sales-Time Relationship

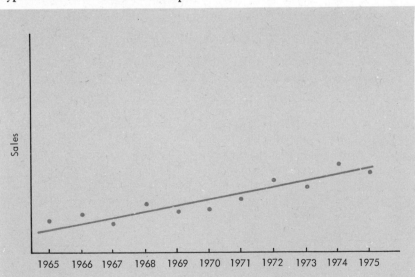

The short-run question of sales during the first quarter of 1976 cannot be answered in Figure 3–3 if there is seasonality in the firm's sales pattern. If such were not the case, the quarterly sales would be approximately one quarter of the annual sales, but the sales of most firms are seasonal. If a company markets fishing equipment, the sharpest demand is during the spring and summer months, declining to quite low levels during the fall and winter. The prediction of annual sales can be attempted from the annual data, provided one is willing to make the assumption that conditions which contributed to previous sales levels will prevail in the future. If not, the forecast must include variables other than time in the analysis.

The reader should not be led to believe that time-series analysis is simply the naive projection of trend. It may be that in the hands of the unskilled, but if skilled analysts are supplied with the right information, they can confront a whole range of questions. The movement of sales over time is due to at least three factors: seasonal, cyclical, and trend; that is, the firm's sales vary in response to seasonal factors, in response to cycles common to business activity generally, and to a trend of long-period duration. The management of a brewery knows that peak sales occur during the summer months, but is also aware of the cyclical nature of beer consumption as beer drinkers shift to liquor when their incomes increase, shifting back when their incomes decline. For long-term planning, the manager must also know something about the trend in beer consumption; consumer tastes change with time and with the introduction of new products. Yet, even the availability of these refinements does not undo the fact that time is the only determinant of sales included in the time-series analyses. Econometric models are means for systematically evaluating the impact of a number of variables on sales.

Econometric models are applications of multiple-correlation techniques to economic analysis. They permit the forecaster to discover the historical relationship between sales and a number of independent variables. These techniques are the most sophisticated of the methods, yet they offer no hope for the elimination of *all* uncertainty; management judgment is still needed.

The econometric approach begins with identification of those independent variables which would be expected to affect the sales of the firm's product. Among the obvious variables are price, competing products, and complementary products. Variables such as the age of existing stocks of the goods, availability of credit, and consumer tastes are less obvious. Measurements of these variables are obtained for previous years and matched with sales of the product for the same years. An equation is then derived which expresses the historical relationship between the variables. For example, if the sales volume of product *Y* is found to be related to variables *X* and *Z*, and the historical relationship is discovered to be

$$Y = 1.25X - 3.7Z,$$

then the forecaster need only predict the *future* values of X and Z to discover the future sales of Y. Now we see that the *forecast* of Y is derived from the *forecast* of X and Z.

No perfect method exists for projecting future sales. Hunches, surveys, and statistical analyses provide estimates which may or may not be reasonable. The estimates coming from these techniques can be no better than the information which goes into them. As technological breakthroughs in information processing occur, we can expect sales forecasts to become more accurate and consequently better guides for planning. At the present time, however, forecasting requires a great deal of managerial judgment.

Resource Forecasts

The sales forecast indicates levels of revenues that can be expected if the firm has the product to sell. But in order to have a product to sell, the firm must have the necessary resources. Accordingly, it is necessary to forecast the future availability of major resource components including personnel, raw materials, and capital. The techniques of forecasting resources are the same as those employed to forecast sales—that is, hunches, market surveys, time-series analysis, and econometric models. The only difference is that the analyst is seeking to know the quantities and prices which can be purchased, rather than sold.

The energy shortage which appeared in the early 1970s brought into sharp focus the necessity for resource forecasting. The effects of the shortage were real at every level in the economy, and the early warning signals had apparently gone unheeded. Yet when it was apparent that energy resources would not be available in assumed quantities, managers could respond only reactively. More astute planning would not necessarily have prevented the energy crisis, but it would have enabled managers to respond in more orderly ways.

Thus, the sales forecast, whether for one year or for ten years, is a prediction of the firm's level of activity. At the same time, the prediction is conditioned by the availability of resources, general economic and social events beyond the province and control of management, and by the predetermined goals. The next phase of the planning function is the allocation of resources necessary to sustain the forecasted level of activity. The principal technique which management uses in this phase of the planning function is the budget.

BUDGETING

The third phase of the planning function is the development of budgets for each important element of the organization. Budgets are widely used in business and government. A considerable body of literature exists dealing with budgeting techniques.[16] We should recognize the very close relationship between budgeting as a planning technique and budgeting as a control technique. In this section, we are concerned only with the preparation of budgets prior to operations. From this perspective, budgeting is a part of planning. However, with the passage of time and as the organization engages in its activities, the actual results are compared with the budgeted (planned) results. This analysis may lead to corrective action and this, as we shall see later, is the essence of controlling. The interrelationship between planning and controlling is well illustrated by budgeting techniques.

Financial Budgeting

The financial budgeting process implements the income goals of the firm and serves as the chief means for integrating the activities of all the various subunits. Budgeting can be viewed as an important method for coordinating the efforts of the firm.

The complexity of the financial budgeting process is revealed in Figure 3–4. The key position of the sales forecast is evident from the placement of the sales budget; all other budgets are related to it either directly or indirectly. For example, the production budget must specify the materials, labor, and other manufacturing expenses required to support the projected sales level. Similarly, the distribution expense budget details the costs associated with the level of sales activity projected for each product in each sales region. Administrative expenses also must be related to the predicted sales volume. The projected sales and expenses are combined in the financial budgets which consist of *pro forma* financial statements, inventory budgets, and the capital additions budget.

Two Budgeting Approaches

The usefulness of financial budgets depends mainly on the degree to which they are flexible to changes in conditions. The forecasted data are based upon certain premises or assumptions regarding the future. If these premises prove wrong, the budgets are inadequate. Two principal means exist to provide flexibility, namely, variable budgeting and moving budgeting.

Variable budgeting provides for the possibility that actual output deviates from planned output. It recognizes that certain costs are related to output (variable costs), while others are unrelated to output (fixed costs). Thus, if actual output is 20 percent less than planned output, it

---

[16] For example: Walter R. Bunge, *Managerial Budgeting for Profit Improvement* (New York: McGraw-Hill Book Co., 1968); Francis C. Dykeman, *Financial Reporting Systems and Techniques* (Englewood Cliffs, N.J.: Prentice-Hall, 1969); J. Brooks Heckert and James D. Wilson, *Business Budgeting and Control* (New York: Ronald Press Co., 1967).

FIGURE 3-4

The Financial Budgeting Process*

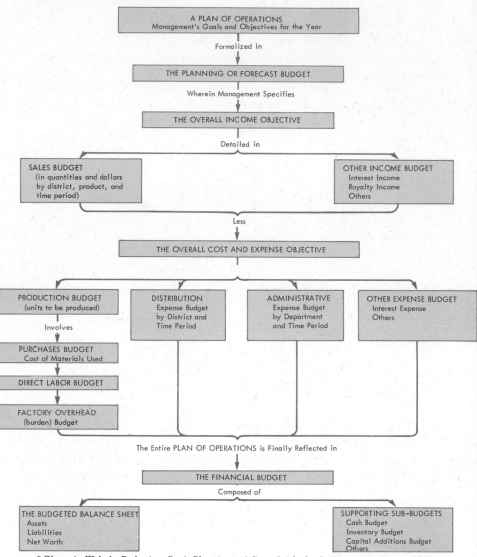

* Glenn A. Welsch, *Budgeting: Profit Planning and Control*, 2d ed., © 1964, p. 50. Reprinted by permission of Prentice-Hall, Inc., Englewood Cliffs, N.J.

does not follow that actual profit will be 20 percent less than that planned. Rather, the actual profit will vary depending upon the quite complex relationship between costs and output. Figure 3–5 demonstrates a hypothetical situation.

The relationships shown in Figure 3–5 take the form of the familiar

FIGURE 3–5

The Relationship between Profit and Output

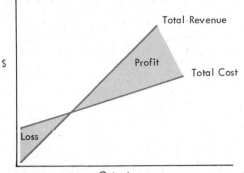

break-even model. The point to be made here is simply that profit varies with output variations, but not proportionately. Table 3–1 shows a variable budget which allows for output variations and which demonstrates the behavior of costs and profits as output varies.

Variable budgeting requires adjustments in all supporting budgets for completeness. The production, distribution, and administrative budgets must likewise allow for the impact of output variation.

Moving budgeting is the preparation of a budget for a fixed period, say, one year, with periodic updating at fixed intervals, say, one month. For example, the budget is prepared in December for the next 12 months, January through December. At the end of January, the budget is revised and projected for the next 12 months, February through January. In this manner, the most recent information is included in the budgeting process. Premises and assumptions are constantly being revised as management learns from experience.

Moving budgets have the advantage of systematic reexamination, but the disadvantage of becoming costly to maintain. Budgets are important instruments for implementing the objectives of the firm; on the other

TABLE 3–1

A Hypothetical Variable Budget

Output (units)	1000	1200	1400	1600
Sales @ $5.00	$5000	$6000	$ 7000	$8000
Variable costs @ $3.00	$3000	$3600	$4200	$4800
Fixed costs	1000	1000	1000	1000
Total costs	4000	4600	5200	5800
Planned profit	$1000	$1400	$1800	$2200

hand, they must be kept in perspective and viewed as competing with other demands for managerial time.

Program Budgeting

A recent development in public administration employs the planning concepts described in this chapter, that is, that plans and budgets should be devised in terms of goals. The development of program budgeting, or PPB, in government began with the attempts of Secretary of Defense McNamara to prepare the 1963 budget of the Department of Defense in a manner which reflected the expected cost of each departmental objective. This effort was in contrast with the historical practice of preparing budgets by objects of expenditure—personnel, operating expenses, and capital improvement expenditures.[17] The traditional governmental budgeting process did not reflect the goals of the department and therefore did not permit rational allocation of resources among those goals.

From those beginnings in the Department of Defense, the concepts of program budgeting spread throughout the federal government as well as state and local governments. For example, Kentucky, Michigan, and Pennsylvania are among the states which have adopted some variant of the program budgeting approach. It is not possible to develop a complete description of PPB here. The important point is to recognize that the logic of planning from goals to resource allocation is well established in business management, yet that logic has only recently been adopted in public management.

POLICY MAKING

The principal means by which management implements plans is through policy making, the fourth phase of planning. *Policies are statements which reflect the basic objectives of the entity and which provide the guidelines for carrying out action throughout the entity.*[18] Policies, like plans, are both specific and general, abstract and concrete, short-run and long-run.

Policy making is an important management tool for assuring that action is goal oriented. Policies explain *how* the goals are to be achieved; they thus direct the behavior of persons in the firm. The interrelation among the managerial functions is reflected in the nature of policies. As we shall see, managerial *control* includes specification of action before the fact, and policies serve this end.

---

[17] See Leonard Merewitz and Stephen H. Sosnick, *The Budget's New Clothes* (Chicago: Markham Publishing Co., 1971), for a more detailed description of program budgeting.

[18] M. Valliant Higginson, *Management Policies I*, AMA Research Study 76 (New York: American Management Association, 1966).

Effective policy making requires recognition of the many dimensions and characteristics of policies. Ziegler[19] has suggested the following characteristics as important for creating effective policies:

1. *Flexibility.* A policy must strike a reasonable balance between stability and flexibility. Conditions change and policies must change accordingly. On the other hand, some degree of stability must prevail if order and a sense of direction are to be achieved. There are no rigid guidelines to specify the exact degree of requisite flexibility; only the judgment of management can determine the balance.

2. *Comprehensiveness.* A policy must be comprehensive to cover any contingency if plans are to be followed. The degree of comprehensiveness depends upon the scope of action controlled by the policy itself. If the policy is directed toward very narrow ranges of activity—for example, hiring policies—it need not be as comprehensive as a policy concerned with public relations.

3. *Coordinative.* A policy must provide for coordination of the various subunits whose actions are interrelated. Without coordinative direction provided by policies, each subunit is tempted to pursue its own goals. The ultimate test of any subunit's activity should be its relationship to the policy statement.

4. *Ethical.* A policy must conform to the canons of ethical behavior which prevail in society. The manager is ultimately responsible for the resolution of issues which involve ethical principles. The increasingly complex and interdependent nature of contemporary society has resulted in a great number of problems involving ethical dimensions which are only vaguely understood.

5. *Clarity.* A policy must be written clearly and logically. It must specify the intended aim of the action which it governs, define the appropriate methods and action, and delineate the limits of freedom of action permitted to those whose actions are to be guided by it.

The ultimate test of the effectiveness of a policy is whether the intended objective is attained. If the policy does not lead to the goal, it should be revised. Thus, policies must be subjected to reexamination on a continual basis.

SUMMARY

The planning function is the fundamental managerial activity. It consists of four distinct phases, or subfunctions: *goal setting, forecasting, budgeting,* and *policy making.* We have seen that planning can have any

---

[19] Raymond J. Ziegler, *Business Policies and Decision Making* (New York: Appleton-Century-Crofts, 1966).

time dimension ranging from the short to long run. We have also surveyed some of the more important forecasting and budgeting techniques. The readers should not assume, however, that they have now surveyed the entire range of problems and issues associated with planning. At the same time, they should recognize that the essence of management is planning, and that all other functions are derived from planning.

The manager who successfully practices the planning function recognizes that much of the task consists of asking the appropriate questions. Table 3–1 suggests the basic ones; other, more specific, questions might well be posed. Yet the fundamental questions are appropriate regardless of the type and size of the organization. Such questions lead to the development of means by which the four phases of the planning function are implemented, and the means will vary depending upon the answers

TABLE 3–2

Key Managerial Planning Issues

Planning Phase	*Key Managerial Decisions*
Goal setting	1. What goals will be sought?
	2. What is the relative importance of each goal?
	3. What are the relationships among the goals?
	4. At what points in time should each goal be achieved?
	5. How can each goal be measured?
	6. What person or organizational unit should be accountable for achieving the goal?
Forecasting	1. What are the important variables which bear on the successful achievement of goals?
	2. What information exists regarding each variable?
	3. What is the appropriate technique for forecasting the future movement of each important variable?
	4. What person or organizational unit should be accountable for the forecasts?
Budgeting	1. What resource components should be included in the budget?
	2. What are the interrelationships among the various budgeted components?
	3. What budgeting technique should be used?
	4. Who or what organizational unit should be accountable for the preparation of the budget?
Policy making	1. What policy statements are necessary to implement the overall plan?
	2. To what extent are the policy statements comprehensive, flexible, coordinative, ethical, and clearly written?
	3. Who or what organizational units should authorize and prepare policy statements?
	4. Who or what organizational units are to be affected by the policy statements?

to the question. We can readily appreciate the fact that the planning function will be undertaken differently in IBM, as compared to a neighborhood grocery store, or in the Department of Health, Education, and Welfare, as compared to a county health department. There are no universally applicable planning aproaches, but the necessity for "advance thinking as a basis for doing" is universal.

DISCUSSION AND REVIEW QUESTIONS

1. Discuss the bases for the statement that planning is the essential management function.
2. A man designated by his employer as a "manager" says: "Plan? Hell, I never have time to plan. I live from day to day just trying to survive." Comment.
3. Is it accurate to say that since planning involves goal setting and goal setting involves value judgments, planning is the implementation of the manager's value system?
4. In what ways are the subgoals of a university suboptimized?
5. Describe potential conflicts between the goals of a production department and the goals of a sales department.
6. Is it true that the planning function is only as good as the underlying forecasts?
7. The budgeting process in government is often described in political terms; to what extent is the budgeting process in business also a political process?
8. How would you measure the results of programs designed to meet a firm's social responsibilities?
9. Do you believe that the *basic* purpose of a business firm is to provide goods or services at a profit?
10. Illustrate the misuse of policy statements from your own experience.
11. What is the only valid test of the appropriateness of a policy?
12. Evaluate the impact on management practice of what Taylor, Fayol, and Urwick said about the planning function.

ADDITIONAL REFERENCES

Ackoff, L. R.   *A Concept of Corporate Planning.* New York: John Wiley and Sons, Inc., 1970.

Ansoff, H. I.   *Corporate Strategy.* New York: McGraw-Hill Book Co., 1965.

Anthony, R. N.   *Planning and Control Systems.* Boston: Harvard University, Graduate School of Business, Division of Research, 1965.

Baur, R. A., and Fenn, D. H.   *The Corporate Social Audit.* New York: Russell Sage Foundation, 1972.

Bierman, H., and Smidt, S.   *The Capital Budgeting Decision.* New York: The Macmillan Co., 1966.

Branch, M. C.   *Planning: Aspects and Applications.* New York: John Wiley and Sons, Inc., 1966.

England, G. W.   *Personal Value Systems of Managers.* Minneapolis: Industrial Relations Center, University of Minnesota, 1973.

Ewing, D. W.   *The Human Side of Planning.* New York: The Macmillan Co., 1969.

Glueck, W. F.   *Business Policy.* New York: McGraw-Hill Book Co., 1972.

Henry, H. W.   *Long-Range Planning Practices in 45 Industrial Companies.* Englewood Cliffs, N.J.: Prentice-Hall, Inc., 1967.

Hughes, C. L.   *Goal Setting: Key to Individual and Organizational Effectiveness.* New York: American Management Association, 1965.

Kolasa, B. J.   *Responsibility in Business.* Englewood Cliffs, N.J.: Prentice-Hall, Inc., 1972.

LeBreton, P. P., and Henning, D. A.   *Planning Theory.* Englewood Cliffs, N.J.: Prentice-Hall, Inc., 1961.

Mockler, R. J.   *Business Planning and Policy Formation.* New York: Appleton-Century-Crofts, 1972.

Paine, F. T., and Naumes, W.   *Strategy and Policy Formation.* Philadelphia: W. B. Saunders Co., 1974.

Payne, B.   *Planning for Company Growth.* New York: McGraw-Hill Book Co., 1963.

Steiner, G. A.   *Managerial Long-Range Planning.* New York: McGraw-Hill Book Co., 1963.

Sweet, F. H.   *Strategic Planning.* Austin, Tex.: University of Texas, Bureau of Business Research, 1964.

Thompson, S.   *How Companies Plan.* New York: American Management Association, 1962.

Warren, E. K.   *Long-Range Planning: The Executive Viewpoint.* Englewood Cliffs, N.J.: Prentice-Hall, Inc., 1966.

Practical Exercise I

Planning in Fast-Food Stores

After serving 20 years in the U.S. Public Health Service, Dr. Joseph Skaggs retired and invested his savings in five fast-food stores. The stores were patterned after the successful Kentucky Fried Chicken national chain. The five stores were previously owned by a small-town banker who had aspirations, at one time, of recreating the Kentucky Fried Chicken success story. When it became apparent that such was not to be the case, he sold the business to Dr. Skaggs.

Dr. Skaggs' preinvestment research convinced him that the five stores could be more profitable than they had been simply through the application of basic management principles and techniques. To begin with, he believed that the previous owner's practice of allowing the five store managers to run their operations without any central direction was a mistake. He reasoned that even though the stores were spread throughout the state, thus precluding day-to-day supervision, coordinated effort should be attempted. At the same time, he did not want to jeopardize the initiative of the store managers by strapping them into rigid rules and procedures. He decided that the best way to introduce "good management" into the system was by beginning with the essential management function—planning.

The concept of planning which Dr. Skaggs presented at his first meeting with the five store managers was based upon his experience in public health administration. The planning concept, termed POAR, is explained as follows: POAR is an acronym which is formed from the four elements of a plan: Problem, Objectives, Activities, Resources. Accordingly the planners, the five store managers in this instance, were instructed to prepare annual plans of action for each problem that they identified in their respective stores. The plans would subsequently be the bases for allocating funds and reporting progress.

The store managers agreed with Dr. Skaggs that greater emphasis on planning should result in greater awareness of what needed to be done to make all the stores more profitable. They also accepted the legitimacy of Dr. Skaggs' right to expect them to follow his direction. Yet they were somewhat skeptical that POAR was applicable to business planning. They asked Dr. Skaggs to explain the concept by using an example. He responded by showing them the following plan for a family-planning program that he had developed during his public health career:

1. Problem Identification
   a. Desired Situation
      All 2,500 women residing in the county, and in the child-bearing age, should be provided family-planning services.
   b. Present Situation
      At present, 500 women are receiving family-planning services either through public or private clinics and physicians' offices.
   c. Specific Problem
      The problem is the difference between the desired situation and the present situation; therefore, the problem is to provide family-planning services to 2,000 women.
2. Objective
   By the end of the fiscal year 1,500 women will have received family-planning services from either public or private sources.
3. Activities
   In order to achieve the objective, the following activities will be required:
   a. Conduct 100 weekly clinics with an estimated 30 patients per clinic for a total of 3,000 patient-visits.
   b. Arrange physician office visits for 100 patients.
   c. Conduct 10 family-planning classes for teachers in 7th–12th grades, reaching approximately 250 teachers and, subsequently, 5,000 school children.
   d. Disseminate information to community and civic groups by giving 20 formal presentations.
4. Resources
   The projected cost of the plan is the total of each activity cost:
   a. Clinic cost .... $2,000.
   b. Office visit cost .... 500.
   c. Classes .... 100.
   d. Information dissemination .... 200.
      Total cost .... $2,800.

After examining the above example, one of the store managers stated that POAR may be appropriate for health management, but he failed to see its relevance for business management.

Questions for Analysis:

1. What would be your response to the store manager concerning the appropriateness of POAR?
2. Do you believe that POAR is appropriate as a format for planning in a fried-chicken store?
3. Do you agree that Dr. Skaggs should have initiated the planning function as he did?

Practical Exercise II

Problem Identification in a Consumer-Products Firm

The top management of a large consumer-products company was preparing for its annual planning session. It was at these sessions that the management identified the company's significant problems, set priorities, and provided guidelines and policies for the preparation of detailed plans. In advance of these sessions, the manager of each of the functional departments was instructed to define the single significant problem facing the company from the perspective of that function. The top management would devise a set of company problems from those provided by the functional managers and place the problems in order of priority.

The seven functional departments of the company were: production, personnel, sales, staff development and training, finance, legal counsel, and engineering. Each of these functions consisted of subunits and operated on annual plans which developed from the planning session.

The problems which were presented for discussion are summarized as follows:

Production: The major problem from the perspective of the production manager was the excessive downtime of machine-paced operations. The amount of downtime was 20 percent more than the previous year. The cause of the problem was the necessity for more intensive preventive maintenance to stay within quality control tolerances imposed by more restrictive consumer protection laws passed by the state legislature.

Personnel: The manager of the personnel department stated that the major company problem was the excessive number of grievances which went to the departmental level for arbitration. The personnel manager indicated that the settlement of grievances at that level was inappropriate as a general rule and reflected the inability of first-line managers to deal with personnel problems.

Sales: The sales manager stated that the major problem was the spiraling cost of product distribution. The company's distribution system was based upon regional warehouses connected to production facilities by a fleet of trucks. The rising cost of fuel was driving up the delivered cost of products in addition to disrupting delivery schedules—all of which indicated the necessity for increasing the delivered price to customers who already were disgruntled by price increases in the previous year.

Staff Development and Training: The manager of this department stated that the major problem was the inability of first-line supervisors to deal effectively with their subordinates. The problem grew out of the company's affirmative response to equal opportunity laws which required the employment of persons formerly considered marginal. For the most part, these new employees required intensive skill training and close supervision. Moreover, they tended to be particularly sensitive to criticism. The problem required a significant expenditure of resources to train supervisors to manage with greater sensitivity.

Finance: According to the finance department, the company must move to reduce its reliance on short-term debt to meet current obligations. The financial manager stated that the company's cash flow was seriously unbalanced, the major cause being the company's liberal credit terms and, subsequently, unpredictable collections from customers.

Legal Counsel: The chief legal officer stated that the company must either meet the recently legislated air quality standards or be brought under injunction. The company's principal source of power was coal. The air quality standards required the removal of air pollutants through the use of filter mechanisms, but at heavy expense to the company.

Engineering: The engineering department's manager stated that the company's significant problem was the high turnover of engineers for better-paying jobs with other companies. He stated that salaries must be upgraded or else face the continued drain of engineering talent.

Questions for Analysis:

1. In what order of priority would you place these problems?
2. Is there any basis for interrelating the problems, that is, is each a separate, unrelated problem?
3. Once problems are identified, what information is needed for subsequent planning decisions?

4 The Organizing Function

INTRODUCTION

The planning function refers to those activities of the managerial process which determine, in advance, goals and the means for achieving them. In a practical sense the determination of means involves an assignment of tasks to people who must then complete their work in a coordinated manner. The requirement for a coordinated effort derives from the fact that overall goals and tasks are subdivided into subgoals and subtasks. These, in turn, must be accomplished in definite ways and sequences in order to accomplish the overall goals and tasks.

This rather common-sensical idea can be easily grasped: As Mooney pointed out, whenever goals and tasks require the efforts of two or more persons, the need for organizing arises. He illustrated the point by referring to the efforts of two men attempting to lift an object that is too heavy for either to lift alone. In order to lift and move the object, the two men must act together; that is, the efforts of the two men must be coordinated through organization.[1] If one man lifts while the other rests, the object would not be moved and, thus, the goal not accomplished.

Throughout this book, the terms "organize," "organizing," and "organization" appear. We should at this time fix the meanings of the terms as they will be used:

---

[1] James D. Mooney, *The Principles of Organization* (New York: Harper and Brothers, 1947, p. 5.

Organize refers to the act of achieving coordinated effort. In this sense, we state that it is the manager's responsibility to organize work.

Organizing refers to the process of achieving coordinated effort. Thus, we say that the organizing function is part of the overall management process.

Organization refers to the final product of the organizing function, that is, the predetermined relationships between subtasks; but the term is also used to refer to an entity. In the latter context, we speak of firms, governmental agencies, hospitals, universities, and the like as organizations.

The recurring theme throughout these usages is predetermined effort to achieve coordination. Thus, we arrive at the definition of the organizing function as: *The means by which management seeks to achieve a coordinated effort through the design of a structure of task and authority relationships.* This definition highlights the importance of such concepts as design, structure, tasks, and authority. The term "design" connotes a conscious effort to predetermine the way tasks will be done in the organization; "structure" refers to the relatively fixed relationships among tasks that are sought in the design. Finally, the term "authority" is used in the traditional sense to refer to the assignment of a right to use resources (including human resources) in carrying out an assigned task.

When viewed in rather abstract terms, the organizing function is the process of breaking down the overall task into individual assignments and then putting them back together in units, or departments, along with a delegation of authority to a manager of the unit, or department. Thus, we can describe the organizing function in terms of *dividing* tasks, *departmentalizing* tasks, and *delegating* authority. But when we move from an abstract discussion of the organizing function to its concrete, practical application, simplicity is soon replaced by complexity.

The classical school of management attempted to deal with the complexity of the organizing function by espousing certain "principles of organization." We have already introduced these principles in our discussion of Taylor, Fayol, Mooney, and Urwick. Here we will apply these principles in the context of the four fundamental problems of organizing, namely:

1. What should determine the nature and content of each job? The principle of specialization of labor addresses itself to this problem.
2. What should determine the way in which jobs are grouped together? The principle of departmentalization suggests bases for grouping jobs.
3. What should determine the size of the groups? The span-of-control principle provides guidelines for solving this issue.
4. How should authority be distributed? The unity-of-command principle is relevant to this issue.

Through the application of these principles the design of a formal structure is created. We shall discuss the application of each principle and conclude the chapter with a summary which compares classical organization theory with the familiar bureaucratic organization.

THE PRINCIPLE OF SPECIALIZATION OF LABOR

Probably the most important single principle in an analysis of the classical approach to organizational design is specialization of labor. This principle affects everyone in society everyday. For example, in the construction of a single-family home, a number of divisions of work occur in every phase of construction. The workers perform tasks with a specialized framework, and include bricklaying specialists, electrical specialists, plumbing specialists, and carpentry specialists. Each performs a narrow range of duties that he is trained and qualified to handle. The overall task of building the home is too large for any one group of specialists to handle within a reasonable period of time. The "jack of all trades" has moved aside for the "master" of a specialized task in home construction.

The narrow work capacity of one group of specialists (for example, plumbers) is one of many reasons why high degrees of division of labor are popular in the classical management approach. The overall production efficiencies generated by dividing labor are viewed as beneficial. This belief is certainly not new and is still accepted as valid.

The gains derived from narrow divisions of labor can be calculated in purely economic terms. Figure 4–1 shows this relationship. As the job

FIGURE 4–1

The Economics of Specialization

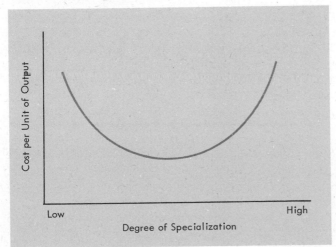

is divided into ever smaller elements, additional output is obtained; but more men and capital must be employed to do the smaller jobs. At some point, the costs of specialization (labor and capital) begin to outweigh the increased efficiency of specialization (output), and the cost per unit of output begins to rise.[2]

The problem of determining the appropriate degree of specialization becomes more difficult as the task becomes more abstract and less amenable to measurement. Nevertheless, the principle of specialization states that one must investigate the potential for gains due to specialization.

The end results of implementing the specialization-of-labor principle are job descriptions which define the *depth* and *scope*[3] of each job. The *depth* reflects the relative freedom that the job holder has in planning and controlling his duties. Ordinarily, one expects the depth of a job to increase as one moves up in the levels of the organization. An obvious contrast can be drawn between the work of the chief executive and the work of an assembly-line worker. But there can also be differences in job depth among persons at the same level. For example, a maintenance man has considerably more job depth than does a lathe worker. The *scope* of a job refers to the length of time of the job cycle; that is, the more often the job is repeated in a given time period, the more limited is its scope. We can expect to find differences in job scope among jobs at the same level and at different levels in the organization.

The writers of the Classical School of management went to great lengths in the application of specialization of labor to manual tasks. F. W. Taylor and the Gilbreths were instrumental in the development of analyses termed motion and time study. We have earlier alluded to this development in the context of goal clarity; here the emphasis is on the design of particular jobs, particularly those which involve expenditures of physical, rather than mental, energy. According to the classical writers, the work of lathe operators, assemblers, iron workers, bricklayers, and similar work can be broken down into separable and discrete hand, eye, and body movements. These movements, termed Therbligs, are defined in Table 4–1.

The identification of Therbligs enabled the classical writers to believe that high degrees of specialization could be achieved in many different settings.[4] Their calculations of the net benefits to be derived from

---

[2] Minimization of average cost is a solution under certain conditions; a generalized solution is to equate the marginal cost of specialization and the marginal gain of specialization. The reader who has had a course in basic economics will be familiar with the idea of marginal cost and gain.

[3] Alan C. Filley and Robert J. House, *Managerial Process and Organizational Behavior* (Glenview, Ill.: Scott, Foresman and Co., 1969), pp. 214–16.

[4] The design of individual tasks is an ongoing activity in most modern organizations. See Carl F. Lutz and Albert P. Ingraham, "Design and Management of Positions," *Personnel Journal*, vol. 51 (April 1972), pp. 234–40.

TABLE 4–1

The Basic Hand Movements of Manual Work

Therblig	*Objective*
1. Grasp	To gain control of an object
2. Position	To line up, orient, or change position of a part
3. Pre-position	To line up part or tool for use in another place
4. Use	To apply tool
5. Assembly	To assemble parts or objects
6. Disassemble	To separate objects
7. Release load	To release a part or object
8. Transport empty	To reach for something
9. Transport loaded	To change location of an object
10. Search	To seek to find an object
11. Select	To locate an object from a group of objects
12. Hold	To hold object in fixed position and location
13. Unavoidable delay	To wait for other body member or machine as a part of the work movement
14. Avoidable delay	To wait for other body member or machine not a part of the work movement
15. Rest for fatigue	To remain idle as a part of the cycle to overcome fatigue
16. Plan	To determine course of action
17. Inspect	To determine quality of item

Source: Adapted from Marvin E. Mundel, "Motion and Time Study," *Industrial Engineering* (Englewood Cliffs, N.J.: Prentice-Hall, Inc., 1955), pp. 296–98.

specialization did not include certain cost factors which have, more recently, been identified by the writers of the Behavioral School. The costs of overspecialization include excessive monotony, boredom, and fatigue which in turn can induce absenteeism, turnover, and shoddy workmanship. As we will see in Chapter 7, the contemporary thinking in management is that while the very essence of work in organizations requires the division of labor, the calculation of the optimum degree of specialization must include psychological as well as economical costs and benefits.

The principle of specialization of labor guides managers in determining the content of individual jobs. From a different perspective, the principle also guides them in determining how jobs should be grouped together.

THE PRINCIPLE OF DEPARTMENTALIZATION

The managerial problems associated with departmentalization are directly related to the degree to which individual jobs have been specialized. That is, the number of ways to group jobs increases with the number of different (specialized) jobs. Moreover, as Adam Smith observed some 200 years ago, the extent of specialization is limited by the extent of the market. Thus, the owner-manager of a small-town clothing store specializing in men's clothing and employing three persons has little difficulty determining the way jobs should be grouped, as compared to the management of Sears, Roebuck and Co.

In general, the bases for grouping jobs can be classified into two major categories: (1) outputs, or clients, and (2) internal operations, or functions. In terms of concepts developed in the discussion of the planning function, these two categories could be termed (1) goals or outcomes, and (2) means, or activity bases. Thus jobs could be grouped according to common goals regardless of activities, or jobs could be grouped according to activities regardless of goals.[5] These two general categories of bases for departmentalization are elaborated below.

Output-Oriented Bases

The three commonly used bases which will be discussed in this section are product, client, and geographic.

FIGURE 4–2

Departmentalization along Product Lines

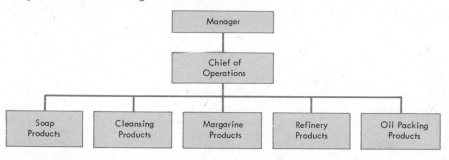

Product departmentalization involves the grouping together of all activities necessary to manufacture a product or product line. As the organization grows in size, it becomes difficult for managers to coordinate the activities of the expanding product lines. One commonly adopted strategy is to establish departments based upon product. The grouping of activities along product lines permits the utilization of the specialized skills of those people affiliated with a particular product or product line. An example of this type of departmentalization is presented in a partial organization chart, Figure 4–2.

---

[5] See Luther Gulick, "Notes on the Theory of Organization," in Luther Gulick and Lyndall F. Urwick, eds., *Papers on the Science of Administration* (New York: Columbia University, 1947), pp. 15–30, for the classical discussion of the departmentalization bases.

FIGURE 4–3

Departmentalization along Customer Lines

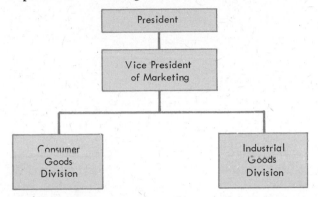

Customer departmentalization is the grouping of activities based upon the customers served. For example, a company may have two sales departments that deal with two major groups of customers. One department may service the general public, while the other may be designed to provide goods to an industrial group of customers. The customer departmentalization design is presented in Figure 4–3.

Geographical departmentalization, grouping activities according to location, is popular in organizations that have physically dispersed markets to serve. The assumption is that if markets are widely dispersed, an improved cost-and-profit situation will result if all activities affecting a product or product line in a specific geographical region are grouped together. Figure 4–4 illustrates an example of geographical departmentalization.

The first classification for grouping work—that is, product, customer,

FIGURE 4–4

Departmentalization along Geographical Lines

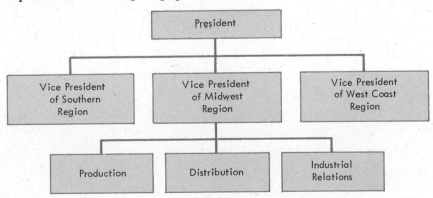

and geography—is oriented toward factors which are external to the actual operations of the firm. For example, the customer is a factor "out there" in the market. The geographical territory is also "out there," as is the distribution of the product.

Internal Operations-Oriented Bases

Two bases in this category are discussed: functional and process. *Functional departmentalization* is used when organizations are designed on the basis of the operations performed by a unit. For example, in a food-processing firm, all job-related activities involved in recruiting and selecting management trainees might be assigned to the personnel department, all marketing-related activities to the marketing department, and all activities concerned with the actual production of goods would

FIGURE 4–5

Departmentalization along Functional Lines

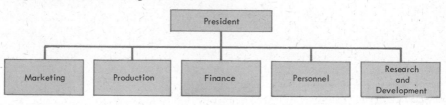

be grouped in the production department. The functional organization design is used extensively in manufacturing firms. Figure 4–5 illustrates the design.

Process departmentalization is the grouping of jobs according to technical functions. For example, the manufacturing of a product may include cutting the materials on a lathe, heat-treating the materials, and finally painting the product. The same type of technical division of work may be found in an office of a business administration department at a college. A number of typists may be assigned specific duties to perform. One types manuscripts; another typist is concerned with correspondence; and the third handles the telephone and the typing of classroom materials. In Figure 4–6, the division of work along process lines is presented.

A Final Word on Departmentalization

The methods cited above for dividing work are not exhaustive; there are many other ways. Furthermore, in most large organizations a

FIGURE 4–6

Departmentalization along Process Lines

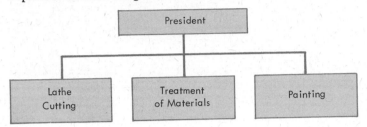

number of different methods of dividing work are used at the same time. For example, at the upper levels of management, the vice presidents reporting to the president represent different product groups. At the level directly below the vice presidents, the managers may be part of a particular function. At the next level in the organization, there may be a number of different technical classifications. This approach is illustrated in Figure 4–7.

The principle of departmentalization specifies the general objective to be followed in grouping activities, but the basis actually chosen is a matter of balancing advantages and disadvantages. For example, the advantage of departmentalizing on the basis of customers or products is that of bringing together under the control of a single manager all the resources necessary to make the product and/or service for the customers. Additionally, the specification of goals is considerably easier when the emphasis is on the final product. Yet, at the same time, the ease of goal identification and measurement can encourage the individual depart-

FIGURE 4–7

Organizational Design Using Mixed Departmentalization

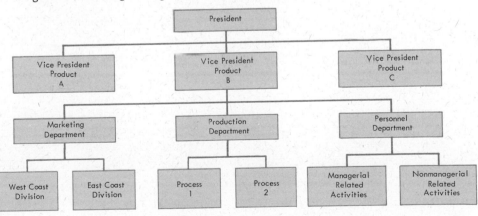

ments to pursue their own goals at the expense of company goals; we referred to this possibility in the discussion of goal structure and the problem of suboptimization in Chapter 3. A second disadvantage of product and customer departmentalization is that the task of coordinating the activities tends to be more complex. Reporting to the unit manager are the managers of the various functions (production, marketing, and personnel, for example) whose diverse but interdependent activities must be coordinated.

Departmentalization based upon internal operations (function and process departments) has advantages as well as disadvantages. The primary advantage is that such departments are based upon specific skills and training; and activities assigned to the department emphasize the skills which individual members bring to the job. The managerial task of coordinating the activities of process departments is considerably less complex than in the product department because of the similarity of the subordinates' tasks. At the same time, the disadvantages of process departments must be recognized, the principal disadvantage being the difficulty of providing job depth for the managers of such groups. Since process departmentalization involves breaking up a natural work flow and assigning parts of this flow to different departments, each departmental manager must coordinate the task with those of other departmental managers. As shown in Figure 4–6, the president must necessarily limit the freedom of the managers of each of the three process departments in order to coordinate their activities.

The relative advantages of the alternative departmentalization bases can be evaluated in terms of three criteria:[6]

1.   Which approach (basis) permits the maximum use of special technical knowledge?
2.   Which provides the most efficient utilization of machinery and equipment?
3.   Which provides the best hope of obtaining the required control and coordination?

These three criteria represent the essential thinking of the Classical School regarding the choice of bases. But as Walker and Lorsch state, they fail to recognize the complex trade-offs between them. Whereas the classical writers left it to managerial judgment to determine these trade-offs, contemporary writers are turning to researchers for help. Yet even if the combination of judgment and research leads to the correct bases for departmentalization in a given situation, the question of size of each group, or department, must be confronted; this is the question of span of control.

THE PRINCIPLE OF SPAN OF CONTROL

The span-of-control principle concerns the number of subordinates who directly report to a supervisor; it therefore determines the size of the department. In a general sense, classical theory suggests that the span of control of a supervisor should be kept small. A number of individuals typically identified with the classical approach support their interpretation of limited span of control with both quantitative and qualitative reasoning.

Graicunas' Theory of Limited Span of Control

A. V. Graicunas, a Lithuanian management consultant, applied deductive reasoning to the span-of-control problem.[7] He demonstrated that, as the number of subordinates reporting to a manager increases arithmetically, the number of potential interactions between the manager and the subordinates increases geometrically.

As Graicunas explained, the manager can relate directly to each individual subordinate (direct single) or to each possible group of subordinates (direct group). Moreover, it is possible for subordinates to relate with each other (cross). For example, a manager (M) is assigned two subordinates (A and B). The total number of relationships is six, as shown in Figure 4–8. But if only one more subordinate (C) is assigned to the manager, the total number of potential relationships increases from 6 to 18, as shown in Figure 4–8.

To demonstrate the impact of increasing the manager's span of control, Graicunas devised a formula which can be used to calculate the total number of potential relationships for any number of subordinates. The formula is as follows:

$$C - N\left[\frac{2^N}{2} + N - 1\right].$$

In this formula, C designates the total potential contacts and N, the number of subordinates reporting directly to the manager. Table 4–2 clearly shows the geometric increase in the number of possible relationships if the number of subordinates increases arithmetically.

If it is assumed that each of the potential relationships is important for successfully managing a group of subordinates, then the argument in favor of limiting the span of control gains some credence. It is, of course,

---

[7] A. V. Graicunas, "Relationships in Organization," in Gulick and Urwick, eds., *Papers on Science of Administration*, pp. 183–87.

FIGURE 4-8

Potential Relationships among a Manager and Two/Three Subordinates

A Manager (M) and Two Subordinates (A and B)			*A Manager (M) and Three Subordinates (A, B, and C)*		
Direct single.....	1.	$M{\rightarrow}A$	Direct single.....	1.	$M{\rightarrow}A$
	2.	$M{\rightarrow}B$		2.	$M{\rightarrow}B$
				3.	$M{\rightarrow}C$
Direct group.....	3.	$M{\rightarrow}A$ with B	Direct group.....	4.	$M{\rightarrow}A$ with B
	4.	$M{\rightarrow}B$ with A		5.	$M{\rightarrow}A$ with C
				6.	$M{\rightarrow}B$ with A
				7.	$M{\rightarrow}B$ with C
				8.	$M{\rightarrow}C$ with A
				9.	$M{\rightarrow}C$ with B
				10.	$M{\rightarrow}A$ with B and C
				11.	$M{\rightarrow}B$ with A and C
				12.	$M{\rightarrow}C$ with A and B
Cross..........	5.	$A{\rightarrow}B$	Cross..........	13.	$A{\rightarrow}B$
	6.	$B{\rightarrow}A$		14.	$A{\rightarrow}C$
				15.	$B{\rightarrow}A$
				16.	$B{\rightarrow}C$
				17.	$C{\rightarrow}A$
				18.	$C{\rightarrow}B$

unlikely that each of the potential relationships occurs on a daily basis. However, Graicunas' presentation of geometric increases in potential relationships provides a striking example of the increase in complexities as the span of control increases.

TABLE 4-2

Potential Relationships with Variable Number of Subordinates*

Number of Subordinates	*Number of Relationships*
1...............................	1
2...............................	6
3...............................	18
4...............................	44
5...............................	100
6...............................	222
7...............................	490
8...............................	1,080
9...............................	2,376
10...............................	5,210
11...............................	11,374
12...............................	24,708
18...............................	2,359,602

* From Harold Koontz and Cyril O'Donnell, *Principles of Management*, 5th ed. (New York: McGraw-Hill Book Co., 1972), p. 253.

Davis' Opinion on Span of Control

R. C. Davis distinguishes between two categories of span of control.[8] He discusses an *executive span* and an *operative span*. It is Davis' contention that the executive span includes the middle and top management positions in an organization structure. The span for managers at these levels should vary from three to nine, depending upon the nature of the managers' jobs and responsibilities and the rate of growth of the company, among other factors. The operative span applies to the lowest level of management. Davis proposes that the operative span can be effective with as many as 30 subordinates.

Urwick's Opinion on Span of Control

Urwick contends that managers should have a limited span of control because man in general has a limited span of attention.[9] That is, a limit exists as to the number of other people or objects to which persons can attend at the same time. Urwick recognizes that, though managers with ten subordinates can be involved with over 5,210 contacts, they typically do not enter into every potential contact in the course of a day. However, if only a portion of the potential 5,210 relationships actually occurs in a day, there is a definite limit on their time. Based upon his interpretation of span of control and the potential relationships, Urwick proposes that the ideal span for top management is four, but that at other supervisory levels, the number may be eight to twelve.

The classical version of the span-of-control principle is thus seen to be flexible in specifying the exact span. Both Davis and Urwick recognize that the optimum span depends upon a number of considerations. A latter-day statement of the principle recognizes that the optimum span is related to at least the following considerations:[10]

1. The competence of both the superior and the subordinates.
2. The degree of interaction between the units or personnel being supervised.
3. The extent to which the supervisor must carry out nonmanagerial responsibilities and the demands on his time from other people and units.
4. The similarity or dissimilarity of the activities being supervised.
5. The incidence of new problems in his unit.

[8] Ralph C. Davis, *Fundamentals of Top Management* (New York: Harper and Row, 1951).

[9] Lyndall F. Urwick, "The Manager's Span of Control," *Harvard Business Review*, vol. 35 (May–June 1956), pp. 39–47.

[10] Harold Steiglitz, *Organization Planning* (New York: National Industrial Conference Board, 1966), p. 15.

6.   The extent of standardized procedures.
7.   The degree of physical dispersion.

Depending upon the relative importance of each of these factors, the optimum span of control could vary quite considerably. Classical management theory leaves unanswered the manner in which the optimum can be determined for any particular situation. Such determination had to await the development of more sophisticated analyses than were available to the classicists. It is fair to say, however, that the tendency in classical theory is toward a narrow span of control, because the emphasis in classical literature is on stability and predictability.

THE PRINCIPLE OF UNITY OF COMMAND

One of the most fundamental relationships presented in the classical approach to organizational design is that existing between superior and subordinate. The classical interpretation of unity of command can be

FIGURE 4–9

Chain of Command

President

Vice President of Operations

Plant Manager

Department Manager

Foreman

described easily once the concept of chain of command is understood. The chain-of-command relationship is viewed as a series of superior-subordinate relationships. Starting at the top of the organization with the president and progressing down to the unskilled employee, the managerial chain of command is viewed as a pyramid. Figure 4–9 depicts the chain of command in a hypothetical managerial hierarchy.

Chain of Command

The chain of command is the formal channel which determines authority, responsibility, and communications. It is postulated that because of the complexity of these phenomena, no individual should be subject to the direct command of more than one superior, as defined by the unity-of-command principle. Thus, in a simplistic way, unity of command stresses that a subordinate is delegated authority and decision-making power from, and communicates with, one superior.

The classical management reasoning for advocating the unity-of-command principle is that receiving commands from two or more superiors is likely to bring about confusion and frustration. According to the classicists, which superior's command should be followed poses a frustrating and confusing dilemma for the subordinate.

The unity-of-command principle is *directly related to the* authority principle which specifies that an unbroken chain of command must be instituted from top to bottom. At the same time, the classicists recognized

FIGURE 4–10

Fayol's Bridge

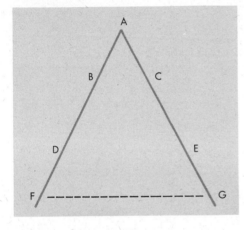

the need for providing the opportunity to bypass the formal chain when conditions warrant. Fayol had this in mind when he proposed that a subordinate should be empowered to communicate directly with a peer outside the chain, provided that the appropriate superiors approve beforehand the circumstances which permit the crossovers. Figure 4–10 shows a bridge between *F* and *G* which *D* and *E* have approved. Under special circumstances, *F* and *G* may communicate directly without going through channels, yet neither *F* nor *G* would be accountable to anyone but their immediate superiors—in this case, *D* and *E*.

Unity of Command and the Staff Function

The classicists also invoked the unity-of-command principle to guide the use of staff personnel. An important point in examining organizational design in terms of the classical theory is to distinguish between line and staff. Many different definitions of line and staff can be found in the management literature. Perhaps the most concise and least confusing definition is one which defines *line* as deriving from operational activities in a direct sense—creating, financing, and distributing a good or service, while *staff* is viewed as an advisory and facilitative function for the line.[11] The crux of this viewpoint of line and staff is the degree to which the function contributes directly to the attainment of organizational objectives. The *line functions* contribute directly to accomplishing the firm's objectives, while *staff functions* facilitate the accomplishment of the major organizational objectives in an indirect manner. Figure 4–11 illustrates a line-and-staff organizational design.

Assuming that the organization depicted in Figure 4–11 is a manu-

FIGURE 4–11

A Line-and-Staff Design

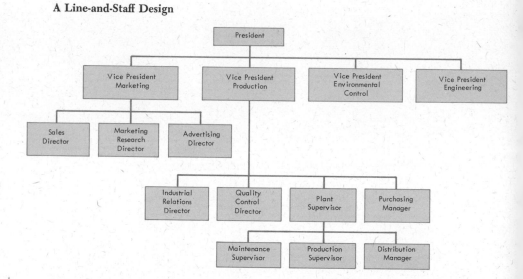

facturing firm would enable one to conclude which of the positions are line and which are staff. Using the criterion that the line function contributes directly to the firm's objectives would lead to the conclusion that the marketing and production departments perform activities directly related to the attainment of a most important organizational goal—placing an acceptable product on the market. The activities of the managers of environmental control and engineering are advisory in nature. That is, they are helpful in enabling the firm to produce and

---

[11] Our choice of this particular distinction is arbitrary. For a complete discussion of various line-staff conceptualizations, see Robert T. Golembiewski, *Organizing Men and Power: Patterns of Behavior and Line-Staff Models* (Chicago: Rand McNally and Co., 1967).

market its product, but do not directly contribute to the process. Thus they are considered to be staff departments in this particular firm.

The unity-of-command principle quite clearly defines the appropriate role of the staff specialist in the organization: The staff advises and provides information, but has no authority over the work of a particular line manager's subordinates. To place a subordinate under the jurisdiction of a staff official as well as a line manager would violate the span-of-control principle and would weaken the chain of command.

SUMMARY

The classical approach emphasizes the design of the formal structure of the organization to achieve coordinated effort. Various principles of management such as division of labor, span of control, unity of command, departmentalization, and authority provide the cornerstones of the classical approach. It is generally concluded that the main emphasis of classical design theory is upon the structure of the organization.

It has also been observed that the classical theory of organizing includes certain assumptions about the participants. These assumptions in turn greatly influenced the classical approach.[12] Douglas McGregor referred to them as Theory X and described them as follows:[13]

1. *The employees of the firm inherently dislike their jobs and will resort to many secretive and disruptive practices to avoid work.* This assumption illustrates a mistrust of the employee since productivity is a desired goal of the Theory X advocate and, consequently, if work is disliked and avoided when possible, the hoped-for goal may not be achieved.
2. *Since employees dislike work, most people must be coerced, controlled and literally threatened with punishment if the firm's desired goals are to be achieved.* This contention is a logical extension and result of the first assumption. If people dislike and avoid work, they must be brought in line by the managers in the organization.
3. *Most workers in an organization want to be directed and want to avoid job responsibilities whenever possible.* This assumption stresses the importance of structuring work in such a manner that the workers will be led and directed by a recognized authority figure in the organization.

---

[12] For a survey of the literature with emphasis on the underlying assumptions of various theories of organization, see James L. Gibson, "Organization Theory and the Nature of Man," *Academy of Management Journal*, vol. 9 (September 1966), pp. 233–45.

[13] Douglas McGregor, *The Human Side of Enterprise* (New York: McGraw-Hill Book Co., 1960).

4. *Most workers want security above all other factors which can be associated with their work.* McGregor included the security factor in his third assumption; however, since it is such an important concept today, the security item is viewed here as a separate assumption. It suggests that managers believe that, in motivating workers or organizing work, they can derive more positive results in performance by considering the high levels of insecurity among the work force.

We can understand how these assumptions influenced classical organization theory by examining them in the context of bureaucratic organization. The bureaucracy, as described by Max Weber, is a highly structured, formalized, and impersonal organization.[14] Weber, writing at the same time as the classical management theorists, argued that the bureaucracy is the most efficient form of organization for achieving goals such as production efficiency. He recognized that the degree of bureaucratization varied widely in practice; but he proposed that certain characteristics define the most efficient organization, which he termed the "ideal" type, as follows:

1. A clear division of labor exists, so that each task to be performed by employees is systematically established and legitimatized by formal recognition as an official duty.
2. The functions within the organizational system are officially arranged in a hierarchical manner. That is, a chain of command from the top down is established. This is referred to in the management literature as the *scalar chain.*
3. The actions of employees are governed by rules and procedures which are formally prescribed and which are utilized in a uniform manner in every situation.
4. The officials of the bureaucracy apply the rules and procedures as impersonally as is humanly possible. The "people" element is given consideration after the entity itself.
5. Admission to the bureaucracy is based upon rigid selection criteria which apply uniformly and impersonally to each candidate applying or being considered for a position. The criteria for selection are based upon objective standards for the job which have been established by the officials of the organization.

Examination of these five characteristics shows that they are similar in many ways to classical organization principles, and that they implement Theory *X* assumptions. In Theory *X*, it is assumed that human behavior requires a rigid organizational structure which is developed and operated by officials. The bureaucratic form of organization is most

---

[14] Max Weber, "The Essentials of Bureaucratic Organization: An Ideal-Type Construction," in Robert K. Merton, et al., eds., *A Reader in Bureaucracy* (Glencoe, Ill.: The Free Press, 1952), pp. 18–27.

compatible with the desires of people who are characterized by Theory X. Table 4–3 demonstrates this compatibility.

In Table 4–3, the chain of command is connected to three McGregor assumptions: (1) dislike of work; (2) control, coercion, and threats; and (3) direction. This indicates how the chain-of-command concept may be viewed as overcoming and satisfying the characteristics of people postulated by McGregor. Further, the rules and procedure requirement of Weber is related to two McGregor assumptions. This is due to the reasoning that rules and procedures give some people the security they

TABLE 4–3
Bureaucracy and Theory X

Characteristics of Bureaucratic Organizations	Theory X Assumptions That They Satisfy
1. Division of Labor.....................	People Need to be Directed.
2. Chain of Command...................	People Dislike Work; People Need to be Coerced, Controlled, and Threatened; People Need to be Directed.
3. Specified Rules and Procedures..........	People Need to be Coerced, Controlled, and Threatened; People Need Security.
4. Impersonality.......................	People Need to be Coerced, Controlled, and Threatened.
5. Rigid Selection Criteria..............	People Dislike Work.

desire and the control mechanisms they need. The other relationships in the table should be interpreted in a similar manner.

The Theory X assumptions and the "ideal" bureaucracy character-istics offer insight into the principles of management and concepts employed in the classical organization theory. As discussed in this chapter, the organizing function in classical theory is concerned with providing a formal structure within which work takes place. However, the structure does not guarantee that the desired activities will auto-matically be realized. The efforts undertaken by management to assure that actual activity conforms to planned activity constitute the control function. Control from the classical viewpoint is discussed in the next chapter.

DISCUSSION AND REVIEW QUESTIONS

1. What objectives do managers seek through the organizing function, and what are the indications that they have achieved them?

2. In what specific ways are the organizing and planning functions inter-related? What kinds of work would you expect to find in a unit titled "Organization Planning"?

3. Use the classical organizing principles to describe and evaluate an organization to which you belong. For example, describe and evaluate the formal structure in terms of division of labor, bases of departmentalization, span of control, and unity of command.

4. What are the bases of departmentalization in the college in which you are enrolled? What alternative bases might be used to group faculty together? Which one is the "best"?

5. How does the manager know that he has designed the right organization structure?

6. A critic of capitalism states that the cost of specialization of labor is alienation from the work place. Is he correct? If he is, so what? What is the alternative?

7. How can the use of staff personnel conflict with the unity-of-command principle? How could such conflicts be resolved?

8. What is the relationship between Taylor's "functional foremanship" and the use of staff?

9. Do you believe that Theory X describes the nature of man? Do you believe that classical organization theory is based upon Theory X?

10. What is the meaning of bureaucracy to a political scientist?

11. Is it true that all organizations have some of the characteristics of bureaucracy? Moreover, can it be argued that "bureaucracy" is necessarily a poor form of organization?

12. Classical organization theory proposed that stability and predictability are appropriate objectives of organization. Do these objectives conflict with creativity and innovativeness?

ADDITIONAL REFERENCES

Baker, A. W., and Davis, R. C.   *Ratios of Staff to Line Employees and Stages of Differentiations of Staff Functions.* Columbus: Ohio State University, Bureau of Business Research, 1954.

Brown, A.   *Organization of Industry.* Englewood Cliffs, N.J.: Prentice-Hall, Inc., 1947.

Dale, E.   *Organization.* New York: American Management Association, 1967.

————.   *Planning and Developing the Company Organization Structure.* New York: American Management Association, 1952.

Dale, E., and Urwick, L. F.   *Staff in Organization.* New York: McGraw-Hill Book Company, 1960.

Davis, R. C.   *The Fundamentals of Top Management.* New York: Harper and Brothers, 1951.

Downs, A. *Inside Bureaucracy*. Boston: Little, Brown. 1967.

Famularo, J. J. *Organization Planning Manual*. New York: American Management Association, 1970.

Fox, W. M. *The Management Process*. Homewood, Ill.: Richard D. Irwin, Inc., 1963.

Frank, H. E. *Organization Structuring*. New York: McGraw-Hill Book Co., 1971.

Hall, C. L. *The Management Guide*. Standard Oil Company of California, Department of Organization, 1948.

Holden, P. E., Fish, L. S., and Smith, H. L. *Top-Management Organization and Control*, New York: McGraw-Hill Book Company, 1941.

Pfiffner, J. M., and Sherwood, F. P. *Administrative Organization*, Englewood Cliffs, N.J.: Prentice-Hall, Inc., 1960.

Practical Exercise I

Organizational Problems in an Electronic Products Company

The plant superintendent and the personnel manager of a large electronic products manufacturing facility were discussing current problems. It was their practice to meet at least twice a month to "review the situation," particularly with respect to personnel. The plant had been opened less than a year ago and the management had spent the better part of its time recruiting and training employees. The superintendent believed that sufficient time had been spent in gearing up the plant and that it was now time to begin to expect that problems would be the exception, rather than the rule. He specifically was concerned with the high levels of downtime, scrappage, labor cost, and absenteeism.

The personnel manager argued for more patience. She stated that the new employees had not had sufficient time to develop the basis for understanding and relating to one another. "Nonsense," replied the plant manager. "We have organization charts, job descriptions, and policy manuals. There is no reason for the work to go undone or half done if the people are trained to do it. And they are trained because you trained them!"

The personnel manager could agree with most of the superintendent's comments. She had to agree that the employees were trained. But she went on to suggest that the existence of a formal structure does not assure that employees will behave in the correct manner. She persuaded the superintendent of the wisdom of using an employee opinion questionnaire to determine the extent to which employees understand the organization.

The opinion questionnaire was completed by all 600 employees, managers and nonmanagers alike, on company time. It included approximately 100 questions dealing with a variety of issues concerning the organization structure. The responses to the questionnaire were tabulated by the personnel manager's staff and a summary was prepared for discussion with the plant superintendent.

Some highlights of the summary are as follows:

1. Thirty-five percent of the nonmanagerial employees stated that they very often felt that there is day-to-day uncertainty concerning the goals of their job.
2. Twenty percent of the nonmanagerial employees stated that they often had difficulty getting necessary job-related information from their supervisors.
3. Twenty percent of the managerial personnel believed that there was seldom enough communication between their units and those with which they came in contact.
4. Forty percent of the nonmanagerial personnel believed that strict enforcement of rules and procedures usually prevented appropriate action.
5. Thirty percent of the managerial personnel believed that they seldom had authority commensurate with their responsibility.
6. Twenty percent of the managerial personnel believed that coordination was rarely achieved through planning.

The plant superintendent read the summary report and stated: "How is it possible for people to believe these ways? After all, we have all kinds of documents, procedures, and policies which define our organization structure. The only explanation that I can accept is that they simply haven't been told."

Questions for Analysis:

1. What would be your response to the superintendent if you were the personnel manager?
2. Do you, as the personnel manager, believe that the evidence from the opinion survey warrants a critical analysis of the organization structure? Why?
3. How would the superintendent know that the organization structure of the plant is the best one?

Practical Exercise II

Reorganizing State Human Resources Agencies

The governor of a southeastern state had pledged during his campaign to reorganize state government. The purpose of the reorganization was to simplify the structure, eliminate overlapping functions, and, consequently, obtain more effective and efficient delivery of governmental services. The governor ran a successful race and was sworn into office.

Within a few weeks after taking office, the governor set in motion the process that would result in reorganization. One of the first areas to be reorganized was human resources. The state agencies which previously were concerned with a range of activities directed toward the health and welfare of people included the Departments of Health, Economic Security, Mental Health, Child Welfare, Handicapped Children, Veterans Affairs, and Aging. The combined budgets of these agencies totaled nearly $650 million and represented one-half of the total state budget. By executive order, the governor placed all of these and other smaller agencies into a single unit, named the Department for Human Resources. The new organization was to be headed by a Secretary who was also named by the governor with the issuance of the executive order. He also named the commissioners of the five bureaus of the new department.

One of the first acts of the Secretary was to issue the following directive to the bureau commissioners:

> The executive order reorganized several formerly independent agencies into a Department for Human Resources. That executive order defined the new department as composed of the Bureaus for Health Services, Social Services, Manpower Services, Social Insurance, and Administration and Operations. The internal structure of each of these bureaus was not specified. The executive order only outlined the broad function of these larger units and allocated various organizational entities from the former agencies to the respective bureaus. The executive order did not define the organizational structure inside these units to allow the commissioners to assist in the development of this organizational refinement. This paper outlines the steps, procedures, checkpoints, and expectations of the Secretary for Human Resources with regard to that organizational refinement.

TASK I. *Inventory of Present Situation* (Due September 24)

The executive order defined the broad purpose of the bureaus of the department and transferred organization subunits of the former agencies into the Department for Human Resources and placed them within the various bureaus. The Human Resources commissioners are directed to prepare an inventory of:

A. *Outline of Mission*

The executive order outlines the overall function of each bureau. Discussion between the secretary and each of the commissioners has amplified that definition of organizational purpose. Each commissioner should now commit to paper the purpose of his bureau as he now understands it, with specific reference to any issues on which there is still confusion and on which further discussion with the secretary is required.

B. *Organizational Resources*

Each commissioner should inventory the organizational units that have been transferred from the former Human Resources agencies to his bureau. The subunits of each of these organizational units, so transferred, should be identified. Each commissioner should identify any organizational units that were not transferred into his bureau that should have been to fulfill the *intent* of the executive order. Each commissioner should identify organizational units or subunits that were transferred into his bureau that should not have been so transferred in accordance with the *intent* of the executive order.

C. *Available Resources*

Each commissioner should present to the secretary a list of his field offices, personnel, and other nonmonetary resources that will affect the eventual development of refined organizational structures. Special note should be taken of personnel within the bureaus that have particularly high levels of competence and will have to be considered for appointment as division directors or other officials of major responsibility within each bureau.

TASK II. *Organization Principles and Alternative Structures* (Due October 8)

Following a discussion between the secretary and each commissioner on the Task I products, each commissioner should prepare the following:

A. *Mission Statement*

Each commissioner should prepare a proposed detailed mission statement for his bureau. These mission statements should reflect refinement in the statement of purpose resulting from discussions with the secretary. The secretary will review these documents to assure that responsibilities do not overlap and that the potential for confusion has been minimized. Upon adoption by the secretary, these mission statements will be the formal basis for subsequent policy and organizational refinement.

B. *Organizational Principles*

Each commissioner should prepare a statement of proposed organizational principles. These organizational principles will guide the development of the organizational structure in each bureau. The organizational principles should reflect the mission of each bureau rather than the overall responsibility of the Department for Human Resources.

C. *Alternative Structures*

Since any organizational structure may be subdivided according to four different rationales—programmatic functions, clientele, activity, and geography—there are four alternatives available for consideration at each level of an organizational hierarchy. The results or implications, both positive and negative, of each reasonable alternative should be presented for the consideration of the Secretary.

Note: Just as the department is functionally divided between program areas of income maintenance, health services, social services, and manpower services, each bureau may be further divided according to any of the four rationales we have defined. The organizational outline or alternatives presented by each commissioner should include all reasonable alternatives and should include them to all levels of organizational hierarchy for which there will be formal structure within each bureau.

Since the Department for Human Resources was designed to acquire and benefit from important programmatic and informational interaction across bureau lines, no recommendation should be presented until all alternatives for all bureaus have been reviewed in light of interbureau relationships. That is, the development of the internal organizational structure of a bureau is not a purely internal question, it is dependent upon the alternative chosen for the other bureaus. This particular factor will be most important in the Bureau for Administration and Operations which must be designed to reflect and support the organizational structure of all program bureaus.

TASK III. *Organizational Recommendations* (Due October 22)

After consideration of all alternatives presented on October 8, and after adequate discussion between the secretary and each of the commissioners individually, and the executive staff of the department collectively, a formal, detailed organizational recommendation will be prepared by each commissioner for submission to the secretary.

Questions for Analysis:

1. Assume that you are a management consultant employed by the Secretary to assist him in the work of organizing the Department for Human Resources. As a consultant, what would you be looking for in the reports which each of the bureau commissioners would submit in response to the directive?

2. As a consultant, what would be your advice to the Secretary in his discussions with the commissioners regarding the missions of each bureau?

3. Again, as a management consultant, how would you advise the Secretary to proceed in the evaluation of the proposed alternative structures?

5 The Controlling Function

INTRODUCTION

The third function comprising the management process as identified and analyzed in classical theory is controlling. This function includes *all activities which the manager undertakes in attempting to assure that actual operations conform to planned operations.* We can see that control was the emphasis of scientific management. The development of standard methods was the result of concerted efforts by Taylor, the Gilbreths, and others to implement managerial control. They recommended a complete separation of duties between workers and managers, with workers executing tasks in consistent and uniform ways as defined by management.

The control function was discussed in considerable detail by Urwick, who synthesized the previous work of Fayol, Mooney, and Taylor to arrive at a framework for analyzing the controlling function. According to Urwick, the desired effect of managerial control is a *stable* work force which pursues its prescribed (planned) activities with a spirit of *initiative* and a *sense of unity.* The means to these ends include staffing the firm with competent managers, and selection and placement of qualified workers, augmented by the use of rewards and sanctions. The classicists emphasized impersonal means for control, but they stressed that the competence of managers crucially determines the outcome of control efforts.

The plan of this chapter is to present the controlling function in terms of three primary topics. First, we will describe the conditions which must be present in order to realize the objectives of the controlling function. In a simplistic sense, managerial control is effective when standards can be established for the variables that are to be controlled, when information is available to measure the established standards, and when managers can take corrective action whenever the actual state of the variable deviates from its desired, or standard, state. Second, we will provide a basis for classifying and understanding managerial control procedures. This classification scheme is then used to discuss the third topic: managerial control procedures. Contemporary management practice utilizes a number of different procedures which derive from the ideas of the Classical School and it is these *practical* applications which receive our most extended attention.

NECESSARY CONDITIONS FOR CONTROL

The implementation of control requires three basic conditions: (1) *Standards* must be established, (2) *information* which indicates deviations between actual and standard results must be available, and (3) *action* to bring about correction of any deviations between actual and standard must be possible. The logic is evident: Without standards, there can be no basis for evaluating the effectiveness of actual performance; without information there can be no way of knowing the situation; without provision for action to correct deviations, the entire control process becomes a pointless exercise.

Standards are derived from goals and have many of the characteristics of goals. Like goals, they are targets; to be effective, they must be clearly stated and logically related to the larger goals of the unit. Standards are the criteria against which future, current, or past actions are compared. They are measured in a variety of ways, including physical, monetary, quantitative, and qualitative terms. The various forms which standards can take will be made clear in subsequent discussions of control methods.

Information which reports actual performance and which permits appraisal of the performance against standards must be provided. Such information is most easily acquired for activities which produce specific and concrete results; for example, production and sales activities have end products which are easily identifiable and for which information is readily obtainable. The performances of legal departments, research-and-development units, and personnel departments are quite difficult to appraise because the outcomes of such activities are difficult to measure.

Managerial actions to correct deviations are stimulated by the discovery of the need for action and from the ability to implement the desired action. People responsible for taking the corrective steps must know that they are indeed responsible and they have the assigned authority to take the action. Unless the job and position descriptions include specific statements which clearly delineate these two requirements, the control function will surely fall short of its objective.

The control function, then, involves the implementation of methods which provide answers to three basic questions, namely: What are the planned and expected results? By what means can the actual results be compared to planned results? What corrective action is appropriate from which authorized person? Let us go on to describe more specifically the relationship between controlling, planning, and organizing by identifying three major types of control.

THREE TYPES OF CONTROL[1]

The control function can be broken down into three types on the basis of the focus of control activity. Figure 5–1 describes the three types.

FIGURE 5–1

The Controlling Function

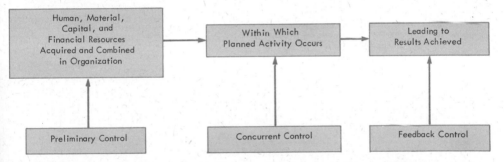

Preliminary control focuses on the problem of preventing deviations in the quality and quantity of resources used in the organization. Human resources must meet the job requirements as defined by the organization structure; employees must have the capability, whether physical or intellectual, to perform the assigned tasks. The materials must meet acceptable levels of quality and must be available at the proper time and place. In addition, capital must be on hand to assure the adequate supply of plant and equipment. Finally, financial resources must be available in the right amounts and at the right times. Methods exist which enable management to implement preliminary control. Some of these are described in this chapter.

---

[1] In this section we identify *feedback* control as a separate type. Many students will recognize that feedback can also be viewed as part of the broader concept of control where it refers to the information which reports results to the manager.

Concurrent control monitors actual ongoing operations to assure that objectives are pursued. The principal means by which concurrent control is implemented are the directing or supervisory activities of managers. Through personal, on-the-spot observation, managers determine whether the work of others is proceeding in the manner defined by policies and procedures. The delegation of authority provides managers with the power to use financial and nonfinancial incentives to affect concurrent control. The standards guiding ongoing activity are derived from job descriptions and from policies which result from the planning function.

Feedback control methods focus on end-results. The corrective action, if taken, is directed at improving either the resource acquisition process or the actual operations. This type of control derives its name from the fact that *historical* results guide *future* actions. An illustration of feedback control is a thermostat, which automatically regulates the temperature of a room by constantly measuring actual temperature and comparing it with the desired temperature. Figure 5–2 shows feedback control

FIGURE 5–2

A Simple Feedback Control System

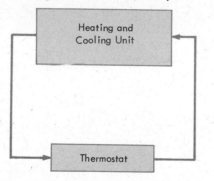

applied to the temperature example. Since the thermostat maintains the preset temperature (goal) by constantly monitoring the actual temperature, future results (temperature) are directly and continually determined by actual results (again, temperature). The feedback methods employed in business include budgets, standard costs, financial statements, and quality control.

At this point, the three types of control can be described and distinguished by examining the *focus* of corrective action. As shown in Figure 5–3, preliminary control methods are based upon information which measures some attribute or characteristic of resources; the focus of corrective action is directed, in turn, at the resources. That is, the variable measured is the variable acted upon. Similarly, concurrent control meth-

FIGURE 5–3

The Three Types of Control as Distinguished by Focus of Corrective Action

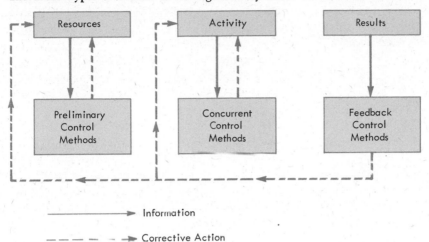

ods are based upon information related to activity, and it is activity that is acted upon. However, the focus of corrective action associated with feedback control is not that which is measured—results. Rather, resources and activity are acted upon. It is this distinction that is used to classify the control methods discussed below.

PRELIMINARY CONTROL PROCEDURES

Preliminary control procedures include all managerial efforts to increase the probability that future actual results will compare favorably with planned results. From this perspective, we can see that policies are important means for implementing preliminary control, since policies are by nature guidelines for future action. Yet we want to distinguish between *setting* policies and *implementing* them. Setting policy is included in the planning function, whereas implementing policy is a part of the control function. Similarly, we might include job descriptions in the control function since job descriptions predetermine the activity of the jobholder. At the same time, however, we want to distinguish between *defining* and *staffing* the task structure. The former is a part of the organizing function, and the latter of the controlling function.

Preliminary Control of Human Resources

The organization structure defines the job requirements and predetermines the skill requirements of the job holders. These requirements vary in the degree of specificity depending upon the nature of the task. At the shop level the skill requirements can be specified in terms of physical attributes and manual dexterity. On the other hand, the job requirements of management and staff personnel are more difficult to define in terms of concrete measurements.

As implied in Chapter 4, preliminary control is effected through procedures which include the selection and placement of managerial and nonmanagerial personnel.[2] We should distinguish between those procedures which are designed to obtain qualified subordinate managers (staffing) and those which are designed to obtain qualified nonmanagers and operatives (selection and placement). The basic procedures and objectives are essentially the same; yet classical theory makes the distinction because of its emphasis upon managerial competence as the fundamental determiner of the organization's success.

The candidates for positions must be recruited from inside or outside the firm and the most promising applicant selected from the list of candidates. The selection decision is based upon the congruence of the applicant's skills, personal characteristics, and the job requirements. The successful candidate must be trained in methods and procedures appropriate for the job—a managerial responsibility that is clearly defined in classical theory by Taylor. Most modern organizations have elaborate procedures for providing training on a continual basis.

Preliminary Control of Materials

The raw material which is converted into the finished product must conform to standards of quality. At the same time, a sufficient inventory must be maintained to insure a continuous flow to meet customer demands. The techniques of inventory control are discussed in a later chapter; at this point, we should only be concerned with the quality of incoming materials.

In recent years numerous methods have been devised which use statistical sampling to control the quality of materials by the inspection of samples rather than of the entire lot. These methods are less costly in terms of inspection time, but there is the risk of accepting defective material if the sample does not happen to contain any of the defectives.

A complete discussion of statistical sampling is beyond the scope of

---

[2] This phase of preliminary control is an aspect of personnel management. See Leon C. Megginson, *Personnel: A Behavioral Science Approach to Administration* (Homewood, Ill.: Richard D. Irwin, Inc., 1972); Paul S. Greenlaw and Robert D. Smith, *Personnel Management* (Scranton, Pa.: International Textbook Co., 1970); John B. Miner and Mary G. Miner, *Personnel and Industrial Relations* (New York: The Macmillan Co., 1973).

this text, but the essence of the procedure can be understood easily.[3] Suppose, for example, that management sets a standard 3 percent level of defective items as the maximum that it will accept from the supplier. The material is then inspected by selecting a random sample and calculating the percentage of defective items in that sample. The decision that must then be made, based on the sample, is whether to accept or reject the entire order, or to take another sample. Errors can be made in sampling so that a lot is accepted when in fact it contains more than 3 percent defectives, or a lot is rejected when in fact it contains less than 3 percent defectives. The control system will be constructed based upon a careful balancing of the relative costs of these two types of errors.

The characteristics of materials preliminary control are illustrative of control systems which are quite routine. The decision to accept or reject materials recurs frequently and must be made on a fairly routine basis. The standard is easily measured and information (the sample) is readily available. The decision to accept or reject (or take another sample) is based upon straightforward instructions; given the sample results, the decision is automatic. The inspector's instructions may read: "If sample defectives are equal to or less than 3 percent, accept the lot; if sample defectives are equal to or more than 5 percent, reject the lot; if sample defectives are between 3 and 5 percent, take another sample." If a second sample is required, the inspector's actions will be determined by another set of instructions.

Preliminary Control of Capital

The acquisition of capital reflects the need to replace existing equipment or to expand the firm's productive capacity. Capital acquisitions are controlled by establishing criteria of potential profitability which must be met before the proposal is authorized. Such acquisitions are ordinarily included in the *capital budget,* which is an intermediate and long-run planning document that details the alternative sources and uses of funds. The decisions to be made by the manager, which involve the commitment of present funds in exchange for future funds, are termed *investment decisions;* and the methods which serve to screen investment proposals derive from economic analysis.[4] In this section a

---

[3] See Lloyd A. Knowler, *Quality Control by Statistical Methods* (New York: McGraw-Hill Book Co., 1969); Eugene L. Grant, *Statistical Quality Control* (New York: McGraw-Hill Book Co., 1952); Acheson J. Duncan, *Quality Control and Industrial Statistics* (Homewood, Ill.: Richard D. Irwin, Inc., 1959).

[4] The analysis of investment opportunities is a highly developed topic in financial management. See Adolph E. Grunewald and Erwin E. Nemmers, *Basic Managerial Finance* (New York: Holt, Rinehart, and Winston, 1970); Curtis W. Symonds, *Basic Financial Management* (New York: American Management Association, 1969);

number of methods in widespread practice will be discussed. Each of these methods involves the formulation of a standard which must be met in order to accept the prospective capital acquisition.

The Payback Method.   The simplest and apparently most widely used method is the payback method. This approach calculates the number of years needed for the proposed capital acquisition to repay its original cost out of future cash earnings. For example, a manager is considering a machine which will reduce labor costs by $4,000 per year for each of the four years of its estimated life. The cost of the machine is $8,000 and the tax rate is 50 percent. The additional after-tax cash inflow from which the machine cost must be paid is calculated as follows:

Additional cash inflow before taxes (labor cost savings)		$4,000
Less additional taxes:		
Additional income	$4,000	
Less depreciation ($8,000 ÷ 4)	2,000	
Additional taxable income	$2,000	
Tax rate	.5	
Additional tax payment		1,000
Additional cash inflow after taxes		$3,000

After additional taxes are deducted from the labor savings, the payback period can be calculated as follows:

$$\frac{\$8,000}{\$3,000} = 2.67 \text{ years.}$$

The proposed machine will repay its original cost in two and two-thirds years; if the standard requires a payback of at most three years, the machine would be deemed an appropriate investment.

The payback method suffers many limitations as a standard for evaluating capital resources. It does not produce a measurement of profitability and, more importantly, it does not take into account the time value of money, that is, it does not recognize that a dollar today is worth more than a dollar at a future date. Other methods can be employed which include these important considerations.

Rate of Return on Investment.   One alternative which produces a measure of profitability and which is consistent with methods ordinarily employed in accounting is the simple rate of return. Using the above example, the calculation would be as follows:

Harold Bierman and Seymour Smidt, *The Capital Budgeting Decision* (New York: The Macmillan Co., 1972); William R. Park, *Cost Engineering Analysis* (New York: John Wiley & Sons, Inc., 1973); Arnold C. Harberger, *Project Evaluation* (Chicago: Markham Publishing Co., 1973).

Additional gross income....................		$4,000
Less depreciation ($8,000 ÷ 4).............	$2,000	
Less taxes...............................	1,000	
Total additional expenses................		3,000
Additional net income after taxes...........		$1,000

The rate of return is the ratio of additional net income to the original cost:

$$\frac{\$1,000}{\$8,000} = 12.5\%.$$

The calculated rate of return would then be compared to some standard of minimum acceptability, and the decision to accept or reject would depend upon that comparison.

The measurement of the simple rate of return has the advantage of being easily understood. It has the disadvantage, however, of not including the time value of money. The discounted rate of return method overcomes this deficiency.

Discounted Rate of Return.   A measurement of profitability which can be used as a standard for screening potential capital acquisitions, and which takes into account the time value of money is the discounted rate of return. This method is similar to the payback method, in that only cash inflows and outflows are considered. The method itself is not widely used because of its apparent complexity and difficulty, yet it is considered the "correct" method for calculating the rate of return. It proceeds as follows, based upon the above example:

$$\$8,000 = \frac{\$3,000}{(1+r)} + \frac{\$3,000}{(1+r)^2} + \frac{\$3,000}{(1+r)^3} + \frac{\$3,000}{(1+r)^4};$$
$$r - 18\%.$$

The discounted rate of return (r) is 18 percent, which is interpreted to mean that an $8,000 investment which repays $3,000 in cash at the end of each of four years yields a return of 18 percent.

The rationale of the method can be understood by thinking of the $3,000 inflows as cash payments received by the firm. In exchange for each of these four payments of $3,000 the firm must pay $8,000. The rate of return, 18 percent, is the factor which equates future cash inflows and present cash outflow.

The time value of money is explicitly considered in the method in the following way: If we remember that 18 percent is the rate of return and that there are four distinct and separate future receipts of $3,000, we can see that $8,000 is the *present value* of the future proceeds.[5]

$2,542 = present value of $3,000 to be received in 1 year
 or $2,542 × (1.18) = $3,000
2,155 = present value of $3,000 to be received in 2 years
 or $2,155 × (1.18)^2 = $3,000
1,826 = present value of $3,000 to be received in 3 years
 or $1,826 × (1.18)^3 = $3,000
1,547 = present value of $3,000 to be received in 4 years
 or $1,547 × (1.18)^4 = $3,000
$8,070 = Total present value.[6]

Preliminary Control of Financial Resources

An adequate supply of financial resources must be available to assure the payment of current obligations arising from current operations. Materials must be purchased, wages paid, interest charges and due dates met. The principal means of controlling the availability and cost of financial resources is budgeting—particularly cash and working capital budgets.[7]

These budgets anticipate the ebb and flow of business activity when materials are purchased, finished goods are produced and inventoried, goods are sold, and cash received. This cycle of activity, the operating cycle, results in a problem of *timing* the availability of cash to meet the obligations. The simple relationship between cash and inventory is shown in Figure 5–4. As inventories of finished goods increase, the supply of cash decreases while materials, labor, and other expenses are incurred and paid. As inventory is depleted through sales, cash increases. Preliminary control of cash requires that cash be available during the period of inventory buildup and be used wisely during periods of abundance. This requires the careful consideration of alternative sources of short-term financing during inventory buildup and of alternative short-run investment opportunities during periods of inventory depletion.

To aid in the process, attention is given by managers to certain financial ratios. For example, the standard may be in terms of the current ratio (the ratio of current assets to current liabilities) and a minimum and a maximum are set. The minimum ratio could be set at 2:1, and the maximum, at 3:1, a practice which recognizes the cost of both too little

---

[5] For a complete discussion of the relationships between discounted rate of return and present value, see Bierman and Smidt, *Capital Budgeting Decision*, pp. 39–43; and G. David Quirin, *The Capital Expenditure Decision* (Homewood, Ill.: Richard D. Irwin, Inc., 1967) pp. 39–55.

[6] Not exactly equal to $8000 because of rounding.

[7] Yair E. Ogler, *Cash Management* (Belmont, Calif.: Wadsworth Publishing Co., Inc., 1969); William J. Vatter, *Operating Budgets* (Belmont, Calif.: Wadsworth Publishing Co., Inc., 1969); Colin Park and John W. Gladson, *Working Capital* (New York: The Macmillan Co., 1963); Walter Rautenstrauch and Raymond Villers, *Budgetary Control* (New York: Funk and Wagnalls, 1968).

FIGURE 5–4

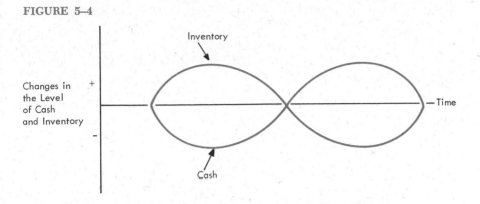

and too much investment in liquid assets. The control would be in terms of corrective action when the actual current ratio deviates from the standard. Other financial ratios which contribute to control of financial resources include the acid test ratio, inventory turnover, and average collection period. These ratios are discussed in greater detail in the section on feedback control methods.

CONCURRENT CONTROL PROCEDURES

Concurrent control consists of methods which monitor the actual execution of plans. In most cases, the focus of concurrent control is the work of subordinates. The direction and supervision phases of the control function encompass all activity of the subordinates. The responsibility of the manager when directing and supervising subordinates is (1) to instruct them in the proper methods and procedures and (2) to assure that they are following instructions.

The direction phase follows the formal chain of command since the responsibility of each superior is to interpret for subordinates the orders received from higher echelons. The relative importance of direction depends almost entirely upon the nature of the tasks which are performed by subordinates. The foreman of an assembly line which produces a simple component part requiring relatively simple manual operations may seldom engage in direction. On the other hand, the manager of a research-and-development unit must devote considerable time to direction. Research work is inherently more complex and varied than manual work, thus requiring more interpretation and instruction.

The scope and content of the direction phase varies, depending upon the nature of work being supervised, as noted above. We can also distinguish a number of other factors which determine differences in the form of direction. For example, if we recognize that direction is basically the process of personal communication, then we can see that the amount

and clarity of information are important factors. Subordinates must receive sufficient information to carry out the task and must understand the
information that they receive. On the other hand, too much information
and too much detail can be damaging. We should also recognize that the
manager's mode and tone of expression greatly influence the effectiveness
of direction.

Supervision is the process of overseeing the work of subordinates. The
purpose is to assure that plans are being carried out in accordance with
instructions. Supervision is "primarily a mental activity that involves
face-to-face leadership."[8] This recognition permits us to place supervision within the context of a leadership framework. Our objective at this
stage is to identify the place of supervision (leadership) in the fundamentals of management.

FEEDBACK CONTROL PROCEDURES

The distinguishing feature of feedback control methods is focusing
attention upon *historical* outcomes as the bases for correcting *future*
actions. For example, the financial statements of a firm are used to
evaluate the acceptability of historical results and to determine the desirability of making changes in future resource acquisitions or operational
activities. In this section we outline three feedback control methods
which are widely used in business; they are: financial statement analysis,
standard cost analysis, and quality control. Our objective is to demonstrate the general features of feedback control techniques through
these three examples.

Financial Statement Analysis

A principal source of information from which managers can evaluate
historical results is the firm's accounting system. Periodically, the manager receives a set of financial statements which usually includes a balance sheet, an income statement, and a sources and uses of funds
statement. These statements summarize and classify the effects of trans-
actions in terms of assets, liabilities, equity, revenues, and expenses—the
principal components of the firm's financial structure.[9]

A detailed analysis of the information contained in the financial statements enables management to ascertain the adequacy of the firm's earning power and its ability to meet current and long-term obligations; that
is, the manager must have measures of and standards for profitability,

---

[8] Ralph C. Davis, *The Fundamentals of Top Management* (New York: Harper
and Brothers, 1951), p. 709.

[9] See John N. Meyer, *Financial Statement Analysis* (Englewood Cliffs, N.J.:
Prentice-Hall, Inc., 1969); S. Winston Korn and Thomas Boyd, *Accounting for Man-
agement Planning and Decision Making* (New York: John Wiley and Sons, 1969);
Leopold A. Bernstein, *Financial Statement Analysis* (Homewood, Ill.: Richard D.
Irwin, 1974).

liquidity, and solvency. The various measures of profitability were discussed in Chapter 3. The planning discussion described the various profitability measures and presented arguments for each. Whether the manager prefers the rate of return on sales, on owner's equity, or on total assets, or a combination of all three, it is important to establish a meaningful norm—one that is appropriate to the particular firm, given its industry and stage of growth. An inadequate rate of return will negatively affect the firm's ability to attract funds for expansion, particularly if a downward trend over time is evident.

The measures of liquidity reflect the firm's ability to meet current obligations as they become due. The widest known and most often used measure is the *ratio of current assets to current liabilities*. The standard of acceptability depends upon the particular firm's own operating characteristics. Bases for comparison are available from trade associations which publish industry averages. A more rigorous test of liquidity is the *acid test ratio*, which relates only cash and near cash items (current assets excluding inventories and prepaid expenses) to current liabilities.

The relationship between current assets and current liabilities is an important determinate of liquidity. Equally important is the *composition* of current assets. Two measures which indicate composition and which rely upon information found in both the balance sheet and income statement are the *accounts receivable turnover* and the *inventory turnover*. The accounts receivable turnover is the ratio of credit sales to average accounts receivable. The higher the turnover, the more rapid is the conversion of accounts receivable to cash. A low turnover would indicate a time lag in the collection of receivables, which in turn, could strain the firm's ability to meet its own obligations. The appropriate corrective action might be a tightening of credit standards or a more vigorous effort to collect outstanding accounts. The inventory turnover also facilitates the analysis of appropriate balances in current assets. It is calculated as the ratio of cost of goods sold to average inventory. A high ratio could indicate a dangerously low inventory balance in relation to sales with the possibility of missed sales or production slowdowns; conversely, a low ratio might indicate an overinvestment in inventory to the exclusion of other, more profitable, assets. Whatever the case, the appropriate ratio must be established by the manager based upon the firm's experience within its industry and market.

Another financial measure is solvency, the ability of the firm to meet its long-term obligations—its fixed commitments. The solvency measure relates the claims of creditors and owners on the assets of the firm. An appropriate balance must be maintained—a balance which protects the interests of the owners, yet does not ignore the advantages of long-term debt as a source of funds. A commonly used measure of solvency is the *ratio of net income before interest and taxes to interest expense*. This indicates the margin of safety and, ordinarily, a high ratio is preferred.

However, a very high ratio combined with a low *debt-to-equity ratio* could indicate that management has not taken advantage of debt as a source of funds. The appropriate balance between debt and equity depends upon a great number of factors; and the issue is an important topic in financial management. But, as a general rule, one can say that the proportion of debt should vary directly with the stability of the firm's earnings.

The ratios discussed above are only suggestive of the great number and variety of methods used to evaluate the financial results of the firm. Accounting as a tool of analysis in business management has a long history predating scientific management.[10] Our point here is that financial statement analysis as a part of the management process is clearly a feedback control method.

Standard Cost Analysis

Standard cost accounting systems date from and are considered a major contribution of the scientific management era. A standard cost system provides information that enables management to compare actual costs with predetermined (standard) costs. Management can then take appropriate corrective action or assign the authority to take action to others. The first use of standard costing was affecting control over manufacturing costs; but, in recent years, standard costing has been applied to selling, general, and administrative expenses. Here we discuss standard manufacturing costs.

The three elements of manufacturing costs are direct labor, direct materials, and overhead. For each of these, an estimate must be made of the element's cost per unit of output. For example, the direct labor cost per unit of output consists of the standard usage of labor and the standard price of labor. The standard usage derives from time studies which fix the expected output per man-hour; the standard price of labor will be fixed by the salary schedule appropriate for the kind of work necessary to produce the output. A similar determination is made for direct materials. Thus, the standard labor and standard materials costs might be as follows:

Standard labor usage per unit..............	2 hours
Standard wage rate per hour...............	$3.00
Standard labor cost (2 × $3.00)............	$6.00
Standard material usage per unit...........	6 pounds
Standard material price per pound..........	$ .30
Standard material cost (6 × $.30)..........	$1.80

---

[10] A. C. Littleton, *Accounting Evolution to 1900* (New York: Russell and Russell, 1966).

The accounting system produces information which enables the manager to compare incurred costs and standard costs. For example, if during the period covered by the report, 200 units of output were produced, the standard labor cost is $1,200 (200 × $6.00) and the standard material cost is $360 (200 × $1.80). Assume that the actual payroll cost for that same time period was $1,500 and the actual material cost was $400. That is, there was an *unfavorable labor variance* of $300 and an *unfavorable material variance* of $40. Management must determine the reasons for the variances and decide what corrective action is appropriate.

Assuming that the standards are correct, the manager must analyze the variance and fix the responsibility for restoring the balance between standard and actual costs. It is obvious that if actual labor cost exceeds standard cost, the reason for the difference is found in labor usage and labor wage rates. Either actual labor usage exceeded standard labor usage or actual wage rates exceeded standard wage rates, or some combination of both. Suppose that, in this example, the accountant reports the actual payroll consisted of 450 actual hours at an average wage rate of $3.33. The questions management must resolve are now narrowed to two: What happened during the period to cause output per man-hour to go down (to produce 200 units of output should require 400 labor hours); and, why was the average wage rate more than the standard wage rate. The answers to these questions are found in the resources and activity stages of the cycle (see Figure 5–3).

Similar analyses are made to discover the causes for the unfavorable material variance. The first step is discovering the relationships between actual and standard usage and between actual and standard price. As with the labor, the manager may find actual material usage exceeded that specified by standard; and/or the manager may find the actual price exceeds the standard price. Once the cause is isolated, the analysis must proceed to fix responsibility for corrective action.

The analysis of manufacturing overhead variances is considerably more complicated than that for labor and material. A complete discussion would carry us far afield.[11] Suffice to say that it is necessary to isolate the causes through comparisons with standards and budgets

Quality Control Analysis

A final illustration of feedback control is quality control of the finished product. This approach uses information regarding attributes and char-

---

[11] The reader can consult any text in cost accounting and managerial accounting for discussions of standard cost analysis. For example, see: Charles T. Horngren, *Accounting for Management Control* (Englewood Cliffs, N.J.: Prentice-Hall, Inc., 1974); Gerald Crowningshield and Kenneth Gorman, *Cost Accounting* (Boston: Houghton Mifflin, 1974); Nicholas Dopuch, Jacob G. Birnberg, and Joel Demski, *Cost Accounting* (New York: Harcourt, Brace, Jovanovich, Inc., 1974).

acteristics of output to ascertain whether the manufacturing process is "in control," that is, producing acceptable output. To make this determination, the manager must specify the product characteristic that is considered critical. This may be weight, length, consistency, or defects. Once the characteristic is defined, it must be measured.

For an example, consider one problem of a manufacturer of peanut butter: maintaining a minimum quantity of peanut butter in each container, say, 12 ounces.

One approach would be to weigh each container when it is filled, that is, 100 percent of the output could be inspected. An alternative is to inspect samples of output to make inferences about the process based upon the sample information. The latter approach is termed *statistical quality control.* This method makes use of statistical sampling theory, and since the amount of time devoted to inspection is reduced, the cost of inspection is also reduced.

THE CLASSICAL SCHOOL IN PERSPECTIVE

This chapter concludes our discussion of the Classical School. In a very general sense, classical writers believed that the performance of business firms, governmental agencies, churches, military units—indeed all instances of consciously organized group endeavor—could be improved through the application of fundamental management principles. These principles, or guidelines, were derived primarily from the writers' personal experiences as managers, but also from logical deduction. In retrospect a major contribution of the classical writers was to popularize management as a field of scientific inquiry.

The analyses of Taylor, the Gilbreths, Fayol, Mooney, Urwick, and others produced a conceptual framework for analyzing and practicing the managerial process. That framework defines the managerial process as consisting of three functions—planning, organizing, and controlling. Whether these three functions completely describe management is more a matter of definition than conceptualization. For example, one might well argue that the managerial process consists of planning, organizing, staffing, directing, coordinating, reviewing, and controlling. It all depends upon the definitions of the concepts. We have chosen to present the classical interpretation of management in terms of only three major concepts; we believe that they are sufficient, simple to understand, and adequately represent the classical framework. Moreover, as we have tried to show, the Classical Management School contributed much more than a lengthy list of functions which the aspiring manager could commit to memory.

Identifying the primary management functions as planning, organizing, and controlling does not end the discussion. Rather, it simply initiates further discussion about how managers do and should perform each function. Moreover, it is necessary to understand the interrelationships among and within the functions. At the highest level of abstraction, we know that the practice of management is a continual process of determining what should be done (planning), how it should be done (organizing), and whether it was done (controlling). Yet one should not infer that the process is as simple as the statement which describes it. The discovery of the interrelationships between and among these three functions is the continuing challenge to students, teachers, and practitioners of management.

At this point in our discussion of management fundamentals, a foundation for meeting this challenge has been developed. What remains is to build on this foundation by considering the contributions of the Behavioral School and the Management Science School. It is reasonable to state that the classical writers did not take into account the potential contributions of these schools if, for no other reason, than that they had not been fully developed. The significant advances in psychology, sociology, anthropology, statistics, and mathematics have occurred in the past 40 years. We shall, in the remainder of this book, review the impact of these advances on the study and practice of management.

DISCUSSION AND REVIEW QUESTIONS

1. It is said by some management experts that the term "control" should not be used in the management literature. These experts argue that control implies some loss of freedom and individuality and that such implications should be avoided. Do you agree with these experts and what is your reasoning?

2. Illustrate the relationship between goals, policies, and standards in the context of an organization in which you are a member.

3. Why are preliminary and concurrent control procedures so widely used in universities, hospitals, governmental agencies, and other nonmarket institutions?

4. The term "cybernetics" was coined by modern system theorists such as Norbert Wiener. As an extra-classroom exercise, research this term and relate it to the chapter discussion of feedback control procedures.

5. Some management writers have argued the point that the creation of organization structures is basically a form of the controlling function, and not a separate managerial function. What would be your response to this argument?

6. A number of standards have been discussed as measures of investment profitability. These measures include the payback period, the rate of return, and the discounted rate of return. If only one measure is "correct," why do the others exist in management practice?

7. Do you believe that the classical writers' distinction between supervision and direction is useful in the practice of management?

8. Financial managers state that financial ratios are similar to other statistical data in the way that they can be used, or misused, to prove a point. How can the nonfinancial expert, such as a plant superintendent, know whether his financial expert is misusing such ratios to press for his own point of view in an executive decision?

9. Under what circumstances would the use of feedback control procedures be inappropriate?

10. The concept of "responsibility accounting" has received much attention in the accounting literature. Research this concept in terms of its relationship to the chapter discussion of necessary conditions for effective managerial control.

ADDITIONAL REFERENCES

Chruden, H. J. *Personnel Management*. Cincinnati: South-Western Publishing Co., 1972.

Duncan, A. J. *Quality Control and Industrial Statistics*. Homewood, Ill.: Richard D. Irwin, Inc., 1965.

Emery, J. C. *Organizational Planning and Control Systems: Theory and Technology*. New York: Macmillan, 1969.

Foulke, R. A. *Practical Financial Statement Analysis*. New York: McGraw-Hill Book Co., 1957.

Gardner, F. V. *Profit Management and Control*. New York: McGraw-Hill Book Co., 1955.

Hamner, W. C. and Schmidt, F. L. *Contemporary Problems in Personnel*. Chicago: St. Clair Press, 1974.

Jerome, W. T. *Executive Control—The Catalyst*. New York: John Wiley and Sons, Inc., 1961.

King-Scott, P. *Industrial Supervision*. London: Sir Isaac Pitman and Sons, Ltd., 1969.

Martindell, J. W. *The Appraisal of Management*. New York: Harper and Row, 1962.

Pigors, P., and Myers, C. A. *Personnel Administration*. New York: McGraw-Hill Book Co., 1973.

Rose, T. G. *Top Management Accounting*. London: Sir Isaac Pitman and Sons, Ltd., 1958.

Rose, T. G., and Farr, D. E. *Higher Management Control*. New York: McGraw-Hill Book Co., 1957.

Sartain, A. Q., and Baker, A. W. *The Supervisor and His Job*. New York: McGraw-Hill Book Co., 1972.

Terry, G. R. *Supervisory Management*. Homewood, Ill.: Richard D. Irwin, Inc., 1974.

Practical Exercise I

The New Dean

The College of Business, Midwestern State University, was made up of five academic departments: accounting, economics, finance, management, and marketing. Each department was headed by a chairman who reported to the dean of the College of Business. The faculty numbered approximately 50, and they were evenly distributed among the five departments. The 2,500 students enrolled in the college were required to "major" in one of the five departments as a part of the requirements for the Bachelor of Business Administration (B.B.A.) degree. The course work in the student's major comprised one-third of the total required course work; the remaining two-thirds were taken in other departments in the college and the university. In a general sense, the College of Business was typical of those in any land-grant state university.

In 1974, the dean of the college retired after serving in that post for 26 years. He was, at the time of his retirement, the senior member of the college faculty; he had hired all of the 50 members of the faculty and he had appointed each of the five chairmen. During the 26 years of his tenure, the retiring dean had managed the college in a highly autocratic style. He personally hired and fired faculty members, determined their salaries and promotions, and defined the course requirements for each of the departmental majors. He would arrive at his decisions, announce them to the five department chairmen, and expect them to carry out his decisions. With the passage of time, those professors who disagreed with the dean's management style would resign and go elsewhere.

The president of Midwestern State University moved very quickly to replace the retired dean. The procedures required the president to appoint a search committee which would screen candidates and make recommendations to the president. The search committee was formed from the faculty of the College of Business as well as from other parts of the University. The committee reviewed the credentials of a number of candidates and brought many of them to the campus for interviews. It reached a decision and recommended to the president that he offer the appointment to a youthful and successful business executive. The

117

executive had a Ph.D. degree from a prestigious university, but rather than go into teaching, he had opted for a business career. The committee's recommendation was accepted by the president. On July 1, 1974 the new dean of the College of Business moved into his office.

One of the first acts of the new dean was to meet with the college's five department chairmen. After inviting each of them to remain as chairmen, he stated that he intended to manage the College of Business according to fundamental management principles. In a sense, he said, "I believe that we should practice what we teach." The dean explained that he was primarily concerned with establishing management procedures for controlling the teaching function of the college. "How do we know," he asked, "whether we are teaching the appropriate subject matter? How do we know whether the professors are actually teaching the subject matter they are assigned? How do we know whether students have learned the subject matter, or, for that matter, how do we know whether the students have received any benefit from their courses? Finally, how do we know which professors are doing the most effective job in the classroom?"

The dean stated that he fully appreciated the fact that the faculty of the college engaged in activities other than teaching. He anticipated that the faculty would continue to engage in research and service activities. "I want us to submit all of our activities to the same set of questions that I have posed about teaching, but, for the moment, I only want to concentrate on teaching." The dean stated that he believed that teaching was the appropriate activity for which to initiate control procedures because of the existence of tangible standards. Research and service activities were less tangible, according to the dean, and therefore less amenable to the development of standards. But as far as the dean was concerned, the teaching function lent itself to the development of standards for which information either was or could be made available, and corrective action could be taken whenever necessary.

The dean directed each of the chairmen to prepare a draft statement which analyzed the most suitable procedures for obtaining answers to the questions he had posed. He stated that he wanted each chairman to appoint a committee of key departmental faculty members to work with him in the preparation of the analysis. He reasoned that college-wide procedures could be devised to meet each department's needs, only after department-level analyses had been completed. The draft statements were to be available for the dean's review within a month.

After this first meeting, the dean was approached by the chairman of the economics department. "Look," he said, "I and my colleagues in the department want to work with you in constructive ways. But quite frankly, I haven't the slightest idea about how to do what you have asked. We economists are not business types, and when you say that you are going to use management fundamentals to control the teaching functions, I don't know what you mean. All that I ever did as chairman was to tell the faculty what the dean said they were to teach. If you want me and a committee of economists to analyze and evaluate procedures for controlling our teaching, you are going to have to be much more specific."

Questions for Analysis:

1. What should be the dean's response to the chairman of the economics department?
2. If you, as the dean, were to meet with the economics department to explain your intentions, what should you be saying?
3. Assume the role of one of the chairmen and prepare an analysis of how preliminary, concurrent, and feedback control procedures can be utilized in controlling the teaching function.

Practical Exercise II

Developing a New Product

In the summer of 1974, the plant manager of a major electronics manufacturer called a meeting with his immediate subordinates to discuss and decide whether to go into full-scale production and marketing of a new product, a miniature thermostat. The miniature thermostat, MT, had been in the developmental process for the past three years, and the manager believed that it was time to make a decision. The meeting was to be attended by the marketing manager, the production superintendent, the purchasing manager, and the plant cost accountant. The plant manager instructed each official to bring appropriate information and to be prepared to make a final decision regarding the MT.

Prior to the meeting, the plant manager noted the following facts concerning the MT.

1. Developmental efforts had been undertaken in 1972 in response to the introduction of a similar product by a major competitor.
2. Initial manufacturing studies had indicated that much of the technology and know-how to produce the MT already existed in the plant and its work force.
3. A prototype model had been approved by Underwriter's Laboratory.
4. A pilot production line had been designed and installed. Several thousand thermostats had already been produced and tested.

5. Market projections indicated that the trend toward miniaturization of components such as thermostats was likely to continue.
6. The competitor who had introduced the product was successfully marketing it at a price of $0.80 each.
7. The cost estimates derived by the cost accountant over the past two years consistently indicated that the firm could not meet the competitor's price and at the same time follow its policy of marking up all products to 14 percent of the selling price.

Because of his concern for the cost of the MT, the plant manager asked the cost accountant to brief the group at the outset of its meeting. The accountant's data are shown below:

	Actual Costs	Standard Costs
Direct labor..............................	$0.059	$0.052
Direct material...........................	0.340	0.194
Manufacturing overhead (438% of standard direct labor)............................	0.228	0.228
Total manufacturing cost....................	$0.627	$0.474
Spoilage (10%)............................	0.063	0.047
Selling and administrative costs (40% of direct labor and overhead)......	0.115	0.112
Total cost per MT.........................	$0.805	$0.633
Required price to achieve 14% markup on selling price............................	$0.936	$0.736

The accountant noted for the group that the firm would not be able to manufacture and sell the MT for less than $0.805 each, given present actual costs. In fact, to meet their markup objective would require a selling price of approximately $0.94 each, but that would be impossible since the competitor was selling the same product for $0.80. She explained that if the MT could be manufactured at standard costs, the product could compete successfully with the competitor's thermostat.

The marketing manager stated that the MT was an important product and that it was critical for the firm to have an entry in the market. He maintained that in a few years the MT would be used by all major customers; he also stated that competition had already moved into the area with a strong sales program. He added that he personally did not place too much reliance on the cost estimates because the plant had so little experience with full-scale production of the MT.

The manufacturing superintendent stated that he was working with engineers to develop a new method for welding contacts and that if the technique proved successful, direct labor cost would be reduced significantly. This would have a cumulative effect on cost since overhead, spoilage, and selling and administrative expenses are based on direct labor. He also believed that with a little more experience, the workers could reach standard times on the assembly operations. He stated that much progress in this direction had been made in the past four weeks.

The purchasing manager stated that material costs were high because the plant did not procure materials in sufficient quantity. She stated that with full-scale production, material costs should reduce to standard.

Questions for Analysis:

1. If you were the plant manager, what would be your decision regarding the MT?
2. If you decided to manufacture the MT, would your decision indicate that the standard of 14 percent markup is not valid?
3. What is the cost of the MT? What concept of cost would be appropriate for basing pricing decisions?

part two

The Behavioral School

Foundations of the Behavioral School
Motivation
Work Groups
Leadership
Organizational Design
Organizational Change and
  Development

6 Foundations of the Behavioral School

INTRODUCTION

As noted in previous chapters, early approaches to management were built on the concept of economic man, which placed emphasis on an individual's rational pursuit of economic objectives. From this assumption followed the logic that if the industrial engineer could properly design a job and if management could devise the right kind of incentive, then productivity would be maximized. Finally, the early industrial psychologist was supposed to aid the whole process by properly selecting and training workers. As is readily apparent the entire approach was very impersonal. Therefore, it is not surprising that a school of thought developed which challenged some established classical theories. Specifically, they began to challenge the economic man assumptions of earlier writers. While this school has been described in several ways, we shall entitle it the *Behavioral School of Management*.[1] Its first branch may be identified as the *"human relations"* approach, and became popular in the 1940s and early 1950s. The second branch was the *"behavioral science"* approach, which came into popular use in the early 1950s and today receives much emphasis in the literature on management. Both branches and important characteristics of each are illustrated in Figure 6–1. Both

---

[1] Some writers describe this school as the "human relations" or "neoclassical" school and distinguish it from the behavioral science school, which they consider as part of "modern" management theory. However, in this text the human relations and behavioral science theories will be examined under the general heading of the Behavioral School of Management.

FIGURE 6–1

The Behavioral School of Management

Human Relations Approach
—Stimulated by Hawthorne Studies
  (1927–1932)
—1940s and early 1950s
—Emphasis on human element

Behavioral Science Approach
—1950s to the present
—Integration of behavioral sciences
—Emphasis on scientific analysis of human
  behavior in organizations

will be discussed in this chapter, in which we shall touch briefly upon the foundations of the Behavioral School of Management.

THE HUMAN RELATIONS APPROACH

Human relations writers brought to the attention of management the important role played by individuals in determining the success or failure of an organization. They dealt with the critical task of compensating for some of the deficiencies in classical theory. Basically, the human relations approach accepted the major premises of the Classical School. However, it showed how these premises should be modified because of differences in individual behavior and the influence of work groups upon the individual, and *vice versa*. Thus, human relations theory concentrated on the *social* environment surrounding the job, whereas classical writers were concerned mainly with the *physical* environment. For the student of management, the human relations movement has left a wealth of important ideas, research findings, and values about the role of the individual in an organization. Let us examine some of these contributions.

The Hawthorne Studies

The human relations approach began when a group of researchers from Harvard University was invited to conduct studies at the Chicago Hawthorne Plant of Western Electric.[2] The researchers originally set out to study the relationship between productivity and physical working conditions.

The general progression of the research at Hawthorne can be grouped in four phases.[3] However, it should be noted that each of the last three

---

[2] For a complete account of these studies, see Fritz J. Roethlisberger and W. J. Dickson, *Management and the Worker* (Boston: Harvard University Press, 1939).

[3] Paul R. Lawrence and John A. Seiler, *Organizational Behavior and Administration* (Homewood, Ill.: Richard D. Irwin, Inc., 1965), p. 165.

developed as an attempt on the part of the researchers to answer questions raised by the previous phase. The four phases were:

1. Experiments to determine the effects of changes in illumination on productivity.
2. Experiments to determine the effects of changes in hours and other working conditions (for example, rest periods, refreshments) on productivity (The Relay Assembly Test Room Experiment).
3. Conducting a plant-wide interview program to determine worker attitudes and sentiments.
4. Determination and analysis of social organization at work (The Bank Wiring Observation Room Experiment).

Experiments in Illumination. In the first series of experiments a group of workers was chosen and placed in two separate groups. One group was exposed to varying intensities of illumination. Since this group was subjected to experimental changes, it was termed the *experimental* group. Another group, the *control* group, continued to work under constant intensities of illumination. Surprisingly, the researchers found that, as they increased the illumination in the experimental group, both groups increased production. When the researchers decreased the intensity, output continued to rise for both groups. Finally, the illumination in the experimental group was reduced to that of moonlight. Then, and only then, was there a significant decline in output. The researchers concluded that illumination in the workplace had little or no effect on the productivity of the two groups.

Relay Assembly Test Room Experiment. In the second phase of the study, several persons volunteered to work under controlled conditions isolated from the other workers. Several changes were made in the conditions of the job (for example, refreshments, work-place temperature) with little effect on productivity. In another phase, a group of women employees was placed together in an isolated part of the assembly department. The experimental group was given a special group incentive as a wage payment. In this case, output increased for each operator.

Overall, the relay assembly test room experiment was designed to determine the effect of changes in various job conditions on group productivity. The researchers concluded that these factors had little or no effect.

Employee Interviews. After the first two phases, the researchers concluded that their attempt to relate physical conditions of the job to productivity did not produce any significant results. They therefore postulated that the *human element* in the work environment apparently had a significantly greater impact on the rate of productivity than the technical and physical aspects of the job. The researchers summarized this as follows:

> In brief, the increase in the output rate of the girls in the Relay Assembly Test Room could not be related to any change in their physical

conditions of work, whether experimentally induced or not. It could, however, be related to what can only be spoken of as the development of an organized social group and a peculiar and effective relation with its supervisors.[4]

On the basis of their extensive interview program, the researchers proposed the premise that the work group as a whole determined the production output of individual group members by enforcing an informal norm of what a fair day's work should be.

Bank Wiring Observation Room Experiment.   In order to test the premise formulated at the conclusion of the interview program, the researchers decided to conduct a final experiment. The procedure in this part of the study was similar to that in the relay assembly test room procedure, except that nine male operators who assembled terminal banks for telephone exchanges were used.

In this experiment, an attempt was made to determine the effect of a group piecework incentive pay plan. The assumption was that the workers would seek their own economic interests by maximizing their productivity and that faster workers would pressure the slower ones to improve their efficiency. However, the researchers found that pressure was actually a form of social behavior. In order to be accepted in the work group, the worker had to act in accord with group norms and not be a "rate buster" by overproducing, or a "chiseler" by underproducing. The group defined what constituted a day's work, and as soon as they knew that they could reach this output level, they slacked off. This process was more marked among the faster than the slower workers.

The researchers concluded that the social standards of the work group set the fair rates for each of its members. They found no relationship between productivity and intelligence, dexterity, and other skills. They concluded that the wage incentive plan was less important in determining an individual worker's output than group acceptance and security.

A Review of the Hawthorne Studies

Probably the major contribution of the Hawthorne studies is that they generated a great deal of interest in human problems of the workplace. They were also the catalyst for a number of future studies of human behavior in organizational settings.

The Hawthorne studies have been widely criticized by some behavioral scientists because of the lack of scientific objectivity in arriving at conclusions. Some critics feel that there was bias and preconception on the part of the researchers. One writer developed a detailed comparison between the conclusions drawn by the researchers and the evidence

---

[4] Ibid., p. 173.

they presented, and found that their conclusions were almost entirely unsupported.[5] He asks the question ". . . how it was possible for studies so nearly devoid of scientific merit, and conclusions so little supported by evidence, to gain so influential and respected a place within scientific disciplines and to hold this place for so long."[6]

Other criticisms have also been leveled at the Hawthorne studies.[7] For example:

1. The Hawthorne researchers did not give sufficient attention to the attitudes that people bring with them to the workplace. They did not recognize such forces as class consciousness, the role of unions and other extraplant forces on attitudes of workers.
2. The Hawthorne plant was not a typical plant because it was a thoroughly unpleasant place in which to work.
3. The Hawthorne studies look upon the worker as a means to an end, not an end in himself. They assume acceptance of management's goals and look on the worker as someone to be manipulated by management.

Although they have been criticized, the Hawthorne studies had a significant impact on management practice, teaching, and research. An obvious one was that the individualistic economic man assumptions of classical writers began to be questioned. Subsequent studies of the behavior of workers confirmed this criticism and led to revised assumptions about human nature.[8] Behavioral scientists began attacking the "dehumanizing" aspects of the scientific management approach and bureaucratic forms of organization. There were a great number of training programs undertaken to teach foremen how to better understand people and groups in the work situation. With this, the pendulum began to swing away from the supposed depersonalized view of classical management to a more personalized view (some would say overpersonalized). Consequently, the worker, rather than the job or production standards, became the focus.

Most of the training programs were a spill-over from the Training Within Industry Program of the War Manpower Commission. This was a supervisory training program to make up for the shortage of civilian supervisory skills during World War II. This and similar programs had as an underlying rationale the belief that a happy worker would be a

[5] Alex Carey, "The Hawthorne Studies: A Radical Criticism," *American Sociological Review*, vol. 32 (June 1967), pp. 403–16.

[6] Ibid., p. 403.

[7] Henry A. Landsberger, *Hawthorne Revisited* (Ithaca, N.Y.: New York State School of Industrial and Labor Relations, Cornell University, 1958).

[8] Elton Mayo, *The Social Problems of an Industrial Civilization* (Cambridge, Mass.; Harvard University Press, 1945).

productive worker. It was not until later that behavioral scientists found that such training programs might have no influence on productivity.

While we do not hold up the Hawthorne studies as a model in the application of scientific methodology to problems of human behavior, it does represent pioneering effort in such studies. If it did nothing else, it stimulated an interest in the human problems of management. Although the assumptions and methods of human relations and behavioral science are not the same, it was the human relations branch that provided the impetus for the present-day behavioral science emphasis in management theory.

HUMAN RELATIONS MODIFICATIONS
OF SELECTED PRINCIPLES OF ORGANIZATION

The human relations approach to management regarded the classical principles of organization as given. However, an attempt was made to modify classical doctrine by injecting the human element either through individual behavior or through the influence of the work group. Let us examine these modifications of the principles of classical organization theory.[9]

1. Division of Labor. The division of labor received a great deal of attention from human relations writers. Special attention was given to the social isolation of workers and their feelings of anonymity, resulting from insignificant jobs and lack of feeling of task completion because of negligible contributions to the final product.

Human relations writers generally assumed that, as the division of labor increases, the need for motivating and coordinating the activities of others arises. Thus a large volume of their writing focuses upon the consequences of dividing work into smaller and smaller units. The emphasis of many of these writers is on procedures that can be used to minimize some of the negative consequences (for example, boredom, fatigue) of the division of labor.

2. Scalar and Functional Processes. The human relations writers believed that the scalar and functional processes are sound, but break down once the human element enters the picture. They believed that the classical writers assumed perfection in the delegation and functionalization processes, but that human problems result through imperfections in the manner in which these processes are handled.

For example, too much or not enough delegation may render a manager incapable of action; or the failure to delegate sufficient authority, or

---

[9] The following discussion is based upon William G. Scott, "Organization Theory: An Overview and an Appraisal," *Journal of the Academy of Management*, vol. 4 (April 1961), pp. 7–26. Also see William G. Scott and Terence R. Mitchell, *Organization Theory: A Structural and Behavioral Analysis* (Homewood, Ill.: Richard D. Irwin, Inc., 1972), chap. 3.

to delegate authority and responsibility unequally, may cause frustration for the delegatee. These and other human relations implications of the scalar and functional processes were examined and discussed by human relations writers.

3. *Structure.* The human relations writers were quick to point out that human behavior can disrupt the best-laid organizational plans. Once the human element entered the picture, much of the neatness and the logical relationships set forth in the formal structure changed. They also noted the internal frictions that can develop among people who perform different functions. One of the often-mentioned areas of friction was that between line and staff functions. The human relations writers offered prescriptions for the management of conflict within the organization structure. Two of the most frequently mentioned prescriptions were participation and better communication. The latter, however, was not necessarily a new prescription since classical writers such as Fayol, Mooney, and Barnard were also interested in communications.

4. *Span of Control.* The human relations writers believed that it was not possible to reduce the problem of span of control to an accurate, universally applicable ratio. They were concerned with the various situational factors that affect span of control, believing that the key determinants were individual differences in managerial abilities, the kind of people and the type of function supervised, and the effectiveness of communication between superior and subordinate.

Another problem relating to span of control examined by human relations writers was the type of organization structure which developed. In other words, is a tall structure with a short span of control or a flat structure with a wide span of control more conducive to high morale and good human relations? Here again they concluded that the answer is situational; that is, because of differences in the people or the organization, one is sometimes more effective than the other.

In addition to modifying the principles of organization, human relations writers also focused attention on the informal work group, which the classical writers did not fully recognize. By informal groups we mean natural formations of people in the work situation, not specified in the formal organization. The Hawthorne studies stimulated interest in the study of groups in the work situation. Human relations writers, and later behavioral science writers, began to examine the underlying determinants, types, characteristics, and roles of work groups. We shall devote an entire chapter to work groups in this section of the book.

THE BEHAVIORAL SCIENCE APPROACH

The behavioral science approach to management became popular in the early 1950s. It was at this time that an organization known as the

Foundation for Research on Human Behavior was established. The goals and objectives of this organization were to promote and support behavioral science research in business, government, and other types of organizations. We shall define the behavioral science approach to the study of management as follows:

> . . . the study of observable and verifiable human behavior in organizations, using scientific procedures. It is largely inductive and problem centered, focusing on the issue of human behavior, and drawing from any relevant literature, especially in psychology, sociology and anthropology.[10]

There were many things about the classical management and human relations approaches that bothered advocates of the behavioral science approach. For example, they recognized that managers did indeed plan, organize, and control but believed that viewing management solely in this way led mainly to descriptions of what a manager does rather than an analysis and understanding of what he does.

Many individuals also believed that while the economic man model of the classical writers was an oversimplification, the "social man" model of the human relations approach was likewise oversimplified. We shall see later that the emphasis of the behavioral science approach has shifted more and more to the nature of work itself and the degree to which it can fulfill man's needs to use skills and abilities.

Finally, advocates of the behavioral science approach were bothered by the fact that both practitioners and scholars had accepted without scientific validation so much of the management theory that preceded them. Their own scientific approach has added greatly to the earlier body of knowledge, since they provided a means to test the earlier theories. Through their work some aspects of the prior theory have been modified while others withstood the test of scientific validation. Because of the emphasis on the behavioral sciences and on science itself, let us examine each of these briefly.

The Behavioral Sciences

First we must distinguish between the social sciences and the behavioral sciences. The term "social sciences" usually refers to six disciplines: anthropology, economics, history, political science, psychology, and sociology. When we use the term "behavioral sciences," we refer to the disciplines of psychology, sociology, and anthropology.

Psychology is the study of human behavior. There are many branches of general psychology which have provided concepts and theories useful

---

[10] Alan C. Filley and Robert J. House, *Managerial Process and Organizational Behavior* (Glenview, Ill.: Scott, Foresman and Company, 1969), p. 8.

to the study of management, for example, *social psychology,* which deals with behavior as it relates to other individuals. It studies how groups and individuals influence and modify each other's behavior. *Organizational psychology* is a relatively new branch which deals with man's behavior and attitudes within an organizational setting. It studies the effect of the organization upon the individual and the individual's effect upon the organization. It is easy to see that these areas of psychology have direct relevance to the field of management.

Of all the behavioral sciences, psychology has probably played the biggest role in influencing management thought and practice. Psychologists have shown that people have a great variety of needs which they attempt to satisfy at work. In the next chapter in this section, we shall see that these include social and psychological as well as economic needs.

Sociology attempts to isolate, define, and describe human behavior in groups. It strives to develop laws and generalizations about human nature, social interaction, culture, and social organization.

One of the major contributions of sociologists to management thought has been their focus on small groups, which are often treated in the management literature as the informal components of organizations. Sociologists also have an interest in formal organizations, which they approach as the study of bureaucracy, focusing on bureaucratic behavior as well as the structural relationships in bureaucratic organizations. Sociologists have provided managers with knowledge regarding leader and follower roles and the patterns of power and authority in organizations.

Anthropology examines all the behaviors of man which have been learned, including all of the social, technical, and family behaviors which are a part of the broad concept of "culture." This is the major theme of cultural anthropology, the science devoted to the study of different peoples and cultures of the world, and is a key concept in the behavioral sciences. In fact, the ways in which individuals behave, the priority of needs they attempt to satisfy, and the means they choose to satisfy them are functions of culture.

While psychology and sociology have had a greater impact in shaping management thought, cultural anthropology has made significant contributions regarding the impact of culture on organizations. In the future, as firms expand their activities overseas, anthropology will undoubtedly provide managers with valuable insights as they attempt to perform the functions of planning, organizing, and controlling in different cultural environments.

Science and Human Behavior

Thus far, we have emphasized that the behavioral science approach to management attempts to study human behavior in organizations by using scientific procedures. Hence it is necessary to examine the nature of science as it is applied to human behavior. We do not, however, intend to get into arguments whether (1) there can be such a thing as a science of human behavior, (2) management is a science or not, and (3) the same scientific procedures used so successfully in the physical sciences can be adapted to the study of humans, especially humans in an organizational setting. The authors assume that science is applicable to management and behavioral studies. We fully realize that there are means other than scientific procedures (for example, observation, intuition) which have provided insights into human behavior.

The scientific approach, however, has a great deal to offer in the study of human behavior. First, it has made great strides in many other fields such as the physical sciences. In addition, it has produced information about human behavior that has become established knowledge. The greatest advantage of the scientific approach has been summarized as follows:

> The scientific approach has one characteristic that no other method of attaining knowledge has: self-correction. There are built-in checks all along the way to scientific knowledge. These checks are so conceived and used that they control and verify the scientist's activities and conclusions to the end of attaining dependable knowledge outside himself.[11]

The one word that best describes this approach is *objectivity*. Most writers agree that there is no single scientific method, but rather several methods that scientists can and do use. Thus, it is probably better to say that there is a *scientific approach*.

Characteristics of the Scientific Approach

While only an "ideal" science would exhibit each of the following characteristics, they nevertheless are the hallmarks of the scientific approach.[12]

1. The Procedures Are Public. This means that a scientific report contains a complete description of what was done, to enable other researchers in the field to follow each step of the investigation as if they were actually present.

2. The Definitions Are Precise. The procedures used, the variables measured, and how they were measured must be clearly stated. For example, if we were examining motivation among employees in a given plant, it would be necessary to define what we mean by motivation and

---

[11] Fred N. Kerlinger, *Foundations of Behavioral Research* (New York: Holt, Rinehart, and Winston, Inc., 1973), p. 6.

[12] Bernard Berelson and Gary A. Steiner, *Human Behavior: An Inventory of Scientific Findings* (New York: Harcourt, Brace and World, Inc., 1964), pp. 16–18.

how we measured it (for example, number of units produced, number of absences).

3. *The Data Collecting Is Objective.* Bias in collecting data as well as in the interpretation of results has no place in science. Objectivity throughout is a key feature of the scientific approach.

4. *The Findings Must Be Replicable.* This enables any researcher in the field to test the findings or results of a study by attempting to reproduce them.

5. *The Approach Is Systematic and Cumulative.* This relates to one of the underlying purposes of science, to develop a unified body of knowledge. Thus, a major purpose of the behavioral science approach to management is to develop an organized system of verified propositions about human behavior in organizations.

6. *The Purposes Are Explanation, Understanding and Prediction.* Every scientist wants to know "why" and "how." If one determines "why" and "how" and is able to provide proof, one can then predict the particular conditions under which specific events (behavior in this case) will occur. Prediction is the ultimate objective of behavioral science, as it is of all science.

These six characteristics exhibit the basic nature of the scientific approach. Throughout the discussion we have stressed the objective, systematic, and controlled nature of the scientific approach, which enables others to have confidence in research outcomes. What is important is the overall fundamental idea that the scientific approach is a controlled rational process.

Methods of Inquiry Used by Behavioral Scientists

Just as other scientists have certain tools and methods for obtaining information so does the behavioral scientist. These are usually referred to as *research designs.* In broad terms, there are three basic designs used by behavioral scientists: the experiment, the sample survey, and the case study.[10]

The Experiment. An investigation that can be considered an experiment must contain two elements—manipulation of some variable by the researcher and observation or measurement of the results. There are several different forms which an experiment can take, but we shall not examine them here.[14] An example of a simple experiment might be one in which management is trying to determine the effect of increases in piecerates on productivity. Since they probably already have measures

---

[13] Ibid., pp. 18–27.

[14] The interested reader should consult Kerlinger, *Foundations of Behavioral Research,* chaps. 17–21.

of present levels of productivity, they would have a "before" measure with which to compare the results. Their first step would be to assign workers randomly to two groups. The *experimental* group would have its rates altered while the *control* group would continue working under the existing rates. After a period of time (for example, six months), the output of both groups would be compared with their productivity before the experiment began. This might give some idea as to the effect of a higher piecerate on productivity. This experiment is an oversimplification used for illustrative purposes. Obviously, there would have to be provisions made to keep the results from being distorted (for example, workers being aware that they are participating in an experiment). However, this example does illustrate the two major elements of an experiment, manipulation of some variable by the researcher (piecerates) and observation or measurement of the results (productivity).

Obviously, practical aspects often preclude experimentation in an ongoing organization. As a result, some of the findings of behavioral scientists which are being applied in the field of management have resulted from experimental studies outside organizations.

The Sample Survey.   In this type of study, the collection of data is from a limited number of subjects which are assumed to be representative of an entire group. For example, suppose we decide to study college students. This is the group or "population" we are concerned about. We then select a sample of this group and collect some measures on particular characteristics in which we are interested (for example, attitudes toward big business). It should be clear that there are certain kinds of questions such as the attitudes of college students toward big business that can only be answered by a sample survey. However, it is often necessary to develop provisions to study changes in attitudes over time in order to improve the usefulness of the findings.

The Case Study.   Unlike the sample survey which attempts to measure one or more characteristics in many people, usually at one point in time, the case study attempts to examine numerous characteristics of one person or group, usually over an extended time period. A behavioral scientist who spends time living with a mountain tribe or working with a group of blue-collar workers will usually report the results in the form of a case study (for example, the key factors and incidents leading up to a strike).

While this method is extremely valuable in answering questions concerning development (for example, factors leading up to the strike) and for exploratory purposes, its major limitation is that the ability to generalize from it is uncertain, since the results are usually based on a sample of one instance. Perhaps, in another firm, the same incidents may not result in a strike. A case study, therefore, usually does not prove or disprove anything.

CONTRIBUTIONS OF THE BEHAVIORAL SCHOOL
TO THE PRACTICE OF MANAGEMENT

The Behavioral School has gained much attention during the 1960s and 1970s. An underlying rationale of the school is that since a manager must "get work done through others," management is really applied behavioral science because a manager must know how to motivate, be a leader, and understand interpersonal relations and the operation of groups, among other things. Therefore, the logic is that future managers must be prepared in these behavioral areas. While we would argue that management is more than solely applied behavioral science, the basic assumption of the behavioral science approach that managers must know how to deal with people appears valid.

One of the vital tasks performed by managers is decision making. To make decisions they must have possible alternatives from which to choose, authority to implement the alternative, and information. This last factor is our concern in this section. Managers need two kinds of information: First, they must have facts about the particular system, the men and machines involved, and the cost. Second, they need theory to aid in explaining what will happen if one variable is altered, and they must know how the different variables are related to each other. The Behavioral School focuses upon the theory and research concerning human behavior in organizations developed by behavioral scientists.

If the Behavioral School is to be useful to managers, it must tell them what to do in problem situations, provide them with a description of their environment, or provide them with a conceptual framework on which to rely in problem solving situations to help them explain their organizational environment. In other words, it must provide them with guides for defining a problem correctly, problem solving, explanation of behavior, and control of variables. In order to be useful, it must make them better practitioners.

This section of the book should in no way be viewed separately from the Classical School. Early management writers identified management as a process consisting of the functions of planning, organizing and controlling and provided insights into the nature and demands of these tasks. The question the reader should now ask is "How can the behavioral sciences help a manager better perform these tasks?"[15] The behavioral science approach should be regarded as an addition to the "people-oriented" management functions of *organizing* and *controlling*. The sole purpose in presenting the behavioral material in the following chapters is to provide readers with knowledge from the be-

---

[15] An excellent reference on this subject is Edwin B. Flippo, "The Underutilization of Behavioral Science By Management," in Joseph W. McGuire, ed., *Contemporary Management* (Englewood Cliffs, N.J.: Prentice-Hall, Inc., 1974), pp. 36–41.

havioral sciences that will make them better managers. Since the functions of management include organizing and controlling, the findings of the behavioral scientists must assist them in performing these functions. Otherwise they would be of little value to managers and would have no place in this text.

While the Behavioral School has not yet produced an integrated body of knowledge, it has provided much useful information for practitioners and students of management. In subsequent chapters of this section, we shall examine such behavioral topics as motivation, leadership, groups, organizational design, and organizational change and development. In doing so, we will draw upon material from the behavioral sciences. While the disciplines may differ, the material will, for the most part, have a common thread. It will have been arrived at through the use of the methods described in this chapter for gaining knowledge in the behavioral sciences.

DISCUSSION AND REVIEW QUESTIONS

1. Why do you think the behavioral approach to management developed?
2. The Hawthorne studies are considered to have provided the impetus for human relations theory. Discuss in detail the four phases of the Hawthorne studies.
3. What are the differences between the human relations approach and the behavioral science approach?
4. Assume that the dean of your college has asked you to study the problem of student motivation. You have decided to use the scientific approach. What are some questions you would need to answer before you could begin to study?
5. Assume that your instructor is undecided which of two textbooks would be best suited for the management course. Can you devise a simple experiment that might help with the decision?
6. Discuss briefly the three basic study designs used by behavioral scientists. Give an actual example of one of them with which you are familiar.
7. A sales manager was overheard saying the following: "I've got enough to do *planning* the work of my sales force, *organizing* their activities and routes, and *controlling* their actions and expenses. I haven't got the time to mess around with that behavioral science stuff. Besides that theory business belongs in school, I can't use it in my world." Is the sales manager right? Of what value is theory to the practicing manager?
8. A popular women's magazine offers the following title on its front page: "Thirty-Five Days as a Women's Libber." Upon reading the article you find that it is actually a case study where a woman reporter spent 35

days as an active member of a women's liberation organization in New York City. Evaluate the study method based upon what you know about the characteristics of the scientific approach in the behavioral sciences and the methods of inquiry used by behavioral scientists.

ADDITIONAL REFERENCES

Argyris, C. *Integrating the Individual and the Organization.* New York: John Wiley and Sons, 1964.

Barnard, C. I. *The Functions of the Executive.* Boston: Harvard University Press, 1938.

Cyert, R. M., and March, J. G. *A Behavioral Theory of the Firm.* Englewood Cliffs, N.J.: Prentice-Hall, Inc., 1963.

Flippo, E. B. *Management: A Behavioral Approach.* Boston: Allyn and Bacon, Inc., 1970.

Gibson, J. L. Ivancevich, J. M., and Donnelly, J. D. *Organizations: Structure, Processes, Behavior.* Dallas, Tex.: Business Publications, Inc., 1973.

Helmstadter, G. C. *Research Concepts in Human Behavior.* New York: Appleton-Century-Crofts, Inc., 1970.

Hodge, B. J., and Johnson, H. J. *Management and Organizational Behavior: A Multidimensional Approach.* New York: John Wiley and Sons, Inc., 1970.

Leavitt, H. J. *Managerial Psychology.* Chicago: The University of Chicago Press, 1972.

Leavitt, H. J., Dill, W. R., and Eyring, H. B. *The Organizational World.* New York: Harcourt Brace Jovanovich, Inc., 1973.

Luthans, F. *Organizational Behavior: A Modern Behavioral Approach to Management.* New York: McGraw-Hill Book Co., 1973.

Mayo, E. *The Human Problems of Industrial Civilization.* New York: Macmillan and Company, 1933.

Roethlisberger, F. J. *Management and Morale.* Boston: Harvard University Press, 1941

Schein, E. H. *Organizational Psychology.* Englewood Cliffs, N.J.: Prentice-Hall, Inc., 1970.

7 Motivation

INTRODUCTION

Motivation is concerned with the "why" of human behavior, what it is that makes people do things. Why does Harry have frequent run-ins with the boss, or why does Dianne work so much harder than Jim? These questions can be partially answered with an understanding of human motivation. An understanding of motivation is a necessity for the student of management and it is an area which receives a great deal of attention in the Behavioral School. Behavioralists are concerned with the relationship between the satisfaction of individual needs and the work place. They believe that, in order to perform effectively, a manager must understand why people are motivated to behave as they do. In this way the manager can make the kinds of decisions which will encourage subordinates to direct their efforts toward achievement of organizational goals.

THE NATURE OF MOTIVATION

Before examining the elements of motivation, it is vital that we clearly understand exactly what the term means. Berelson and Steiner define motivation as "all those inner striving conditions described as wishes, desires, drives, etc. . . . . It is an inner state that activates or moves."[1]

---

[1] Bernard Berelson and Gary A. Steiner, *Human Behavior: An Inventory of Scientific Findings* (New York: Harcourt, Brace, and World, 1964), p. 239.

More specifically, the term motivation has often been called an *intervening variable*.[2] Intervening variables are internal and psychological processes which are not directly observable and which, in turn, account for behavior.[3] Thus, motivation is an intervening variable for it cannot be seen, heard, or felt, and can only be inferred from behavior. In other words we can only judge how motivated a person is by observing his behavior; we cannot measure it directly because it is unobservable. This means that we must first operationally define what motivation is, since we can only measure presumed indicators of motivation. For example, if one student consistently achieves higher grades than other students with similar intelligence we might infer that he or she is highly motivated. If a typist completes more purchase orders with no more errors than other typists with comparable skills we might infer that the typist is motivated. However, note that in each case we did not measure motivation directly; we observed a presumed indicator of motivation (grades and purchase orders completed) and made inferences from our observations.

Motivation and Behavior

Psychologists generally agree that all behavior is motivated, and that people have reasons for doing the things they do or for behaving in the manner that they do. In other words, all human behavior is designed to achieve certain goals and objectives. Such goal-directed behavior revolves around the desire for need satisfaction.

An unsatisfied need is the starting point in the process of motivation. It is a deficiency of something within the individual and provides the spark which begins the chain of events leading to behavior. An unsatisfied need causes tension (physical or psychological) within the individual, leading the individual to engage in some kind of behavior (seek a means) to satisfy the need, and thereby reduce the tension. Note that this activity is directed toward a goal; arrival at the goal satisfies the need, and the process of motivation is complete. For example, a thirsty person *needs* water, is *driven* by thirst, and *motivated* by a desire for water in order to satisfy his need.

Thus, the continuous process begins with an unsatisfied need and ends with need satisfaction with goal-directed behavior as a part of the process. This can be illustrated in a diagram (Figure 7-1). Since needs are such an important part of the process of motivation, let us examine them in more detail.

---

[2] E. Tolman, *Behavior and Psychological Man* (Berkeley, Calif.: University of California Press, 1958), pp. 115–29.

[3] Fred N. Kerlinger, *Foundations of Behavioral Research* (New York: Holt, Rinehart, and Winston, Inc., 1973), p. 40.

FIGURE 7–1

The Process of Motivation

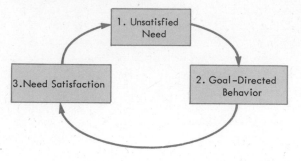

INDIVIDUAL NEEDS AND MOTIVATION

As we have already mentioned, unsatisfied needs are the starting point in the process of motivation. These needs may be classified in different ways.

Motivation and Early Management Writers

Many of the early writers on management emphasized monetary incentives as prime means for motivating the individual. These writers were influenced by the classical economists of the 18th and 19th centuries who placed emphasis on man's rational pursuit of economic objectives and believed that economic behavior was characterized by rational economic calculations. Today, most psychologists agree that while money is obviously an important motivator, man seeks to satisfy other than purely economic needs. In fact, Freud was the first psychologist to hypothesize that much of man's behavior may not even be rational, but that it may be influenced by needs of which the individual is not aware.

While most psychologists agree that man is motivated by the desire to satisfy many needs, there is a wide difference of opinion as to what these needs and their relative importance are. Most, however, take the pluralistic view, emphasizing many different types of needs the satisfaction of which is a key determinant of behavior. Let us now examine one of the most widely adopted theories of human motivation.

The Hierarchy of Needs

A widely adopted pluralistic framework is that presented by psychologist A. H. Maslow.[4] His theory of motivation stresses two fundamental premises:

---

[4] Abraham H. Maslow, *Motivation and Personality* (New York: Harper and Brothers, 1954), chap. 5.

FIGURE 7–2
Hierarchy of Needs

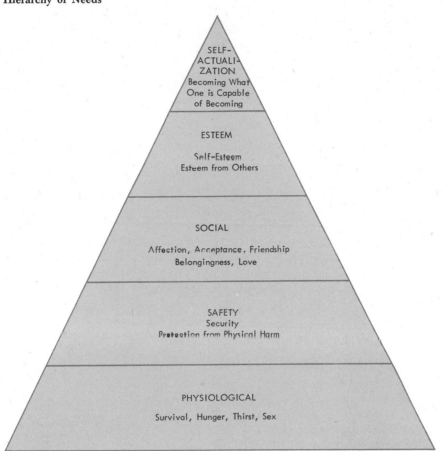

SELF-
ACTUALI-
ZATION
Becoming What
One is Capable
of Becoming

ESTEEM

Self-Esteem
Esteem from Others

SOCIAL

Affection, Acceptance, Friendship
Belongingness, Love

SAFETY
Security
Protection from Physical Harm

PHYSIOLOGICAL

Survival, Hunger, Thirst, Sex

1. Man is a wanting animal whose needs depend on what he already
   has. Only needs not yet satisfied can influence behavior. In other
   words, a satisfied need is not a motivator.
2. Man's needs are arranged in a hierarchy of importance. Once one
   need is satisfied, another emerges and demands satisfaction.

Maslow hypothesized five levels of needs. These needs are (1) physiological, (2) safety, (3) social, (4) esteem, and (5) self-actualization.[5]

---

[5] Less described, and hence not as well known are the cognitive and aesthetic
needs hypothesized by Maslow. Examples of cognitive needs are the need to know or
to understand, and the manipulation of the environment as the result of curiosity.
The aesthetic needs are satisfied by moving from ugliness toward beauty. Maslow
did not include them in the formal hierarchy framework. Ibid., pp. 93–98.

He placed them in a framework referred to as the *hierarchy of needs* because of the different levels of importance indicated. This framework is presented in Figure 7–2.

Maslow states that if all of a person's needs are unsatisfied at a particular time, satisfaction of the most predominant needs will be more pressing than the others. Those which come first must be satisfied before a higher level need comes into play, and only when they are sufficiently satisfied are the next ones in line significant. Let us briefly examine each need level.

Physiological Needs

This category consists of the primary needs of the human body such as food, water, and sex. Physiological needs will dominate when all needs are unsatisfied. In such a case, no other needs will serve as a basis for motivation. As Maslow states, "a person who is lacking food, safety, love, and esteem would probably hunger for food more strongly than for anything else."[6]

Since these types of situations probably do not arise often these days, particularly in the United States, the important needs, at least from a managerial standpoint, would appear to be those higher in the hierarchy.

Safety Needs

With the physiological needs met, the next higher level assumes importance. Safety needs include protection from physical harm, ill health, economic disaster, and avoidance of the unexpected. From a managerial standpoint, safety needs manifest themselves in attempts to insure job security and attempts to move toward greater financial support. For example, in the early days of labor unions, the primary demands which unions presented to management consisted of monetary increases. In recent times, however, many unions are making demands on management for such things as fringe benefits and job security, with less emphasis on increases in pay.

Social Needs

These needs are related to the social and gregarious nature of man and his need for companionship. This level in the hierarchy is the point of departure from the physical or quasi-physical needs of the two previous levels. Nonsatisfaction of this level of need may affect the mental health of the individual.

---

[6] Ibid., p. 82.

Esteem Needs

These needs consist both of the need for the awareness of importance to others (self-esteem) and the actual esteem from others. Esteem from others must also be felt as warranted and deserved. Satisfaction of these needs leads to a feeling of self-confidence and prestige.

Self-Actualization Needs

Maslow defines this need as the "desire to become more and more what one is, to become everything one is capable of becoming."[7] This means that the individual will fully realize the potentialities of talents and capabilities.

Obviously, as the role of the individual varies, so will the external aspects of self-actualization. In other words, whether the person is a college professor, a corporate manager, a parent, or an athlete, the drive is to be effective and efficient in the particular role. Maslow assumes that satisfaction of these needs is possibly only after the satisfaction of all other needs in the hierarchy.

Management's Use of the Need-Hierarchy Model

The need-hierarchy model is widely referred to by practitioners, for it is easy to comprehend, has a great deal of "common-sense" validity, and points out some of the factors that motivate people in business and other types of organizations. Most organizations in the United States have been extremely successful in satisfying lower-level needs. Through the salary they receive, individuals are able to satisfy the physiological needs of themselves and their families. Organizations also aid in satisfying security or safety needs through both salary and fringe benefit programs. Finally, they aid in satisfying social and affiliation needs by allowing interaction and association with others on the job. In one way, all of this may have created a future problem for management. Since human behavior is primarily directed toward fulfilling unsatisfied needs, how successful a manager is in the future in motivating subordinates may be a function of the ability to satisfy their higher-level needs.

While Maslow's need hierarchy does not provide a complete understanding of human motivation or the means to motivate people, it does provide an excellent starting point for the student of management. We shall use it in this chapter as the foundation for an understanding of motivation in organizations.

---

[7] Ibid., p. 92.

NONSATISFACTION OF NEEDS

Unsatisfied needs are the starting points for the understanding of motivation. However, many times an individual is unsuccessful in attempts to satisfy needs. In order to improve our understanding of motivation, it is necessary to explore what happens when needs are not satisfied.

As noted previously, unsatisfied needs produce tensions within the individual. (The reader is encouraged to think of these unsatisfied needs as occurring at any level in the need hierarchy. An unsatisfied social need can produce as much tension as an unsatisfied physiological need such as hunger.) These unsatisfied needs motivate the individual to behavior which will relieve the tension. When the individual is unable to satisfy needs (and thereby reduce the tension), *frustration* is the result. The college male who plots conscientiously for half a semester to secure a date with a co-ed in his management class only to have her refuse is an example of an individual who would probably be quite frustrated. His goal of getting a date, the attainment of which would have brought the satisfaction of several needs, has been blocked. Reactions to frustration will vary from person to person. Some people will react in a positive manner (constructive behavior), and others in a negative manner (defensive behavior).

Constructive Behavior

The reader is undoubtedly familiar with the constructive adaptive behavior in which a person engages when faced with frustration in attempts to satisfy needs. An assembly-line worker frustrated in attempts for recognition because of the nature of the job may seek recognition off the job by seeking election to leadership posts in fraternal or civic organizations. In order to satisfy social and belonging needs, a worker may conform to the norms and values of a group which bowls together on weekends. Finally, the college male mentioned previously may settle for a date with a less desirable co-ed or attend a party without a date but with some friends. Each of these is an example of constructive adaptive behavior which individuals employ to reduce frustration and satisfy needs.

Defensive Behavior

When individuals are blocked in attempts to satisfy their needs, they may evoke one or more defense mechanisms instead of adopting constructive behavior to solve problems. All of us employ defense mechanisms in one way or another because they perform an important protective function in our attempts to cope with reality. In most cases, they do not handicap the individual to any great degree. Ordinarily, however, they are not adequate for the task of protecting the self. As a result, adults whose behavior is continually dominated by defensive behavior will usually have great difficulty in adapting to the responsibilities of work and of other people.

What happens when needs are not satisfied is a complex area of inquiry still being investigated by psychologists. However, there are some general patterns of defensive behavior which have been identified, some of the most common being:

Withdrawal. One obvious way to avoid reality is to withdraw or avoid those situations which will prove frustrating The withdrawal may be physical (leaving the scene), but more than likely will be internalized and manifested in apathy. Workers whose jobs provide little in the way of need satisfaction may "withdraw" in the form of excessive absences, latenesses, or turnover.

Aggression. A very common reaction to frustration is aggression. In some cases, there may be a direct attack on the source of the frustration. However, this may often not be possible (for example, to fight the boss). Unfortunately, all too often the aggression is directed toward another object or party. This is known as *displacement*. Thus, a foreman may displace aggression on a subordinate production worker who, in turn, might displace his aggression on his wife.

Substitution. This occurs when the individual puts something else in the place of the original object. An employee frustrated in attempts to be promoted may substitute achieving leadership status in a work group whose objectives are to resist management policies.

Compensation. When a person goes overboard in one area or activity to make up for deficiencies in another, this defense mechanism is being evoked. A superior who has a disagreeable personality may overcompensate in any kind of attempts to practice good "human relations" with subordinates.

Repression. Many times the individual will repress a situation and a problem in order to keep frustration down. At times repression is an almost automatic response whereby the individual loses awareness of incidents that would cause anxiety or frustration if allowed to remain at the conscious level of the mind. Thus an unpleasant situation with the superior may be quickly "forgotten" by a subordinate.

Regression. When confronted with frustration, some individuals will revert back (regress) to childlike forms of behavior in their attempts to avoid the unpleasant reality. In the work situation, this often manifests itself in some form of horseplay.

Projection. This involves attributing one's own feelings to someone else. A subordinate may dislike a superior for some particular reason and attempt to make the superior appear ineffective whenever possible. The subordinate will attempt to justify this by saying, "My boss never liked me from the moment I got here."

Rationalization. This occurs when an individual presents a reason for behavior which is less ego-deflating or more socially acceptable than the true reason. An example of this defense mechanism is an employee perceiving poor performance as the result of obsolete equipment rather than personal deficiency.

Since every individual relies to some extent on defense mechanisms, this kind of behavior is difficult to eliminate completely in organizations. In fact, it performs a useful role in maintaining mental health. However,

FIGURE 7–3

A Motivation Model

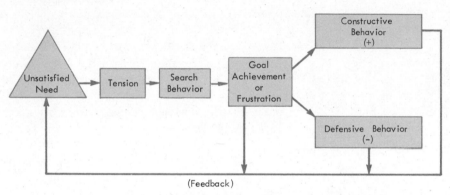

(Feedback)

its occurrence may be minimized to the extent that managerial decisions provide conditions under which employees experience minimum frustration. In addition, understanding of such behavior gives the manager greater empathy in everyday interactions with superiors and subordinates, and encourages awareness that an individual's behavior may not be a true indication of the person, since defense mechanisms may hide the true personality.

We can summarize what has been said thus far about motivation in the model presented in Figure 7–3. The diagram indicates that an unsatisfied need results in tensions within the individual and motivates a search for ways to relieve the tension. The diagram indicates that, if one is successful in achieving a goal, the next unsatisfied need emerges. If, however, attempts are met with frustration, one either engages in constructive behavior (note the plus sign to indicate its adaptive/positive nature), or resorts to defensive types of behavior (indicated with a minus sign because of its often negative effects). In either case, the individual returns to the next unsatisfied need which emerges.

PERSONALITY, BEHAVIOR, AND MOTIVATION

In the previous section we presented a conceptual framework for the relationship between needs and motivation. It is obvious that this is a general behavioral model which does not consider individual differences in motivation and behavior; otherwise, based on this model, one should be able to predict behavior. The reader should see that this is not possible: Given similar needs, different people react in different ways, not only in the goals they select and the means they choose to achieve them, but also in their reactions to frustration. Evidently there is some element missing in our explanation of motivation. This important element is the individual *personality*. Though each of us may be motivated to fulfill similar kinds of needs, the particular patterns of behavior we choose will differ from those of others because of our personalities.

Personality

The term personality means many things to behavioral scientists. We shall define it as *the general sum of traits or characteristics of an individual*. The reader should note that when we use the term, we do not mean what people often refer to when they describe an outstanding aspect of the impression which an individual creates on others. Personality is a conglomerate of forces within the individual and can be thought of as a dynamic system.

Determinants of Personality. Man is like all other men, and yet like no other man. One of the unique areas of his development is the personality. In order to understand how personality relates to motivation and behavior, we must first examine the determinants of personality.

The formation of the human personality is influenced by the mutual interaction of many factors. While the list could be unending, experts agree that there are four general classifications of influencing factors.[8]

1. *Constitutional Determinants.* These are inborn characteristics which the individual inherits. For example, different genetic structures result in varying potentials for learning, energy, activity, and tolerance for frustration. Age is also an important constitutional determinant of personality. These characteristics influence an individual's needs and expectations.

2. *Group Membership Determinants.* Individuals within any culture are exposed to the beliefs, values, and mores of the culture in different ways. These are usually transmitted through the various groups (for example, family, education, religion) with which they come into contact.

[8] Clyde Kluckhohn and Henry A. Murray, *Personality* (New York: Alfred A. Knopf, Inc., 1956), chap. 2.

The relationships which individuals develop are likely to have a lasting influence on their personalities and ways of viewing life.

3. *Role Determinants.* In a sense, role determinants of personality can be considered a special class of group membership determinants. Each of us has a number of different roles which we play at different times. The roles an individual plays to fulfill a given position are determined by the group within which the position exists. For example, the roles of a husband and wife are determined by the cultural environment within which the positions exist, while the roles of a military officer and a college professor are determined by their reference groups. While it is incorrect to accept a person's behavior in a particular situation (for example, a college professor's behavior in the classroom or on campus) as representative of the total personality, the roles which people play every day have a great influence upon their personalities.

4. *Situational Determinants.* Situational determinants of personality include the unique factors which influence an individual's personality. For example, a student who is undecided which functional area of business to major in while at college may have in his first management course a dynamic, persuasive bank executive as a guest speaker. While this event may not directly and immediately alter the student's personality, it may put into motion events which will be decisive in influencing his personality.

While each of the determinants discussed has an important influence on personality development, it is necessary to recognize their interdependence rather than considering them as isolated factors. In other words, it is incorrect to view a single determinant as the cause of personality. Instead, the personality of an individual is conditioned by several mutually interdependent and interacting variables and must be viewed as a dynamic system.

Personality and Motivation. In our earlier discussion of motivation, we constructed a motivational model which indicated that most behavior is directed toward satisfying an unsatisfied need, and that whenever need gratification is blocked, the individual experiences frustration. We saw that the individual may react to frustration either by engaging in some kind of constructive behavior to solve the problem or evoking one or more defense mechanisms. Now that we have discussed personality, how does this important determinant of behavior fit into the motivation process? Personality differences influence the process of motivation in the following ways:[9]

[9] Max D. Richard and Paul S. Greenlaw, *Management: Decisions and Behavior* (Homewood, Ill.: Richard D. Irwin, Inc., 1972), pp. 149–53. Also see an earlier edition, *Management Decision Making* (1966), pp. 112–15. The discussion here is based largely on the earlier edition.

1. *Strength of Needs.* The strength and importance of various needs will differ from one individual to another depending on the individual's personality. For example, some people have strong esteem needs which lead them to seek different kinds of employment or buy a whole different range of products than people whose esteem needs are not as strong.

2. *Aspiration Level.* Aspiration levels differ among individuals depending upon the strength of their needs. One individual may not be satisfied until reaching a position of power and influence in an organization, while another may be quite satisfied in a middle management position.

3. *Types of Behavior.* Although individuals may experience the same needs, the strategies or types of behavior which an individual utilizes to achieve need satisfaction are a function of personality. For example, one person may satisfy esteem needs by gaining on-the-job recognition from superiors, while another may satisfy the same need by striving to become a respected member of a professional or peer group. The need is the same but the behavior used to satisfy it differs.

4. *Reaction to Frustration.* How a person reacts to nonsatisfaction of needs is also a function of personality. Personality differences affect the types of situations which cause frustration, the degree to which defense mechanisms are evoked, and the kinds of defense mechanisms that are employed. For example, one individual frustrated in attempts to move up in an organization may instead seek leadership positions in external political or civic organizations (constructive behavior), while another individual experiencing the same frustration might engage in sabotage activities against the organization (defensive behavior).

In this section, we have presented a motivational model based upon the need-hierarchy framework. We have also noted that both motivation and behavior will vary from person to person as a result of differences in personality.

OTHER MODELS OF MOTIVATION

Before leaving the subject of motivation, let us examine two other widely discussed models of motivation which are especially useful for students of management because they are specifically concerned with motivation in the work situation.

Herzberg's Model

This approach to motivation was first advanced by Frederick Herzberg who based his theory on a study of need satisfactions and on the reported motivational effects of these satisfactions on 200 engineers and accountants. It is often referred to as the "two-factor" theory of motivation.[10]

In this study, Herzberg and his associates asked these subjects to think of times when they felt especially good, and times when they felt especially bad about their jobs. Each employee was then asked to describe the conditions which led to these particular feelings. It was found that the employees named different kinds of conditions which caused each of the feelings. For example, if recognition led to a good feeling about the job, the lack of recognition was seldom indicated as a cause of bad feelings.

Based on this research, Herzberg reached the following two conclusions:

1. There are some conditions of a job which operate primarily to dissatisfy employees when they are not present. However, the presence of these conditions does not build strong motivation. Herzberg called these factors *maintenance* or *hygiene* factors since they are necessary to maintain a reasonable level of satisfaction. He also noted that many of these have often been perceived by managers as factors which can motivate subordinates, but that they are, in fact, more potent as dissatisfiers when they are absent. He concluded that there were ten maintenance factors, namely:

a. Company policy and administration.
b. Technical supervision.
c. Interpersonal relations with supervisor.
d. Interpersonal relations with peers.
e. Interpersonal relations with subordinates.
f. Salary.
g. Job security.
h. Personal life.
i. Work conditions.
j. Status.

2. There are some job conditions which, if present, build high levels of motivation and job satisfaction. However, if these conditions are not present, they do not prove highly dissatisfying. Herzberg described six of these factors as *motivational* factors or satisfiers:

a. Achievement.
b. Recognition.
c. Advancement.
d. The work itself.
e. The possibility of personal growth.
f. Responsibility.

Summarizing the maintenance factors cause much dissatisfaction when they are not present, but do not provide strong motivation when they are present. On the other hand, the factors in the second group lead to strong motivation and satisfaction when they are present, but do not cause much dissatisfaction when they are absent.

The reader has probably noted that the *motivational factors* are job-

---

[10] See Frederick Herzberg, B. Mausner, and B. Snyderman, *The Motivation to Work* (New York: John Wiley and Sons, Inc., 1959).

centered; that is, they relate directly to the job content itself, the individual's performance of it, its responsibilities, and the growth and recognition obtained from. *Maintenance factors* are peripheral to the job itself and more related to the external environment of work. Another important finding of the study is that when employees are highly motivated, they have a high tolerance for dissatisfaction arising from the peripheral factors. However, the reverse is not true.

One limitation of Herzberg's original study and conclusions is that the subjects consisted of engineers and accountants. The fact that these individuals were in such positions indicates that they had the motivation to seek advanced education and expect to be rewarded for it. The same may not hold true for the nonprofessional worker. In fact, some testing of Herzberg's model on blue-collar workers showed that some of the factors considered as maintenance factors by Herzberg (pay, job security) are considered by blue-collar workers to be motivational factors.[11]

Another limitation of Herzberg's work has been cited by Vroom.[12] He believes that Herzberg's inference concerning differences between dissatisfiers and motivators cannot be completely accepted, and that the differences between stated sources of satisfaction and dissatisfaction in Herzberg's study may be the result of defensive processes within those responding. Vroom points out that people are apt to attribute the causes of satisfaction to their own achievements, but more likely to attribute their dissatisfaction to obstacles presented by company policies or superiors than to their own deficiencies.

Another group of writers believe that the two-factor theory is an oversimplification of the true relationship between motivation and dissatisfaction as well as between the sources of job satisfaction and dissatisfaction.[13] They reviewed several studies which showed that one factor can cause job satisfaction for one person and job dissatisfaction for another. They concluded that further research is needed to be able to predict in what situations worker satisfaction will produce greater productivity.

Since his original study, Herzberg has cited numerous and diverse replications of the original study which support his position.[14] These

[11] Michael R. Malinovsky and John R. Barry, "Determinants of Work Attitudes," *Journal of Applied Psychology*, vol. 49 (December 1965), pp. 446–51. For a discussion of other alternative interpretations of the two-factor theory and the research support for the various interpretations, see N. King, "Clarification and Evaluation of the Two-Factor Theory of Job Satisfaction," *Psychological Bulletin*, vol. 74 (July 1970), pp. 18–31.

[12] Victor H. Vroom, *Work and Motivation* (New York: John Wiley and Sons, Inc., 1964), pp. 128–29.

[13] R. J. House and L. A. Wigdor, "Herzberg's Dual-Factor Theory of Job Satisfaction and Motivation: A Review of the Evidence and a Criticism," *Personnel Psychology*, vol. 20 (Winter 1967), pp. 369–89.

[14] Frederick Herzberg, *Work and the Nature of Man* (Cleveland: World Publishing Co., 1966).

subsequent studies were conducted on professional women, hospital maintenance personnel, agricultural administrators, nurses, food handlers, manufacturing supervisors, engineers, scientists, military·officers, managers ready for retirement, teachers, technicians, and assemblers; and some were conducted in other cultural settings—Finland, Hungary, Russia, and Yugoslavia. However, other researchers who have used the same research methods employed by Herzberg have obtained results different from what his theory would predict,[15] while several others using different methods have also obtained contradictory results.[16]

This discussion indicates that Herzberg's theory has generated a great deal of controversy. Therefore readers should view this theory not as a panacea for all motivation problems in organizations, but as a starting point which they can use when attempting to develop their own approaches to motivation in the work situation.

Even after considering the legitimate criticisms, few would argue that Herzberg has not contributed substantially to our thinking on motivation at work. He certainly has extended Maslow's ideas and made them more applicable to the work situation. Finally, he has drawn attention to the critical importance of job-centered factors in work motivation which previously had been given little attention by behavioral scientists.

Comparison of Herzberg's and Maslow's Models

There is much similarity between Herzberg's and Maslow's models. A close examination of Herzberg's ideas indicates that what he is actually saying is that some employees may have achieved a level of social and economic progress in our society such that the higher-level needs of Maslow (esteem and self-actualization) are the primary motivators. However, they still must satisfy the lower-level needs for the maintenance of their current state. Thus, we can see that money might still be a motivator for nonmanagement workers (particularly those at a minimum wage level) and for some managerial employees. In addition, Herzberg's model adds to the need hierarchy model because it draws a

---

[15] Donald P. Schwab, H. William DeVitt, and Larry L. Cummings, "A Test of the Adequacy of the Two-Factor Theory as a Predictor of Self-Report Performance Effects," *Personnel Psychology*, vol. 24 (Summer 1971), pp. 293–303.

[16] Marvin D. Dunnette, John P. Campbell, and Milton D. Hakel, "Factors Contributing To Job Satisfaction and Job Dissatisfaction in Six Occupational Groups," *Organizational Behavior and Human Performance*, vol. 2 (May 1967), pp. 143–74; C. L. Hulin and P. A. Smith, "An Empirical Investigation of Two Implications of the Two-Factor Theory of Job Satisfaction," *Journal of Applied Psychology*, vol. 51 (October 1967), pp. 396–402; and C. A. Lindsay, E. Marks, and L. Gorlow, "The Herzberg Theory: A Critique and Reformulation," *Journal of Applied Psychology*, vol. 51 (August 1967), pp. 330–39.

FIGURE 7–4

A Comparison of the Maslow and Herzberg Models*

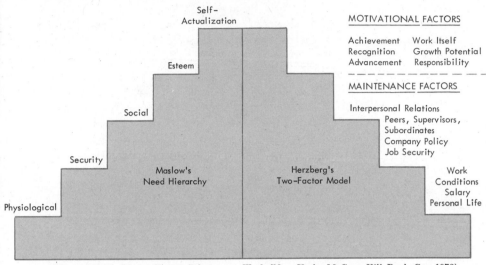

*Also see Keith Davis, *Human Relations at Work* (New York: McGraw-Hill Book Co., 1972), p. 59.

distinction between the two groups of motivational and maintenance factors, and points out that the motivational factors are often derived from the job itself. Figure 7–4 compares the two models.

Vroom's Model

One of the most recent models of motivation has been developed by Vroom and expands upon those developed by Maslow and Herzberg.[17] The Vroom model views motivation as a process governing choices. Thus, if an individual has a particular goal, in order to achieve the goal, some behavior must be performed. The individual, therefore, weighs the likelihood that various behaviors will achieve the desired goal, and if certain behavior is expected to be more successful than others, that type of behavior will likely be elected.

An important contribution of Vroom's model is that it explains how the *goals* of individuals influence their *effort* and that the behavior individuals select depends upon their assessment of the probability that the behavior will successfully lead to the goal. For example, all members of an organization may not place the same value on such job factors as promotion, high pay, job security, and working conditions. In other

[17] Vroom, *Work and Motivation.*

words, they may rank them differently. Vroom believes that what is important is the perception and value the individual places upon certain goals. Suppose that one individual places high value on salary increases and perceives superior performance as instrumental in reaching that goal. According to Vroom, this individual will strive toward superior performance in order to achieve the salary increases. On the other hand, another individual may value a promotion and perceive political behavior as instrumental in achieving it. This individual, therefore, is not likely to emphasize superior performance to achieve the goal. The reader is now encouraged to think of this in terms of student motivation, where one student has the goal of an A grade and another the goal of a C grade in a particular course. How might their respective efforts and behaviors in the course vary?

In summary, Vroom emphasizes the importance of individual perceptions and assessments of organizational behavior. What is important here is that what the individual perceives as the consequence of a particular behavior is far more important than what the manager (or professor) believes the individual should perceive.[18]

Since the Vroom model is relatively new there are few tests of its validity.[19] It is certainly more abstract than the Maslow and Herzberg models, and, as such, it may be some time before it is of any practical use to a manager. However, despite the lack of tested validity it would seem that the Vroom model adds additional insight into the study of motivation at work since it attempts to explain how *individual goals* influence *individual effort*. Note that the common thread running through each of the three models discussed in this chapter is that behavior is

---

[18] Using Vroom's terminology, the behavior of an individual is based upon the strength (*valance*) of the desire for achieving a particular outcome. This is related to perception of how the *first-level* outcome (for example, superior performance, extensive outside reading) is associated with the *second-level* outcome (for example, promotion, an A grade). The individual's perception of this relationship is called *instrumentality*. Finally, *expectancy* is the probability that a particular action will lead to a first-level outcome. It differs from instrumentality in that it relates efforts to first-level outcomes where instrumentality relates first- and second-level outcomes to each other. Thus, Vroom's model is often referred to as the Expectancy/Valence Model.

[19] See V. H. Vroom, "Organizational Choice: A Study of Pre- and Post-Decision Processes," *Organizational Behavior and Human Performance*, vol. 1 (August 1966), pp. 212–25; and J. Galbraith and L. L. Cummings, "An Empirical Investigation of the Motivational Determinants of Task Performance: Interactive Effects Between Instrumentality—Valence and Motivation—Ability," *Organizational Behavior and Human Performance*, vol. 2 (August 1967), pp. 237–57. For a critical review of field research on expectancy theory predictions of employee performance, see H. G. Heneman, III, and D. P. Schwab, "Expectancy Theory Predictions of Employee Performance: A Review of the Theory and Evidence," *Psychological Bulletin*, vol. 78 (July 1972), pp. 1–9.

goal directed. Thus, the process of motivation as it was presented earlier in the chapter serves as the cornerstone of the Maslow, Herzberg, and Vroom models of motivation.

TWO MANAGEMENT TECHNIQUES DESIGNED TO INCREASE MOTIVATION

Interest in improving the performance and overall contribution of organization members has been growing ever since behavioral scientists have provided evidence that certain appraisal and motivational programs yield positive results. Two of these programs, *management by objectives* and *job enrichment,* are excellent examples of the types of motivation techniques being proposed by behavioral scientists. While others could be cited, the two discussed here appear to be among the most widely used.

Management by Objectives

One management technique which has acquired many loyal supporters since it was first introduced in the early 1950s is management by objectives (MBO). Exactly what MBO entails has been presented in slightly different styles by those who advocate its use. For example, Peter Drucker who first introduced the concept of MBO describes it as follows:

> . . . the objectives of the district manager's job should be defined by the contribution he and his district sales force have to make to the sales department, the objectives of the project engineer's job by the contribution he, his engineers and draftsmen make to the engineering department. . . .
>
> This requires each manager to develop and set the objectives of his unit himself. Higher management must, of course, reserve the power to approve or disapprove these objectives. But their development is part of a manager's responsibility; indeed, it is his first responsibility. . . .[20]

Drucker believes that the greatest advantage of MBO is that it allows the manager to control his own performance. This self-control is supposed to result in stronger motivation to do the best rather than just to get by.

Another slightly different presentation of the basic fundamentals and overall philosophy of MBO is provided by Odiorne:

> . . . a process whereby the superior and subordinate managers of an organization jointly identify its common goals, define each individual's major areas of responsibility in terms of the results expected of him, and

---

[20] Peter Drucker, *The Practice of Management* (New York: Harper and Brothers, 1954), pp. 128–29.

use these measures as guides for operating the unit and assessing the contribution of each of its members.[21]

An important factor in Odiorne's viewpoint is for the subordinate and superior to have an understanding regarding the subordinate's major areas of responsibility, what will constitute an acceptable level of performance, and what needs to be done to improve performance. A common thread found in both the Drucker and Odiorne conceptions is that MBO should lead to improved motivation of participants.

Other well-known management scholars have also written extensively on MBO.[22] Their contentions are similar to those offered by Drucker and Odiorne. Synthesizing the works of these experts enables one to develop a set of three guidelines which provide an operational understanding of management by objectives. The guidelines emphasize that, in MBO programs:

1. Superiors and subordinates meet and discuss goals (results) for the subordinates which are in line with overall organizational goals;
2. The superiors and subordinates jointly establish attainable goals for subordinates,
3. The superiors and subordinates meet again after the initial goals are established, and evaluate the subordinates' performance in terms of the goals. The essential feature is that *feedback* on performance is provided the subordinates. The subordinates know where they stand with regard to their contributions to their organizational unit and the firm.

The exact procedures employed in implementing the goal-setting and performance evaluation program will vary from organization to organization or from unit to unit. The anticipated end results, however, will hopefully be the same: (1) improved participant contribution, (2) improved morale and attitudes of the participants, (3) reduced anxiety resulting from ambiguity as to where they stand with their superior, and (4) implementing Vroom's concept of attempting to establish a direct linkage between individual and organizational objectives.

Research on MBO

A number of firms have implemented MBO-type programs on a company or departmental basis. A number of recent studies report some of the effects of such programs.

---

[21] George Odiorne, *Management by Objectives* (New York: Pitman Publishing Co., 1965), p. 26. Also see George Odiorne, *Personnel Administration by Objectives* (Homewood, Ill.: Richard D. Irwin, Inc., 1971).

[22] See Douglas McGregor, "An Uneasy Look at Performance Appraisal," *Harvard Business Review*, vol. 35 (May–June 1957), pp. 89–94; E. C. Schleh, *Management by Results* (New York: McGraw-Hill Book Co., 1961); and W. J. Reddin, *Effective Management by Objectives* (New York: McGraw-Hill Book Co., 1970).

A two-part study of a type of MBO program referred to as "Goal Setting and Self-Control" was undertaken during 1965 and 1966 at the Purex Corporation.[23] The result of the research was that after the goal-setting program had been initiated, participants at Purex were more concerned about and aware of the firm's goals and future activities. In the initial study it was also found that the goal-setting procedure improved communications and understanding among those involved.

However, the follow-up study showed that many of the participants perceived the program as being a weak incentive for improving performance levels. Evidently they had changed their opinions about the program after it had been in operation over a four-year period. Their reasons for changing their opinions about the program were divided into five categories:

1. Managers reported that the program was used as a whip.
2. The program increased the amount of paperwork.
3. The program failed to reach the lower managerial levels.
4. There was an overemphasis placed on production.
5. The program failed to provide adequate incentives to improve performance.

Another study was made on the effects of a form of MBO program known as "Work Planning and Review."[24] The research design included an experimental and control group of managers. The control group operated under a traditional performance appraisal system which involved an annual appraisal of a subordinate's performance by the manager. The experimental group was encouraged to prepare a set of goals for achieving improved job performance and to submit them for the superior's review and approval.

Managers using the "Work Planning and Review" goal-setting program were compared to those operating under the traditional appraisal program. The managers using the goal-setting program expressed significantly more favorable attitudes. Specifically, their attitudes changed in a favorable direction over the one-year study in the four areas which are as follow:

1. Extent to which the managers made use of their abilities and experiences.
2. Ability of the managers to plan.

[23] Anthony P. Raia, "Goal Setting and Self Control," *Journal of Management Studies*, vol. 2 (September 1965), pp. 34–53; and Anthony P. Raia, "A Second Look at Management Goals and Controls," *California Management Review*, vol. 8 (Summer 1966), pp. 49–58.

[24] Herbert H. Meyer, Emanuel Kay, and John R. P. French, Jr., "Split Roles in Performance Appraisal," *Harvard Business Review*, vol. 43 (January–February 1965), pp. 21–27.

3. Degree to which the managers were receptive to new ideas and suggestions.
4. Degree to which they felt the goals for which they were aiming were what they should be.

A more recent study dealt with managerial reactions to management by objectives in a large manufacturing firm.[25] The researchers were concerned with the manager's perceptions associated with the MBO approach. The rationale of the program most cited by participants was that the objectives-setting process was intended to link the evaluation of an individual to actual performance rather than to personality or other characteristics. It was also found that a majority of the participating managers believed that the most significant advantage of the program was that one was more likely "to know what was expected by the boss." A major problem cited by the managers was that excessive formal requirements were imposed because of the program; that is, the need to process, complete, and update forms, and to provide other data to the coordinator of the program were major irritants.

In the studies cited thus far, the major purpose of each was to determine some of the effects of MBO programs rather than the impact of MBO upon managers. Two recent studies, however, were designed to determine the impact of MBO on participant job satisfaction.[26] In these studies the researchers administered a psychological test which measures an individual's perceived need satisfactions. It was found that the need satisfaction of participants was influenced by the MBO program. However, the findings indicated that the manner in which MBO was implemented in the two companies had some impact on the perceived need satisfactions of the participants.

Implementing MBO Programs

Despite the evident advantages of MBO, there are several key factors which must be considered in the implementation phase. For ex-

---

[25] Henry L. Tosi and Stephen J. Carroll, "Managerial Reaction to Management by Objectives," *Academy of Management Journal*, vol. 11 (December 1968), pp. 415–26. For other related work, see Stephen J. Carroll and Henry L. Tosi, "The Relation of Characteristics of the Review Process as Moderated by Personality and Situational Factors to the Success of the 'Management by Objectives' Approach," *Academy of Management Journal*, vol. 12 (September 1969), pp. 139–43; and Stephen J. Carroll and Henry L. Tosi, "Goal Characteristics and Personality Factors in a Management by Objectives Program," *Administrative Science Quarterly*, vol. 15 (September 1970), pp. 295–305.

[26] John M. Ivancevich, "A Longitudinal Assessment of Management by Objectives," *Administrative Science Quarterly*, vol. 17 (March 1972), pp. 126–38; and John M. Ivancevich, James H. Donnelly, Jr., and Herbert L. Lyon, "A Study of the Impact of Management by Objectives on Perceived Need Satisfactions," *Personnel Psychology*, vol. 23 (Summer 1970), pp. 139–51.

ample, managers who are about to engage in MBO programs must first be conditioned and psychologically prepared.[27] With the introduction of MBO, changes will often occur in organizational variables such as the flow of communications both horizontally and vertically, the intensity of inter-group interaction, and the number of personal contacts between superiors and subordinates. Thus, the dynamic nature of these variables and their impact on the functioning of the organization necessitate complete understanding of MBO by managers, to insure that managerial resistance to implementation and participation is minimal.

Another critical factor in the implementation of MBO programs is the supportive managerial climate which pervades the organization. Two important conclusions have been cited concerning implementation:[28]

1. Top management must not assume a passive role. The most effective manner to implement MBO is to allow the top-level executives to explain, coordinate, and guide the program. When top managers are actively involved, the philosophy and mechanics of the program filter through and penetrate the entire organization. Thus, a possible motivation strategy to improve need satisfaction at lower levels of management would be to involve the top-level management group in the MBO program.

2. Improvements in need satisfaction are higher in the company where the MBO program is instituted by upper-level executives than in organizations where it is implemented by the personnel department.

Management by objectives is not being offered here as a cure-all for motivation problems, but it is an approach which warrants careful consideration, especially since some evidence of its effectiveness is available.

Job Enrichment

The "quality of life" at work is currently receiving much attention from practicing managers, professors, government officials, and union leaders. It appears that many workers are becoming increasingly dissatisfied and frustrated by routine, mechanically paced tasks and are reacting negatively with output restrictions, poor quality work, absenteeism, high turnover, militant demands for higher wages, expanded fringe benefits, and greater participation in decisions which directly affect their jobs. Earlier we discussed the motivational and maintenance factors model developed by Herzberg. In recent efforts, he has gone farther and attempted to increase employee motivation by actually

---

[27] Henry L. Tosi, Jr., "Management Development and Management by Objectives —An Interrelationship," *Management of Personnel Quarterly*, vol. 4 (Summer 1965), p. 24.

[28] Ivancevich, Donnelly, and Lyon, "Impact of MBO on Need Satisfactions," pp. 148–50.

building up the motivational factors in a job. This practical contribution of Herzberg is a motivational technique known as *job enrichment* and has been supported by many as a solution to the problem of the "quality of life" at work. He first reported the successful application of his approach using stockholder correspondents employed by a large corporation.[29] Job enrichment as Herzberg describes it,

> . . . seeks to improve both task efficiency and human satisfaction by means of building into people's jobs, quite specifically, greater scope for personal achievement and recognition, more challenging and responsible work, and more opportunity for individual advancement and growth. It is concerned only incidentally with matters such as pay and working conditions, organizational structure, communications, and training, important and necessary though these may be in their own right.[30]

In another series of experiments, Herzberg studied five British firms to determine among other things, the generality of his original findings.[31] The five studies covered widely different business areas and company functions as well as many types and levels of jobs. The five groups were laboratory technicians in a research and development department, sales representatives, design engineers, production foremen on shift work, and enginering foremen on day work. There were three main features to the study:

1. The hygiene factors were held constant. This means that no deliberate changes were made in pay, security, and other maintenance factors, because the researchers were only interested in determining gains which were brought about through change in job content.
2. An "experimental" group was formed for whom the specific changes in job content were made, and a "control" group was formed whose job content remained the same.
3. The fact that the studies were being done was kept confidential. This was done to avoid the well-known tendency of people to behave differently when they are aware that they are part of a study.

The researchers sought to measure job satisfaction and performance for both groups over the study period, which generally lasted one year. Performance measures were specific to the group concerned and, in addition, were determined by the local management of the participating company.

How were the jobs in the experimental group "enriched"? Rather than

---

[29] Frederick Herzberg, "One More Time: How Do You Motivate Employees?" *Harvard Business Review*, vol. 46 (January–February 1968), p. 53.

[30] William J. Paul, Jr., Keith B. Robertson, and Frederick Herzberg, "Job Enrichment Pays Off," *Harvard Business Review*, vol. 47 (March–April 1969), p. 61.

[31] Ibid.

examine all five groups, let us review the program of action devised and implemented for the sales representatives.

> Sales representatives were no longer obliged to write reports on every customer call. They were asked simply to pass on information when they thought it appropriate or request action as they thought it was required.
>
> Responsibility for determining calling frequencies was put wholly with the representatives themselves, who kept the only records for purposes such as staff reviews.
>
> The technical service department agreed to provide service "on demand" from the representatives; nominated technicians regarded such calls as their first priority. Communication was by direct contact, paperwork being cleared after the event.[32]

Following the changes in job content of the sales representatives, there resulted an increase in sales of 19 percent over the same period of the previous year for the experimental group. In the control group, sales declined during the study period by 5 percent. The equivalent change for both groups the previous year had been a decline of 3 percent.

The content of the jobs in the remaining four groups was "enriched" in a fashion similar to that for the sales representatives. The specific changes are not detailed here. However, it is necessary to note that similar positive results were found for each of the other four types of jobs when specific changes were made in the job content of the workers in each "experimental" group. The researchers concluded among other things that "tasks have to be motivational—that is, the more they draw upon the motivators, the more likely they are to produce an effective contribution to business objectives."[33]

Herzberg emphasizes the importance of differentiating between *job enrichment* and *job enlargement*. He views job enrichment as providing the employee with an opportunity to grow psychologically and mature in his job, while job enlargement merely makes a job structurally larger by increasing the number of tasks. Job enlargement will be discussed in Chapter 10 (Organizational Design).

Job Enrichment at Texas Instruments.   Over a period of years a study of motivation in the work place has been conducted at Texas Instruments, Inc. (TI).[34] The company grew during the 1950s from a firm with 1,700 to one with 17,000 employees. The management of the company and their consultants believed that they could best cope with this significant growth by implementing a management philosophy that

---

[32] Ibid., p. 66.

[33] Ibid., p. 77.

[34] See M. Scott Meyers, "Who Are Your Motivated Workers?" *Harvard Business Review*, vol. 42 (January–February 1964), pp. 73–88, for an excellent account of the work at Texas Instruments.

encouraged individual self-actualization. The basic premise was that TI goals could be achieved more readily by providing opportunities for employees to attain their personal goals.

As a result, behavioral research began at TI on motivational problems in 1961. A number of randomly selected employees participated in the research which used Herzberg's motivational model as a cornerstone for determining maintenance and motivation factors. Five classifications of employees were included in the sample—scientists, engineers, manufacturing supervisors, technicians, and assemblers.

The research found that all of the five occupational groups, except assemblers, were largely comprised of actual or potential motivation seekers. That is, they sought achievement, recognition, and growth among other things. The scientists were the group most oriented toward motivational factors, while the group most oriented toward maintenance factors (for example, pay, supplemental benefits) was that of the assemblers.

Based upon these and other research findings, TI has implemented a program which attempts to make supervisors aware of the two-factor (Herzberg) theory so that it can aid them in designing jobs. For example, the supervisors analyzed the functions performed by their subordinates in terms of the potential for serving maintenance or motivation needs. The company implemented a training program for supervisors to facilitate the understanding of employee motivation. Group meetings were used so that skills in motivating people could be developed. Thus, the research at Texas Instruments has sought to implement Herzberg's theory over a period of time by integrating it into the total management system of the firm.

SUMMARY

We have examined an area of prime importance in the Behavioral School. We have seen that motivation is closely related to needs and to the individual personality. A knowledge of these behavioral concepts provides managers with insight into the complex area of human motivation.

We have also examined two management techniques—management by objectives and job enrichment—whose supporters believe can lead to many positive consequences if utilized correctly. The authors do not contend that either of these techniques is free of limitations for managers. There are also many additional techniques not discussed in this text for lack of space. We do not mean to imply by omission that these other techniques will not result in positive consequences if they are utilized.

One final comment is in order: The reader should note that a common thread (participation by subordinates in planning and goal setting) can be found in both the MBO and job enrichment approaches. We shall see in the following chapters that advocates of the behavioral science approach to management place a great deal of emphasis on the participative approach.

DISCUSSION AND REVIEW QUESTIONS

1. Discuss the following statement: "Motivation can be directly and accurately measured."

2. The manager of a fast-food restaurant was overheard saying, "I believe that money is the best of all possible motivators. You can say what you please about all that other nonsense, but when it comes right down to it, if you give a guy a raise, you'll motivate him. That's all there is to it." In light of what was discussed in the chapter, advise this restaurant manager.

3. Think of a situation from your personal experiences where two individuals reacted differently to frustration. Discuss each situation and the reactions of the two individuals. Can you give a possible explanation why the two individuals reacted differently?

4. In the chapter it was emphasized that managers must be familiar with the fundamental needs of man in order to motivate employees successfully. Select two individuals with whom you are well acquainted. Do they differ, in your opinion, with respect to the strength of various needs? Discuss these differences and indicate how this could affect their behavior. If you were attempting to motivate them, could these differences cause you to use different approaches for each individual? Why?

5. Can a student's "job" be enriched? Assume that your professor has asked you to consult with him concerning applying the "two-factor" motivation model in your class. You are to answer two questions for him: (1) Can you apply this approach to the classroom? Why? and (2) If so, differentiate between maintenance and motivational factors and develop a list of motivational factors your professor can use to "enrich" the student's job.

6. Assume that you have just read Vroom's thoughts on how the *goals* of individuals influence their *effort* and that the behavior the individual selects depends upon his assessment of the probability that the behavior will successfully lead to the goal. What is your goal in this management course? Is it influencing your effort? Do you suppose another individual in your class might have a different goal? Is his or her effort (behavior) different from yours? If your professor was aware of this, could it be of any value to him?

7. Compare and contrast job enrichment and management by objectives (MBO).

8. Assume you have just completed college and have accepted a job with a large corporation. Discuss the factors you feel would motivate you to superior performance during your first three years with the firm. Do the same thing again, except assume you have been out of college for 15 years. Do the factors differ? Explain why.

ADDITIONAL REFERENCES

Bolles, R. C. *Theory of Motivation.* New York: Harper and Row Publishers, 1967.

Carroll, S. J., and Tosi, H. L. *Management by Objectives.* New York: The Macmillan Co., 1973.

Cummings, L. L., and Schwab, D. P. *Performance in Organizations: Determinants and Appraisal.* Glenview, Ill.: Scott, Foresman and Co., 1973.

Dalton, G. W., and Lawrence, P. *Motivation and Control in Organizations.* Homewood, Ill.: Richard D. Irwin, Inc., 1970.

Gellerman, S. W. *Motivation and Productivity.* New York: American Management Association, 1963.

Hunt, J. G., and Hill, H. W. "The New Look in Motivational Theory for Organizational Research," *Human Organization* 28 (Summer 1969): 100–109.

Likert, R. *The Human Organization,* New York: McGraw-Hill Book Co., Inc., 1967.

McClelland, D. C. *The Achieving Society.* Princeton, N.J.: Van Nostrand Company, 1961.

Maslow, A. H. *Eupsychian Management.* Homewood, Ill.: Richard D. Irwin, Inc., 1965.

Opsahl, R. L., and Dunnette, M. D. "The Role of Financial Compensation in Industrial Motivation," *Psychological Bulletin* 66 (August 1966): 94–118.

Porter, L. W., and Lawler, E. E. *Managerial Attitudes and Performance.* Homewood, Ill.: Richard D. Irwin, Inc., 1968.

Raia, A. P. *Managing By Objectives.* Glenview, Ill.: Scott, Foresman and Co., 1974.

Practical Exercise I

John Sloane

Since he was in between his sophomore and junior years in college, Jeff Bailey considered himself very fortunate to land a summer job in the stock transfer department at one of the largest stock brokers in his home town. Not only would the job provide him with some spending money for his junior year but perhaps also give him some practical work experience. Since he was a business administration major he thought this might be especially valuable.

His job consisted of the following: When a purchase order for securities was received, it was typed on a purchase order form which consisted of four different colored carbon copies. When the form was pulled apart each colored carbon went to a specific department in the firm. Jeff's group received the pink copy. Jeff sat at a long table with five other men. The forms would come in batches, and their task was to look up the closing price of the security for the previous day, multiply it by the number of shares purchased, and write the total figure on the form. It was not necessary to be precise as it was only an estimate since stock prices fluctuated. On a busy day the forms would pile up. If they were not completed by the end of the day, the group had to work overtime until all work was completed. The job wasn't much of a challenge, Jeff thought, but at least it was spending money.

After his first week on the job Jeff learned that two of his co-workers were students like himself, two others were attending a local university part-time in the evening while working during the day. The other was John Sloane. John had been employed by the firm for 37 years in various clerical jobs and had been doing his present job for over five years. He knew his job so well that unlike the others, he did not consult a list to identify the prices of securities. He had the approximate prices committed to memory. Jeff heard that Sloane was paid $140 per week which was double the amount he was making. Sloane stayed by himself mostly and rarely talked with other members of the group.

Jeff worked well with the group and they often went to lunch together and dinner on the nights when overtime was necessary. One night on returning early from dinner Jeff saw John Sloane stuffing a large batch of purchase forms into his coat pocket in the cloak room. Jeff didn't say anything but was embarrassed. John Sloane said nothing.

A few days later when the two were alone John confided in Jeff that he did it occasionally when work piled up in order to get home at a reasonable time. He said, "What difference does it make? By the time it shows up it might be two or three months and they can't trace it to any department. Besides there are three other carbon copies floating around the company. Believe me, kid, this company doesn't give a damn about you or me so don't give them an inch more than you have to."

Jeff never said anything about his conversation with Sloane. During the summer he became pretty friendly with John and found him to be a likable person.

As he sat on the plane returning to school in the fall, Jeff thought about John Sloane. Actually he didn't know really what to think about John—whether to like him or dislike him, respect him or not respect him. Frankly, he was puzzled.

Questions for Analysis:

1. Assume you had just been hired as head of the stock transfer department and were made aware of John Sloane's behavior. In terms of what you have just read in the chapter can you provide a possible explanation for his behavior?

2. What do you believe are the causes of John Sloane's behavior?

3. Can anything be done to motivate John Sloane in a positive direction? Explain.

Practical Exercise II

Motivating Different Individuals

Below are brief descriptions of several individuals. Assume that you are their manager. Select from the following the strategy that you feel would be most likely to motivate each person to improved performance. Explain your reasons for selecting it.

a. Management by objectives.
b. An individual incentive plan.
c. Recognition for achievement.
d. A salary increase.
e. Threat of demotion or discharge.

f. Additional status (for example, bigger office, title, carpeting in office, secretary).
g. A group profit-sharing plan.
h. Job enrichment.
i. Additional fringe benefits.
j. More participation in management decisions.
k. More freedom of action (that is, less supervision).

1. Jim Hammer is a marketing representative for a large pharmaceutical firm. His job involves calling on medical doctors to promote the firm's line of prescription drugs. He is 27 years old, married with one child, and holds a college degree in business administration. He has been with the firm five years and earns $15,700 annually.

2. Barbara Oldec is head pediatrics nurse at a large public hospital. She is 29 years old, married with two children, and is currently pursuing a masters degree. She has a reputation among staff physicians as an extremely competent nurse. Her yearly salary is $12,000.

3. John Ekard is vice president of operations for one of the nation's largest fast-food franchisers. He is 51 years old, divorced, and has three children—two attend college and one is married. He has been with the company for nine years and earns a salary of $52,500 per year. He is among a group of top-level executives in the company who share in company profits through a bonus system.

4. Dave Noe is a part-time employee for a large supermarket chain. He is 26 years old, an Air Force veteran, and has worked for the firm before entering and after being discharged from the service. He is a highly valued employee and earns approximately $4.50 per hour. He also attends a local university and is presently completing the final 12 hours for a degree in business administration.

5. Marie Glass is assistant director of market development for a new space industry firm. She is 25 years old, single, bright, witty, and energetic. She exemplifies the "new woman." Her annual salary is $14,000. She has just completed her master's degree.

6. Bill Porter is assistant manager of a low priced restaurant which is part of a 14-unit chain. He is 25 years old, single, and has three years of college. He works six days each week and earns $150 per week. He receives about $4,000 per year from a family inheritance.

7. Betty Harris is the administrative assistant to the dean of a liberal arts college. She is 31 years old, single, and has had one year of secretarial training. Her duties involve counseling students on degree requirements, supervising registration, and keeping student records. She earns $9,500 per year. She has been at the college for 12 years where she began as a typist.

8. John Richards is a research chemist for one of the nation's largest

chemical companies. He joined the firm four years ago upon graduating from a leading university. He is 26 years old and his present annual salary is $13,500 per year. He is getting married in two months.

9. Sam Wilson supervises the 16-man night cleaning crew in a large office building. He has been supervisor for two years, being promoted to his present job after performing various cleaning jobs for 11 years. He is 44 years old, married, and has two children. He earns $10,000 per year. Three days each week he holds a part-time job on the cleaning crew at a local hospital. During the baseball season he works Sundays at the local stadium when the home team is playing.

10. Dr. Thomas Pryor is professor of history at a well-known university. He is well recognized in his field of American history, having authored several articles in respected professional journals and having authored one well-recognized text. However, he has not written anything during the past four years. He is a full professor with tenure, earning the top salary in his department, $25,000. He is 40 years old, is married, and has three children under ten years of age. His interest and enthusiasm for teaching appears to have declined during the last two years, and his excellent teacher ratings by students have begun to decline slightly.

8 Work Groups

INTRODUCTION

Few managers question the existence of work groups. This chapter is concerned with the general concept of groups in all types of organizations. Beginning with the famous Hawthorne studies of the 1920s, behavioral scientists have paid special attention to the processes occurring within groups which affect individuals and organizations. Thus, any presentation of a behavioral approach to management would certainly be incomplete if the reader were not provided with a framework for understanding the nature and characteristics of work groups.

The purpose of this chapter is to provide (1) a classification system which can be used to sort the different types of work groups; (2) some knowledge about the reasons for formation of work groups; (3) some explanation of methods utilized to study work groups; (4) some insights into the results of group membership; (5) an understanding of some of the structural characteristics of groups; and (6) a brief presentation of some studies on groups which are relevant to actual organizational situations.

An appropriate definition of the term "work group" is essential to an analysis of the way in which behavioral scientists discuss groups in the management literature. The list of elaborate definitions proposed by individuals studying work groups is endless. However, a concise definition which is appropriate for the present chapter is as follows: *A work group is a collection of employees (managerial or nonmanagerial), sharing certain norms, who are striving toward member need satisfaction through the attainment of a group goal(s).*

171

Many individuals ask why work groups should be studied in a management text. There are, of course, many different answers which can be provided. Some of the more relevant responses are:

1.   The formation of work group(s) is inevitable and ubiquitous.[1] Consequently, no matter how rewarding or satisfying it is to work in a particular organization, it is almost certain that work groups will be formed. Thus it is in management's interest to understand what happens within work groups because they are found throughout the organization.
2.   Work groups strongly influence the overall behavior and performance of members. To understand the forces of influence exerted by the group requires a systematic analysis.
3.   Group membership can have both positive and negative consequences as far as the organization is concerned. If managers are to avoid the negative consequences generated by work groups, it behooves them to learn about groups.

These three answers are typical of the numerous explanations provided when writers are attempting to justify their discussion of work groups. The common thread found in most answers is that groups exist and are a force which affect the attitudes and behaviors of employees. This is the most obvious and pragmatic reason for the study of groups; no further justification or explanation is needed.

REASONS FOR THE FORMATION OF WORK GROUPS

An explanation of the reasons for group formation can center around a number of factors which may be physical, economic, and sociopsychological. All of these factors can be viewed as categories of determinants for group formation.

Location

When people are put in close proximity to each other, there is a tendency for them to interact and communicate with each other. If workers are not able to do this on a fairly regular basis, there is less tendency to form a group.[2] This is not to say that workers must communicate daily or hourly before a work group forms. Instead, it should be obvious that some degree of interaction and communication is necessary.

In organizations, a typical procedure is to locate workers in similar

---

[1] Dorwin Cartwright and Ronald Lippett, "Group Dynamics and the Individual," *International Journal of Group Psychotherapy*, vol. 7 (January 1957), p. 88.

[2] William G. Scott and Terence R. Mitchell, *Organization Theory* (Homewood, Ill., Richard D. Irwin, Inc., 1972), p. 124.

occupations together. For example, in the construction of a home, the bricklayers perform their jobs in close proximity to each other. The same situation exists in offices where secretaries are located next to each other.[3]

Economic Reasons

In some cases, work groups form because individuals believe that they can derive more economic benefits on their jobs if they form into groups. For example, individuals (strangers) working at different stations on an assembly line may be paid on a group incentive basis. Whatever the particular group produces determines the wages for each member. Because of the interest of the workers in their wages, they would interact and communicate with each other. By working as a group instead of as individuals, the employees may perceive and actually obtain higher economic benefits.

Another example of the economic motive for work group formation could definitely exist in a nonunion organization, where the workers may form into a group to bring pressure against management for more economic benefits. The group members have a common interest—increased economic benefits—which leads to group affiliation.

A number of older workers may form into a work group because of economic motives, such as the administration and payment of their pensions after retirement. Assuming that they wanted to handle discussions of the pension plan outside the jurisdiction of their union (if they are in a unionized plant), they would be considered a work group.

Socio-Psychological Reasons

Workers in organizations are also motivated to form work groups so that certain needs can be more adequately satisfied. The safety, social, esteem, and self-actualization needs can be satisfied to some degree by work groups.

Safety. Work groups protect members from outside pressures such as management demands for better quality and quantity of production, punching the clock on time, and recommendations for changing the individual's work area layout. By being members of a group, the employees can immerse themselves in the group activities and openly discuss these management demands with individuals who usually support their viewpoint. Without the group to lean on when various management demands are made, employees often assume that they are standing alone facing management and the entire organization. This "aloneness" leads to a degree of insecurity.

---

[3] Ibid., p. 125.

The interactions and communications existing between members of a work group serve as a buffer to management demands. Another form of security need satisfaction occurs in instances when an individual is a new employee and is asked to perform a difficult job task over an extended period of time. The employee may not want to continually contact the supervisor for help in correctly performing the job, and therefore depends largely upon the group. This reliance can certainly be interpreted as providing the new employee with a form of security need satisfaction. New employees are often very concerned with performing well so that they can continue on the job. Thus, continually requesting help from the supervisor is thought of by some new employees as indicating that they are not able to handle the job. Consequently they turn to the group for help so that their new position is not threatened. Whether the supervisor believes that a subordinate continually asking for help is a sign of inability to perform the job is not the main issue. The important point is how new workers perceive their situation and job security.

Social. Employees often join work groups because of their need for affiliation. The basis of affiliation ranges from wanting to interact with and enjoy other employees to more complex desires for group support of self-image.[4] A management atmosphere which does not permit interaction and communication is suppressing the desire of employees to feel a sense of belongingness.

The desire to belong and to be a part of a group points up the intensity of the social needs. An excellent discusion of the social needs of Americans is offered by Edgar Schein. He discusses the concern which was voiced about the behavior of United States prisoners of war in North Korea. Since there were few escapes and numerous instances of apparent collaboration, many citizens of the United States were distressed. Schein suggests that one of the reasons for the POW situation was the manner in which prisoners were treated.[5]

In the North Korean POW camps, officers were separated from enlisted men. Groups were systematically broken up and prisoners were regularly transferred between barracks to forestall the development of groups. The fact that groups could not be formed on a continuing basis could explain the low escape rate: Because the men could not get organized, they could not develop the type of plan that was needed by POWs to break free. Also, they could not develop the trust in each other that is so essential for escape. Without the required trust, the "belongingness"

---

[4] David R. Hampton, Charles E. Summer, and Ross A. Webber, *Organization Behavior and the Practice of Management* (Glenview, Ill.: Scott, Foresman and Company, 1973), p. 215.

[5] Edgar Schein, "The Chinese Indoctrination Program for Prisoners of War," *Psychiatry,* vol. 19 (May 1956), pp. 149–72.

need was greatly undermined, as was the morale in the POW camps.

Schein's discussion of POWs certainly has implications for managers in organizations. Work groups appear to satisfy an individual's social needs. The group affiliation enables the individual to identify and to deal with the environment (for example, POW camp or the organization). Research findings indicate that employees who are isolated from each other because of plant layout report that their jobs are less satisfying than those of group members who are able to socialize on the job.[6]

Esteem. Some employees are attracted to a work group because they perceive themselves as having more prestige by being inside the group. In an organization, a particular group may be viewed by employees as being a top-notch work group. Consequently, membership in the elite group bestows prestige upon the members which is not enjoyed by non-members. This prestige is conferred on members by other employees (nonmembers), and this often leads to more gratification of the esteem need. By sharing in the activities of a high-prestige work group the individual identifies more closely with the group. This form of identification is valued highly by some employees.

Self-Actualization. The desire of individuals to utilize their skills to maximum efficiency and to grow and develop psychologically on the job is interpreted as the self-actualization need. Employees often believe that rigid job requirements and rules imposed by managers do not enable them to satisfy this need sufficiently. One reaction to rigid requirements, rules, and regulations is to join a work group, which is viewed as a vehicle for communicating among friends about the use of a job-related skill. The jargon utilized and the skill employed are appreciated by the knowledgeable group members. This appreciation can lead to a feeling of accomplishing a worthwhile task. This feeling, and other similar feelings which are related to a belief that one is creative and skillful, often lead to more satisfaction of the self-actualization need.

A Final Note on Work Group Formation

The above reasons for group formation are by no means to be interpreted as being mutually exclusive or the only specific reasons for group formation. They do, however, have a behavioral overtone, and this is why they are presented. The main theme in the discussion of the reasons for group formation is that group membership is closely related to individual satisfaction. This is not meant to be an indictment that the organization does not or cannot sufficiently provide an atmosphere of work conducive to high levels of satisfaction. Although this may be true

---

[6] Elton Mayo, *The Human Problems of an Industrial Civilization* (Boston: Graduate School of Business Administration, Harvard University, 1946), pp. 42–52.

in many cases, it would seem that both the organization and work groups can be compatible and provide the employee with opportunities to satisfy their needs.

DEVELOPMENT OF WORK GROUPS

The development of work groups is distinctly related to learning—learning to work together, to accept each other, and to trust each other. These phases are referred to as the maturation of a group.[7] Bass has succinctly presented a four-phase group development process which points out clearly some of the problems and frustrations inherent in group development.[8]

First Phase: Mutual Acceptance

Employees are often hampered by their mistrust of each other, of the organization, and of their superiors. They are fearful that they do not have the necessary training or skill to perform the job or to compete with others on the job. These feelings of insecurity motivate employees to seek out others in the same predicament and to begin to express their feelings openly. A group results, and the mistrust is significantly reduced. Thus, after an initial period of uneasiness and learning about the feelings of others, individuals begin to accept each other.

Second Phase: Decision Making

During this phase, open communication and expression of thoughts concerning the job are the rule. Problem solving and decision making are undertaken. The workers trust each other's viewpoints and beliefs and develop strategies to make the job easier to help members perform more efficiently.

Third Phase: Motivation

The group has reached maturity and the problems of its members are known. It is accepted that it is better for the group to have cooperation instead of competition from the members. Thus, the emphasis is on group solidarity in the form of cooperating with each other so that the job is more rewarding both economically and socio-psychologically.

---

[7] Warren G. Bennis and Herbert A. Shepard, "A Theory of Group Development," *Human Relations*, vol. 9 (Summer 1963), p. 415–57.

[8] The discussion of the development of groups is based largely upon Bernard Bass, *Organizational Psychology* (Boston: Allyn and Bacon, Inc., 1965), pp. 197–98. A number of alterations were made by the authors.

Fourth Phase: Control

The group has successfully organized itself and members contribute according to their abilities and interests. The group exercises sanctions when control is needed to bring members into line with the group's norms.

The structures and processes which are found in work groups develop over a period of time. The motivation or control of members' behavior is not an overnight occurrence. The four phases of development show that a learning process is involved. Performance and motivation of group members depend on individual learning and on the degree to which the group coordinates the efforts and desires of members. The degree of maturity of the group will have important implications concerning the perceived and actual level of satisfaction derived by belonging to the group.

TYPES OF GROUPS IN AN ORGANIZATION

Both managers and nonmanagers belong to a number of different groups within the organization. The membership in these groups often overlap.[9] In some instances, individuals are members of a group because of formal position in the organization. However, through the contacts they make in the group, they begin to affiliate with some of its members on an informal basis. The overlapping form of groups is illustrated in Figure 8–1.

There are five overlapping groups presented in Figure 8–1.

Group 1—John, Ralph, Mike, George;
Group 2—Ralph, Sam, Tony, Nick;
Group 3—Ralph, Nick, Bob;
Group 4—George, Stu, Phil;
Group 5—Mike, George, Pete, Stu.

Group 1 is a formal organization group which causes John, Ralph, Mike, and George to communicate with each other. By position, John is the leader in this group. The leaders of the other four work groups which have formed are not indicated. Any one of the individuals in these overlapping groups may be the leader. An individual will emerge as a leader in some groups and, in others, will be one of many followers.

In examining groups in a general framework, it becomes apparent that organizational demands and processes lead to the formation of different types of work groups. One classification system used to describe

---

[9] Rensis Likert, *New Patterns of Management* (New York: McGraw-Hill Book Company, 1961), chap. 8.

FIGURE 8–1

Group Overlay

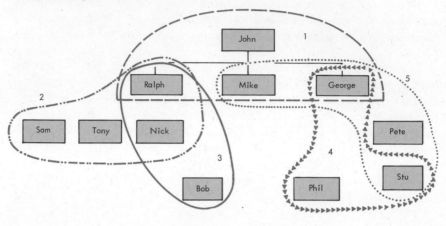

groups is the command, task, interest, and friendship framework.[10] Command and task groups are referred to as *formal* groups because they are defined by the organization structure; interest and friendship groups are not defined by the organization structure and are termed *informal* groups.

Command Group

The command group is specified by the organization chart. The subordinates who report directly to a given supervisor make up a command group. The relationship between the department manager and the three foremen in a machine shop is spelled out in the organization chart (Figure 8–2).

As the span of control of the department manager increases, his command group increases in size. For example, if John had four subordinates directly reporting to him he would have a larger span of control than his present span of three (Ralph, Mike, and George).

Task Group

A number of employees that work together to complete a project or job are considered a task group. A manufacturing or office work process that requires a great deal of interdependency is an example of a task group. Assume that three office clerks are required for (1) securing

---

[10] This is the widely used and insightful framework offered by Leonard R. Sayles, "Research in Industrial Human Relations," *Industrial Relations Research Association* (New York: Harper and Row, 1957), pp. 131–45.

FIGURE 8–2

Command Group Structure

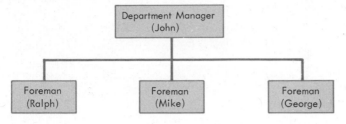

a file of an automobile accident claim; (2) checking the accuracy of the claim by contacting persons involved; and (3) typing the claim, securing the required signatures of those involved, and refiling the claim.

The activation of the file and the steps required before the claim is refiled constitute required tasks. These activities create a situation in which three clerks must communicate and coordinate with each other if the file is to be handled properly. Their activities and interactions facilitate the formation of the task group.

Interest Group

In discussing the economic determinant of group formation, an example of older workers grouping together to present a united front was cited. This type of group can be viewed as an interest group, for the members have joined together to achieve some objective such as an equitable pension payment. The members of the group may or may not be members of the same command or task group.

When the desired objective has been achieved or is thought to be within reach, the interest group might disband. Thus, this type of group typically exists for a shorter period of time than other types of groups.

Friendship Group

In the workplace, employees, because of some common characteristic such as age, ethnic background, political sentiment, interest in sports, or desire to drink coffee in the lounge at 10:30 A.M., often form a friendship group. These groups often extend their interaction and communication to off-the-job activities. For example, they get to know each other in the work place because of friendship and then bowl together, or attend sporting events together, or take their families on picnics.

If an individual's affiliation patterns are reviewed, it becomes readily apparent that managerial and nonmanagerial personnel belong to many different and occasionally overlapping groups. Membership in command

and task groups is designated by the formal organization, which specifies who will be the superior and who will be the subordinate in the command group. The flow of work specified by management and the job description designate the composition of command and task groups.

The membership patterns of interest and friendship groups are not tightly controlled by the organization. However, managerial actions such as laying out a work area, allowing workers to take coffee breaks at a specified time, and demanding a certain level of productivity influence the interaction and communication patterns of employees, causing individuals to affiliate with each other so that interest and friendship groups emerge.

CHARACTERISTICS OF WORK GROUPS

The creation of an organization structure results in characteristics such as specified relationships between subordinates, superiors, and peers, leaders assigned to positions, communication networks, standards of performance, and a status rank order according to the position an individual is filling. The logic behind these formally established characteristics is that, if the organization is to accomplish its goals, retain its personnel, and project a favorable image to the public, it must have structure and a favorable work atmosphere (that is, the employees must enjoy going to work to some extent). Work groups have characteristics which are similar to those of formal organizations and include standards of conduct, communication systems, and reward and sanction mechanisms.[11] These and other characteristics of groups are discussed below.

The Emergent Leader

As a group strives to complete some objective and the individual members begin to know each other, members begin to fill one or more of the many group roles. One of the most important roles is that of the group leader. The leader is accepted by the group members and emerges from within. In the formal organization, the leader is appointed.

The leaders in the formal organization are followed and obeyed because employees perceive them as possessing power and influence to reward or punish them for not complying with requests. The formal leaders possess the power to regulate the formal rewards of the members of a work group. On the other hand, informal group leaders do not possess this power.

---

[11] Leonard R. Sayles and George Strauss, *Human Behavior in Organizations* (Englewood Cliffs, N.J.: Prentice-Hall, Inc., 1966), pp. 90–100.

The informal leader emerges from within and serves a number of facilitating functions. First, any group of individuals that does not have a plan or some coordination becomes an ineffective unit. The individuals are not directed toward the accomplishment of goals, and this leads to a breakdown in group effectiveness. The leader serves to initiate action and provide direction. If there are differences of opinions on a group-related matter, the leader attempts to compromise differences of opinion and move the group toward accomplishing its goals.

Second, some individual must communicate the group's beliefs about policies, the job, the organization, the supervision, and other related matters to nonmembers. The nonmembership category could include members of other groups, supervisory personnel, and the union. In effect, the group leader communicates the values of the group.

A number of research studies have been reported which focus upon the personal characteristics of group leaders, which can be summarized as follows:

1. The leadership role is filled by an individual who possesses the attributes which the members perceive as being critical for satisfying their needs.
2. The leader embodies the values of the group and is able to perceive these values, organize them into an intelligible philosophy, and verbalize them to nonmembers.[12]
3. The leader who is able to receive and decipher communication relevant to the group and effectively communicate important information to group members can be thought of as an information center.[13]

Status in a Group

Managers in an organization are accorded status because of position in the hierarchy; that is, the top management group of the firm has more prestige or status than middle managers in the organization, while middle managers have more prestige or status than lower-level managers. The basic cornerstone of status in the formal organization is a comparative process. The top-level positions embody more authority, responsibility, power, and influence, and thus are accorded more status. In effect, a status hierarchy emerges with the top-level positions listed first and the lower-level positions listed last.

In an informal group a similar type of status system develops. For many different reasons, individuals are accorded status by the group in

---

[12] Scott and Mitchell, *Organization Theory,* p. 127.
[13] Ibid.

which they interact and communicate. The individuals performing in leadership roles possess prestige because of their role. Consequently they are ranked by group members as being at a particular level in the group-status hierarchy.

There are a number of other factors which influence the status systems developed in groups. The seniority of a member is a factor which many groups consider to be important. A worker having more seniority is often thought of as being "organizationally intelligent," which means that person knows how to adapt to the demands of supervisors, subordinates, or peers. This ability to adjust is an important status factor with group members.

The skill of an individual in performing a job is another factor related to status. An individual who is an expert in the technical aspects, managerial or nonmanagerial, of the job is given a high status ranking in some groups. This type of status does not mean that the individual actually utilizes the skill to perform more efficiently, but that the group members perceive this skill in the individual.

Thus, the status system in a work group is formed on the basis of such factors as whether the member is a leader, has seniority, and skill. These and other factors are weighted differently by each type of work group; the varying amount of importance placed on them affects the status system.

Work Group Norms and Control

A *norm* is an agreement among the group membership as to how members in the group should behave.[14] The more an individual complies with norms, the more one is accepting the group's standards of behavior. The teen-age girl who dresses exactly like her friends at school is being influenced by the group norm concerning dress behavior.

Work groups also utilize norms to bring about job performance that is acceptable to the group. In the workplace a number of different production-related norms are evident. The following are typical: (1) Don't agree with management in its campaign to change the wage structure; (2) present a united front to the supervisor concerning the displeasure of the group about firing Mr. Jones; (3) resist the suggestions of the new college graduate assigned to the group's work area; (4) do not produce above the group leader's level of production; (5) help members of the group to achieve an acceptable production level if they are having difficulty and you have time; and (6) don't allow the union steward to convince you to vote for his favorite union presidential candidate in the upcoming election.

---

[14] Joseph A. Litterer, *The Analysis of Organizations* (New York: John Wiley and Sons, Inc., 1973), p. 96.

Three specific social processes bring about compliance with group norms,[15] namely, group pressure, group review and enforcement, and the personalization of norms.

Group Pressure. The process of group pressure is clearly illustrated by Asch in a series of experiments[16] in which he was concerned with studying how social forces constrain opinions and attitudes. Asch utilized groups of college students to conduct a "psychological experiment" in visual judgment. The experimenter informed the members of the group that they would be comparing the lengths of lines. Two sets of cards, similar to those presented in Figure 8–3, were used for each

FIGURE 8–3

Asch-Type Comparisons

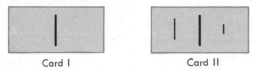

Card I   Card II

comparison. The individuals had to choose the line on the second card that matched the line on the first card in length. These comparisons were made a number of times.

Prior to the actual visual observation of the lengths of lines on various sets of cards, the experimenter "rigged" the results. He informed all but one member of the group that they should choose on the third comparison a line that did not match the length of the line shown in the first card of the set. The reaction of the uninformed member in each group of students was observed and recorded.

The results of the Asch experiments showed that when individuals were confronted with only one other group member who was giving incorrect responses, they continued to stick with their correct answer. When the opposition (those giving incorrect answers) was increased to two, the group pressure influence became noticeable: The uninformed group members accepted the incorrect answer 13.6 percent of the time. Under the group pressures provided by three incorrect responses, the uninformed members gave incorrect responses 31.8 percent of the time.

This experiment illustrates how group pressures and support for one's viewpoint are related. If individuals stand alone, they are inclined to succumb to group pressures; but when they find their attitude supported by even one group member, they resist pressure to change.

---

[15] Ibid., pp. 245–47.

[16] Solomon E. Asch, "Opinions and Social Pressures," *Scientific American*, vol. 193 (November 1955), pp. 31–35.

Individuals who value their group membership highly and who satisfy some combination of personal needs by being a part of a group allow group pressures to influence their behavior and performance. This premise leads to a second type of group process designated here as group review and enforcement.

Group Review and Enforcement. When individuals become members of a group, especially task groups, they quickly become aware of group norms. The group position on such matters as production, absenteeism, and quality of output is communicated. The group members then observe the actions and language of new members to determine whether the group norms are being followed.

If individual members, both oldtimers and newcomers, are not complying with generally accepted norms, a number of different approaches may be employed. A "soft" approach would be a discussion between respected leaders and those persons deviating from the norm. If this does not prove effective, more rigid corrective action such as the membership scolding the individual or individuals both privately and publicly is used. The ultimate type of enforcement would be to ostracize the nonconforming members, which might very well take the form of not communicating with them.

These are only a few of the numerous strategies which may be implemented to bring deviants back into line. Other, more severe techniques such as sabotaging the nonconformers' performance have also been utilized. It should be made clear that review and enforcement occur at the managerial levels in a form similar to that in the nonmanagerial ranks.

Personal Values and Norms. The behavioral patterns of individuals are influenced significantly by their value systems.[17] The values of people are influenced by the events occurring around them; they are learned and become personalized. For example, the norm of a work group to which a person belongs may encourage the group member to treat college graduates and noncollege individuals equally and courteously. This norm may be accepted by the individual as morally and ethically correct. Prior to group affiliation, one may have displayed little interest in a "fair treatment of all" philosophy. However, based on a latent feeling of fairness, one personalizes this group-learned norm. It becomes a standard of conduct which is correct from a group as well as from a social vantage point.

In some, but definitely not in all instances, group pressures, group review and enforcement, and personalization of norms may conflict with organizational objectives such as higher production, improved quality of output, lower absenteeism, and loyalty to the firm. The emphasis here is

---

[17] Litterer, *Analysis of Organizations*, p. 96.

FIGURE 8–4

Formal Communication Flow

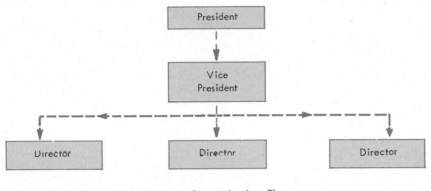

```
        ┌──────────────┐
        │  President   │
        └──────────────┘
               │
               ▼
        ┌──────────────┐
        │    Vice      │
        │  President   │
        └──────────────┘
```

         ▫ ▫ ▫ ▫ ▶ = Communication Flow

on the word "some." It is nonsense to assume that all groups are established to resist the achievement of organizational goals.

Communication Network

In classical organization theory, the specified communication network is represented by the superior-subordinate relationships shown in the organization chart. The formal communication network follows the chain of command (Figure 8–4).

In informal groups the communication patterns are not rigidly set. In the formal organization system, the top-level executives possessing the most status direct their messages to lower-status members. However, research conducted within groups generally indicates that low-status group members direct more communication toward higher-status group members.[18]

A detailed study by Bavelas clearly illustrated some of the communication networks that can exist in groups. He was interested in the efficiency with which groups completed their tasks. In the Bavelas experiments, members of a group were isolated so that no cross-communication could occur, as illustrated in Figure 8–5 (ⓧ designates the leader).[19]

Bavelas provided some interesting insights into the results of these four networks on leaders and problem-solving abilities. The location of a person in a central position (for example, the circled ⓧ in the chain net-

---

[18] Harold H. Kelly, "Communication in Experimentally Created Hierarchies," *Human Relations*, vol. 4 (February 1951), pp. 39–56.

[19] Alex Bavelas, "Communication Patterns In Task-Oriented Groups," *Journal of the Accoustical Society of America*, vol. 22 (1950), pp. 725–30.

FIGURE 8–5

Bavelas Communication Networks

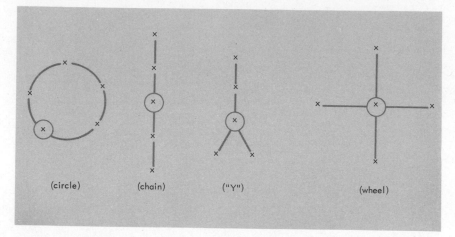

work of five individuals) produces group leaders. The centrally located person is in the best position to facilitate the smooth flow of information among group members.

It was also determined that when simple problems had to be solved, the wheel network was the fastest and most efficient. The members of the group fed information to the central figure, and it was acted upon rapidly. When difficult tasks had to be solved and interaction and exchange of ideas were important to task completion, the circle arrangement proved fastest.

Although the Bavelas research was conducted in a laboratory situation, it indicates clearly some of the events that may occur in small-group communication networks. The leader is at the center of the group and is a facilitator. The networks are similar to the formal organization chain-of-command pattern and enable problems to be solved efficiently.

Some examples of the four communication networks would be the following:

Circle—A committee in a College of Business is given the charge to study the long-range plans of the college. A faculty member is appointed the chairman, ⓧ, and four other faculty members serve with him on the committee. The communication flow is circular, emanating from the appointed chairman.

"Y"—A merchandise buyer in a large clothing store is designated as ⓧ . She is the third most important person in the organization's chain of command. She is in charge of both men's and women's

clothing. Thus, the president, vice president, merchandise buyer, director of men's sales, and director of women's sales constitute the "Y."

Chain—A regional sales director in an insurance company is specified as Ⓧ . He reports directly to the vice president of sales, who reports to the president of the company. Reporting directly to the regional sales director is the district manager, who has salesmen reporting to him.

Wheel—The wheel, Ⓧ , could be an advertising layout manager. She reports to the director of marketing and must work closely with two other advertising layout managers who have the same authority and responsibility in the organizational hierarchy. The advertising layout manager, Ⓧ , has an assistant called an art coordinator who reports only to her.

In reviewing the characteristics of work groups, it becomes apparent that many similarities and some differences exist between formal and informal groups. Characteristics such as leaders, status systems, norms and control mechanisms, and communication networks are found in both types. The major differences between formal and informal groups are that the leader of the formal group is appointed, and that the status, norms, and communication systems flow from this preestablished structuring. An individual who is a formal leader has a certain degree of status and is expected to perform at a norm which is established by the organization. In the informal group, a leader emerges and is given a status ranking by the members.

Group Cohesiveness

Cohesiveness is another important concept which must be understood if the behavioral analysis of groups is to be complete. In a simplistic manner, this concept involves the "stick-together" characteristics of groups and their impact on group members. In a more refined definition, group cohesiveness is stated as the attraction of members to the group in terms of the strength of forces on the individual member to remain active in the group and to resist leaving it.[20]

All of the above characteristics of groups are influenced in some degree by the cohesiveness within the group.[21] For example, the greater the at-

---

[20] This definition is based upon the group cohesiveness concept presented by Stanley E. Seashore, *Group Cohesiveness in the Industrial Work Group* (Ann Arbor, Mich.: University of Michigan, Institute for Social Research, 1954).

[21] Sayles and Strauss, *Human Behavior in Organizations,* p. 101.

FIGURE 8–6

Factors Contributing to Group Cohesiveness

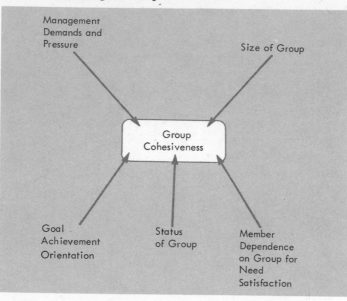

traction within the group, the more likely it is that the membership will adhere closely to a group norm such as production level.

Research findings have allowed those interested in work group cohesiveness to isolate some of the more important factors which affect it. Some of the conditions which influence cohesiveness are presented in Figure 8–6. The factors which are identified are only examples of some of the variables uncovered in research studies, but they are representative of the types of factors that can enhance or reduce cohesiveness of work groups.

Size of Work Group.   One of the important and necessary conditions for the existence of a group is that members interact and communicate with each other. If the group is so large that members do not get to know each other, there is little likelihood that the group will be high in cohesiveness. This is a logical assumption that would be made by those who understand the difficulties of communicating in large groups.

Research studies found in behavioral literature indicate that the logical assumption is accurate and that an inverse relationship does exist between size of group and group cohesiveness.[22] As the size of a group increases, its cohesiveness decreases.

---

[22] Seashore, *Group Cohesiveness*, pp. 90–95. This study will be discussed in detail later in the chapter. Also see Robert C. Cummins and Donald C. King, "The Interaction of Group Size and Task Structure in an Industrial Organization," *Personnel Psychology*, vol. 26 (Spring 1973), pp. 87–94.

Dependence of Members upon the Work Group. As stated previously, individuals join groups because they perceive the group as a unit which can help them satisfy economic and sociopsychological needs. A group that is able to satisfy a significant portion of an individual's needs will appear attractive to that individual. Group processes such as communication and overall friendship make the group a key factor in the individual's life. Thus, what the group stands for, its norms, and its membership are bonds which relate the individual to the group. These are examples of the forces of attraction discussed by behavioralists. The greater the individual's dependency upon the group, the stronger will be these bonds of attraction.

Achievement of Goals. The attainment of some set of group-established goals (for example, better production than another group) has an influence on members. For example, a work group that attains a highly desired rating for completing a task enhances the value of being a group member; individuals within the group feel a pride in being members of a work group that has performed in such a manner that they are recognized as being superior.

The group has proved through task completion efforts that it possesses the individual skills and coordination necessary for organizational performance that is viewed as successful.

Work groups that have successfully attained pre-established goals are likely to be highly cohesive units, the members tending to be more attracted toward each other because they have worked together in the past and because their efforts have resulted in achieving a desired goal. Thus, success and cohesiveness are interrelated: Success in goal achievement encourages cohesiveness, and cohesive work groups are more likely to attain preestablished goals. It is important to consider that, although group cohesiveness can lead to successful achievement of goals, that some cohesiveness can prove detrimental when group and organization goals are not congruent.

Status of Group. In an organizational setting work groups are typically ranked in a status hierarchy. An intergroup status hierarchy may develop for many different reasons, including the following:

1. One group is rated higher than another in overall performance; this is a measure of success in the organization.
2. To become a member of the group, individuals must display a high level of skill.
3. The work being done by the group is dangerous or financially more rewarding or more challenging than other work.
4. The group is less closely supervised in comparison to other groups.
5. In the past, members of the group have been considered for promotion more often than members of other groups.

These are only some of the criteria which affect the status hierarchy of groups.[23] Generally, the higher a group ranks in the intergroup status hierarchy, the greater its cohesiveness. However, the higher-status groups appear attractive only to some nonmembers. Individuals on the outside of the group very well may not want to become members of a high-status group because membership then entails close adherence to group norms.

Management Demands and Pressure. The last determinant of group cohesiveness discussed in this section should not be viewed as the least significant factor because of its ranking in our discussion. It is certainly true in many organizations that management has a significant impact on group cohesiveness. The members of work groups tend to "stick together" when they are pressured by superiors to conform to some organizational norm (for example, punching in at 8:00 and not 8:05 A.M., or publishing at least 5 articles every year).

The group cohesiveness attributed to managerial demands may be a short-run or long-run phenomenon. In some cases, a group may be loosely knit (low in cohesiveness), and a company policy statement may be interpreted as a threat to the job security of group members. Consequently the members of the group become a more cohesive and unified whole in order to withstand the perceived management threat. After the danger is past (that is, the policy statement is rescinded), the group gradually drifts back toward low cohesiveness. In other cases, the cohesiveness may be a longer-lasting phenomenon.

AN END RESULT: MEMBER SATISFACTION

An end result or consequence of group membership is satisfaction of members. Social psychologists have, in recent years, increased their efforts to unravel some of the mysteries of member satisfaction within groups.

Perhaps the most provocative integrative analysis of work group member satisfaction is presented by Heslin and Dunphy.[24] They report on a survey of 37 studies which show specific relationships between work group member satisfaction and (1) perceived freedom to partici-pate, (2) perceived goal attainment, and (3) status consensus.

Perceived Freedom to Participate

Heslin and Dunphy, through their analysis of small-group studies, indicate that a member's perception of freedom to participate influences

---

[23] For a listing of other status criteria, see Sayles and Strauss, *Human Behavior in Organizations,* p. 102.

[24] Richard Heslin and Dexter Dunphy, "Three Dimensions of Member Satisfaction in Sr   Groups," *Human Relations,* vol. 17 (May 1964), pp. 99–112.

need satisfaction. The individuals who perceived themselves as active participators reported themselves more satisfied,[25] while those who perceived their freedom to participate to be insignificant typically were the least satisfied members in a work group.

The freedom-to-participate phenomenon is related to the entire spectrum of economic and socio-psychological needs. For example, the perceived ability to participate may lead individuals to believe that they are valued members of the group. This assumption can lead to satisfaction of social esteem, and self-actualization needs.

Perceived Goal Attainment

A number of studies indicate that a group member's perception of progress toward the attainment of desired goals is an important factor which is related to member satisfaction.[26] Groups which progressed toward the attainment of goals indicated higher levels of member satisfaction, while members of groups not adequately progressing toward the attainment of group goals showed a lower satisfaction level.

Status Consensus

This concept is defined as agreement about the relative status of all group members. Several studies reviewed by Heslin and Dunphy indicate that, when the degree of status consensus is high, member satisfaction tends to be high; where status consensus within the group is low, member satisfaction tends to be low.

It is also concluded that status consensus is more readily achieved in groups where

1. The group task specialist is perceived to be competent by the membership,
2. A leader emerges who plays a role that is considered an important group task, and
3. A leadership role emerges and is filled by an individual who concentrates on coordinating and maintaining the activities of the group.

The insightful review of Heslin and Dunphy suggests that the perception of the membership concerning freedom to participate, movement toward goal attainment, and status consensus significantly influence the level of need satisfaction attained by group members. Their review also clearly indicates that when an individual member's goals and needs are

---

[25] This was indicated in Bavelas' experiments with communication networks in Bavelas, "Communication Patterns," p. 729.

[26] Clovis R. Shepherd, *Small Groups: Some Sociological Perspectives* (San Francisco: Chandler Publishing Co., 1964), p. 101.

in conflict with the goals and needs of the overall group, lower levels of membership satisfaction are the result.

A WORK GROUP MODEL

Our discussion of work groups now enables us to develop a model of work group behavior. This model is shown in Figure 8–7. The diagram has a distinct behavioral character, since it contains the "why," "how," and "when" of work groups as found in the behavioral literature. Figure 8–7 summarizes what has been discussed concerning reasons for group formation, the types of groups, the characteristics of group membership, and one of the major end results, membership satisfaction.

FIGURE 8–7

A Model of Work Group Behavior

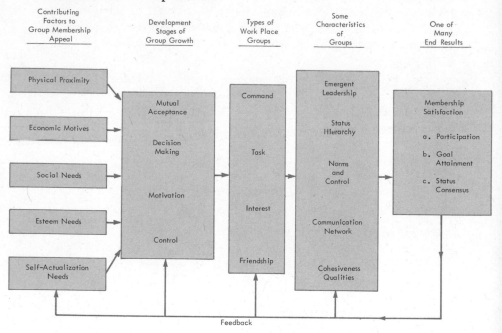

Another important aspect of the work group model is the feedback cycle. As designated in Figure 8–7, feedback on the end results of group membership influences each of the elements in the framework. For example, the perceived goal attainment in a work group influences its cohesiveness.

As stated previously, groups that achieve or are moving toward success (goal attainment) have the greatest attraction (cohesiveness) within the group.

TECHNIQUES FOR STUDYING GROUPS

Behavioral scientists believe that systematic research is needed if managers are to continue acquiring vital knowledge about factors such as characteristics of group structure, the impact of groups on the attitudes of members, and how the membership influences phenomena like group culture and attractiveness. The methods typically suggested by behavioral scientists have, in most instances, proved successful in studying group behavior in a laboratory setting. The college classroom, management development seminar, or boys' day camp are often used as settings for investigating group phenomena. Although these settings are not exactly similar to a company office or production department work area, an internal revenue service office, or an emergency room in a hospital there are many perceptive insights provided by laboratory group behavior studies. For example, the flow of communication and personal interaction, the emergence of leaders, and the exercise of pressure upon members are some of the phenomena that can be examined in laboratory settings.

Several methods for studying group behavior are proposed in the behavioral literature. Two methods, developed over a decade ago, yet continually found in contemporary literature are Bales' interaction analysis and Moreno's sociometric analysis.

Bales Laboratory Technique

R. F. Bales developed what is called the interaction analysis to obtain work group behavior data by observing directly what is occurring within a group. He studied groups attempting to reach a decision (for example, solving a business case). After studying groups in the laboratory setting, Bales concluded that group behavior can be classified as task oriented and human-relations oriented. He proposed that through group interaction, a number of task and human-relations reactions occur in both positive and negative forms.[27]

Bales observed the interactions and recorded the group discussion that occurred in leaderless groups attempting to analyze a case in human relations. He identified 12 categories of interactions which occurred within the groups as they attempted to resolve the case. The 12 categories were briefly described as follows:[28]

---

[27] R. F. Bales and F. L. Strodbeck, "Phases in Group Problem Solving," *The Journal of Abnormal and Social Psychology*, vol. 46 (October 1951), pp. 485–95. For a complete discussion of the interaction analysis, see R. F. Bales, *Interaction Process Analysis: A Method for the Study of Small Groups* (Cambridge, Mass.: Addison-Wesley, Inc., 1950).

[28] Ibid.

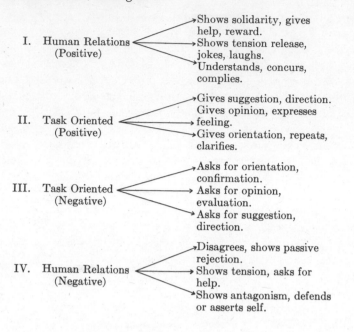

I. Human Relations (Positive)
- Shows solidarity, gives help, reward.
- Shows tension release, jokes, laughs.
- Understands, concurs, complies.

II. Task Oriented (Positive)
- Gives suggestion, direction.
- Gives opinion, expresses feeling.
- Gives orientation, repeats, clarifies.

III. Task Oriented (Negative)
- Asks for orientation, confirmation.
- Asks for opinion, evaluation.
- Asks for suggestion, direction.

IV. Human Relations (Negative)
- Disagrees, shows passive rejection.
- Shows tension, asks for help.
- Shows antagonism, defends or asserts self.

After the group case-solving sessions, members completed a questionnaire concerning their reactions, their satisfactions, their relations to each other, and their opinions about their discussion group. From the questionnaire answers and from observation, Bales developed an interaction profile of satisfied and dissatisfied case-solving groups using the 12-category descriptive system he developed.

The Who-to-Whom Matrix

Another procedure developed by Bales for acquiring a better understanding of work group behavior and interaction is the who-to-whom matrix. Bales tabulated the number of discussions between individuals, who initiated the discussion, and who addressed discussion to the group as a whole.

Bales found that the patterns of discussion varied under different circumstances. For example, groups with no designated leader generally tend to have more equal participation than groups with designated leaders of higher status. It was also found that the size of the group is an important factor affecting within-group discussion patterns. The leader in groups larger than five tends to speak considerably more to the group as a whole than to specific members. All other members tend to speak more to specific individuals than to the group as a whole. As groups increase in size, a larger and larger proportion of the activity tends to be addressed to the leader, and a smaller and smaller proportion to other members. In effect, the communication pattern tends to "centralize" around the leader.

In addition to tracing communication patterns, Bales also studied the roles of group members. Specifically, he investigated the roles of the best idea person, best guidance person, best liked, and scapegoat. The individual who had the best ideas and gave the most guidance was classified as the group task specialist, while the best-liked person was viewed as the group human relations specialist.

By using these two classifications, Bales introduced an interesting analysis of what could happen if, for example, the human relations specialist attempts to take over the group from the task specialist. This type of internal struggling can disrupt the activities and overall performance of the group. The implication of this part of the Bales analysis is that groups work more effectively with two members filling the two separate leader roles.

Bales' interaction process analysis furnishes a valuable technique for analyzing small-group functioning in laboratory settings. The findings and insights of his research provide managers with insights about communication patterns, roles, and the relationship between communication initiation and the status systems within work groups. Thus, although it would be extremely difficult, if not impossible, to perform interaction process analysis in an office or on the production floor, the laboratory-based findings provide needed knowledge about groups. The vital questions regarding what makes a group "tick," what is the pattern of group communications, and who is the task leader and human relations leader can be coped with more effectively if research findings similar to those of Bales are common knowledge among managers.

Moreno's Sociometric Analysis

The sociometric-analysis method of studying work group behavior and structural characteristics involves the use of self-reports from group members. These reports indicate the preference and repulsion patterns of group members. Based on the expressed choices of members, insights about the leaders and status hierarchy of the group and about communication patterns can be provided to those interested in such phenomena.[29]

For the purpose of understanding the complex communication patterns and interactions of groups, Moreno developed questions which asked group members whom they liked and disliked within the

---

[29] J. L. Moreno, "Contributions of Sociometry to Research Methodology in Sociology," *American Sociological Review*, vol. 12 (June 1947), pp. 287–92.

group,[30] enabling Moreno to gain knowledge about group relations. From the data collected by interview and/or questionnaire, Moreno was able to construct a *sociogram.*

The *sociogram* is a diagram which illustrates the interpersonal relationships existing within a group. Figure 8–8 presents a simple sociogram

FIGURE 8–8

Sociogram Patterns of Attraction

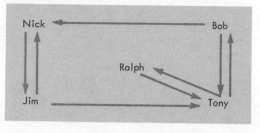

based upon feelings of attraction reported by a group of workers. The line from Nick to Jim represents an expressed choice by Nick. That is, Nick likes to work with Jim. The Jim-to-Nick line shows that Jim likes to work with Nick. This is a mutual-choice pair (Nick to Jim and Jim to Nick). The relationship reported between Bob and Nick, however, is a single choice pattern: Bob likes to work with Nick. The same type of procedure can be used to depict rejections, that is, asking with whom someone dislikes working would show rejection choices.

Questions concerning the choice by group members when they have technical problems with their work can help management identify those members with respected technical expertise. Sociometric-choice data concerning individuals whom the group members contact for technical assistance are shown in Figure 8–9.

Ralph is the overwhelming choice of the group members. Other similar patterns of choice and rejection can identify isolates and scapegoats of groups. The isolate would not be the choice of other group members; and the scapegoat would be designated verbally as a poor group member.

The sociometric procedures recommended by Moreno have value for managers. For example, if managers could identify the leader(s) of the group, they could hopefully work with the leader(s) in bringing about change. Of course, many factors such as the type of change being introduced, the groups' past relations with management, and the influence of

[30] J. H. Jacobs, "The Application of Sociometry to Industry," *Sociometry,* vol. 8 (May 1954), pp. 181–98.

FIGURE 8–9

Technical Expert Preferences

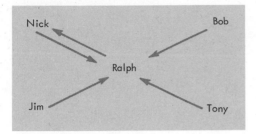

the leader within the group would be critical to the success of dealing with work group leaders.[31]

STUDIES OF GROUPS WITH RELEVANCE TO MANAGEMENT

Group studies have involved college students, housewives, children, religious sects, executives, police officers, military personnel, and many other segments of society. There have been some studies involving organizations that stress some of the group characteristics discussed in this chapter. These studies show how group characteristics influence the on-the-job attitudes and performance of individuals within an organizational setting. Three such studies are briefly presented.

Van Zelst Construction Industry Study

In the building trades, work groups are typically formed on a piece-meal basis. For example, bricklayers are sent to a job location from the union hall and are assigned work by the supervisor. The task group is structured by management, and, once the job is completed, the group is generally disbanded.

Van Zelst theorized that if construction workers were allowed to select their own partners and form their own groups, overall group performance would improve.[32] He used two groups of workers, carpenters and bricklayers, to test his theory. These workers were allowed to select their

---

[31] For an excellent discussion of some of the limitations of sociometric analysis (for example, inadequate attention to the selection of sociometric criteria), see Gardner Lindzey and Edgar F. Borgatta, "Sociometric Measurement," in Gardner Lindzey, ed., *Handbook of Social Psychology* (Reading, Mass.: Addison-Wesley, Inc., 1954), pp. 405–48.

[32] R. H. Van Zelst, "Sociometrically Selected Work Teams Increase Production," *Personnel Psychology,* vol. 5 (Autumn 1952), pp. 175–85.

partners, and work assignments were rearranged to conform to these preferences—first into mutual-choice teams of two (Moreno sociometric choice, Figure 8–8); then, when technically necessary, these pairs were combined into larger work teams.

The group established by the usual methods and those established by allowing workers to select their partners were compared on such measures as job satisfaction, turnover, labor cost, and material cost. The results clearly indicated that the groups established on the basis of peer selection were superior on each of these measures.

The results of Van Zelst's investigation should not be interpreted as a "one best way" answer to establishing task groups. In some instances, for example, those workers selecting each other may be low producers and/or troublemakers who, by getting together, can cause more disruption in the work place than if they were apart. These employees may have goals of interacting and socializing, while a basic organizational goal such as higher productivity is not achieved. Thus the feasibility and wisdom of allowing workers to select their task group partners can result in positive or negative consequences for an organization.

Whyte's Restaurant Study

The artificial connotation associated with laboratory studies of work group behavior causes many practicing managers concern. They fear that what is being observed and analyzed at some university is not what is occurring in their company. However, an interesting study conducted and supervised by Whyte[33] in restaurants illustrates how many of the group characteristics discovered through interaction process analysis and sociometric analysis are also found in an ongoing organization.

The Whyte-led team of behavioral science consultants studied such factors as the work flow in the restaurant, the group status hierarchies, the communication patterns between members of different status groups, and conflict between members of different groups. They discovered that the flow of work begins when the customer places an order with the waitress. Figure 8–10 depicts the work-flow pattern.

The Whyte team included a sociologist, a psychologist, and an anthropologist. They each visited a number of the company's restaurants in order to study work-flow patterns and prepare a report on their observations. The three agreed that the problems between customers, runners, cooks, and waitresses were most severe during rush hours. During these hours, the cooks had trouble meeting the volume of orders, the

---

[33] William F. Whyte, *Human Relations in the Restaurant Industry* (New York: McGraw-Hill Book Co., 1948). For a thorough analysis of the Whyte study, see Elias H. Porter, "The Parable of the Spindle," *Harvard Business Review*, vol. 40 (May–June 1962), pp. 58–66.

FIGURE 8–10

Restaurant Work Flow

1. Customer ⟶ enters

2. Order taken by ⟶ waitress

3. Order taken to pantry where it is assembled (salad) or not be assembled (meat)

4. Runner as- ⟶ signed to take meat requests

5. Runner informs ⟶ cook of customer meat request

6. Cook prepares meat

7. Runner ⟶ takes meat to pantry to complete order

8. Waitress checks to ⟶ see that portions are the proper size

9. Waitress delivers completed order to the customer

waitresses had problems with complaining customers, and the runners had trouble communicating with the cook, especially with regard to requests for special dishes. The rush-hour hostility and confusion appeared to carry over to nonrush hours.

The consultants also observed that informal groups were created among the restaurant employees. These friendship and interest groups were formed among employees on the basis of age, sex, and similar interests.

Despite these similarities in assessing the company's problems, the consultants seemed to differ in the issues that they emphasized. The sociologist reported stress between the various individuals in the restaurant. It was the sociologist's opinion that it was not correct for the lower-status runners and waitresses to give orders, or appear to do so, to a higher-status person such as a cook.

The psychologist viewed the manager as the father figure, the cook as the son, and the waitress as the daughter. If the son or daughter refuses to obey the father, this can affect the ego of the father. Thus, it was the psychologist's conclusion that to maintain harmony and allow the father to sustain his ego, it was necessary to break up the practice of the daughter and son not obeying the father and arguing with each other.

The anthropologist assumed that people behave according to their value systems. The manager wanted the restaurant to become more efficient and effective. The cooks also shared this orientation. The waitresses, however, were most concerned with supplanting their family incomes. They were concerned with having a decent place to work and did not concentrate on efficiency and effectiveness. Thus, it was the anthropologist's conclusion that it was necessary to reduce the interaction between people with different value systems, the cooks and the waitresses.

Although each consultant emphasized a different set of issues in investigating the problem, there is a common thread in their viewpoints. Each identified behavioral factors: The sociologist focused on status conflict, the psychologist identified ego factors, and the anthropologist emphasized a conflict of values. Their analysis led the restaurant people to adopt the suggestion of using a spindle. The waitress placed an order on a spindle and did not have to call it out to the cook. Many restaurants today still use the spindle which was recommended by the Whyte team.

Seashore's Manufacturing Study

In the early 1950s, Seashore studied work group cohesiveness (defined as attraction to the group or resistance to leaving it) and various measures of group member attitudes and productivity.[34] He reached a number of insightful conclusions based on responses to questions concerning cohesiveness and on production records.

First, Seashore reports that high group cohesiveness is associated with less anxiety about job-related matters, as shown in Figure 8–11. For example, high cohesive group members were significantly less likely than low cohesive group members to report (1) feeling under pressure for higher productivity, (2) feeling lack of supportiveness (that is, individuals see their on-the-job experiences as contributing to or maintaining their sense of personal worth), (3) feeling "jumpy" or "nervous" about the job.

Seashore's results suggest that an employee who is a member of a highly cohesive group receives the type of support that reduces typical work-place anxieties (pressure to produce). The group serves as an anxiety-reducing mechanism.

Secondly, it was found that the greater the cohesiveness of the group, the greater the influence which the goals of the group have on the performance of members. In work groups with high cohesiveness, the variation in productivity among members is less than in groups with low cohesiveness. Seashore concluded that, on the average, highly cohesive groups are somewhat more productive than low cohesive groups. However, a key factor specified by him is that those groups that tend to support company goals and also are cohesive produce at higher levels. Thus, an important qualification is that the cohesive group perceive as supportive both management and company goals.

Seashore's productivity findings are summarized in Figure 8–12. It shows that a work group can produce significantly below formally established norms, especially if the group is cohesive and perceives management as being nonsupportive.

---

[34] Seashore, *Group Cohesiveness*, p. 20.

FIGURE 8–11

Group Cohesiveness as Related to Anxiety

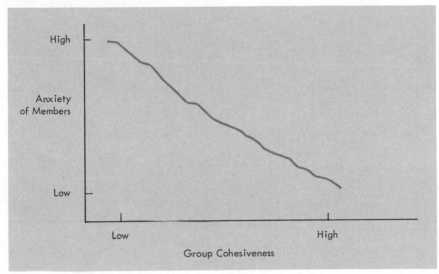

The Seashore studies indicate that cohesiveness factors influence be-havior, anxiety and productivity. They imply that supervisors who can foster a cohesive work group that perceives the company and them as being supportive should be rewarded with higher levels of productivity. The difficulty, of course, lies in determining group cohesiveness initially. Like so many behavioral concepts, group cohesiveness is difficult to measure. Also, it is certainly difficult to measure productivity for many groups. For example, how do we measure the productivity of

FIGURE 8–12

Cohesiveness and Productivity

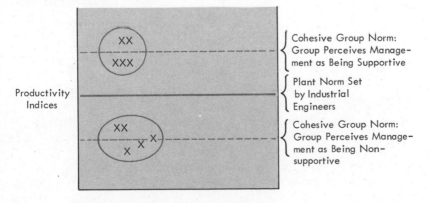

group members engaged in managerial work or in work where it is difficult to determine the output of each individual member? Despite these perplexing problems, the findings of Van Zelst, Whyte, and Seashore clearly indicate that many of the group phenomena observed in the laboratory also exist in the work place. Consequently, to supervise more effectively, it is in management's best interest to learn more about group behavior.

SUMMARY

The Behavioral School's approach to management is replete with discussions, theories, and research findings concerning work groups. This intense interest in groups is based upon premises such as (1) groups are ubiquitous; (2) groups influence an employee's perceptions and attitudes; (3) groups influence the productivity of employees; (4) groups aid an individual in satisfying unfulfilled needs; and (5) groups facilitate communications.

The interest in groups and their dynamics has not waned and is not expected to do so. What has been and is presently being learned about group phenomena are being put to greater use in organizations. Awareness of the practical importance of groups to the continued effectiveness of an organization should generate more studies which should lead to additional understanding of group behavior and group influence in organizational settings.

DISCUSSION AND REVIEW QUESTIONS

1. Distinguish between intragroup and intergroup status.
2. Why would it be difficult to utilize the Bales interaction analysis method and the sociometric analysis technique of Moreno in an actual organizational setting?
3. What would be some of the reasons for an individual to become an isolate (a member not in good standing) in a work group?
4. Should management encourage and aid in the development of cohesive work groups? Why?
5. What factors other than those shown in Figure 8–6 could possibly lead to the development of cohesive work groups?
6. Would behavioralists agree that the emergent leaders of informal work groups would typically utilize democratic leadership in their roles of leading the group? Why?
7. Discuss and compare the type of reward procedures that can be utilized by informal groups and by the formal organization.

8. In what type of work would it be feasible to utilize the sociometric peer choice arrangement used by Van Zelst in his construction industry study?

9. It is generally agreed that a group influences individual behavior. Can an individual significantly influence a group's overall behavior? Why?

10. Why is it difficult to achieve status consensus in some work groups?

ADDITIONAL REFERENCES

Bridges, E. M., et al. "Effects of Hierarchical Differentiation on Group Productivity, Efficiency, and Risk Taking," *Administrative Science Quarterly* 13 (1968): 305–19.

Bucklow, M. "A New Role for the Work Group," *Administrative Science Quarterly* 7 (1962): 236–57.

Forehand, G. A., and Gilmer, B. "Environmental Variation in Studies of Organizational Behavior," *Psychological Bulletin* 62 (1965): 361–82.

Hare, A. Paul. *Handbook of Small Group Research*. New York: The Free Press of Glencoe, 1962.

Holloman, Charles R., and Hendrick, Hal W. "Adequacy of Group Decisions as a Function of the Decision-Making Process," *Academy of Management Journal* 15 (June 1972): 175–84.

Homans, G. C. *The Human Group*. New York: Harcourt, Brace & World, 1950.

Maier, Norman R. F. "Prior Commitment as a Deterrent to Group Problem Solving," *Personnel Psychology* 26 (Spring 1973): 117–26.

Patchen, M. "The Effect of Reference Group Standards on Job Satisfactions," *Human Relations* 11 (1958): 303–14.

Patchen, M. "Supervisory Methods and Group Performance Norms," *Administrative Science Quarterly* 7 (1962): 275–94.

Hinton, Bernard L., and Reitz, H. Joseph, eds. *Groups and Organizations*. Belmont, California: Wadsworth Publishing Co., 1971.

Slater, P. E. *Microcosm: Structural, Psychological and Religious Evolution in Groups*. New York: John Wiley & Sons, Inc., 1966.

Stogdill, R. M. *Individual Behavior and Group Achievement*. New York: Oxford Press, 1959.

Thomas, E. J., and Fink, C. F. "Effects of Group Size," *Psychological Bulletin* 60 (1963): 371–84.

Practical Exercise I

The Lonely Keypunch Operator

Anne Martin has worked for the past eight years as a keypunch operator for the Pullman Steel Company. In the last six months she has been troubled about her relationships with the other nine keypunch operators in her work unit. Anne believes that the other members of the group are being extremely cold toward her.

Prior to the last six months, the keypunch operators would communicate throughout the day about such matters as their jobs, the company, their families, and a number of other personal matters such as problems with their children and their husbands. The ten keypunch operators were considered a very cohesive work group. The keypunch operators were women ranging in age from 25 to 55. None of the girls had a college education. They were of varied ethnic and religious backgrounds. For example, two of the operators were Italian, two were black, one was Irish, and one was English-German.

Anne was the oldest member of the group at 55. She had been well liked until about January of this year. At this time the girls no longer openly communicated with Anne, and they stopped asking her to eat lunch with them in what is referred to as "Keypunch Korner" in the cafeteria.

Over the past two years Anne has been known as one of the fastest and most accurate keypunch operators in the unit. She has had little difficulty adjusting to the new supervisors who are trained on the job in the keypunch unit. The keypunch unit has had ten supervisors since Anne began working at Pullman.

In January, the informal keypunch unit leader Phyllis Pizzuto had a heated disagreement with management about her work. The supervisor, Mary Castille, told Phyllis that her work would have to improve in both speed and accuracy. Anne liked both Phyllis and Mary and did not want to get involved in this dispute. In fact everytime Phyllis brought up the subject on the job or at lunch, Anne tried to change the subject. On a number of occasions Phyllis asked Anne, "Why are you taking the side of management?"

Since January, Phyllis Pizzuto and her best personal friend, another keypunch operator, Joy Flynn, have looked at Anne's daily production sheet. On five separate occasions Anne has seen one of them "peeking" at her output sheet.

Although none of the other operators have tried to determine Anne's productivity, they have also ostracized her. Because the group is important to her personally, Anne is trying to analyze the situation and take the best action. She is thinking about a number of alternatives:

1. Report her problem to the supervisor.
2. Request a transfer to the other keypunch unit in the plant.
3. Confront Phyllis Pizzuto and ask her why the group is cold toward her.
4. Talk to the group, excluding Phyllis and Joy, and ask them why they are cold toward her.
5. Quit her job.

Anne wants to do the best thing and really wants to get back on good terms with all of the keypunch operators. She thinks that her problems at work have carried over into her home and are affecting her relationship with her husband.

Questions for Analysis:

1. What is the problem with which Anne is faced?
2. Why do you feel that the keypunch operators are a cohesive work group?
3. What course of action would you recommend for Anne? Why?

Practical Exercise II

Rudy Garcia's Department

The prototype–project development department of Torando Electronics Company played an essential role in the development of the product lines sold by the firm. The department consisted of 12 engineers and 35 technicians who worked on the first floor of the Baltimore, Maryland plant. Each project worked on in the department usually had at least two engineers and five technicians working together under the direction of a project supervisor.

When each project was started, the engineers submitted a written work order, and the department manager would assign the technicians to work with the engineers. Upon completion of each project a quality control assessor would inspect the work. The engineers were recognized by the top management of the company as having the expertise to submit top quality work orders and in only a few instances were their requests rejected. The engineers were college graduates and were paid on a salary basis.

Most of the 35 technicians had previously worked as assembly workers at Torando and they knew the plant operations very well. They were paid on an hourly basis and most of their pay raises were based primarily on seniority. The majority of technicians worked the day shift, although some had to work the other two shifts. Seniority was used to schedule the shift assignments.

The technicians interacted with each other off the job, either through activities such as softball, bowling, card games, or professional football parties on the weekends during the season. The technicians ate lunch and took coffee breaks together.

The engineers rarely, if ever, spent any off-the-job time with the technicians. They had an engineering office where they took coffee breaks and often met after work to schedule some activity for the evening.

Rudy Garcia, the department manager, was concerned about the strained relationship that existed between the technicians and engineers. He noticed the engineers complaining about the slowness and poor quality of work being done by the technicians. These complaints were occurring regularly. The productivity of the department became a part of Rudy Garcia's performance file, and his salary increments and promotion opportunities were based on his file. It was obvious to Rudy that the production of the department was extremely low compared to other similar departments in other plants in the company.

Because of the perceived problems in the department, Rudy started to investigate the relationship between the engineers and technicians. For two weeks he talked to a number of the technicians and most of the engineers to learn more about the interaction between the groups. He found that the technicians believed that the engineers requested work orders and set up projects that were poorly developed. They also thought that their suggestions on how to accomplish projects were never followed.

Rudy discovered that the engineers believed that they were a part of the management team and needed control over the technicians. The engineers believed that the technicians were feared by management because they were unionized. In addition, the engineers thought that the technicians were "dragging their feet" and passively resisting any suggestions or recommendations initiated by the engineers.

After his preliminary investigation of the situation Rudy concluded that immediate action had to be taken. He wanted to be fair, but firm, in the steps that he needed to take to try to minimize or resolve the friction.

Questions for Analysis:

1. Would you have predicted problems between the engineering and technician groups? Why?
2. What type(s) of groups are described in the exercise?
3. Is the friction among the engineers and technicians creating more or less cohesion within the groups? Why?
4. What action would you recommend that Rudy Garcia take?

9 Leadership

INTRODUCTION

Scholars and management practitioners have been perplexed for years by the phenomenon of leadership in organizations. Concerted effort has been expended to describe and analyze the relationships between the way in which a leader functions and the way in which followers perform their tasks. Despite numerous theories and research studies the impact of the leader on followers in organizational settings is still not clear.[1]

Behavioralists have attempted to apply their logic and methodologies to clarify some of the variables normally associated with leading people. However, although some of the many leadership variables have been clarified, numerous incongruous and contradictory theories and research findings still exist. In this chapter, some of the theories and research findings are organized into a practical framework. The material presented here shows that no one theory of leadership is universally accepted. It will show, however, that many of the theories of leadership overlap. Although the terms used are different, the underlying rationales, premises, and tentative conclusions of the various theories are similar.

WHAT IS LEADERSHIP?

Some writers have projected the impression that leadership is a synonym for managership. This assumption is not correct. Leaders are

---

[1] Gary Yukl, "Toward a Behavioral Theory of Leadership," *Organizational Behavior and Human Performance*, vol. 6 (July 1971), p. 414.

found not only in the managerial hierarchy, but also in informal work groups. The discussion in this chapter is directed toward the exercise of leadership by individuals in the formal managerial hierarchy.

In the management literature, there are many definitions of leadership. Listed below are a few of the more popular ones:

1. Leadership is one form of dominance, in which the followers more or less willingly accept direction and control by another person.[2]
2. Leadership is the process of influencing the activities of an organized group in efforts toward goal setting and goal achievement.[3]
3. Leadership is the process of inducing a subordinate to behave in a desired manner.[4]
4. Leadership is an influence process, the dynamics of which are a function of the personal characteristics of the leader and followers, and of the nature of the specific situation.[5]

A review of the four leadership definitions indicates that although (1) was stated in 1946 and (4) was proposed in 1972, they are very similar. The common thread running through these four definitions is that leadership is a process whereby one individual exerts influence over others. Several attempts have been made to clarify and depict the basis upon which a superior might influence a subordinate or a group of subordinates. One of the most concise and insightful approaches is offered by French and Raven.[6] These researchers define influence in terms of power —the control which a person possesses and can exercise on others.

It is proposed by French and Raven that there are five different bases of power:

1. *Coercive Power.* This is power based upon fear. A subordinate perceives that failure to comply with the wishes of a superior would lead to punishment (for example, an undesirable work assignment, a reprimand). Coercive power is based upon the expectations of individuals that punishment is the consequence for not agreeing with the actions, attitudes, or directives of a superior.

---

[2] K. Young, *Handbook of Social Psychology* (London: Routledge & Kegan Paul, Ltd., 1946).

[3] Ralph M. Stogdill, "Leadership, Membership and Organization," *Psychological Bulletin,* vol. 52 (January 1950), p. 4.

[4] Warren G. Bennis, "Leadership Theory and Administrative Behavior: The Problem of Authority," *Administrative Science Quarterly,* vol. 4 (December 1959), p. 261.

[5] Max D. Richards and Paul S. Greenlaw, *Management Decision Making* (Homewood, Ill.: Richard D. Irwin, Inc., 1972), p. 166.

[6] John R. P. French and Bertram Raven, "The Bases of Social Power," in Dorwin Cartwright and A. F. Zander, eds., *Group Dynamics,* 2d ed. (Evanston, Ill.: Row, Peterson, and Company, 1960), pp. 607–23.

2. *Reward Power.* This is the opposite of coercive power. A subordinate perceives that compliance with the wishes of a superior will lead to positive rewards. These rewards could be monetary (increases in pay) or psychological (a compliment for a job well done).

3. *Legitimate Power.* This type of power derives from the position of a superior in the organizational hierarchy. For example, the president of a corporation possesses more legitimate power than the vice president, and the department manager has more legitimate power than the first line foreman.

4. *Expert Power.* An individual with this type of power is one with some expertise, special skill, or knowledge. The possession of one or more of these attributes gains the respect and compliance of peers or subordinates.

5. *Referent Power.* This power is based on a follower's identification with a leader. The leader is admired because of one or more personal traits, and the follower can be influenced because of this admiration.

This fivefold framework offers the student of management a conceptual distinction between the bases of power. These can be summarized into two major categories: (1) power based primarily on organizational factors and (2) power based on individual factors.

Coercive, reward, and legitimate power are specified primarily by the individual's position in the organization. The foreman in an organization is at a lower managerial level than the department manager, and consequently has significantly less coercive, reward, and legitimate power than does the department manager. Upper level managers are allowed various company facilities and resources, while managers at the lower levels cannot utilize these. The head operating room nurse has more freedom to make job-related decisions than a floor nurse. Position also affects the use of power in regard to the discipline process. A foreman can reprimand subordinates (coercive power), while the department manager can reprimand the foreman.

The degree and scope of a manager's referent and expert power bases are dictated primarily by individual characteristics. Some managers possess specific qualities (for example, skills or attributes) that make them attractive to subordinates. Managers could be viewed attractive because of an ability to express themselves clearly or because they appear completely confident in performing the job. Thus, the individual superior controls the referent and expert power bases while the organization controls the coercive, reward, and legitimate power bases.

Katz and Kahn have added another concept to the fivefold power framework for studying leadership. They propose an incremental influence category in the following manner: ". . . we consider the essence of organizational leadership to be the influential increment over and above the mechanical compliance with routine directives of the organization."[7]

The incremental influence factor can be described in the French and Raven approach as a combination of the referent and expert bases.[8] The essence of this influence concept is that the organizational and individual characteristics of managers are related to each other. Thus, the act of influencing or leading of others depends on the organization system and on the perceptions which subordinates hold of their leaders, among other things.

The influence framework can be utilized to identify the functions which a leader is supposed to perform in an organization. Many distinct behavioral viewpoints of leadership functions are espoused by individuals studying leadership behavior. Two interpretations of what the leader should do have been classified as the psychological view and the sociological view.[9]

THE LEADERSHIP JOB: PSYCHOLOGICAL VIEW

The psychological view proposes that the primary function of a leader is to develop effective motivation systems. The leader must be able to stimulate subordinates in such a manner that they contribute positively to organizational goals and are also able to satisfy various personal needs.

The Maslow need hierarchy could serve as a model for the leader in developing the most effective motivation system. The leader, by being familiar with the premise that "man does not live by bread alone," but is interested in psychological growth, can develop programs that achieve optimum contribution from subordinates. A program that focuses upon the entire need spectrum—physiological, safety, social, esteem, and self-actualization—is assumed to have a higher probability for motivating successfully than a partial program.

In the psychological view, the French and Raven influence concept is an integral part. To consider only organizationally controlled power sources—coercive, reward, and legitimate—leads to the development of incomplete and often misdirected motivational programs. Leaders must also consider referent and expert power bases when developing motivation programs.

The theme stressed in the psychological view of the leader's job

---

[7] Daniel Katz and Robert L. Kahn, *The Social Psychology of Organizations* (New York: John Wiley and Sons, Inc., 1966), p. 302.

[8] Kurt R. Student, "Supervisory Influence and Work-Group Performance, *Journal of Applied Psychology,* vol. 52 (June 1968), pp. 188–94.

[9] Also see Harold Koontz and Cyril O'Donnell, *Principles of Management* (New York: McGraw-Hill Book Co., 1972), pp. 556–59.

is this aiding of subordinates in satisfying their various needs. The satisfaction of these needs in such a manner that the organization is more successful and the employees happier is the function which a leader must perform. Any leader not accomplishing this complex task would be rated low according to the psychological view.

THE LEADERSHIP JOB: SOCIOLOGICAL VIEW

Other behavioralists perceive the leadership function as a facilitative activity. For example, the leader establishes goals and reconciles organizational conflict between followers, exerting influence by performing these activities.

The establishment of goals provides the direction which followers often require. It provides the followers with guidance so that they know what type of performance or attitude is expected of them. The goals also influence the interaction patterns that develop between followers. This leads to group characteristics such as the development of communication networks, group cohesiveness, and status hierarchies.

Conflict among followers can become so disruptive that nothing positive is contributed to the organization. When this occurs, a leader's influence must be exercised to minimize the disruptive conflict within or between groups.

The sociological view can be criticized from a pragmatic viewpoint. While it is accurate to assume that leaders facilitate the activities of followers, it is misleading to contend that leaders can always set goals and resolve conflict. These are large orders for any leader, which are once again made more difficult by differences in people, and by leadership ability and situations. In the sociological view the leader has to be a facilitator and also has to conduct the planning, organizing, and controlling functions.

In summary, the psychological and sociological views are too broad to be of much value to those practicing managers interested in learning about leadership behavior. A much better system for studying leadership would be one which is narrower and is based, if possible, on a more scientific foundation.

SELECTED LEADERSHIP THEORIES

Recent efforts by behavioralists have indicated that there is interest among them to organize the numerous theories. Instead of creating more theories of leadership behavior, the focus here is upon systematically organizing and categorizing what is already available. There appear to be three broad leadership theory categories. They are (1) the trait theories, (2) the personal-behavioral theories, and (3) the situational or contingency theories. Figure 9–1 illustrates that the trait and

FIGURE 9–1

Overlap of Theories of Leadership

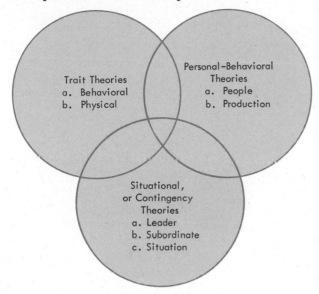

personal-behavioral approaches can be integrated to some degree to yield the situational approach. Some of the situational theories emerging have borrowed from the trait approaches and from various personal-behavioral approaches. Therefore it is best to consider each of the approaches as having many similarities and some differences.

Trait Theories

The identification of various personal traits of leaders as criteria for describing or predicting success has been used for some time. Many executives engaged in recruitment and selection of managers believe that the trait approach is as valid as any other method. However, the comparison of leaders by various physical, personality, and intelligence traits has resulted in little agreement among researchers.

Physical Traits. There are advocates of the trait theory who contend that the physical stature of a person affects ability to influence followers. For example, in an extensive review of 12 leadership investigations, Stogdill determined that in 9 of the studies leaders were found to be taller than followers; 2 found them to be shorter, while 1 concluded that height was not the most important factor.[10] Other physical

---

[10] Ralph Stogdill, "Personal Factors Associated with Leadership," *Journal of Applied Psychology*, vol. 25 (January 1948), pp. 35–71.

traits that have been studied with no conclusive results include weight, physique, and personal appearance.

Personality. A research study by Ghiselli[11] reports on several personality factors that are related in most, though not all cases to effective leadership. He found that leaders who have the drive to act independently and are self-assured (for example, have confidence in their leadership skills) are successful in achieving organizational goals.

The work of Fiedler suggests that successful leaders may be more perceptive than nonsuccessful leaders.[12] He found that effective leaders are more proficient in differentiating between their best and poorest followers than are the less effective leaders. The leaders of the more effective groups maintain greater psychological distance between themselves and their followers than do leaders of less effective groups.

Intelligence. After surveying the literature, Stogdill concluded that leadership ability is associated with the judgment and verbal facility of the leader.[13] Ghiselli also concluded that an individual's intelligence is an accurate predictor of managerial success within a certain range. Above and below this range the chances of successful prediction significantly decrease.[14] It should be noted, however, that the leader's intelligence should be close to the followers. The leader who is too smart or not smart enough may lose the followers' respect.

There are some shortcomings in the method of employing a trait approach and assuming that if one is confident, independent, and intelligent, one has a higher probability of succeeding. First, the trait theory of leadership ignores the subordinates. The followers have a significant effect on the job accomplished by the leader. Second, trait theorists do not specify the relative importance of various traits. Should an organization attempt to find managers who are confident or those who act independently—which should be weighted more? Third, the research evidence is inconsistent. For every study that supports the idea that a particular trait is positively related to improved effectiveness there seems to be one that shows a negative or no relationship. Finally, though endless lists of traits have already been uncovered, the list grows annually, so that the numerous traits already uncovered suggest that others will be found in the future. The cumbersome listings lead to confusion and disputes, and provide little insight into leadership.

The manager in the real world searches for answers and suggestions

---

[11] Edwin E. Ghiselli, "Managerial Talent," *American Psychologist,* vol. 18 (October 1963), pp. 631–41.

[12] Fred Fiedler, "The Leader's Psychological Distance and Group Effectiveness," in Cartwright and Zander, eds., *Group Dynamics,* pp. 586–605.

[13] Stogdill, "Personal Factors."

[14] Ghiselli, "Managerial Talent."

and is not concerned about theoretical arguments. Perhaps the most significant limitation is that trait-related research findings do not allow us to generalize such findings from one situation to another.

Personal-Behavioral Theories

Personal-behavioral theories contend that leaders may best be classified by personal qualities or behavioral patterns (styles). A number of individuals have presented theories of leadership which fit into the personal-behavioral (P-B) category. In all cases, however, the P-B theories of leadership focus upon what the leader does in carrying out the managerial job. Of these there is no specific style that is universally accepted.

A Continuum of Leadership. Tannenbaum and Schmidt postulate that managers often have difficulty in deciding what type of action is

FIGURE 9–2

Continuum of Leadership Behavior

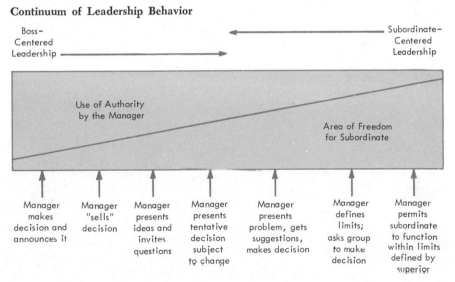

most appropriate for handling a particular problem.[15] They are not sure whether to make the decision or to delegate the decision-making authority to subordinates. To provide insight into the meaning of leadership behavior with regard to decision making, Tannenbaum and Schmidt suggest a continuum.

Figure 9–2 presents this leadership continuum. Leadership actions

[15] Robert Tannenbaum and Warren H. Schmidt, "How to Choose a Leadership Pattern," *Harvard Business Review* (May–June 1973), pp. 162–80.

are related to the degree of authority used by managers, and to the amount of freedom available to the subordinates in reaching decisions. The managerial actions depicted on the left characterize managers who maintain a high degree of control, while those on the right designate managers who delegate decision-making authority. The continuum clearly illustrates that there are a number of leadership styles that can be employed. Leaders who would be most effective would be those who are adaptable, that is, who can delegate authority effectively because they consider their capabilities, subordinates' capabilities, and goals to be accomplished.

Thus, Tannenbaum and Schmidt imply that leaders should not choose a strict "autocratic" or "democratic" style, but should be flexible enough to cope with different situations.

Benevolent Autocracy. McMurry believes that the realities of organizational life have doomed what is referred to as democratic leadership.[16] The democratic leader and the autocratic leader both must set objectives and guide subordinates. However, the democratic leader encourages two-way communication. The benevolent autocrat is powerful and prestigious, can be communicated with, and is personally interested in subordinates' problems. Subordinates perceive this type of leader as being able to take prompt remedial action in matters that affect them.

To support the benevolent-autocrat theory, McMurry offers the following reasons for the demise of democratic leadership:

1. The climate within organizations is unfavorable. The "captains" of industry have worked hard to attain their positions in the managerial hierarchy. Thus, they are likely to be hard driving and would like to control the destinies of their firms. These individuals are not likely to favor delegation of decision-making power.

2. Since most organizations must make rapid and difficult decisions, it is in their best interest to maintain the control of operations in a centralized group of managers. Thus, freedom of action is constrained by the need to make rapid decisions, and democratic leadership is not feasible because it encourages freedom of action.

3. Democratic leadership concepts are relatively new and unproven. Historically, successful firms have followed classical organization principles. These principles are generally compatible with autocratic and not with democratic leadership. Once a firm has begun to follow classical

---

[16] Robert N. McMurry, "The Case for Benevolent Autocracy," *Harvard Business Review*, vol. 36 (January–February 1958), pp. 82–90. For a discussion of other theories, see Douglas McGregor, *The Human Side of Enterprise* (New York: McGraw-Hill Book Co., 1960); and Chris Argyris, *Personality and Organization* (New York: Harper and Row, 1957).

guidelines and develop autocratic leaders, these leaders perpetuate themselves.

These three reasons, among others, are the evidence offered by McMurry to justify his claim that the benevolent autocrat is the most effective leader. This type of leader structures subordinates' work activities; makes the policy decisions affecting them; and enforces discipline. The benevolent autocrat may encourage participation in the planning of a course of action, but is the "chief" in executing a decision. The benevolent autocrat is concerned about subordinates' feelings, attitudes, and productivity; but despite these humanistic feelings uses rules, regulations, and specified policies.

Over a decade has passed since McMurry first stated his leadership approach. What has occurred in society recently seems to indicate that the arguments have weakened. It appears that there are growing numbers of organizations willing to attempt more humanistic and less autocratic leadership approaches. This is not to say that the autocrat is not found in organizations or is not successful in the modern corporation.

Job-Centered–Employee-Centered Leaders. The Tannenbaum and Schmidt and McMurry theories are based upon opinion. They are not supported by performance data demanded by executives. Since 1947, Likert and his associates at the Institute for Social Research at the University of Michigan have conducted studies of leadership.[17] They have studied leaders in industry, hospitals, and government, obtaining data from thousands of employees.

After extensive analyses, the leaders studied were classified as job-centered or employee-centered. The *job-centered leader* structures the jobs of subordinates, closely supervises to see that designated tasks are performed, uses incentives to spur production, and determines satisfactory rates of production based on procedures such as time study.

The *employee-centered leader* focuses attention on the human aspects of subordinates' problems and on building effective work groups with high performance goals. Such a leader specifies objectives, communicates them to subordinates and gives subordinates considerable freedom to accomplish their job tasks and goals. Figure 9–3 presents the findings from one study which compared employee-centered and job-centered managers.

As indicated, the majority of high-producing sections were led by supervisors who displayed an employee-centered style. In a study of clerical workers the employee-centered manager was described as a general supervisor and the job-centered manager as a close supervisor.

[17] Rensis Likert, *New Patterns of Management* (New York: McGraw-Hill Book Company, Inc., 1961). Figures 9–3 and 9–4 are based upon Likert's research findings.

FIGURE 9–3

Number of Supervisors Who Are:

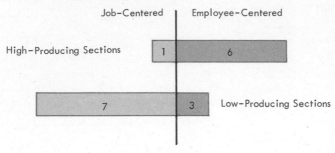

Once again, productivity data clearly indicated that the general type of supervision (employee centered) was more effective than the close supervision style (job centered). Figure 9–4 presents a summary of the findings from the study of clerical workers.

Based on his extensive research, Likert suggests that the type of leadership style significantly influences various end-result variables. Such variables as productivity, absenteeism, attitudes, turnover, and defective units were found to be more favorable from an organizational standpoint when employee-centered or general supervision was utilized. Likert implies that the choice is of the either–or variety, that is, management can be categorized and practiced as employee-centered or job-centered. His recommendation is to develop employee-centered managers whenever possible.

Two-Dimensional Theory.   In 1945, a group of researchers at Ohio State University began extensive investigations of leadership. The central focus of their work was to study in depth the work of a leader. Their effort uncovered many provocative insights concerning leadership behavior. Perhaps the most publicized aspect of the Ohio State leadership

FIGURE 9–4

Number of Supervisors Who Are:

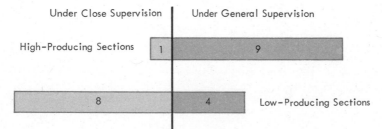

studies was the isolation of two dimensions of leadership behavior, identified as "consideration" and "initiating structure."[18]

These two dimensions were used to describe leadership behavior in organizational settings. The researchers assessed how supervisors think they should behave in leadership roles. They also attempted to ascertain subordinate perceptions of supervisory behavior. Analyses allowed the Ohio State researchers to classify leaders on "consideration" and "initiating structure."

Leaders who were high on the "consideration" dimension reflected that they had developed a work atmosphere of mutual trust, respect for subordinates' ideas, and consideration of subordinates' feelings. Such leaders encouraged good superior-subordinate rapport and two-way communication. A low "consideration" score indicates that leaders are more impersonal in their dealings with subordinates.

A high "initiating structure" score indicates that leaders structure their roles and those of subordinates toward the attainment of goals. They are actively involved in planning work activities, communicating pertinent information, and scheduling work.

One research study attempted to compare foremen having different "consideration" and "initiating structure" scores with various performance measures.[19] The first measure was obtained from proficiency ratings made by plant management. Other measures were unexcused absenteeism, accidents, formally filed grievances, and employee turnover. Indices for each of these measures were computed for each foreman's work group for an 11-month period.

Foremen who worked in production divisions were compared to foremen in nonproduction divisions on "consideration" scores, "initiating structure" scores, and proficiency ratings. In the production divisions there was a positive relationship between proficiency and "initiating structure" and a negative relationship with "consideration." In other words, the foremen who were rated by their superiors as most proficient scored high on "structure" and low on "consideration." In the nonproduction divisions the relationships were reversed.

After comparing the leadership scores and foreman proficiency ratings,

---

[18] See any of the following for excellent presentations of the two-dimensional theory: E. A. Fleishman, "The Measurement of Leadership Attitudes in Industry," *Journal of Applied Psychology,* vol. 37 (June 1953), pp. 153–58; E. A. Fleishman and D. A. Peters, "Interpersonal Values, Leadership Attitudes and Managerial Success," *Personnel Psychology,* vol. 15 (Summer 1962), pp. 127–43; and Abraham K. Korman, "Consideration, Initiating Structure, and Organizational Criteria—A Review," *Personnel Psychology,* vol. 19 (Winter 1966), pp. 349–61.

[19] E. A. Fleishman, E. F. Harris, and H. E. Burtt, *Leadership and Supervision in Industry* (Columbus, Ohio: Bureau of Educational Research, Ohio State University, 1955).

the researchers compared leadership scores to the other performance measures—unexcused absenteeism, accidents, formally filed grievances, and employee turnover. In general, it was determined that high structure and low consideration were related to more absenteeism, accidents, grievances, and turnover.

A number of other studies have supported the general findings cited above, while other research findings present contradictory evidence.[20] Despite these differences, it certainly is true that the Ohio State researchers have stimulated the interest of laymen and researchers in systematically studying leadership. More effort along the lines of the Ohio State studies is needed if some of the mysteries of leadership in an organization are to be understood.

The Managerial Grid Theory.   Thus far, we have examined personal opinions and research findings concerning leadership behavior. Another P-B theory which is based on research findings is the managerial grid concept. Blake and Mouton propose that leadership styles can be plotted on a two-dimensional grid.[21] This grid is presented in Figure 9–5.

Five specific leadership styles are indicated in the grid. Of course these are only a few of the many possible styles of leadership that can be, and are utilized.

1,1–*Impoverished*—a minimum effort to accomplish the work is exerted by the leader.

9,1–*Task*—the leader concentrates on task efficiency but shows little regard for the development and morale of subordinates.

1,9–*Country Club*—the leader focuses on being supportive and considerate of employees. However, task efficiency is not a primary concern of this easygoing style.

5,5–*Middle of the Road*—adequate task efficiency and satisfactory morale are the goals of this style.

9,9–*Team*—the leader facilitates production and morale by coordinating and integrating work-related activities.

It is assumed by Blake and Mouton that the leader who is a (9,9) individual would be using the most effective style. However, defining a (9,9) leader for every type of job is very difficult. But Blake and Mouton imply that a managerial development program can move leaders *toward* a (9,9) style. They recommend a number of management development phases. It is assumed that the development experience will aid the manager in acquiring concern for fellow employees and expertise

---

[20] For a number of studies which dispute some of the findings of the Ohio State researchers, see Korman, "Consideration."

[21] Robert R. Blake and Jane S. Mouton, *The Managerial Grid* (Houston, Texas: Gulf Publishing, 1964).

FIGURE 9–5

Managerial grid

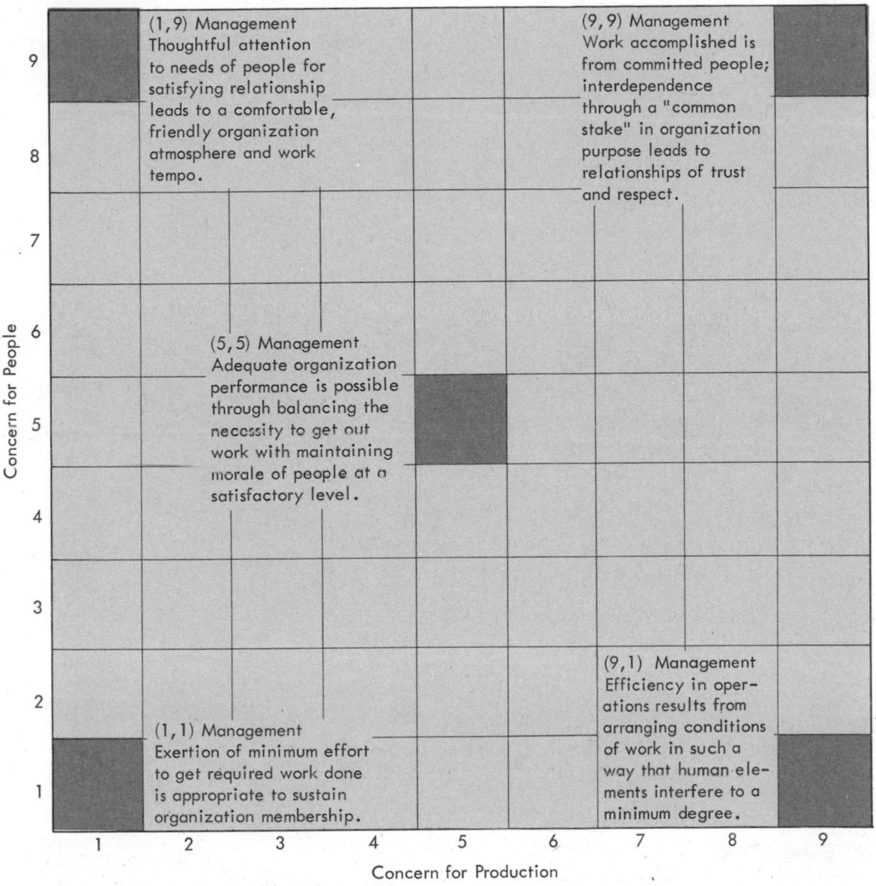

Concern for People (vertical axis, scale 1–9)
Concern for Production (horizontal axis, scale 1–9)

(1,9) Management
Thoughtful attention
to needs of people for
satisfying relationship
leads to a comfortable,
friendly organization
atmosphere and work
tempo.

(9,9) Management
Work accomplished is
from committed people;
interdependence
through a "common
stake" in organization
purpose leads to
relationships of trust
and respect.

(5,5) Management
Adequate organization
performance is possible
through balancing the
necessity to get out
work with maintaining
morale of people at a
satisfactory level.

(1,1) Management
Exertion of minimum effort
to get required work done
is appropriate to sustain
organization membership.

(9,1) Management
Efficiency in oper-
ations results from
arranging conditions
of work in such a
way that human ele-
ments interfere to a
minimum degree.

Source: Robert R. Blake and Jane S. Mouton, *The Managerial Grid* (Houston: Gulf Publishing Company, 1964), p. 10.

to accomplish task objectives such as productivity and quality. Four of these phases are outlined below:

Phase 1: Laboratory-seminar groups. Typically, one-week conferences are used to introduce the leaders to the grid approach and philosophy. The training of the leaders in the conferences is conducted by line managers of the firm who are already familiar with the ideas of Blake and Mouton. A key part of the phase is to analyze and assess one's own leadership style.

Phase 2: Teamwork. Each department works out and specifies its own (9,9) description. This phase is an extension of Phase 1, which included leaders from different departments in the conference groups. Thus, in the second phase, managers from the same department are brought together. The intent of Phases 1 and 2 is to enable leaders to learn the grid philosophy, improve their ability to assess their own leadership style, and to develop cohesiveness among the participants.

Phase 3: Intergroup Interaction. This phase involves intergroup discussion and analysis of (9,9) specifications. Situations are created whereby tensions and conflicts that exist between groups are analyzed by group members.

Phase 4: Organizational Goal Setting. Goal setting on the part of the leaders in the program is discussed and analyzed. Such problems as profits, cost control, and safety are placed in a goal-setting context (for example, one participant vows to reduce direct expenses 20 percent over the next six-month period).

The managerial grid approach relates task effectiveness and human satisfaction to a formal managerial development program. This program is unique in that (1) line managers, not academicians or consultants, run the program, (2) a conceptual framework of management (the grid) is utilized, and (3) the entire managerial hierarchy undergoes development, not just one group level (for example, first-line supervisors).

A Synopsis of the Personal-Behavioral Approach

Some readers may suggest that instead of discussing an approach, we should talk about approaches. However, examination of the various

TABLE 9–1

Personal-Behavioral Theories

Theories	*Two Concepts and Derivation*
1. Leadership continuum	1. Boss centered and subordinate centered; opinions of Tannenbaum and Schmidt.
2. Benevolent autocrat	2. Benevolent autocrat and democrat; opinion of McMurry.
3. Supportive theory	3. Job-centered and employee-centered; research at the University of Michigan.
4. Two-dimensional theory	4. "Consideration" and "initiating structure"; research at Ohio State University.
5. Managerial grid	5. Concern for people and concern for production; research of Blake and Mouton.

P-B theories presented in this section indicates that similar concepts are discussed, but different labels are utilized. For example, the continuum, the benevolent-autocrat proposition, Likert, the Ohio State researchers, and the managerial grid approach each utilize two broadly defined concepts which are summarized in Table 9–1.

Each of the five approaches summarized in Table 9–1 focuses upon two concepts; however, some differences should be emphasized. The first two theories are based primarily upon personal opinions. Although the opinions of the originators are respected, they should be supported with research evidence before more faith can be placed in each particular theory. Likert implies that the most successful leadership style is employee centeredness. He suggests that we need look no further to find the best leadership style. The critical question is whether the employee-

FIGURE 9–6

Overlay of Grid and Ohio State Leadership Theories

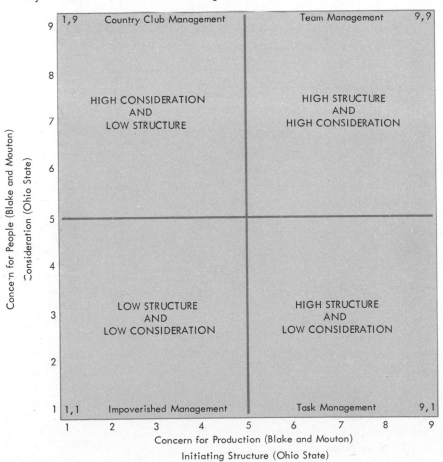

centered style works in all situations. Some studies dispute Likert's claim. The Ohio State researchers found that from a production standpoint, the leader with a high "initiating structure" score was preferred by the executives of the company. Thus, Likert's claim, or any other claim, that one best leadership approach has been discovered is subject to debate.

Finally, two of the theories can be fitted together to present an overlay view of leadership. Merging the other theories is a great deal more difficult because of the differences in definitions and contentions of the originators.

The Ohio State theory and the managerial grid approach can be integrated into an overlay of leadership, "overlay" meaning that they are merged into one.[22] Perhaps more integrative work along the lines of the overlay (Figure 9–6) would provide the student of management with a better understanding of the P-B theories of leadership. This is not to suggest that an ultimate theory of leadership has been discovered, but that the endless list of styles causes semantic difficulties by referring to the same basic leadership behavior with different terminology.

Situational or Contingency Theory

An increasing number of behavioral scientists are questioning the premise that a particular leadership style is effective in all situations. They believe that a manager, behaving as a democratic leader, for example, cannot be assured of effective results in every situation. As noted earlier in this chapter, the Ohio State researchers found that supervisors who scored high on initiating structure were relatively more proficient when managing production rather than non-production workers. Thus evidence exists even in the literature on personal-behavioral theories to support the view that effective leadership depends upon the interaction of the situation and the leader's behavior.

The identification of key situational factors and the determination of their relative importance are difficult undertakings. One behavioral scientist who has devoted considerable time and energy to such undertakings is Professor Fred Fiedler.

Fiedler Theory of Leadership. With a considerable body of research evidence behind him, Fiedler has developed a dynamic situational or contingency theory of leadership.[23] Three important situational factors,

---

[22] The merging idea was originally proposed and presented by Paul Hersey and Kenneth H. Blanchard, *Management of Organizational Behavior* (Englewood Cliffs, N.J.: Prentice-Hall, Inc., 1972), p. 76.

[23] Fred E. Fiedler, *A Theory of Leadership Effectiveness* (New York: McGraw-Hill Book Co., 1967).

or dimensions, are specified and are assumed to influence the leader's effectiveness.

The dimensions identified are:

1. *Leader-member relations*—This refers to the degree of confidence the subordinates have in the leader. It also entails the loyalty shown and attractiveness of the leader.
2. *Task structure*—This refers to the degree to which the followers' jobs are routine versus being ill-structured and undefined.
3. *Position Power*—This refers to the power inherent in the leadership position. It includes the rewards and punishments which are typically associated with the position, the leader's official authority (based on ranking in managerial hierarchy), and the support which the leader receives from superiors and the overall organization.

Fiedler measures leadership style by evaluating leader responses to what is called a Least-Preferred Co-Worker (LPC) questionnaire. The leaders who rate their least-preferred co-worker in favorable terms (high LPC) are assumed to be people oriented and supportive. Those leaders with low LPC ratings are more task oriented.

By utilizing the three-dimensional model, LPC scores, and research findings, Fiedler has specified the type of leadership style that is most appropriate in different situations. He has assembled data which relate leadership style to the three-dimensional measures of conditions favorable or unfavorable to the leader. The LPC measure of leadership style is assumed to discriminate between leaders who tend to be permissive, considerate, and foster good interpersonal relations among group members (permissive) and leaders who tend to be directive, controlling, more oriented toward task than toward people (directive). For example, permissive leaders obtain optimal group performance in situations where the task is structured, but the leader is disliked and must be diplomatic. This type of leadership style is also effective in situations where the leader is liked, but the group is faced with an unstructured task. When the task is structured, directive leadership is more effective.

In effect, the Fiedler model suggests that leaders who are directive and leaders who are permissive can function best in certain types of situations. Instead of stating that a leader must adopt this or that type of style, Fiedler identifies the type of leader that functions best in a situation. According to Fiedler we should not talk simply about good leaders or poor leaders. A leader who achieves effectiveness in one situation may or may not be effective in another. The implication of this logic is that managers should think about the situation in which a particular leader (subordinate manager) performs well or badly. Fiedler assumes that managers can enhance the subordinate's effectiveness if they carefully choose the situations that are favorable to the subordinate's style.

In Table 9–2, some of Fiedler's findings about the relationship among the three dimensions to leadership style for such task groups as bomber crews, management groups, high school basketball teams, and open-hearth crews are presented.

TABLE 9–2

Summary of Fiedler's Investigations of Leadership

| Condition | Group Situation | | | Leadership Style Correlating with Productivity |
	Leader-Member Relations	Task Structure	Position Power	
1...............	Good	Structured	Strong	Directive
2...............	Good	Structured	Weak	Directive
3...............	Good	Unstructured	Strong	Directive
4...............	Good	Unstructured	Weak	Permissive
5...............	Moderately poor	Structured	Strong	Permissive
6...............	Moderately poor	Structured	Weak	No Data
7...............	Moderately poor	Unstructured	Strong	No relationship found
8...............	Moderately poor	Unstructured	Weak	Directive

A review of Table 9–2 indicates a correlation between good task performance and a *directive* style under conditions 1, 2, 3, and 8, and a correlation between good task performance and a *permissive* style under conditions 4 and 5. These results indicate that for various situations a particular leadership style achieves the best results.

An example of an effective leader under condition 1 could be the following:

> A well-liked, head nurse in a university medical center who is in charge of getting the nursing team ready for open-heart surgery. The tasks which must be performed by the head nurse are very tightly structured. There is no room for error or indecision, and the duties of everyone on the nursing team are clearly specified. The head nurse has complete power to correct any personnel or performance problems within the nursing team.

A leader who is working under condition 5 shown in Table 9–2 would be the following:

> Dan Pride recently graduated from college. While in school, he took as many management courses as possible. His first job assignment

was to supervise 18 technicians in a manufacturing plant in Chicago. Most of the technicians had little education past the eighth grade and had worked for more than ten years in the plant. They generally believed that college "kids" were either "wise guys" or good people, but they took their time deciding. Because they were genuine experts on their job, a formal leader had very little control over sequencing or structuring the job. The job was structured by the experts, and Dan actually concentrated on paper work, not technical work.

These two brief examples are provided to show that the three dimensions of leader-member relations, task structure, and position power are found in each of the eight conditions. According to Fiedler, these conditions are found throughout various organizations and directly influence the leader's effectiveness.

In various organizational settings there may be a need to "engineer" the situation to fit the leader's style, as described by Fiedler in his contingency model. Fiedler suggests some pragmatic procedures for improving a leader's relations, task structure, and position power. Some of his suggestions are as follows:

1. *Leader-member relations* could be improved by restructuring the leader's group of subordinates so that the group is more compatible in terms of background, education level, technical expertise, or ethnic origin. It should be noted that this would be extremely difficult in a unionized group since it may assume that this restructuring is a management plan to weaken the union.

2. The *task structure* can be modified in the structured or the non-structured direction. The task can be more structured by spelling out the jobs in greater detail. A task can be made less structured by providing only general directions for the work that is to be accomplished. Some workers like minimum task structure, while others want detailed and specific task structure.

3. Leader *position power* can be modified in a number of ways. A leader can be given a higher rank in the organization or given more authority to do the job. A memo could be issued indicating the rank change or the authority which a leader now possesses. In addition, a leader's reward power could be increased if the organization delegates authority to evaluate the performance of subordinates.

Fiedler's suggestions may not be possible in every organization setting. Such factors as unions, technology, time, and costs to accomplish changes must be considered. For example, a unionized company that has a highly routine technology and is currently faced with intense competition in new-product development may not have the patience, time, and energy to modify the three situational dimensions so that its leaders become more effective. The real world tempers many of the logically sound and provocative suggestions offered by the contingency approach to leadership.

In effect, Fiedler has presented a theory of leadership which takes into account the leader's personality as well as such situational variables as the task to be completed and the behavioral characteristics of the group which the leader must influence. Of course, much more research is needed before the theory gains widespread acceptance or even partial agreement from among those studying leadership. There are critics who question Fiedler's methodology of measuring LPC, the subjects he uses in some of his research (for example, basketball teams, Belgian Navy, and students), and the fact that only high and low LPC scores are considered in discussing effectiveness.[24] Despite critics and shortcomings, Fiedler has provided a starting point for leadership research in the 1970s.

UNDERSTANDING LEADERSHIP

So far, the discussion of leadership has emphasized that the search for the one best way to lead has not been exceptionally fruitful. Moreover, the tendency of theorists and researchers to use different terms when referring to similar concepts introduces considerable confusion. Terms such as directive, autocratic, concern for production, initiating structure, appear frequently and refer to an essentially similar form of leader behavior. At the same time it is now recognized that effective leadership behavior in one situation is not necessarily effective in a different situation. The aspiring manager is seemingly left with little established knowledge to draw on in understanding effective leadership behavior.

The authors recognize the tentative nature of all knowledge, but at the same time recognize the necessity for managers to understand and practice leadership. With these two considerations in mind, a framework for understanding and integrating contemporary leadership theory is proposed in Figure 9–7. The framework emphasizes the effect of the *leader's background and experiences* on (1) *qualities* such as communication ability, self-awareness and confidence and on (2) the *leader's perceptions* of subordinates, the situation, and the self. The interaction of all these factors is important for determining the *leader's ability to influence* others. The manner in which these variables interact and the proportionate weight of each is not known with certainty; but there is no doubt of their importance.

The leader should consider a number of important organizational and environmental variables as illustrated in Figure 9–7. In the context of the leadership framework, the effective leader is an individual who in-

---

[24] A thorough review article that is critical of the situational or contingency model of leadership is George Graen, Kenneth Alveris, James B. Orris, and Joseph A. Martella, "Contingency Model of Leadership Effectiveness: Antecedent and Evidential Results," *Psychological Bulletin*, vol. 74 (October 1970), pp. 285–96.

FIGURE 9–7

An Integrative Perspective of Leadership

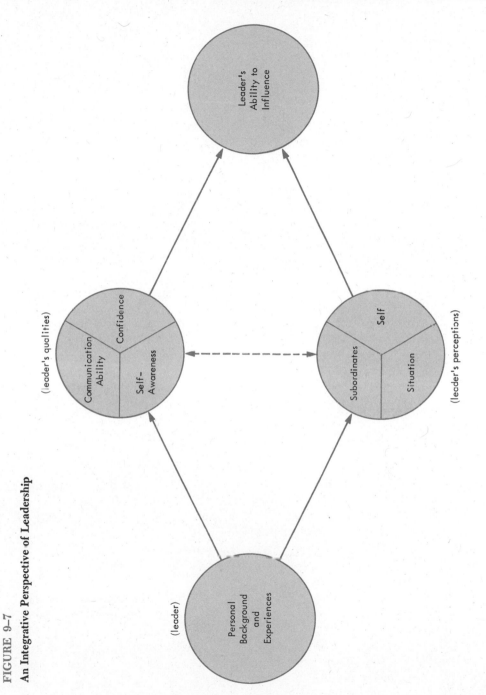

(leader's qualities)

Communication Ability

Confidence

Self-Awareness

(leader)

Personal Background and Experiences

Leader's Ability to Influence

Self

Subordinates

Situation

(leader's perceptions)

fluences followers in such a manner that high productivity is achieved, high group morale exists, low absenteeism, turnover, and accident rates are the rule, and the development of followers is achieved. Figure 9–7 only specifies three personal qualities which contribute significantly to a leader's ability to influence others. This is not intended to be a complete list of relevant factors. The three qualities, however, are suited for most leadership styles and are especially compatible with the situational, or contingency, theory of leadership. They are also related as shown by the dashed line to the perception factors.

Awareness of Self.   One of the most important factors in the situational approach to leadership centers around leader self-awareness.[25] Leaders should be aware of their impact upon those they lead. We are not assuming that they can predict accurately in every situation how their leadership style will affect followers. However, we are suggesting that they should attempt to learn more about their influence upon others. It is assumed that leaders who know themselves are able to perform effectively such necessary functions as planning, organizing, and controlling.

Many of us maintain and develop inaccurate images of our personalities and interaction styles. For example, a leader may perceive "self" as being soft-spoken and easygoing, while subordinates consider the leader sharp-tongued and ill-tempered. This type of counter evaluation or inaccurate self-perception by the leader often reduces a leader's effectiveness.

Confidence.   Leaders differ significantly in the personal confidence which they have in their ability to lead others. Leaders who lack confidence would have difficulty in diagnosing different situations and coping adequately with these situations. These difficulties result in leaders failing to perform certain functions that could lead to desirable results. For example, a leader with little self-confidence will often assume that followers cannot adequately perform their job tasks. This may lead to the leader exercising close supervision over subordinates. The closeness of supervision may prove disruptive because of the type of job being completed, the personality and type of personnel in the work group, and the size of the work group.

A lack of confidence could also result in the leader making decisions which are not adequate or are viewed as being harmful by the group members. In effect, the confidence of a leader is related to some extent to the risk-taking propensities of the leader. The leader that lacks confidence makes decisions in many instances that compromise the followers' morale, rewards, and status ranking among other groups.

---

[25] In Chapter 11, sensitivity training will be discussed. One of the purported advantages of sensitivity training is that it improves the self-awareness of participants.

Ability to Communicate. Every leader must be able to communicate objectives to followers. The leader who fails to communicate with followers may become ineffective as an influencer of others. This results because failing to communicate leads to an inability to coordinate necessary follower activities.

In Table 9–3 the integrative model is used to describe Dan Pride

TABLE 9–3

The Integrative Model and Dan Pride

Leader's Characteristics (background and experience)	Leader's Qualities	Leader's Ability to Influence	Leader's Perceptions
a. 23 years old	a. Shy—but is also impressive when he begins to communicate	a. Performance of group will be assessed every three months by MBO review	a. Perceives that his lack of technical knowledge could be a drawback
b. College graduate	b. Has confidence and ability to influence others	b. Check of group absenteeism and turnover will be continually made	b. Perceives group's attitudes toward college graduates as being cautious
c. Born in Chicago	c. Thinks that he is aggressive with others		c. Perceives the group as being interested in quality at any cost
d. Worked as trainee in manufacturing plant during summers			

who was used to illustrate condition 5 in the Fiedler model. The description of various factors provides a picture of him as a leader.

The emphasis of the authors' model is on leaders' ability to diagnose themselves and their total leadership environment. Perhaps what we are suggesting is that leadership training programs should stress diagnostic and adaptability skill learning. It should not be concluded that managers can be easily trained to accurately diagnose work situations and to develop appropriate leadership abilities. This type of training difficulty is summed up by Fiedler in the following manner:

> Industrial psychologists and personnel men typically view the executive's position as fixed and immutable and the individual as highly plastic and trainable. When we think of improving leadership performance, we generally think first of training the leader. Yet, we know all too well from our experience with psychotherapy, our attempts to rehabilitate prison inmates, drug addicts or juvenile delinquents—not to mention our diffi-

culties with rearing our own progeny—that our ability to change personality has its limitations.[26]

If leaders are to become diagnostically skilled and flexible to the degree of changing their leadership style, depending upon the circumstances at hand, patience is essential. The organization must be willing to plan, and fund development programs which are time-consuming. The model approach we are suggesting is not applicable in those instances where changing the situation is less costly than changing the leader.

SUMMARY

Inevitably, organizations require leaders to utilize the abilities of their followers so that goals may be accomplished. Although an organization may have the necessary requisites for the attainment of goals, if it does not have a leadership team that can influence followers, the probability is high that the organization will not survive in the long run. Consequently, it is obvious that effective leadership is the lifeblood of organizational survival.

The Classical and Behavioral Schools of management have recognized the importance of leadership in organizations. This fact is disclosed by the extensive research and literature devoted to the what, why, and how of leadership. The efforts of behavioralists have resulted in numerous theories of leadership. The theories are based on concepts of influence, power and authority. To highlight the crux of these theories, the French and Raven analysis was employed in this chapter because it focuses upon the relationship between organizational factors (for example, managerial hierarchy) and individual characteristics.

After establishing the fact that influence is the crux of leadership, a number of behavioral leadership theories were presented. The theories presented provide the reader with an indication of (1) the differences of opinion among behavioralists, (2) the different methodologies employed to study leadership, (3) the similarities between various theories, and (4) the fact that increasing research on the situational or contingency approach seems to be the contemporary thrust.

The final tone of the chapter offers the premise that there is no "one best way" to lead. It is felt that more emphasis should be given the situational approach. The key to this approach seems to be the diagnostic skill of the leader. That is, leaders who can ascertain the personality of followers, their own behavioral patterns, and understand organizational requirements are viewed as having a better chance of succeeding in influencing their subordinates.

---

[26] Fiedler, *Leadership Effectiveness*, p. 247.

DISCUSSION AND REVIEW QUESTIONS

1. What appears to be the trend in the Behavioral School for conducting research on leadership behavior?
2. How could the incremental influence concept of Katz and Kahn be related to the trait theory of leadership?
3. What are some of the factors about motivation that a leader should know?
4. Why should leaders be aware of their impact on followers?
5. What are the similarities and differences found when Likert's approach to leadership is compared to the Ohio State theory of leadership?
6. What are some of the terms used in this chapter that are nearly synonymous with democratic leadership and autocratic leadership? Are there any terms that mean exactly the same thing?
7. Why is the diagnostic skill of the leader so vital to the situational approach to leadership?
8. Which of the personal-behavioral approaches is most similar to the situational theory of leadership? Why have you selected this approach?
9. Is it feasible to alter the job so that a particular type of leader will be more effective? Discuss an actual or hypothetical situation where it would be best to alter the job to suit the leader.
10. Explain how the three situational dimensions discussed by Fiedler can be modified in an organization.

ADDITIONAL REFERENCES

Bartol, K. M., "Male versus Female Leaders: The Effect of Leader Need for Dominance on Follower Satisfaction," *Academy of Management Journal* 17 (1974): 209–21.

Bowers, D. G., and Seashore, S. "Predicting Organizational Effectiveness with a Four-Factor Theory of Leadership," *Administrative Science Quarterly* 11 (1966): 238–63.

Campbell, J. P., Dunnette, M. D., Lawler, E. E., III, and Weick, K. E., Jr. *Managerial Behavior, Performance, and Effectiveness.* New York: McGraw-Hill Book Co., 1970.

Cartwright, D. "Power: A Neglected Variable in Social Psychology," in W. G. Bennis, K. D. Benne, and R. Chin, eds., *The Planning of Change.* New York: Holt, Rinehart, and Winston, Inc., 1966.

Fiedler, F. "Engineer the Job to Fit the Manager," *Harvard Business Review* 43 (1965): 115–22.

Hill, W. "Leadership Style: Rigid or Flexible?" *Organizational Behavior and Human Performance* 9 (February 1973): 35–47.

House, R. J. "A Path Goal Theory of Leader Effectiveness," *Administrative Science Quarterly* 16 (September 1971): 321–39.

Hunt, J. G. "Breakthrough in Leadership Research," *Personnel Administration* 30 (1967): 38–44.

Jaques, E. *Measurement of Responsibility.* London: Tavistock Publications 1956.

Jay, A. *Management and Machiavelli.* New York: Holt, Rinehart, & Winston, Inc., 1967.

Maslow, A. H. *Eupsychian Management.* Homewood, Ill.: Richard D. Irwin, Inc. and The Dorsey Press, 1965.

Osborn, R. N., and Hunt, J. G. "An Empirical Investigation of Lateral and Vertical Leadership at Two Organizational Levels," *Journal of Business Research* 2 (1974): 209–21.

Powell, R. M. and Schlacter, J. L. "Participative Management: A Panacea?" *Academy of Management Journal* 14 (1971): 165–73.

Reddin, W. J. *Managerial Effectiveness.* New York: McGraw-Hill Book Co., 1970.

Sales, S. "Supervisory Style and Productivity: Review and Theory," *Personnel Psychology,* 19 (1966): 275–86.

Sayles, L. *Managerial Behavior.* New York: McGraw-Hill Book Co., 1964.

Smith, P. B., Moscow, D., Berger, M., and Cooper, C. "Relationships between Managers and Their Work Associates," *Administrative Science Quarterly,* 14 (1969): 338–45.

Stogdill, R. M. *Handbook of Leadership.* New York: The Free Press, 1974.

PRACTICAL EXERCISES

Practical Exercise I

The New Accounting Unit Leader

Dabney Federated Stores, Incorporated is one of the leading department store chains in the Southwest. The company is known for its quality merchandise and efficient service. The headquarters and general offices of the company are located in the main store in Dallas, Texas. The president of the company is Ralph Simpson and the general manager is Tony Rice. Recently, the chief accountant, Nick Maria, retired, and this created a vacancy in this crucial position. Many people believe that the chief accountant is the second most prestigious and powerful person in the company.

Nick Maria had a reputation throughout the company as being an easygoing and competent accountant. He expected his subordinates to get their jobs done without being closely supervised. He wanted his subordinates to work together and know their jobs. Presently, the accounting office has nine older women, three older men, four younger women, and three younger men. All of the accounting personnel perform some type of accounting duty, which results in the preparation of reports which were used by the chief accountant in briefing Ralph Simpson and Tony Rice.

Two months ago, Joan Wesley was selected as the replacement for Nick Maria. Joan came to Dabney from the Corpon Federated Stores Company, where she was assistant director of accounting for the past seven years. She has a B.S. and an M.S. in accounting from a leading university and was thought to be the right person for the job.

The first two months Joan was on the job she had a number of frustrating experiences. She felt that these experiences had resulted in lower efficiency in her unit. Some of the experiences that she continually thought about are listed below:

1. Joan had to have cost data for the preparation of the two reports to be submitted to Ralph Simpson and Tony Rice. She requested the data from two of the younger women who asked, "What is the big rush about?" This puzzled Joan since she believed that as the chief accountant

235

she had the right to ask for, and receive, any information she wanted.

2. Joan submitted a report to Tony Rice that had a number of errors because of faulty information one of the older men had provided. Joan was embarrassed by this and reprimanded the man at his desk in front of three other accounting department personnel.

3. One of the younger girls needed some time off during the work day to visit a lawyer. Joan discussed this with the girl and concluded that if she let the girl off, others would request time off. The girl became disgusted and a screaming bout between her and Joan ensued.

These problems and others significantly affected Joan. She wondered what she had done wrong and how she could become a more effective leader of the accounting group in the months ahead.

Questions for Analysis:

1. What were the differences in leadership style used by Nick Maria and Joan Wesley?
2. As a leader, what type of influence is Joan attempting to utilize?
3. What can Joan do in the future as a leader to help reduce the frustration which she is now facing in her job?
4. Analyze the situation using Fiedler's model? What type of LPC (high or low) is best suited for this exercise? Is Joan this type of leader? What variables can be modified to improve the unit's effectiveness?

Practical Exercise II

The Troubled Hospital Superintendent

Tyler Medical Center consisted of four buildings, had 475 patient beds, and 1,850 employees. It was known in Illinois as a quality medical institution and a good place for medical researchers and interns to work. The superintendent of the hospital was Don Gloversmen. The Board of Trustees of the hospital relied heavily upon the judgment of the superintendent regarding the administration of the hospital.

Tyler was organized around six functionally defined areas. Each area had a head who reported to Don. The areas were:

1. Medical Services
2. Nursing Services
3. Accounting Services
4. Dietary Services
5. Plant and Housekeeping Services
6. Pharmaceutical Services

Don, as superintendent, had to handle complaints and requests from administrators in each of the areas. He was the only person in the hospital who had legitimate power to make decisions concerning administrative matters. Two areas that were extremely difficult to work with were the Medical Services and Nursing Services. Don analyzed each of the personnel components of these units in the following manner:

Medical Services—Medical doctors and laboratory technicians. Included are such individuals as physician in charge of neurology, physician in charge of pediatrics, director of surgery, director of clinical laboratories, and director of anesthesiology. The medical doctors were largely male, while the technicians were split about even between male and female.

Nursing Services—Primarily females who were in charge of providing nursing care at bedside, staffing operating rooms, delivery rooms, and nurseries. The nursing group and staff included approximately 975 employees.

Don communicated in most instances with the administrators in these two service areas. He found that his leadership style of being frank, open, and direct worked better with the Medical Services administrators than with the Nursing Services administrators. He wanted to be the best superintendent the hospital ever had, but found that his approach of being the same kind of leader for all people he worked with was not effective.

Don reached the conclusion that he was not effective in his relationship with the nursing administrators. They seemed to be hostile toward him and the other functional areas, especially the Medical Service area. In addition, a number of patients had complained about rudeness displayed by the nurses. The strain in his relationship with Nursing Services always seemed to peak at the monthly meeting of nursing administrators. Each month the 42 nursing supervisors who had authority and responsibility for the Nursing Services personnel met with Don. In these sessions, Don attempted to ascertain how the nursing area was performing. The nursing administrators complained that no standards for assessing performance were used to determine effectiveness. They also complained because they were being watched too closely while the Medical Services area never had discussions with the superintendent about performance.

After last month's disruptive and volatile meeting, Don decided to look at the problem. He assumed that there might be a serious flaw in his leadership ability. He also thought about what he read about the situational or contingency approach to leadership.

Questions for Analysis:

1. What are some of the causes of Don's problem with the nursing administrators?

2. As a superintendent in Tyler Medical Center, would it be necessary to consider situational or contingency leadership approaches? Why?

3. What kind of modification in the three situational dimensions—leader-member relations, task structure, and position power—could aid Don in improving his relationship with Nursing Services?

10 Organizational Design

INTRODUCTION

One of the major limitations of classical organization theory is that many of the contentions are offered in the form of broad generalizations. These sweeping statements involving the principles of organization are grounded upon deductive reasoning and personal observations. They also fail to consider the theory and research findings offered by the Behavioral School. This is largely the result of the fact that many of the classical concepts were developed years before behavioral scientists began to analyze organizational design.

The behavioral approach to organizational design does not have what can be considered a set of principles such as the classical approach. Consequently, the behavioral critique of classical organization design will be centered upon four major classical management principles—division of labor, unity of command, line and staff, and span of control. The philosophical cornerstone of the behavioral approach to organization design is

Douglas McGregor's Theory Y, the assumptions of which are:

1. *Employees do not inherently dislike work.* The exercise of physical and mental effort on the job is a natural human phenomenon.
2. *Employees do not want to be rigidly controlled and threatened with punishment.* If employees are committed to specific objectives, they will exercise self-control in attempting to attain these objectives.
3. *Employees under proper conditions do not seek to avoid responsi-*

bility. If the organizational atmosphere and working conditions are functioning effectively, employees will seek responsibility.
4. *Employees desire security but also want to satisfy social, esteem, and self-actualization needs.* In motivating employees the security factor is important but it is not the only consideration. The whole person must be considered and this means the employees' creativity, imagination, and intellectual potentialities must be considered.[1]

The Theory Y assumptions set the stage for the behavioral approach to organizational design. The manager with a Theory Y orientation, as compared to a Theory X, would probably design jobs so that employees could achieve some of the gratification desired. The design effort would focus on building into the job and the total organization challenging work, autonomy, and the opportunity for employees to use a full range of skills.

DIVISION-OF-LABOR CRITIQUE

The classicists emphasized the economic gains to be realized through specialization (Chapter 4). Unlike the classicists, the behavioralists emphasize noneconomic factors which contribute to the eventual negative returns to continued division of labor. If a job is broken down into fewer and fewer operations for an employee, eventually boredom, monotony, dissatisfaction, or some combination of these, and other negative factors will set in. Thus, lower productivity and poor overall efficiency will eventually be the rule rather than the exception. Consequently, many behavioral critiques of excessive division of work have centered upon the depersonalization of the job which may lead to psychological alienation of many workers toward their job and the organization.

One study which supports the alienation premise is that of Walker and Guest.[2] These researchers were concerned with the social and psychological problems associated with mass production jobs in an automobile assembly plant. They found that many workers disliked numerous aspects of their jobs. It was determined that mechanical pacing, repetitiveness of operations, and a lack of a sense of accomplishment were job factors which employees disliked. These and other findings are summarized in Table 10–1.

Walker and Guest outlined some of the problem areas identified by behavioralists when discussing division of labor. They found that a

---

[1] The reader will recall the discussion of Theory X in Chapter 4. For further information see Douglas McGregor, *The Human Side of Enterprise* (New York: McGraw-Hill Book Co., pp. 33–57.

[2] Charles R. Walker and Robert H. Guest, *The Man on the Assembly Line* (Cambridge, Mass.: Harvard University Press, 1952).

TABLE 10-1

Employee Interest and Job Variety

Number of Operations Performed	Number Reporting Work as Very or Fairly Interesting	Number Reporting Work as Not Very or Not at All Interesting	Total Employees
1	19	38	57
2-5	28	36	64
5 or more	41	18	59
Total	88	92	180

Source: Charles R. Walker and Robert H. Guest, *The Man on the Assembly Line* (Cambridge: Harvard University Press, 1952), p. 54.

majority of the automobile workers disliked certain features of their jobs. The mechanical pacing of the line appeared to be disliked the most. Pacing was viewed as a control over the workers. They were not able to slow the line, and this eventually led to much frustration and boredom.

Behavioral Suggestions for Overcoming the Psychological Problems of Division of Labor

The Behavioral School has developed a number of methods for minimizing worker alienation. Some of the most popular behavioral suggestions are covered in this section.

Job Enlargement. The behavioral literature contains many different job enlargement strategies. These strategies focus upon the opposite of dividing work—they are a form of despecialization or increasing the number of tasks which an employee performs. Although, in many instances, an enlarged job requires a longer training period, it is assumed that satisfaction of the worker increases because boredom is reduced. The implication, of course, is that the job enlargement will lead to more productivity and improved overall efficiency.

To support their contentions concerning job enlargement, the behavioralists cite such studies as the often-quoted I.B.M. findings.[3] A parts manufacturing unit of the Endicott plant of I.B.M. reorganized a number of jobs in an attempt to improve worker morale. The job of machine operator after the reorganization included setting up the job, sharpening tools, and inspecting the work, in addition to operating the equipment. The findings of the I.B.M. study suggest that the job enlargement strategy increased worker morale, lowered production costs, increased the interests of employees, as well as improving the quality of output.

---

[3] C. R. Walker, "The Problem of the Repetitive Job," *Harvard Business Review*, vol. 28 (May 1950), pp. 54-58.

Another study which involves the effects of job enlargement is the Maytag Company study.[4] It was concerned with changing the job design on a mass-production assembly line. During different phases of the study, the job was changed. The different phases were as follows:

Phase I: Six operators assembled a washing machine pump on a conveyor line.

Phase II: The assembling of the pump was a four-person operation.

Phase III: The work previously done on the conveyor line was done at four individual workbenches.

Throughout each of these changes, the time required to assemble the pump decreased. The least time-consuming design for assembling involved the individual workbenches. This suggests that reducing assembly-line delays and enlarging the job may increase productivity in some instances.

The job enlargement strategy and research support presented are not to be viewed as a solution for all the ills of excessive division of work. It is only offered as a behaviorally oriented program to offset some of the negative factors associated with job specialization. Of course, too much job enlargement may be as disruptive to the organization as too much specialization.

Job Rotation.   Another strategy to reduce employees' alienation toward performing a smaller number of tasks is referred to as job rotation. In some positions, it is feasible to rotate an individual from one job assignment to another. The person switches jobs periodically so that boredom and disinterest are hopefully reduced. Job rotation provides more flexibility to management because jobs do not have to be redesigned, as is the case with job enlargement. Also it allows management to select the most opportune time to rotate a person.

Companies such as Western Electric, Ford, Bethlehem Steel, and TRW Systems utilize job rotation programs for new college graduates. The new trainee is moved from unit to unit so that an overview and appreciation of the total company are acquired. The rotation practice of recent college recruits is not designed to reduce alienation but is supposed to create more enthusiasm and understanding.

Participation Approaches.   In many organizations, it may be possible to provide decision-making opportunities to employees at lower levels in the organization. In classical theory, authority for decision making is centered primarily among top-level executives; but, the participation concept offered by behavioralists redistributes some of the decision-making authority throughout the organization. The rationale behind the redistribution of authority is that people frequently feel more inclined to accept decisions which they have helped to make.

---

[4] M. D. Kilbridge, "Reduced Costs through Job Enlargement: A Case," *The Journal of Business,* vol. 33 (October 1960), pp. 357–62.

One example of a participation approach is the "multiple management" program at McCormick and Company.[5] This plan involves allowing junior executives to form what is called a junior board of directors. The junior board is used as a monitoring group for decisions made by the senior board of directors and top-level executives and makes decisions which supplement the top-level decisions.

Another example of worker participation in the decision-making process is the approach utilized at the Glacier Metal Company of Great Britain.[6] The approach is referred to as a "consultative hierarchy." The approach was specifically designed for three reasons: (1) to provide for worker representation in making operating and general policy decisions; (2) to improve communications between workers and management; and (3) to provide workers with a feeling of involvement in the consultative hierarchy.[7]

The consultative hierarchy is composed of a network of committees representing all interest groups and levels of personnel in the company. The committees make decisions concerning job design, promotion, salary, retirement plans, and appeals procedures, among other things.

Many other participation methods are suggested by the behavioralists. The theme of most of the others (as is the case in the McCormick and Glacier examples) is that involvement through participation may lead to more positive commitments by the worker to company objectives, even in situations where division of labor is intense.

There is some criticism of participation techniques among managers themselves. Some believe that to invite participation is to give up "managerial rights" and to abdicate your responsibility to manage subordinates. There are also those who question whether participative decisions are better than nonparticipative decisions. These criticisms suggest the need for much more research on the cost and benefits of participative management.

UNITY-OF-COMMAND CRITIQUE

In viewing organizational relationships realistically, it is easy to understand why it is difficult to rigidly adhere to the unity-of-command principle. Even one of the most identified classical theorists, Henri Fayol, recognized the need to sometimes bypass the strict chain of command and suggested an organizational arrangement which enabled individuals

---

[5] Charles P. McCormick, *Multiple Management* (New York: Harper & Row, 1938).

[6] See E. Jaques, *The Changing Culture of a Factory* (London: Tavistock Publications, Ltd., 1951); E. Jaques, *Equitable Payment* (London: William Heinemann, Ltd., 1961); and E. Jaques, *Measurement of Responsibility* (London: Tavistock Publications, Ltd., Cambridge, Mass.: Harvard University Press, 1956).

[7] Jaques, *Changing Culture*.

to bypass the command hierarchy. His suggestion is referred to in Chapter 4, as the "Fayol Bridge."

The "Fayol Bridge" and the "Functional Foremanship" concept of Taylor can be viewed not as behavioral examples which disprove the unity-of-command principle, but as examples from classical theory which show that rigid unity-of-command practices are not generally found in organizations. It is more realistic to state that, typically, subordinates will have one superior who is most dominant in influencing their behavior. The argument of the behavioralists concerning unity of command does not revolve around the reasonableness of the concept but, instead, is centered upon the practicalities of everyday organizational life.

The unity-of-command issue is highlighted in different kinds of work. Imagine a head nurse in a hospital who takes orders from three different doctors or an accountant who must answer questions and carry out directives issued by three different partners in a CPA firm. In each case the subordinate is faced with deciding who will be listened to the most. This dilemma can certainly lead to frustration and confusion. If you had to respond to three different instructors in a management course you would have firsthand experience of a situation that violated the unity-of-command principle.

LINE-AND-STAFF CRITIQUE

It is implied in classical organization theory that the line-and-staff arrangement offers the best potential for growth, profitability, and attainment of overall organizational objectives. The difficulty is not what is discussed by the classical theorists, but how it is presented, and what is missing. In presenting the typical classical line-and-staff discussion, a manufacturing firm is normally utilized to provide insight to the reader. The operations of a manufacturing organization can be separated into activities which relate directly to the achievement of objectives (line) and activities which relate indirectly to the attainment of objectives (staff). Thus, the line-and-staff distinction is orderly. This orderly distinction, however, is more difficult to establish for nonmanufacturing and nonbusiness organizations.

It must be made clear that not only have classical theorists contributed to the confusion in presenting an understandable interpretation of line and staff, but so have the behavioralists. Presentations by both classical theorists and behavioralists concerning line-and-staff design have been discussed in terms of (1) attainment of objectives; (2) authority relationships (for example, line has authority, while staff has little or no authority); or (3) functions.[8]

---

[8] Alan C. Filley and Robert J. House, *Managerial Process and Organizational Behavior* (Glenview, Ill.: Scott, Foresman and Co., 1969), p. 260.

The main focus of the behavioralists has been directed toward conflict and resolution of conflict involving line-and-staff personnel. The behavioralists point out that line-and-staff personnel are different in personal characteristics and this may aggravate the relationships between line and staff.[9] One comparison between the backgrounds of line-and-staff personnel suggests that staff are generally younger, are more educated, and come from different social backgrounds than the line.[10]

Another line-and-staff comparative analysis is the "cosmopolitan" and "local" classification of Gouldner.[11] The professional is described as a "cosmo" and is assumed to be less loyal to the employing organization and more committed to the specialized skills of the profession (for example, accountant, nurse, operations researcher, industrial engineer). The line manager can be compared to the "local" and is assumed to have greater company loyalty and more concern for general knowledge rather than specific knowledge.

Behavioralists study such phenomena as the reasons for line-staff conflict, methods which can minimize conflict so that it does not disrupt operations, and personality and background differences of line-and-staff personnel. Thus, the emphasis is on the human element and not structural variables associated with line and staff. If the line-and-staff approach to organization is to be effective, understanding the mechanics involved is not worth much without knowledge about line-and-staff problems and personnel. The classical approach without interpreting necessary behavioral problems such as conflict is incomplete as is the behavioral approach without coping with the logic and mechanics of line-and-staff structure offered by the classical theorists.

SPAN-OF-CONTROL CRITIQUE

The behavioralists contend that the classicists' approach to span of control is too artificial in that they often state in specific quantitative terms the "ideal" ratio of subordinates to a superior. They believe that it is not realistic to utilize formulas and opinions concerning what managers' spans of control should be if they are located at particular levels in the organizational hierarchy. A better approach than quantifying potential relationships according to behavioralists is to consider people, the environment, and the influence of various spans of control upon the overall organization structure and performance.

---

[9] M. Dalton, "Changing Line-Staff Relations," *Personnel Administration,* vol. 28 (March–April 1966), pp. 3–5.

[10] Ibid.

[11] A. W. Gouldner, "Cosmopolitans and Locals: Toward an Analysis of Social Roles —I and II," *Administrative Science Quarterly,* vol. 2 (September 1957), pp. 281–306.

The behavioralists believe that small spans of control recommended by classical theorists foster close supervision. If an organization has narrow spans of control, it typically has more levels of supervision and takes on a distinct tall pyramidal appearance. For example, assume that a company has 48 nonmanagers and the span of control is 8. There would be six supervisors directing the workers and two senior supervisors directing three supervisors each. This type of structure is illustrated in Figure 10–1 where there are three levels of management: president, senior supervisor, and supervisor.

FIGURE 10–1

Narrow Span of Control

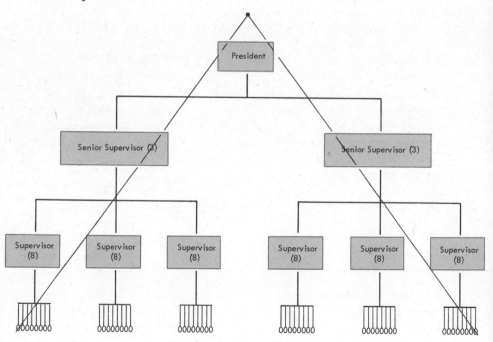

If the same number of workers (48) were supervised by two superiors, an organization with only two managerial levels could be structured. The organizational design resulting from widening the span of control to 24 is presented in Figure 10–2. By increasing the span of control from eight to twenty-four, one level of management and six managerial positions were eliminated from the organization.

The critique of the behavioralists does not center on organization chart presentations (that is, Figures 10–1 and 10–2) but on the results of narrow spans of control. They suggest that a narrow span of control (Figure 10–1) allows managers to exercise close supervision because of the smaller number of subordinates reporting directly to them. The narrow

FIGURE 10–2

Wide Span of Control

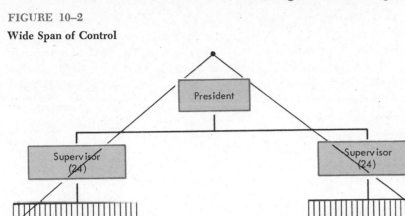

span of control leads to the bureaucratic structure which is presented as a tall pyramid. Furthermore, it is the behavioralists' contention that the wider span forces management to utilize more general supervision.

Individual managerial abilities also must be studied before stating that a span of control should be some specific number. Such characteristics as the personality of the manager, the manager's attitudes toward delegating authority to subordinates, the manager's willingness to utilize staff assistance, and the manager's experience are some of the critical areas of concern. The behavioralists are also very concerned about various characteristics of subordinates. The attitudes, personalities, experience, training, and abilities of the subordinates influence the choice of an effective span of control.

The type and nature of the work to be performed also have some bearing on developing spans of control. If the work is routine in nature and involves little uncertainty in reaching decisions, only minor attention of the manager may be required.[12] This would enable the utilization of a wide span of control. At the other extreme would be jobs that are nonroutine in nature and decision making is often concerned with ill-defined problems. This type of work may necessitate a narrower span of control so that the manager can oversee the work.

The need to coordinate the activities of subordinates in performing their work should also be considered. If the work of one person or one group of workers has a significant influence on other persons or groups, the span of control must be narrower. For example, in food-processing operations, it may be necessary to coordinate the activities of six different groups on an automated line. Each station on the line, other than the first, is dependent upon the work performed at the previous stations:

[12] Justin G. Longenecker, *Principles of Management and Organizational Behavior* (Columbus, Ohio: Charles E. Merrill Co., 1969), p. 209.

In this case it is important for the manager to be able to coordinate the work of each station.

Clearly, the issue of span of control is still being debated by advocates of narrow and wide spans. There appears to be a limit for each job and for each manager. The problem today is similar to the one discovered by the classicists—finding what this limit is.

DECENTRALIZATION

The term decentralization has often been associated with the Behavioral School. It is placed into a behavioral context because such terms as "democratic," "less authoritarian," and "more autonomy" are used when decentralization examples are cited. Instead of joining the argument about whether decentralization is a classical or behavioral phenomenon, the present authors have decided to present only some of the behaviorally oriented ideas being espoused by advocates of decentralization.

Structure

There are basically two methods of decentralizing an organization structure. One is leaving the decentralized units as integral divisions. This is the approach followed by General Motors, the integral and viable divisions being Buick, Oldsmobile, Chevrolet, Pontiac, Cadillac, Allison, and Frigidaire. The other is to decentralize the organization by use of a subsidiary or affiliate company arrangement. The most publicized examples of this decentralized arrangement are the Standard Oil Companies. Each company has its own president and board of directors. Basically, each Standard Oil company is operating autonomously.

In both the divisional and subsidiary arrangements, the major organizational unit develops, manufactures, and distributes its own products; purchases its own materials; recruits, selects, trains, and develops its own group of employees; and purchases its own equipment. The principal point is that appropriate authority is pushed further down into the divisional units and subsidiaries so that the various manufacturing, motivational, purchasing, and distribution problems can be resolved on a decentralized basis.

The People Factor

Since the Behavioral School expends significant effort on learning how people respond to various organizational phenomena, it is best to review some of the consequences of decentralized operations on managers. If this is the main focus, then it would be appropriate to study managerial decentralization as a concept which involves the manager's assigned formal authority and freedom to make decisions. In a simplistic sense, an organizational structure is more decentralized than a typical classical organizational structure if:

1. Decisions are made at lower levels in the management hierarchy.
2. There are fewer controls and checks on decisions made by managers.

These two guidelines are only used as criteria for evaluating or comparing organizations on a centralization-decentralization scale. That is, if two organizations are contrasted and it is found that in one company the decisions concerning production, personnel, and financial matters involving expenditures of $100,000 or more are being made at the very top level of the firm, but, in the second company, it is found that similar decisions are being made at the middle level of the managerial hierarchy, it could be assumed that on the basis of the decisions analyzed, the second firm has a more decentralized organizational design.

Why Decentralization?

There is no universal agreement within the Behavioral School about why it is better to decentralize. The following items are only partially agreed upon by the many different scholars analyzing the decentralization approach. They may or may not be true depending upon such factors as the size of the firm, desire for autonomy of employees, the availability of competent managers, government regulations, and other important factors.

First, advocates assume that decentralization encourages the development of managers. The main point is that as decision-making authority is pushed down in the organization, managers must adapt and prove themselves to advance in the company. That is, managers must become generalists who know something about each factor in the decentralized arrangement.

Second, because managers in a decentralized structure often have to adapt and deal with difficult decisions, they are assumed to be excellently trained for promotions into positions of greater authority and responsibility. Managers can be readily compared with their peers on the basis of actual decision-making performance. In effect, the decentralized arrangement leads to a more equitable performance appraisal program. This can lead to a more satisfied group of managers because they perceive themselves as being evaluated on the basis of results not personalities. It should be remembered, however, that developing performance criteria for managers is an extremely difficult task.

Third, the decentralized arrangement leads to a competitive climate within the organization. The managers are motivated to contribute in this competitive atmosphere since they are being compared with their peers on various performance measures.

Finally, in the decentralized pattern, managers are able to exercise more autonomy and this satisfies their desire to participate in problem solving. This freedom is assumed to lead to managerial creativity, ingenuity, and action that contributes to the growth and development of the firm and the managers.

These are only four of the factors associated with the virtues of decentralization. They are only cited as examples of some of the often-mentioned advantages of decentralized operations. These advantages do not come free of costs. Certainly, the behavioralists are aware that organizational and people costs may have to be incurred if a firm shifts its organizational pattern from a more centralized arrangement to a decentralized design. Some of the *costs* are:

1. Managers must be trained to handle decision making, and this may require expensive formal training programs.
2. Since many managers have worked in centralized organizations, it is very uncomfortable for them to delegate authority in a more decentralized arrangement. These old attitudes are difficult to alter and often lead to resistance and disruptive conflict.
3. To alter accounting and performance appraisal systems so they are compatible with the decentralized arrangement is costly. Administrative costs are incurred because new or altered accounting and performance systems must be tested, implemented, and evaluated.

These are, of course, only some of the costs that the Behavioral School considers when discussing and analyzing the pros and cons of decentralizing. Like most managerial concepts, there is definitely no clear-cut answer about whether decentralization is better or worse for an organization. It would appear that considering each organizational factor (for example, manpower, size, and products) is a prerequisite for reaching design decisions concerning decentralization.

It should now be obvious that centralization and decentralization are the opposite ends of a continuum. The effort of behavioral design experts does not focus upon whether one is good or one is bad because neither is an ideal. The real effort of research and interest is on how much centralization and how much decentralization is most suitable for a company with a certain type of personnel, product line, technology, size, and various locations.

ALTERNATIVES TO CLASSICAL
ORGANIZATIONAL DESIGN

The classical approach is succinctly presented in Figure 10–3. Examples of behavioral type designs are presented in Figure 10–4. Both

FIGURE 10–3

The Pyramid—Classical Design

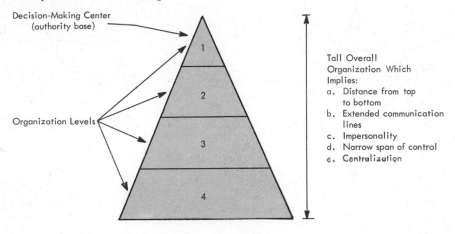

of these figures attempt to capture the main flavor of the two opposing design philosophies and sets of assumptions. Basically, they show that the classicists are identified with the taller, many-layered structure and the behavioralists with the flatter, fewer-layered, and more decentralized structure.

Recently, there has been an emphasis on what is called the *contingency view of organizations*. The classical ideas and the behavioral modifications are not rejected, but they are viewed as being incomplete and not suited for all organizations. Lawrence and Lorsch state the sense of the contingency view as follows:

> During the past few years there has been evident a new trend in the study of organizational phenomena. Underlying this new approach is the idea that the internal functioning of organizations must be consistent with the demands of the organization task, technology, external environment, and the needs of its members if the organization is to be effective. Rather than searching for the panacea of the one best way to organize under all conditions, investigators have more and more tended to examine the functioning of organizations in relation to the needs of their particular members and the external pressures facing them.[13]

This passage suggests that in some cases the pyramid or the bell or the pancake design may be the most effective. Instead of talking about the one best design, the contingency view focuses on what is best for a particular unit or organization that has a particular technology, group of

[13] Jay W. Lorsch and Paul R. Lawrence, eds. *Studies in Organization Design* (Homewood, Ill.: Richard D. Irwin, Inc., 1970), p. 14.

FIGURE 10-4

Behavioral Modifications of the Classical Pyramid

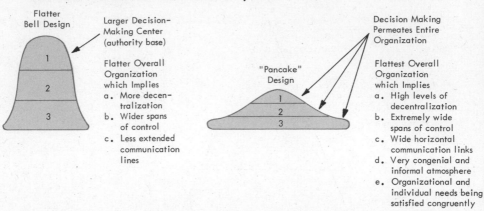

employees, and environment. The relationships and interactions of these kinds of variables are the focus of contingency analyses of organizational design.

STUDIES CONCERNING ORGANIZATIONAL DESIGN

The classical approach, the behavioral approach, and the new contingency approaches to designing an organization continue to remain main topics of debate and controversy. Research concerning organizational design is not conclusive enough today to support any specific organizational design strategy. In fact, the number of research studies involving organization structure *per se* is limited.

There are three popular approaches to the study of organizational designs.[15] These approaches can be applied to the study of the principles of classical theory such as division of labor, span of control, line and staff distinction, and unity of command. The three approaches are as follows:

1. The researcher attempts to relate the behavior of individuals to such phenomena as organization structure and various applications of the principles.
2. The researcher attempts to explain the features of organizational structures and the principles of organizational theory.
3. The researcher conducts comparative research which is concerned

---

[14] Henry L. Tosi and W. Clay Hamner, *Organizational Behavior and Management: A Contingency Approach* (Chicago: St. Clair Press, 1974).

[15] William Scott, "Field Methods in the Study of Organizations," in James March, ed., *Handbook of Organizations* (Chicago: Rand McNally, 1965), pp. 261–304.

with the similarities, dissimilarities and consequences of various organization structures and approaches to designing organizations.

Each of the three research approaches is valuable in providing insights into organizational design from a classical and a behavioral viewpoint. Three studies are presented in this section which have investigated the impact of organizational structure upon morale, job satisfaction, and organizational success.

The Sears, Roebuck Study

Worthy studied the morale of over 100,000 employees at Sears, Roebuck and Company during a 12-year period.[16] He was concerned with determining the morale of Sear's employees with respect to six major factors of their work environment: (1) the company in general, (2) the local organization, (3) the local management, (4) immediate supervision, (5) fellow employees, and (6) job and working conditions.

The results of Worthy's research are basically the following:

1. The more complex the organizational structure, the greater the probability that poor management-employee relationships will result.
2. Dividing work into fewer and fewer units and dividing departments into subdepartments often results in low output and low morale. Those groups which contribute consistently to the organization (for example, salesmen) and display the highest morale are those who complete entire tasks.
3. Overfunctionalization requires close and constant supervision at the work level to maintain production. A consequence of closely supervising employees is rigid control systems which negatively affect morale and productivity.
4. Overfunctionalization does not allow personnel to operate except in closest coordination with others, and the system is often so complex that this coordination cannot occur spontaneously.
5. The overly complex, overly functionalized organizational structure typically requires the type of leader who uses pressure as a supervisory device.

Next, Worthy compared and contrasted various unit structures at Sears. The implication of his analysis is that organizations with fewer levels and wider spans of control yield a less complex organizational system. The wide span of control literally forces management to delegate authority. In addition to delegation, the flattening technique (widening span of control) requires a better trained management team, shortens

[16] James C. Worthy, "Organizational Structure and Employee Morale," *American Sociological Review*, vol. 15 (April 1950), pp. 169–79.

FIGURE 10–5

The Pyramid versus the Flat System

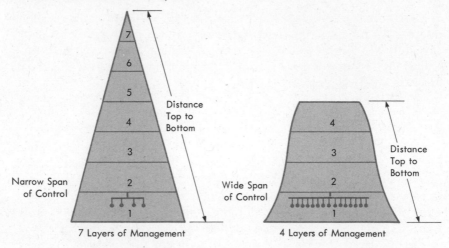

7 Layers of Management   4 Layers of Management

communication networks, and shortens the administrative distance between the levels of management. Figure 10–5 highlights the analysis of
Worthy. According to Worthy, the executives at Sears found that the
flatter organization structure with maximum decentralization develops
self-reliance, initiative, and decision-making abilities.

Worthy's conclusions imply that the flatter structure is the best way
to design an organization. This type of universal assumption is what
contingency design approaches attempt to temper. What is good for
Sears may not be suited for J. C. Penney or Montgomery Ward or
Macys. The contingency proponents would recommend studying the
people, environment, technology, size, and other variables before concluding that a flat design is the most optimal for a retail organization.

Porter and Lawler Study of Attitudes in Tall and
Flat Organizations

A study conducted by Porter and Lawler concentrated upon the job
attitudes of managerial personnel in tall and flat organization structures.[17]
They utilized a need satisfaction questionnaire to ascertain the satisfaction of managers in the tall and flat structures. They were concerned with the security, social, esteem, autonomy, and self-actualization
need satisfactions of the managers studied. Over 1,900 managers par-

---

[17] L. W. Porter and E. E. Lawler, "The Effects of Tall versus Flat Organization
Structures on Managerial Job Satisfaction," *Personnel Psychology*, vol. 17 (Summer
1964), pp. 135–48.

ticipated in this study. The major findings of the investigation are briefly summarized as follows:

1. In firms employing fewer than 5,000 employees, managerial need satisfaction was greater in the flat than in the tall organization structure.
2. In firms employing 5,000 employees and over, the managers in the tall organization structure generally reported more need satisfaction.
3. In the flatter organization structure, more satisfaction of the self-actualization need was found. However, in the taller organization structure, there was more satisfaction of the security and social need categories.
4. Thus, reviewing their findings Porter and Lawler conclude that there is no clear overall superiority of a flat organization structure over a tall organization structure.

The conclusions of Worthy support the behavioralists' contentions regarding the advantages of the flat structure over the tall structure. The Porter and Lawler research, however, prevents one from making sweeping generalizations that a flat organization structure produces more favorable job satisfaction.

The Woodward Contingency Study

A complete and insightful contingency study of organization structures was conducted by Joan Woodward.[18] She and research associates studied 100 firms in Great Britain. All the firms studied manufactured goods and offered them for sale, but the nature of their markets and market share goals differed considerably.

By a combination of research methods (for example, surveys, interviews) various kinds of information were collected. Some of the information obtained for each firm was:

1. History, background and objectives of the firm.
2. Information on the manufacturing processes and methods employed.
3. Forms and routines through which the firm was organized and operated.
4. Organization chart.
5. Labor structure and cost.
6. Qualifications of managers.
7. Assessment of the success of the firm in their respective industries.

Woodward developed a system for classifying firms as above average, average, and below average in success. In constructing the success cri-

---

[18] Joan Woodward, *Industrial Organization: Theory and Practice* (London: Oxford University Press, 1965).

terion such factors as the state of the industry in which the firm operated (for example, new and expanding, old and contracting), the percentage of the total volume of the industry the firm contributed, five-year profit figures and investment figures, the fluctuation of the firm's shares on the Stock Exchange, the reputation of the firm, the salaries it pays, and the union opinion about the firm were some of the items considered.

The researchers became aware of the many variations in manufacturing methods utilized by the firms studied. This led to classifying the firms into three groups.[19]

1. Unit and small-batch (for example, a job shop).
2. Large-batch and mass production (for example, an auto-assembly plant).
3. Long-run process production (for example, a chemical manufacturing plant).

The three groupings suggested differences in technological complexity of operations. The simplest technology involved the production of goods for a single customer in the form of unit or small-batch manufacturing operations. The middle range of technological complexity involved the production of large batches of goods on a mass-production scale, while the highly complex technology included the production of goods utilizing interrelated processes.

The successful firms in the high and low technological scales (that is, long-run process and unit and small batch) tended to adhere more closely to the behavioralist's suggestions concerning organizational design. There was greater delegation of authority and more permissive management.

In the successful firms line-and-staff organization was most developed in the middle ranges of technological complexity. In all the successful large batch firms, there was a clear definition of duties and responsibilities and adherence to the unity of command principle.

In the final analysis, Woodward's research and findings suggest that although there is no one best way of structuring an organization, there seems to be a particular form of structure most appropriate for each technology. The firms engaged in large-batch production appear to operate more successfully if they are organized along classical lines. However, firms in the other two classifications are more successful if a less classical and more behavioral orientation is utilized.

SUMMARY

The Behavioral School perspective of designing an organization structure has been presented in a concise form. There is both agreement and

---

[19] Woodward, *Industrial Organization*, p. 39.

disagreement between the classical and behavioral design approaches. The classical theory of design is associated with such concepts as Theory X management; "ideal" bureaucratic structures, intense division of labor at the job level and departmentalization at the organizational level, unity of command, orderly line and staff distinctions, and narrow spans of control.

The behavioralists relate their organization design strategies to the human element more specifically than the classical theorists. They stress Theory Y, despecialization of job tasks, line-and-staff conflict analysis and procedures to reduce this conflict, wider spans of control which foster flatter organizational structure, more general supervision, and more decentralization.

When research evidence is closely scrutinized, it appears that the classical approach to organization design is not perfectly applicable to all situations and organizations. It is also evident that a pure behavioral approach to design which includes participation by workers and flatter organization structures is also not suited for some situations and organizations. The limited amount of sound research evidence does not allow conclusive statements to be made concerning which type of design is best for a particular organization. The few research studies available in the management literature suggest that the type of managerial and non-managerial personnel, the type of work being performed, the size, and production processes of the organization are some variables that should be given more than passing attention in designing an organization. When management experts more clearly specify the significant organizational factors influencing the success of a particular design, they will be in a better position to design effective organizations. This is a monumental order and there certainly is no one specific classical or behavioral design approach that will be recommended. Instead a *blending* of classical and behavioral concepts would seem to be appropriate when designing organizations. This blending is what is suggested by the contingency approach to organizational design.

DISCUSSION AND REVIEW QUESTIONS

1. Do you consider General Motors Corporation a decentralized organization? Why?

2. Discuss the applicability of the classical principle of division of labor in the 1970s. Will high degrees of specialization be found in organizations in the 1970s? Where?

3. Why do some scholars of management theory refer to the behavioral perspective of organizational design as a motivation-oriented approach?

4. What is the contingency approach to organizational design?

5. What is the major difference between the unity-of-command and chain-of-command principle?

6. What is meant by the term administrative distance? What would the behavioralist viewpoint be concerning the decreasing of the administrative distance between top management and nonmanagers?

7. Can generalizations about satisfaction attained by managers in tall and flat structures in various industries be made based upon the Porter and Lawler research results? Why?

8. What is the classical viewpoint concerning the line-and-staff concept? What are the similarities in the classical and behavioral viewpoints concerning line and staff?

9. Are the advantages of participation consistent with the classical theory of organizational structure? Why?

10. If a manager understands the Theory Y assumptions, can he predict the behavior of the work force he is dealing with? Why?

ADDITIONAL REFERENCES

Argyris, C.   *Integrating the Individual and the Organization.* New York: John Wiley and Sons, Inc., 1964.

Chandler, A. D., Jr.   *Strategy and Structure.* Cambridge, Mass.: The M.I.T. Press, 1962.

Etzioni, A.   *A Comparative Analysis of Complex Organizations.* Glencoe, Ill.: The Free Press, 1961.

Fisch, G. G.   "Line-Staff Is Obsolete," *The Harvard Business Review,* 39 (1961): 67–79.

Hulin, C. L., and Blood, M. R.   "Job Enlargement, Individual Differences, and Worker Responses," *Psychological Bulletin* 69 (1968): 41–55.

Lawrence, P., and Lorsch, J.   *Organization and Environment.* Division of Research, Graduate School of Business, Harvard University, 1967.

Leavitt, H. J., and Whisler, T. L.   "Management in the 1980s," *Harvard Business Review* 36 (1958): 41–48.

March, J. G., and Simon, H. A.   *Organizations.* New York: John Wiley and Sons, Inc., 1958.

Perrow, C.   "The Short and Glorious History of Organizational Theory," *Organizational Dynamics* 1 (1973): 20–27.

Pugh, D. S., Hickson, D. J., Hinings, C. R., and Turner, C.   "Dimensions of Organization Structure," *Administrative Science Quarterly* 13 (1968): 65–105.

Reimann, B. C.   "Dimensions of Structure in Effective Organizations: Some Empirical Evidence," *Academy of Management Journal* 17 (1974): 693–708.

Rubenstein, A. H., and Haberstroh, C. J., eds. *Some Theories of Organization.* Homewood, Ill.: Richard D. Irwin, Inc., 1966.

Schollhammer, H. "Organization Structures of Multinational Corporations," *Academy of Management Journal* 14 (1971): 345–65.

Swinth, R. *Organizational Systems for Management: Designing, Planning and Implementation.* Columbus, Ohio: Grid, Inc., 1974.

Talacchi, S. "Organization Size, Individual Attitudes and Behavior: An Empirical Study," *Administrative Science Quarterly* 5 (1960): 398–420.

Thompson, J. D. *Organizations in Action.* New York: McGraw-Hill Book Company, 1967.

Practical Exercise I

The Reorganization of Donzi's Bakery

Only six months after graduating from the state university, Pete Donzi had to take over his father's bakery business because his dad passed away unexpectedly. Donzi's Bakery Corporation was started as a small store on the South Side of Chicago in 1961. By 1970 Joe Donzi, the owner, had bought eight other bakery stores, owned ten trucks which delivered bakery products to industrial plants throughout the city and the suburbs, and employed about 120 people.

Joe literally ran his business out of his back pocket. Pete had wanted his dad to become more systematic and businesslike in running the company. Pete had continually attempted to convince his dad that an organization chart was needed so that the authority and responsibility of each person in a crucial position were clarified. Joe argued that by not having a chart he was able to give the people assignments that had to be accomplished on short notice. This flexibility is what Joe believed was a key to his success in the bakery business. A formal organization chart would restrict his style and not allow him to cope with changes in the environment and in the capabilities of his employees.

Despite his dad's resistance Pete, during his summer vacation in 1973, developed an organization chart. The chart is shown in Figure 1. The dominant and key person in the entire operation was Joe. He was the decision maker, problem solver, and disciplinarian in the company. Joe's wife, Anne, and his three children, Pete, Maria, and Mario, were given key positions in the company.

When Joe died the family had to decide what to do with the business. They all decided that Pete was the best qualified to succeed Joe as president. They also agreed to give Pete complete control of the organization. This freedom would allow Pete to do whatever he thought was best for the organization.

One of the first jobs Pete undertook was to improve the organizational design of his company. He examined closely the organization chart which he constructed in the summer of 1973. He found that his span of control as president, if he followed this design, would be 13. This he

FIGURE 1

Organization Chart for Donzi's Bakery as of Summer 1973

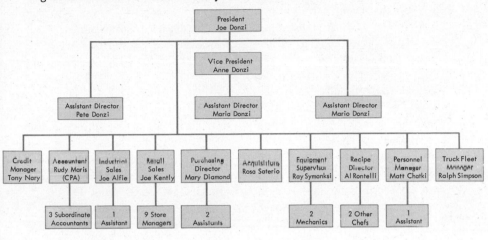

FIGURE 2

Organization Chart for Donzi's Bakery as of January 1975

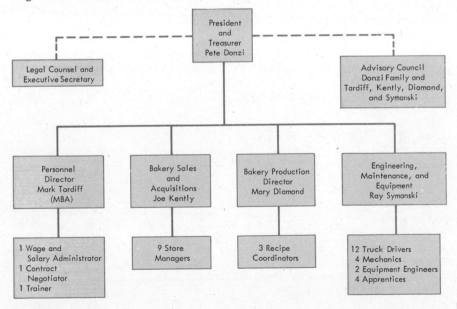

felt was too large and would not enable him to operate like a president should. It was his belief that a president should delegate authority, and should be involved in providing guidance and overall direction to the company. He certainly did not want to abdicate his decision-making responsibility, but he wanted to develop some key subordinates. Pete assumed that he would need competent subordinates to take advantage of growth opportunities in the next ten years.

The organizational design Pete established after taking over the business is shown in Figure 2. He believed that his new organizational design was contingency oriented in that it faced the realities of the bakery industry. That is, it placed the most knowledgeable and promising people in four, key, line positions; it reduced his span of control; it increased the administrative distance between the president and the line-operating employees; and it removed family members from line positions that he felt irritated almost everyone in the company. Of course, Pete felt that his family would be hurt by his reorganization, and he began to prepare an explanation of why this was the way the business had to be operated.

Questions for Analysis:

1. Compare and contrast the two organization charts—Figures 1 and 2.
   a. Is there a reduction in the president's span of control in Figure 2? Explain.
   b. Is Pete correct in his assumptions about administrative distance?
   c. What kind of positions would the family assume under the Figure 2 arrangement?
   d. Why might some of the family members be hurt by Pete's reorganization?
2. Is the organizational design of Figure 1 taller than that reflected in Figure 2? Why?
3. What behavioral problems could a recent college graduate expect in introducing a specific organizational design change like the one illustrated in this case?

Practical Exercise II

The "Flat" Organization

The Dana Lou Corporation is a rapidly growing company that is involved in developing, manufacturing, and distributing precision machine parts to food-processing, machine-manufacturing, and chemical-processing organizations. Dana Lou sells directly to purchasing agents and engineers in these companies. In the past five years the product line of the company has increased from 70, to over 150 precision parts.

The sales force is made up primarily of young engineers, a number of business administration graduates, and some noncollege personnel who have extensive sales experience. Approximately 75 percent of the salesmen have earned undergraduate degrees. The salesmen are paid on a commission basis. The rate paid depends on the type and volume of the products sold. The lowest commission rate is 8 percent and the highest rate is 42 percent. The average annual income for salesmen is $16,350. The sales force presently has 48 salesmen located throughout the United States.

When the company started business 12 years ago, it had seven salesmen. The second year of business these salesmen sold $320,000 worth of precision parts. This past year Dana Lou salesmen have sold approximately $2.6 million worth of parts.

TABLE 1

Location of Dana Lou Sales Force

Base City of Operations	Number of Salesmen
Boston	4
New York	7
Philadelphia	3
Chicago	7
San Francisco	4
Los Angeles	5
Denver	5
San Diego	6
Detroit	5
Cleveland	2

Tony Bertel is currently the vice president of sales. He has carefully scrutinized the sales force and the long-range mission of the company. He firmly believes that the sales force can sell at least $3.5 million. Tony is interested in planning for future sales growth and in organizing the sales team so that it can take advantage of the present market environment which is demanding more and more precision parts.

In attempting to do a better job of managing, Tony constructed Table 1. In this table the geographical location of the salesmen are shown. Most of the salesmen shown in Table 1 live in the large cities and sell to clients in areas surrounding the city. Tony, in reviewing his subordinates, is aware of the fact that two attractive markets are not being serviced—Florida and Texas. He believes that the company must have at least 15 salesmen for Tampa, Miami, Dallas, and Houston.

Presently Tony is the only sales executive who is involved in recruiting, selecting, and training salesmen. He has a billing clerk and two secretaries who work for him. He has worked extremely hard in developing a cohesive and highly motivated sales force. Three times a year Tony brings all of the sales force together at company headquarters. He attempts to introduce the company's sales objectives and new products and allows the salesmen to express complaints and make suggestions.

The company operating committee, of which Tony is a member, has set as the goal a sales volume of $5.75 million. They plan to accomplish this goal within the next five years. They believe that hiring 15 to 20 new salesmen for the Florida and Texas areas and improving their training of present salesmen will allow them to accomplish their goal. In these meetings when the goal was established, Tony had forcefully stated that the present organizational design for the sales division is outmoded and will be a detriment to accomplishing the goal. He has stated that the geographical dispersion of the sales force, his span of control (presently 48 salesmen), and his lack of immediate subordinates to whom he can delegate some of the recruitment, selection, and training duties has not enabled him to plan, organize, and control adequately.

The president is sympathetic to Tony's problems but wants him to show the other committee members the kind of organizational design that will enable the company to achieve its five-year sales goal.

Questions for Analysis:

1. Develop the two-level organizational design as it presently exists.
2. Present an organizational design that you believe would be best suited for the Dana Lou sales organization with 63 salesmen.
3. Would there be any agreement among classicists, behavioralists, and contingency advocates concerning the problems that Tony identified for the company operating committee? Discuss your answer.

11 Organizational Change and Development

INTRODUCTION

Managers must continually consider the necessity for change. If they were able to design an optimally effective organization and if the environment in which it operates were stable and unchanging, there would be little pressure for organizational change. But neither is the case. Organizational change[1] is a pressing problem for modern managers; and in recent years, a great deal of literature has appeared which focuses on the need for *planning* for change. Some companies have instituted staff units whose mission is organizational planning.[2] The planning units are specific responses to the need for systematic, formalized procedures to anticipate and implement changes in the structure, technology, and personnel of the organization.

In this chapter the processes of organizational change and development are discussed. Before beginning, however, we must explain the manner in which we are using the terms *change* and *development*. As even the casual reader of management literature must soon realize, the term organization development connotes a variety of meanings and management strategies. In its most restrictive sense it refers specifically

---

[1] "Organizational change" is broadly interpreted for purposes of this discussion. Some management students restrict the term to changes in the formal structure, but we will include changes in employee behavior and technology.

[2] Paul E. Holden, Carlton A. Pederson, Gayton E. Germane, *Top Management* (New York: McGraw-Hill Book Co., 1968), pp. 66–68.

to some form of sensitivity training; in a larger and more encompassing sense, it refers to any systematically planned, programmatic effort to improve the effectiveness of an organization through the application of behavioral science concepts, theories, and approaches. The change effort may focus on the way in which the organization is structured, the behavior of employees, or the technology that is used in getting the work done. But regardless of the principal focus, the process is consciously managed.

The growing realization that organizations, regardless of whether they are business firms, educational institutions, or governmental agencies, can be changed and made more effective through managerial applications of behavioral science knowledge has created a wealth of literature.[3] This chapter presents some of the established ideas from this literature in the context of practical management. In order to provide a theme, we present the material in terms of a model which describes the important factors of the change and development process. Our purpose is to demonstrate that managers can most effectively respond to the necessity for change through the application of this model which itself reflects the more abiding contributions of the organization development literature. For simplicity we will use the phrase, "the management of change," to include the concept of organization development in its broadest sense.

A MODEL FOR MANAGING CHANGE

The management of change implies a systematic process which can be broken down into subprocesses or steps. The model which describes this process is illustrated in Figure 11–1 and consists of eight subprocesses which are linked in a logical sequence. A manager considers each of them, either explicitly or implicitly, to undertake a change program. The prospects for initiating successful change are enhanced when the manager explicitly and formally goes through each successive step. For this reason, each step is discussed in a separate section of this chapter.

It is our purpose to describe alternative change techniques and strategies, but not to propose that some alternatives are superior to others. No one change technique or change strategy can be judged superior on *a priori* grounds.[4]

---

[3] For a sample of organizational development literature in the context of various settings, see Wendell L. French and Cecil H. Bell, Jr., *Organization Development* (Englewood Cliffs, N.J.: Prentice-Hall, Inc., 1973); Larry Kirkhart and Neely Gardner, eds., "A Symposium: Organization Development," *Public Administration Review*, vol. 34 (March–April 1974), pp. 97–140; Newton Margulies, "Organizational Development in a University Setting: Some Problems in Initiating Change," *Educational Technology*, vol. 12 (October 1972), pp. 48–51.

[4] Jeremiah J. O'Connell, *Managing Organizational Innovation* (Homewood, Ill.: Richard D. Irwin, Inc., 1968), pp. 10, 142–45.

FIGURE 11–1

A Model for the Management of Change

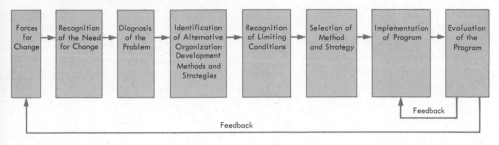

The well-equipped manager is one who recognizes the multiplicity of alternatives, is not predisposed to one particular approach to the exclusion of all others. At the same time, the effective manager avoids the pitfalls of stagnation. The sign of decay, as Greiner has observed, is "managerial behavior that (*a*) is oriented more to the past than to the future, (*b*) recognizes the obligations of ritual more than the challenges of current problems, and (*c*) owes allegiance more to department goals than to overall company objectives."[5] Thus the management of change implies a flexible, forward-looking stance for the manager.[6] This attribute is essential for using the change model outlined in Figure 11–1.

The model presumes that forces for change continually act upon the firm; this assumption reflects the dynamic character of the modern world. At the same time it is the manager's responsibility to sort out the information received from the firm's control system and other sources which reflect the magnitude of change forces. The information is the basis for recognizing the need for change; it is equally desirable to recognize when change is *not* needed. But once the problem is recognized, the manager must diagnose the problem and identify relevant alternative change techniques. The change technique selected must be appropriate to the problem, as constrained by limiting conditions. One example of a limiting condition which we have discussed in an earlier chapter is the prevailing character of group norms. The work groups may support some of the change techniques, but may sabotage others. Other limiting conditions include leadership behavior, legal requirements, and economic conditions.

The fact that a change program can be thwarted underscores the fact

[5] Larry E. Greiner, "Patterns of Organization Change," *Harvard Business Review*, vol. 45 (May–June 1967), p. 119.

[6] See Paul Hersey and Kenneth H. Blanchard, "The Management of Change," *Training and Development Journal*, vol. 26 (January 1972), pp. 6–11, for the first of a three-part discussion of the management of change which parallels the model developed in this chapter.

that the choice of change *strategy* is as important as the change technique itself. One well-documented behavioral phenomenon is that people tend to resist change or at least to be reluctant to undergo change. An appropriate strategy for implementing change is one which seeks to minimize resistance and maximize employee commitment. Finally, managers must implement the change and monitor the change process and change results. The model includes feedback to the implementation phase and to the forces-for-change phase. These feedback loops suggest that the change process itself must be monitored and evaluated. The implementation strategy may be faulty and lead to poor results, but responsive action could correct the situation. Moreover, the feedback loop to the initial step recognizes that *no* change is final. A new situation is created within which other problems and issues will emerge; a new setting is created which will itself become subject to change. The model suggests no "final solution"; rather, it emphasizes that modern managers operate in a dynamic setting wherein the only certainty is change itself.

The process by which the solution to one problem creates new problems is widely recognized. Blau and Scott refer to it as the "dialectic processes of change,"[7] and they illustrate the dilemma by a number of examples. They observe that assembly-line techniques increase productivity but that, at the same time, employee absenteeism and turnover increase. Assembly-line work is monotonous and routine; it alienates workers and creates discontent; morale declines and personnel problems emerge. Thus a different set of difficulties is created by the solution itself. This phenomenon must be taken into account as managers consider changes.

The thoughtful student will, no doubt, argue that many successful changes have been implemented by managers who did not consciously and systematically go through each step of the model. Indeed there are many such cases. However, these managers may not be representative of the population of managers. They may very well be intuitive artists who have the experience and judgment to guide and implement change without a conscious effort. Such men are the geniuses of management. The rest of us might be well advised to follow a more systematic approach, as outlined in this chapter.

FORCES FOR CHANGE

The forces for change can be classified conveniently into two groups, namely, external and internal forces. External forces include changes in the marketplace, technology, and environment; they are beyond the con-

---

[7] Peter M. Blau and W. Richard Scott, *Formal Organizations* (San Francisco: Chandler Publishing Co., 1962), pp. 250–53.

trol of the manager. Internal forces operate inside the firm are generally within the control of management.

External Forces

The manager of a busines firm has historically been concerned with reacting to changes in the *marketplace*. Competitors introduce new products, increase their advertising, reduce their prices, or improve their customer service. In each case a response is required unless the manager is content to permit the erosion of profit and market share. At the same time, changes occur in customer tastes and incomes. The firm's products may no longer have customer appeal; customers may be able to purchase more expensive, higher-quality forms of the same product.

The enterprise system eventually eliminates from the economic scene those firms which do not adjust to market conditions. The isolated-from-reality manager who ignores the signals from the market will soon confront the more vocal and louder signals of discontented stockholders. By that time, however, the appropriate change may well be dissolution of the firm—the final solution.

Another source of market forces is that of the supply of *resources* to the firm. A change in the quality and quantity of human resources can dictate changes in the firm. For example, the adoption of automated processes can be stimulated by a decline in the supply of labor. The techniques of coal mining and tobacco farming have changed greatly during recent years due to labor shortages. We can also understand how changes in the materials supply can cause the firm to substitute one material for another. Rayon stockings and synthetic rubber tires are direct outgrowths of World War II–induced shortages of raw materials. We need not catalog the whole range of possible changes in the resource markets which stimulate organizational change. The potential is great, however, and must be recognized.

The second source of external change forces is *technology*. The knowledge explosion since World War II introduced new technology for nearly every management function. Computers have made possible high-speed data processing and the solution to complex production problems. New machines and new processes have revolutionized the way in which many products are manufactured and distributed. High rates of obsolescence have encouraged many firms to adopt payback criteria as low as two years, so that they will not be caught with obsolete equipment. Computer technology and automation have affected not only the technical conditions of work, but the social conditions as well. New occupations have been created and others have been eliminated. Slowness in adopting new technology which reduces costs and improves quality will show itself in the financial statements sooner or later.

Technological advance is a permanent fixture in contemporary society and, as a force for change, will continue to demand attention.[8]

Finally, the third external force consists of *environmental* changes. Managers must be "tuned in" to great movements over which they have no control but which, in time, control the firm's fate. The 1950s and 1960s witnessed a distinct increase in social activity. The drive for social equality posed new issues for managers, which had not been previously confronted. Sophisticated mass communications and international markets created enormous potential but also posed a great threat to those managers unable to understand what was going on. Finally, to add to the problem, the relationship between government and business became much more involved as new regulations were imposed. These pressures for change reflect the increasing complexity and interdependence of modern living. The traditional function of business is being questioned and new objectives are being advanced. No doubt the events of the future will intensify environmental forces for change.

Internal Forces

The forces for change which occur within the organization can be traced to *process* and *people* causes. Process forces include breakdowns in decision making, communications, and interpersonal relations. Decisions are either not being made, are made too late, or are of poor quality. Communications are short-circuited, redundant, or simply inadequate. Tasks are not undertaken or not completed because the person responsible did not "get the word." A customer order is not filled; a grievance is not processed; or an invoice is not filed; and the supplier is not paid because of inadequate and nonexistent communications. Interpersonal and interdepartmental conflicts reflect breakdowns in the human interactional process.

Low levels of morale and high levels of absenteeism and turnover are symptoms of people problems that must be diagnosed. A wildcat strike or a walkout may be the most tangible sign of a problem, yet such tactics are usually employed because they rouse the management to action. There is in most organizations a certain level of employee discontent; a great danger is to ignore the complaints and suggestions. But the process of change includes the *recognition* phase, and it is at this point that management must decide to act or not to act.

RECOGNITION OF THE NEED FOR CHANGE

Information is the basis on which managers are made aware of the magnitude of the change forces. We noted some of the important sources

[8] Thomas J. Watson, Jr., "Technological Change," in Arthur O. Lewis, Jr., ed., *Of Men and Machines* (New York: E. P. Dutton & Co., Inc., 1963), pp. 295–309.

of information in our discussion above. Certainly the most important information comes from the firm's preliminary, concurrent, and feedback control data. Indeed, the process of change can be viewed as a part of the control function, specifically the corrective-action requirement. Financial statements, quality control data, and budget and standard cost information are important media through which both external and internal forces are revealed. Declining profit margins and market shares are tangible signs that the firm's competitive position is deteriorating and that change may be required. These sources of feedback control information are highly developed in most organizations because of their crucial importance.

The need for change goes unrecognized in many organizations until some major catastrophe occurs. The employees strike or seek the recognition of a union before management finally recognizes the need for action. Whether it takes a whisper or a shout, the need for change must be recognized by some means; and the exact nature of the problem must be diagnosed.

DIAGNOSIS OF THE PROBLEM

Before appropriate action can be taken, the symptoms of the problem must be analyzed to discover the problem itself. Experience and judgment are critical to this phase unless the problem is readily apparent to all observers. Ordinarily, however, persons in management can disagree as to the nature of the problem. There is no magic formula which is available for accurate diagnosis. The objectives of this phase can be described by three questions:

1. What is the problem, as distinct from the symptoms of the problem?
2. What must be changed to resolve the problem?
3. What outcomes (objectives) are expected from the change, and how will such objectives be measured?

The answers to these questions can come from information ordinarily found in organizations, such as financial statements and departmental reports. Or it may be necessary to generate *ad hoc* information through the creation of committees or task forces. Meetings between managers and employees provide a variety of points of view which can be sifted through by a smaller group. Technical operational problems may be easily diagnosed, but more subtle human relations problems usually entail extensive analysis. One approach to diagnosing the problem is the attitude survey.

Attitude surveys can be administered to the entire work force or to a sample of it. The survey permits the respondents to evaluate and rate (1) management, (2) pay and pay-related items, (3) working conditions, (4) equipment, and (5) other job-related items. The appropriate use of such surveys requires that the questionnaire be completed anonymously so that employees can express their views freely and without threat, whether real or fancied. The objective of the survey is to pinpoint the problem or problems as perceived by the members of the organization. Subsequent discussions of the survey results at all levels of the organization can add additional insights into the nature of the problem.[9]

The approach which management uses to diagnose the problem is a crucial part of the total strategy for change. As will be seen in a later section, the manner in which the problem is diagnosed has clear implications for the final success of the proposed change.

Finally, the diagnostic step must specify *objectives* for change. Given the diagnosis of the problem, it is necessary to define objectives to guide as well as to evaluate the outcome of the change. The objectives can be stated in terms of financial and production data, such as profits, market shares, sales volume, productivity, scrappage, or the like. Or they can be stated as attitude and morale objectives derived from attitude survey information. Whatever the objectives, they must be explicit and, if possible, measurable.

ALTERNATIVE CHANGE TECHNIQUES

The choice of the particular change technique depends upon the nature of the problem which management has diagnosed. Management must determine which alternative is most likely to produce the desired outcome, whether it be improvement in the knowledge, attitudes, skills, or job performances of the organization's personnel. As we have noted, diagnosis of the problem includes specification of the outcomes which management desires from the change. In this section, we will describe a number of change techniques. They will be classified according to the major focus of the technique, namely, to change structure, people, or technology.[10] This classification of organizational change techniques in no way implies a distinct division among the three types. On the contrary, the interrelationships among structure, people, and technology must be acknowledged and anticipated.

An important contribution of the Behavioral School is the documentation of the impact of structure on attitudes and behavior. Overspecializa-

[9] Complete discussions of attitude surveys as diagnostic tools are found in Stuart M. Klein, Allen I. Kraut, and Alan Wolfson, "Employee Reactions to Attitude Survey Feedback," *Administrative Science Quarterly*, vol. 16 (December 1971), pp. 497–514; Gary B. Brumback, "Employee Attitude Surveys," *Personnel Administration*, vol. 35 (March–April 1972), pp. 27–34; and Diane Coryell and David Sirota, "Attitude Survey Feedback—Letting the First-Line Manager Know Where He Stands," *Personnel Administration*, vol. 35 (May–June 1972), pp. 53–57.

[10] See Harold J. Leavitt, "Applied Organizational Change in Industry: Structural, Technological and Humanistic Approaches," in James G. March, ed., *Handbook of Organizations* (Chicago: Rand McNally and Co., 1965), pp. 1144–68.

tion and narrow spans of control can lead to low levels of morale and low productivity.[11] At the same time, the technology of production, distribution, and information processing affects the structural characteristics of the firm,[12] as well as attitudes and sentiments.[13] The fact that the interrelationships among structure, people, and technology are so pronounced might suggest a weakness in our classification scheme; but in defense of it, the techniques described below can be distinguished on the basis of their *major* thrust or focus—structure, people, or technology.

Structural Change

Changes in the structure of the organization ordinarily follow changes in strategy.[14] Logically, the organizing function follows the planning function since the structure is a means for achieving the goals established through planning. Structural change in the context of organizational change refers to managerial action which attempts to improve performance by altering the formal structure of task and authority relationships. At the same time, we must recognize that the structure creates human and social relationships which gradually can become ends for the members of the organization. These relationships, when they have been defined and made legitimate by management, introduce an element of stability.[15] Members of the organization may resist efforts to disrupt these relationships.

Structural changes alter some aspect of the formal task and authority definitions. As we have seen, the design of an organization involves the definition and specification of job content and scope, the grouping of jobs in departments, determination of the size of groups reporting to a single manager, and the provision of staff assistance. Within this framework, the communication, decision-making, and human interaction processes occur. We can see, then, that changes in the nature of jobs, bases for departmentalization, and line-staff relationships involve structural change.

Changes in the nature of jobs include any revision in the prescribed

---

[11] Rensis Likert, *The Human Organization* (New York: McGraw-Hill Book Co., 1967).

[12] Joan Woodward, *Industrial Organization* (New York: Oxford University Press, 1967); and Frank J. Jasinski, "Adapting Organization to New Technology," *Harvard Business Review*, vol. 37 (January–February 1959), pp. 79–86.

[13] Harriet O. Ronken and Paul R. Lawrence, *Administering Changes: A Case Study of Human Relations in a Factory* (Boston: Division of Research, Harvard Business School, 1952).

[14] Alfred Chandler, *Strategy and Structure* (Cambridge, Mass.: M.I.T. Press, 1962).

[15] R. K. Ready, *The Administrator's Job* (New York: McGraw-Hill Book Co., 1967), pp. 24–30.

ways for performing assigned tasks. The origins of such changes are the implementation of new methods and new machines. Work simplification and job enrichment are two examples of methods changes. The former narrows job content and scope, whereas the latter widens them. Scientific management introduced significant changes in the way work is done through the use of motion and time studies. These methods tend to create highly specialized jobs. Job enrichment, however, moves in the opposite direction, toward despecialization.

One application of job change which led to significant increases in productivity and decreases in absenteeism occurred at Texas Instruments Incorporated.[16] In 1965, a group of women who had been assembling radar equipment according to methods defined by the engineering department were given the responsibility for devising their own methods, manufacturing processes, and goals. The women had full access to cost and engineering information and staff personnel. After implementation of the group's own methods and goals, the assembly time per unit dropped from 138 hours to 86 hours. At this point a second goal-setting session was held, and the women suggested that they did not need a supervisor; they could, in their judgment, exercise self-control. The women did keep their supervisor informed, but they self-directed their activities. The assembly time for the unit was finally reduced to 36 hours.

In this instance of job change, the employees were encouraged to evaluate their own task performance. They responded by not only enlarging the job along the horizontal dimension—by adding additional tasks—but also by enriching the job along the vertical dimension—by assuming the responsibility for their own supervision. The degree of general applicability to other organizational settings is, of course, a matter of on-site determination; the case does suggest the positive gains from job change which can be realized.

Changes in the bases for departmentalization occur in response to a variety of stimuli. In the study of 30 California-based financial, service, and manufacturing firms which experienced marked growth during the period 1947–1955, McNulty found a considerable increase in the relative importance of product departmentalization relative to other bases.[17] The use of product bases indicates efforts to move toward decentralized forms of organization like those found in General Motors and in General Electric. But the ambivalence of the managers in the study is demonstrated by their tendency to create "taller" rather than "flatter" organiza-

---

[16] Charles L. Hughes, "Applying Behavioral Science in Manufacturing Supervision: Case Report," *Proceedings of the Ninth Annual Midwest Management Conference* (Carbondale, Ill.: Bureau of Business Research, Southern Illinois University, 1966), pp. 85–89.

[17] James E. McNulty, "Organizational Change in Growing Enterprises," *Administrative Science Quarterly*, vol. 7 (June 1962), pp. 1–21.

tions. With decentralization, one expects to find relatively wider spans of control. McNulty's study suggests that the problems of rapid market growth were such that management was reluctant to relinquish too much control over the situation.

Changes in line-staff relationships include two techniques. The first and the usual approach is to create staff assistance as either an *ad hoc* or permanent solution. McNulty reported that one response of manufacturing firms to the problem of market expansion is the creation of separate staff and service units.[18] These units provide the technical expertise to deal with the production, financial, and marketing problems posed by expansion.

An illustrative case is a company which had grown quite rapidly since its entry into the fast-foods industry. Its basic sources of field control were area directors who supervised the operations of sales outlets of a particular region. During the growth period the area directors had considerable autonomy in making the advertising decisions for their regions. They could select their own media, format, and budget within general guidelines. But, as their markets became saturated and as competitors appeared, corporate officials decided to centralize the advertising function in a staff unit located at corporate headquarters. Consequently, the area director's freedom was limited and an essential job aspect was eliminated.[19]

A final illustration of changes in line-staff relationships is based upon the case which O'Connell described.[20] A large insurance company hired a management consulting firm to analyze the problem created by a deteriorating market position. The consulting company recommended that the firm undertake a program of decentralization by changing a staff position to a line manager. This recommendation was based upon the consultants' belief that the company must have its best personnel and resources available at the branch office level to increase premium income. Accordingly, the consultants recommended that assistant managers be converted to first-level supervisors reporting to branch managers. The transformation required a significant change in the work of assistant managers and in the work of managers throughout the organization.

These examples illustrate the range of alternatives which managers must consider. Certainly we have not exhausted the possibilities. The point that should be made in concluding this discussion, however, is not that the list is incomplete, but that students and managers must

---

[18] Ibid.

[19] See Herbert A. Simon et al., *Centralization versus Decentralization in Organizing the Controller's Department* (New York: The Controllership Foundation, 1954) for another discussion of the key issues to be resolved in the decision of where to locate staff units—in this case, an accounting unit.

[20] O'Connell, *Organizational Innovation.*

recognize the interrelationships of structural parts. A change in job content does not take place in a vacuum; on the contrary, the change affects all other directly related jobs, supervisory and nonsupervisory alike. The management of structural change must be guided by the *holistic* point of view that all things are connected.

Behavioral Change

This class of change techniques refers to efforts to redirect and improve employee attitudes, skills, and knowledge bases. The objectives is to enhance the capacity of individuals to perform assigned tasks in coordination with others. The early efforts to engage in behavioral change date to scientific management work improvement and employee training methods. These attempts were primarily directed at improving employee skills and knowledge bases. The employee counseling programs which grew out of the Hawthorne studies were (and remain) primarily directed at improving employee attitudes.

Training programs for managers have typically emphasized supervisory relationships. These programs attempt to provide supervisors and foremen with basic technical and human-relations skills. Since supervisors and foremen are primarily concerned with overseeing the work of others, the content of these traditional programs emphasizes techniques for dealing with people problems: how to deal with the malcontent, the loafer, the troublemaker, the complainer. The programs also include conceptual material dealing with communications, leadership styles, and organizational relationships. The vehicles for training include role playing, discussion groups, lectures, and organized courses offered by universities.[21] A number of programs include materials about the managerial grid, democratic leadership, and other ideas derived from the Behavioral School.[22]

Training continues to be an important technique for introducing people changes. Training has taken on quite a different form in some applications from that which developed in classical management theory.[23] In contemporary management a popular behavioral change approach is sensitivity training.

Sensitivity training is a change technique which attempts to make the

---

[21] Ernest Dale and L. C. Michelon, *Modern Management Methods* (New York: The World Publishing Company, 1966), pp. 15–16.

[22] See T. A. Swann and Russel C. Cox, "How Training Perked Up Morale at Maxwell House," *Management Review*, vol. 61 (February 1972), pp. 4–11.

[23] A survey of alternative training methodologies is presented in Edward C. Ryterband and Bernard M. Bass, "Management Development," in Joseph W. McGuire, ed., *Contemporary Management* (Englewood Cliffs, N.J.: Prentice-Hall, Inc., 1974), pp. 579–609.

participant more aware of himself and of his impact on others. "Sensitivity" in this context means sensitivity to self and to relationships with others. An assumption of sensitivity training is that the causes of poor task performance are the emotional problems of people who must collectively achieve a goal. If these problems can be removed, a major impediment to task performance is consequently eliminated. Sensitivity training stresses "the *process* rather than the *content* of training and . . . *emotional* rather than *conceptual* training."[24] We can see that this form of training is quite different from traditional forms which stress the acquisition of a predetermined body of concepts with immediate application to the work place.

The process of sensitivity training includes a group of managers (Training group or T-group) who in most cases come together at some location other than their place of work. Under the direction of a trainer, the group usually engages in a dialogue which has no agenda and no focus. The objective is to provide an environment which produces its own learning experiences.[25] The unstructured dialogue encourages one to learn about self in dealing with others. One's motives and feelings are revealed through behavior toward others in the group and through the behavior of others. The T-group is typically unstructured. As Marrow points out in a report of his own sensitivity training, "It [sensitivity training] says, 'Open your eyes. Look at yourself. See how you look to others. Then decide what changes, if any, you want to make and in which direction you want to go.' "[26]

The role of the trainer in the T-group is to facilitate the learning process. According to Kelly, the trainer's mission is "to observe, record, interpret, sometimes to lead, and always to learn."[27] The artistry and style of the trainer are critical variables in determining the direction of the T-group's sessions. The trainer must walk the uneasy path of unobtrusive leadership and be able to interpret the roles of participants and encourage them to analyze their contributions without being perceived as a threat. Unlike the group therapist, the T-group trainer is dealing with people who are considered normal, but who have come together to learn. The ordinarily prescribed role of the trainer is that of "permissive, nonauthoritarian, sometimes almost nonparticipative" leadership.[28]

The critical test of sensitivity training is whether the experience itself

[24] Henry C. Smith, *Sensitivity to People* (New York: McGraw-Hill Book Co., 1966), p. 197.

[25] L. P. Bradford, J. R. Gibb, and K. D. Benne, *T-Group Theory and Laboratory Method* (New York: John Wiley & Sons, Inc., 1964).

[26] Alfred J. Marrow, *Behind the Executive Mask* (New York: American Management Association, 1964), p. 51.

[27] Joe Kelly, *Organizational Behaviour* (Homewood, Ill.: Richard D. Irwin, Inc., 1969), p. 419.

[28] Leavitt, "Organizational Change," p. 1154.

is a factor leading to improvement in task performance. It is apparent that even if the training induces positive changes in the participant's sensitivity to self and others, such behavior may be either not possible or not permissible back in the work place. The participant must deal with the same environment and the same people as before the training. The open, supportive, and permissive environment of the training sessions is not likely to be found on the job. Even so, proponents of sensitivity training would reply that it makes the participant better able to deal with the environment. We should also recognize that sensitivity training may well induce negative changes in the participant's ability to perform organizational tasks; the training sessions can be occasions of extreme stress and anxiety. The capacity to deal effectively with stress varies among individuals, and the outcome may be dysfunctional for some participants.

The research evidence to date on the effectiveness of sensitivity training as a change technique suggests mixed results.[29] The manager must critically examine this technique in terms of the kinds of changes which are desired and those which are possible. Our model suggests the existence of conditions which limit the range of possible changes. In this light the manager must determine whether the changes induced by sensitivity training are instrumental for organizational purposes and whether the prospective participant is able to tolerate the potential anxiety of the training.

The recognition that structure must be compatible with behavior and vice versa has stimulated the search for a means to relate the two. A notable contribution is that of Likert. He proposes, on the basis of considerable research, that the most effective organizational form is one which can be clearly distinguished from others; he furthermore proposes that management should make a conscious effort to change to the superior form,[30] which he terms System 4.

System 4 Organization relates people change and structural change.[31] According to Likert an organization can be described in terms of eight operating characteristics. They are (1) leadership, (2) motivation, (3) communication, (4) interaction, (5) decision making, (6) goal setting, (7) control, and (8) performance. The nature of each of these characteristics can be located on a continuum through the use of a questionnaire which members of the firm (usually managers) complete. The

---

[29] See Robert J. House, "T-Group Education and Leadership Effectiveness: A Review of the Empirical Literature and a Critical Evaluation," *Personnel Psychology*, vol. 20 (Spring 1967), pp. 1–32; and John P. Campbell and Marvin D. Dunnette, "Effectiveness of T-Group Experiences in Managerial Training and Development," *Psychological Bulletin*, vol. 70 (August 1968), pp. 73–104.

[30] Likert, *Human Organization*.

[31] A complete review of change efforts based upon the System 4–type technique is Alfred J. Marrow, ed., *The Failure of Success* (New York: The American Management Association, 1972).

arithmetic means (averages) of each response category are calculated and plotted to produce an organizational profile. Figure 11–2 presents superimposed profiles for two plants located in southeastern Kentucky.

FIGURE 11–2

Organizational Profile for Two Manufacturing Firms

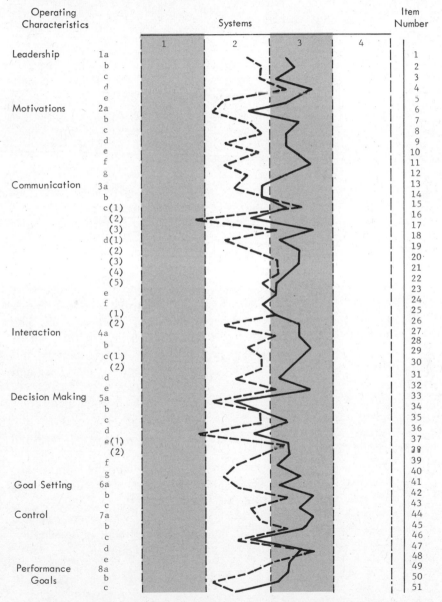

* These two profiles are based upon responses to the 51-item version of Likert's questionnaire. Copies can be obtained from the Foundation for Research on Human Behavior, Ann Arbor, Michigan. A facsimile is included in J. H. Donnelly, et al., *Fundamentals of Management* (Dallas, Tex.: Business Publications, Inc. ,1971), pp. 258-72.

The horizontal dimension of the organizational profile describes four points on the continuum for each of the eight operating characteristics which appear on the vertical dimension. Likert has labelled the four points as follows:

System 1—Exploitive-Authoritative,
System 2—Benevolent-Authoritative,
System 3—Consultative, and
System 4—Participative Group.

Likert no longer uses these value-laden labels since value-free descriptions of each of the systems are obviously desirable. He now defines each system in quantitative terms on the dimensions shown in Figure 11–2.

The System 4 organization is one in which managers (1) use the principle of supportive relationships; (2) use group methods for decision making and supervision; and (3) have high performance goals.[32] More specific characteristics of System 4 organization are:

1. *Leadership processes* which instill confidence and trust between superiors and subordinates and vice versa. Subordinates feel free to discuss job problems with their superiors, who in turn solicit their ideas and opinions.
2. *Motivational processes* which develop a full range of motives through participatory methods. Attitudes are favorable toward the company and toward goals of the company.
3. *Communication processes* are such that information flows freely throughout the organization—upward, downward, and laterally. The information is accurate and undistorted.
4. *Interaction processes* are open and extensive; both superiors and subordinates are able to affect departmental goals, methods, and activities.
5. *Decision-making processes* occur at all levels of the organization through group methods.
6. *Goal-setting processes* encourage group participation in setting high, yet realistic, objectives.
7. *Control processes* are dispersed throughout the company with all participants seeking information to implement self-control; the emphasis of control is problem solving, not blame setting.
8. *Performance goals* are high and actively sought by superiors who also recognize the necessity for making a full commitment to developing, through training, the human resources of the company.

The System 4 organization as described above has no counterpart in

---

[32] Likert, *Human Organization*, p. 47.

reality. Likert himself has studies of companies which *approach* System 4, but he has not discovered any companies which are pure System 4. He assumes that it is an "ideal type," toward which the most successful companies are moving.

The profiles of the two firms presented in Figure 11–2 demonstrate the kinds of differences that can occur in organizational processes. In Likert's terms, the firm represented by the dotted line is clearly a System 2 organization, whereas that represented by the solid line is a System 3 organization with tendencies toward System 2. The profiles (derived from Likert's questionnaire) were used in conjunction with attitude surveys to pinpoint the nature of suspected problems. The profiles suggested the need to examine motivational, communication, and decision-making processes since the most pronounced deviations occurred in these areas. Subsequent analysis of information contained in the attitude survey and interviews with the employees confirmed these observations that problems existed in the areas of motivation, communications, and decision making. The managements of both organizations believed that efforts to move toward System 4 organization should be undertaken.

The change toward System 4 involves measuring the present state of the firm through the use of the questionnaire. Subsequent training programs emphasize the concepts of System 4 management and their application to the present organization. The use of supportive, group-oriented leadership and sustained encouragement to set goals, implement controls, and make decisions should ordinarily lead to higher earnings and productivity, according to Likert. These favorable results derive from positive changes in employee attitudes which are induced by the structural changes. As has been pointed out by others, "To obtain lasting change, one does not try to change people, but rather to change the organizational constraints that operate upon them."[33]

Technological Change

This category of change includes any application of new ways to transform resources into the product or service. In the usual sense of the word, technology means new machines—lathes, presses, computers, and the like. But we should expand the concept to include new techniques with or without new machines. From this perspective, the work improvement methods of scientific management can be considered as

[33] Eliot D. Chapple and Leonard R. Sayles, *The Measure of Management* (New York: The Macmillan Company, 1961), p. 202. Stanley E. Seashore and David G. Bowers, in "Durability of Organizational Change," *American Psychologist*, vol. 25 (1970), pp. 227–32, also report evidence that System 4-type change can be made permanent in an organization.

technological breakthroughs. However, in this section only those changes which are induced by the introduction of a machine or man-machine process are discussed.

The changes in organizational efficiency brought about by a new machine are calculable in economic and engineering terms. Whether the machine is a good investment is a matter of estimating its future profitability in relation to its present cost. These calculations are an important part of the managerial control function. Here, however, we are interested in the impact of the new machine on the structure of the organization and on the behavior of the people in the organization. As some scholars have observed, technology is a key determinant of structure.[34] They tentatively conclude that firms with simple and stable technology should adopt a structure that tends toward bureaucratic organization, whereas firms with complex and dynamic technology ought to tend toward the more open and flexible System 4 structure.[35] Thus it would appear that the adoption of new technology involves a concurrent decision to adapt the organizational structure to that technology. Whether an inexorable and deterministic relationship between technology and structure exists, the fact remains that the introduction of technological innovation has far-reaching effects on the organization.

In order to catalog the impact of technological change on structure and behavior, Floyd C. Mann analyzed a number of actual cases and concluded that the adoption of new machines in the factory involves:

1. Major changes in the division of labor and the content of jobs.
2. Changes in social relations among workers.
3. Improved working conditions.
4. The need for different supervisory skills.
5. Changes in career patterns, promotion procedures, and job security.
6. Generally higher wages.
7. Generally higher prestige for those who work.
8. Around-the-clock operations.[36]

The degree and extent of these observed changes in structure and behavior depend upon the magnitude of the technological change. Obviously, the introduction of a new offset printing press will not cause the great dislocations and changes which Mann observes, but the complete auto-

---

[34] Woodward, *Industrial Organization*, and Jasinski, *Adapting*, among others.

[35] Burns and Stalker make this point in their analysis of the ways Scottish electronic firms responded to technological change. They use the terms "mechanistic" to refer to relatively tight, highly structured organizations and "organic" to refer to relatively loose, flexibly structured organization. Tom Burns and G. M. Stalker, *The Management of Innovation* (London: Tavistock Publications, 1961).

[36] Floyd C. Mann, "Psychological and Organizational Impacts," in John T. Dunlop, ed., *Automation and Technological Change* (Englewood Cliffs, N.J.: Prentice-Hall, Inc., 1962), pp. 50–55.

mation of a previously man-paced manufacturing process would include many, if not all of them.

A widespread structural adaptation to the necessity for utilizing technological innovation with minimum delay is referred to as *project* or *program management*. In this organizational form, the responsibility for achieving the goals of a short-run project is assigned to a project manager, who may then draw upon the expertise of functional experts in production, engineering, finance, or any other, as necessary. The project manager usually has complete authority over all the activities and personnel necessary to carry out the project, including personnel who ordinarily report to a functional department head. This organizational form permits horizontal communications and authority relationships necessary to complete the project but maintains the traditional and permanent vertical relationships. However, the existence of a dual authority system introduces the potential for problems associated with dual command.

The decision to adopt a technological approach to organizational change must include consideration of the potential structural and behavioral impacts. These impacts must, in turn, be reconciled with conditions which limit the scope and magnitude of the proposed change.

RECOGNITION OF LIMITING CONDITIONS

The selection of the change technique is based upon diagnosis of the problem, but the choice is tempered by certain conditions that exist at the time. Filley and House identify three sources of influence on the outcome of management development programs which can be generalized to cover the entire range of organizational change efforts, whether structural, behavioral, or technological. They are the leadership climate, formal organization, and organizational culture.[37]

Leadership climate refers to the nature of the work environment which results from "the leadership style and administrative practices" of superiors. Any change program which does not have the support and commitment of management has a slim chance of success. Managers must be at least neutral toward the change. We also understand that the style of leadership itself may be the subject of change; for example, sensitivity training and System 4 are direct attempts to move managers toward a certain style—open, supportive, and group centered. But, it must be recognized that the participants may be unable to adopt such styles if they are not compatible with their own superiors' styles.

The *formal organization* must be compatible with the proposed change. This includes the effects on the environment that result from the philosophy and policies of top management, as well as "legal precedent, organizational structure, and the system of control." Of

---

[37] Alan C. Filley and Robert J. House, *Managerial Process and Organizational Behavior* (Glenview, Ill.: Scott, Foresman and Company, 1969), pp. 423–34.

course, each of these sources of impact may be the focus of the change effort; the important point is that a change in one must be compatible with all others. For example, a change in technology which will eliminate jobs contradicts a policy of guaranteed employment.

The *organizational culture* refers to the impact on the environment resulting from "group norms, values, and informal activities." The impact of traditional behavior, sanctioned by group norms but not formally acknowledged, was first documented in the Hawthorne studies. A proposed change in work methods or the installation of an automated device can run counter to the expectations and attitudes of work groups. If such is the case, the change strategist must anticipate the resulting resistance.

In a real sense, when managers evaluate the strength of limiting conditions, they are simultaneously considering the problem of objective setting. Many managers have been disappointed by change efforts which fell short of their expectations. Particularly frustrated are those managers who cannot understand why the simple issuance of a directive does not produce the intended response. Thoughtful managers will recognize that even as they operate as forces for change, other conditions are operating as forces for stability. The realities of limiting conditions are such that managers must often be content with modest change or no change at all.[38]

The implementation of change, which does not consider the constraints imposed by prevailing conditions within the present organization, may amplify the problem that initiated the change process. Even if implemented, the groundwork for subsequent problems is made more fertile than what could ordinarily be expected. Taken together, these conditions constitute the climate for change which can be positive or negative.

THE STRATEGY FOR CHANGE

The selection of a strategy for implementing the change technique has consequences in the final outcome. Greiner analyzes a number of organizational changes to determine the relationship of various change strategies to the relative success of the change itself.[39] He identifies three approaches which are located along a continuum, with *unilateral* authority at one extreme and *delegated* authority at the other extreme. In the middle of the continuum are approaches which he terms *shared* authority.

Unilateral approaches can take the form of an edict from top manage-

---

[38] Herbert Kaufman, "The Direction of Organizational Evolution," *Public Administration Review*, vol. 33 (July–August 1974), pp. 300–307, has made a strong plea for reality-centered objectives in organizational change programs.

[39] Greiner, "Patterns of Change."

ment which describes the change and the responsibilities of subordinates in implementing the change. The formal communication may be a memorandum or policy statement. It is, in any form, a one-way, top-down communication.[40] Shared approaches involve lower-level groups in the process of either (1) defining the problem and alternative solutions or (2) defining solutions only after higher-level management has defined the problem. In either case, the process engages the talents and insights of all members at all levels. Finally, delegated approaches relinquish complete authority to subordinate groups. Through freewheeling discussions, the group is ultimately responsible for the analysis of the problem and proposed solutions. According to Greiner, the relatively more successful instances of organizational change are those which tend toward the shared position of the continuum. Why would this be the case?

As has been observed, most instances of organizational change are accompanied by resistance from those who are involved in the change. The actual form of resistance may range in extreme from passive resignation to deliberate sabotage.[41] The objective of the strategy is to at least minimize resistance and at most maximize cooperation and support. The manner in which the change is managed from beginning to end is a key determinant of the reaction of people to change.

The strategy which emphasizes shared authority has the greatest likelihood of minimizing resistance to change. This is the case because it takes into account the "American culture pattern of equivalence between self-reliance and self-respect."[42] Change imposed from the top—unilateral authority—runs the danger of *creating* resistance even though the proposed change may benefit the participants in every conceivable way by any objective standards. As has been recognized by the Behavioral School, an important means for overcoming resistance to change is to involve those who will be affected by the change in the decision to make the change.

The process of shared authority is composed of six phases. According to Greiner, each of these phases accompanies each instance of reported successful change. The six phases, in logical sequence, are:

1. Pressure and Arousal. Instances of successful change are stimulated by strong pressure on the top management of the firm. This pres-

---

[40] Greiner identifies replacement of key personnel and structural changes as two other forms of unilateral change. For our purposes, personnel and structural changes are change techniques, not strategies for implementing change. Techniques specify *what* is to be done; strategies specify *how* it is to be done.

[41] Arnold S. Judson, *A Manager's Guide to Making Changes* (New York: John Wiley and Sons, 1966), p. 41.

[42] Paul C. Agnew and Francis L. K. Hsu, "Introducing Change in a Mental Hospital," *Human Organization*, vol. 19 (Winter 1960), p. 198.

sure ordinarily exerts itself in the form of unmistakable and unambiguous signals that something is wrong and needs attention.

2. Intervention and Reorientation. Because there is a tendency to seek answers in traditional solutions, the intervention of an outsider is necessary to reorient the management away from routine approaches and toward nonroutine approaches. The outsider may be a new management appointee, a corporate staff official, or a consultant. The outsider brings a different perspective into the situation and serves as challenger to the status quo. At this point, top management must commit itself to change.

3. Diagnosis and Recognition. The entire organization from top to bottom joins together to diagnose and specify the problem. Greiner observes that the less successful changes use either unilateral or delegated approaches in this step. The former fails because management presumes that they alone know the problem and its solution and thus ignore the necessity for involving participants. The latter fails because subordinates question the sincerity of managers who totally relinquish their authority. The involvement of all concerned members of the organization and, at the same time, maintenance of the necessary authority relationships approaches a "balance between maximized feelings of independence and the need for enforcing policy and authority."[43]

4. Intervention and Commitment. The outsider actively encourages management and nonmanagement personnel to invent new solutions to its diagnosed problems. All members share in this step. Through the sharing experience, a high degree of commitment to the change can be expected—provided that top management makes a commitment to the proposed new solution.

5. Experimentation and Search. The solution is not implemented on a grand scale; rather, it is implemented on a small scale at various points throughout the organization. The objective is to test the validity of the solution on an experimental basis. This tactic avoids large errors by permitting a test run—a "shakedown" cruise.

6. Reinforcement and Acceptance. As the experimental attempts provide positive signals that the change is proceeding as planned, there is a reinforcement effect which encourages the participants to accept the change and to enlarge, potentially, the scope of their own efforts. "People are rewarded and encouraged" by the success of the experimental changes, thus validating broader applications of the change.

The strategy for implementing change as described above involves superiors and subordinates in the entire process. But, we should recognize that there is no guarantee that the strategy will work in all cases.

[43] Agnew and Hsu, "Introducing Change," p. 198.

Indeed, some very basic preconditions must exist before employees can meaningfully participate in the change process. They are:[44]

a. An intuitively obvious factor is that employees must want to become involved. For any number of reasons, they may reject the invitation. They may have other, more pressing needs, getting on with their own work, for example. Or, they may view the invitation to participate as a subtle (but not too subtle) attempt by managers to manipulate them toward a solution already predetermined. If the leadership climate or organizational culture has created an atmosphere of mistrust and insincerity, any attempt to involve workers will be viewed by them in cynical terms.

b. The employees must be willing and able to voice their ideas. Even if they are willing, they must have expertise in some aspect of the analysis. The technical problems associated with computer installation or automated processes may be beyond the training of assembly-line workers, yet they may have valuable insights into the impact of the machinery on their and co-workers' jobs. But even if they have the knowledge they must be able to articulate their ideas.

c. The managers must be secure in their own positions. Insecure managers would perceive any participation by employees as a threat to their authority. They might view employee participation as a sign of weakness or as undermining their status. They must be able to give credit for good ideas and to give explanations for ideas of questionable merit. As is evident, the managers' personalities and leadership styles must be compatible with the shared-authority approach if it is to be a successful strategy.

d. Finally, the managers must be open-minded to employees' suggestions. If they have predetermined the solution, the participation of employees will soon be recognized for what it is. Certainly, managers have final responsibility for the outcome, and can control the situation by specifying beforehand the latitude of the employees: They may define objectives, establish constraints, or whatever, so long as the employees know the rules prior to their participation.

If any of the conditions which limit effective participation are present, the use of shared or delegated authority approaches must be viewed with caution. As we have seen, the same factors which limit the range of viable alternative change techniques also limit the range of

---

[44] Based upon Judson, *Manager's Guide*, pp. 109–13. Much popular and scientific literature treats employee participation in decision making. For an example of each type, see W. L. Mandry, "Participative Management: The CIL Experience," *The Business Quarterly*, vol. 36 (Winter 1971), pp. 80–87; and Joseph A. Alutto and James A. Belasco, "A Typology for Participation in Organizational Decision-Making," *Administrative Science Quarterly*, vol. 17 (March 1972), pp. 117–25.

alternative change strategies. Leadership style, formal organization, organizational culture, along with characteristics of the employees are key variables which constrain the entire change process. It should be recognized that the nature of the problem itself affects the choice of strategy. If, for example, the problem is one which requires immediate action, a unilateral approach may be the only means since alternative approaches consume time. We can summarize by observing that the appropriate change strategy depends upon three factors: the problem, the participants, and the organizational setting.

IMPLEMENTING AND MONITORING THE PROCESS

The implementation of the proposed change has two dimensions—*timing* and *scope*. Timing is the selection of the appropriate point in time to initiate the change. Scope is the selection of the appropriate scale of the change. The matter of timing is strategic and depends upon a number of factors, particularly the company's operating cycle and the groundwork which has preceded the change. Certainly if a change is of considerable magnitude, it is desirable that it not compete with ordinary business operations. Thus the change might well be implemented during a slack period. On the other hand, if the problem is critical to the survival of the organization, then immediate implementation is in order. The scope of the change depends upon the strategy. The change may be implemented throughout the organization and it becomes an established fact in a short period of time. Or, it may be phased into the organization level by level, department by department. The strategy of successful changes, according to Greiner, makes use of a phased approach, which limits the scope but provides feedback for each subsequent implementation.

The provision of feedback information is termed the *monitoring* phase. From Figure 11–1 we see that information is fed back into the implementation phase. It is also fed back into the forces for change phase because the change itself establishes a new situation which will create problems. The monitoring phase has two problems to overcome: (1) the acquisition of data which measure the desired objectives and (2) the determination of the expected trend of improvement over time.

The acquisition of information which measures the sought-after objective is the relatively easier problem to solve, although it certainly does not lend itself to naive solutions. As we have come to understand, the stimulus for change is the deterioration of performance criteria which management traces to either structural, behavioral, or technological causes. The criteria may be any number of objective indicators, including profit, sales volume, productivity, absenteeism, turnover, scrappage, or costs. The major source of feedback for those variables is the firm's usual information system. But, if the change includes the objective of improving employee attitudes and morale, the usual sources of information are limited, if not invalid. As Likert has shown, it is quite possible for a change to induce increased productivity at the expense of declining employee attitudes and motivation.[45] Thus, if the manager relies on the naive assumption that productivity and employee morale are directly related, the change may be incorrectly judged successful when improved cost and profit reports become available.

To avoid the danger of overreliance on productivity data, the manager can generate *ad hoc* information which measures employee attitudes and morale. The benchmark for evaluation would be available if an attitude survey had been used in the diagnosis phase. The definition of acceptable improvement is difficult when evaluating attitudinal data since the matter of "how much more" positive should be the attitude of employees is quite different than the matter of "how much more" productive they should be. Nevertheless, if a complete analysis of results is to be undertaken, attitudinal measurements must be combined with productivity measurements.

The second problem of the monitoring phase is the determination of

FIGURE 11–3

Three Patterns of Change in Results through Time

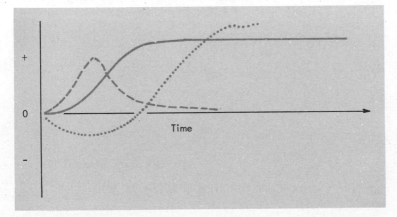

the trend of improvement over time. The trend itself has three dimensions: (1) the first indication of improvement, (2) the magnitude of improvement, and (3) the duration of the improvement. In Figure 11–3 three different patterns of change for a particular performance, behavioral, or attitudinal measure are illustrated. In the change illustrated by the solid line, improvement is slight during the early periods of time,

[45] Likert, *Human Organization*, pp. 84–91.

but rises and maintains itself at a positive level. The dashed line illustrates a marked increase, but followed by a deterioration and a return to the original position. The dotted line describes a situation in which the early signs indicate a decrease, but followed by a sharp rise toward substantial improvement. The figure illustrates only three of a number of possible change patterns. A well-devised change strategy should include an analysis of what pattern can be expected. The actual pattern can then be compared to the expected.

Ideally, the pattern would consist of an index which measures all relevant variables. Figure 11–4 illustrates a model which describes the

FIGURE 11–4

Expected and Actual Pattern of Results*

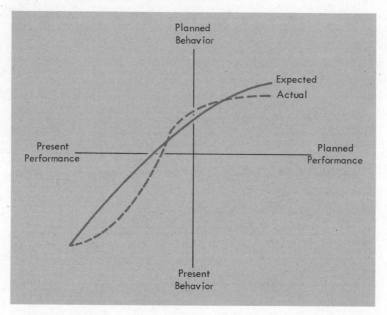

* Based upon Jeremiah J. O'Connell, *Managing Organizational Innovation* (Homewood, Ill.: Richard D. Irwin, Inc., 1968), p. 156.

necessary information for an index measuring performance and behavioral variables. The solid line is the expected pattern through time. It shows a movement into acceptable behavior prior to a movement into acceptable performance. The expected pattern may, of course, assume any configuration. The dashed line is the plot of actual change through time. It reflects not only what is happening but also the impact of corrective action which management takes to keep the change program on course. If the expected pattern is valid as originally conceived, the management's objective is to minimize the oscillations around the planned results.

In general, the monitoring phase is a specific application of management control. Before it can be effective, management must provide for a measurement of the objective, information to compare actual results with planned results, and action to correct any deviations.

SUMMARY

This chapter concludes the discussion of the Behavioral School of management. In the context of a model which describes the process of managing organizational change and development, a number of behavioral science concepts are shown to have considerable relevance. Motivation, attitudes, work groups, and leadership styles are all key concepts in an overall change framework which stresses the dynamic nature of the managerial process. Indeed, since change itself has become such a pervasive fact of the modern world, it is both appropriate and logical to cast management in a framework which emphasizes change. At the same time, the management of change certainly does not imply random and unplanned responses to a changing environment. On the contrary, we have repeatedly stressed the need for systematic analyses of all facets of the proposed change program.

The literature which reports changes undertaken in various organizations indicates the critical need for planning, organizing, and controlling the change process. We have emphasized that the manner in which the change is implemented bears heavily on the ultimate outcome. In fact, we should recognize that a change technique may fail because of ineffective implementation. We have also stressed the necessity for evaluating techniques and strategies in the context of the particular organization. Thus, even though there is evidence that certain strategies (for example, shared authority) and certain techniques (for example, sensitivity training) are appropriate in many instances, their validity in the specific instance is a matter of on-site analysis.

DISCUSSION AND REVIEW QUESTIONS

1. Review your understanding of the change model by using it to evaluate a change which you implemented recently in your approach to getting a college degree.

2. Which step in the change model is most important for the ultimate success of a particular proposed change? Explain your reasoning.

3. Which step in the change model is most difficult and most likely to be

ignored because of its difficulty? Can you think of examples from your own experience?

4. What are the dangers of the uncritical use of sensitivity training?

5. A young manager states: "It took me 30 years to develop a set of defense mechanisms that enable me to live and function in this crazy world. I refuse to participate in any training program whose objective is to tear them down." Comment.

6. Why is the creation of staff departments such a widespread reaction to organizational problems? What are the dangers of this strategy?

7. "The successful manager is one who knows how to play the role of a change agent." Comment.

8. How can supervisors and foremen provide management with feedback information which monitors a change process? How can managers validate the correctness of such information?

9. What changes do you believe are necessary within your own college or university? Why do you think so? What is your evidence? What are the limiting conditions? What are the objectives? How would you evaluate your proposed changes once implemented?

10. Even though structure should follow strategy, can you cite from experience any instances of structural change preceding the development of strategy?

ADDITIONAL REFERENCES

Argyris, C. *Intervention Theory and Method: A Behavioral Science View.* Reading, Mass.: Addison-Wesley Publishing Co., 1970.

Bennis, W. G., Benne, K. D., and Chin, R. *The Planning of Change.* New York: Holt, Rinehart, and Winston, Inc., 1961.

Coch, L., and French, J. R. P. "Overcoming Resistance to Change." *Human Relations* 1 (1948): 512–32.

Dalton, G. W., Lawrence, P. R., and Greiner, L. E. *Organizational Change and Development.* Homewood, Ill.: Richard D. Irwin, Inc., 1970.

Dickson, W. J., and Roethlisberger, F. J. *Counseling in an Organization.* Boston: Harvard University Division of Research, 1966.

Ginzberg, E., and Reilley, E. W. *Effecting Change in Large Organizations.* New York: Columbia University Press, 1957.

Gouldner, A. *Patterns of Industrial Bureaucracy.* Glencoe, Ill.: The Free Press, 1964.

Grossman, L. *The Change Agent.* New York: Amacom, 1974.

Guest, R. H. *Organizational Change: The Effect of Successful Leadership.* Homewood, Ill.: Richard D. Irwin, Inc., 1962.

Jaques, E. *The Changing Culture of a Factory.* London: Tavistock Publications, Ltd., 1951.

Kaufman, H.   *The Limits of Organizational Change.* University, Ala.: University of Alabama Press, 1971.

Levinson, H., Molinari, J., and Spohn, A. G.   *Organizational Diagnosis.* Cambridge, Mass.: Harvard University Press, 1972.

Lippitt, R., Watson, J., and Westley, B.   *The Dynamics of Planned Change.* New York: Harcourt, Brace and World, Inc., 1958.

Mann, F. C., and Neff, F. W., eds.   *Managing Major Changes in Organization.* Ann Arbor, Mich.: Foundation for Research on Human Behavior, 1961.

Morgan, J. S.   *Managing Change.* New York: McGraw-Hill Book Company, 1972.

Seashore, S. E., and Bowers, D. G.   *Changing the Structure and Functioning of an Organization.* Ann Arbor, Michigan: University of Michigan Survey Research Center, 1963.

Sofer, C.   *The Organization from Within.* London: Tavistock Publications, Ltd., 1961.

Trist, E. L., Higgin, G. W., and Pollack, A. B.   *Organizational Choice.* London: Oxford University Press, 1965.

Practical Exercise I

Organizational Change in a State Department of Health

In late 1970 the governor of a southeastern state appointed a new commissioner of health. The previous commissioner had retired from public service after spending over 20 years as the state's commissioner of health. During that time the state's Department of Health had grown from a relatively small organization employing less than 100 people to a relatively large one employing some 600 people. Its annual budget had increased from thousands to millions of dollars devoted to a wide range of personal and environmental health services. The services of the department were delivered through a state-wide network of county and regional health departments, all of which received policy direction from the commissioner's office.

The newly appointed commissioner was a licensed physician with considerable experience in federal and state public health administration. He was also a member of the American Management Association and had attended many of the association's management training programs. He was a habitual reader of the management literature. His public statements and speeches typically were strongly worded appeals for the application of management fundamentals in public health administration. His general philosophy articulated the case for strong policy direction through the management hierarchy, with policy implemented through plans developed at the operating level—the county and regional health departments, in this instance.

At the time that the commissioner took office in 1971, the organization was structured such that 15 different division and program directors reported directly to him. In addition to these formally established lines, there was an informal practice of by-passing the chain of command and going directly to the commissioner. This informal practice had been encouraged by the previous commissioner in order for him to be involved in much of the day-to-day routine of all the divisions and programs. In a very short period of time after assuming the office, the new commissioner found himself much more involved with routine affairs than he thought was appropriate. Even though the wide span of control should theoretically facilitate the development of decentralized management, the historically defined practice was quite the opposite. Division and program directors had simply not been permitted by the previous commissioner to exercise discretion and, as it happened, had not developed the skills and initiative to do so.

The commissioner was generally aware of the situation when he took office. Briefings with the governor's staff and public health experts indicated considerable dissatisfaction with the department's programs. The consensus was that the department had not aggressively sought new approaches and that its response to public health, particularly environmental needs, had been disappointing. Terms such as "drift" and "indecisiveness" were generally used to describe the department's performance during the past ten years. In response to these expressions of concern, the commissioner appointed a task force of division directors to propose initiatives for change. The task force consisted of physicians and engineers who had credibility within the organization and among public health professionals. His charge to the task force was to prepare recommendations based upon diagnosis. He reminded them that they should approach the problem with the same scientific point of view that buttressed their professional practices of medicine and engineering.

The task force met on many occasions during a two-month period of time. They evaluated the solicited comments of departmental employees and clients. The commissioner himself met with the group and offered his observations about the future direction of the Department of Health and the appropriate organization structure and management practices to sustain that direction.

The task force reviewed the information available to it and recommended that the commissioner make a basic change in the way the Health Department was structured. The recommended structural change would involve the establishment of three deputy commissioners who would specialize in three different functions: administration, personal health, and environmental health. All the former divisions and programs would be grouped together into one of the three functions, and the managers of these units would report to them instead of to the commissioner. The recommendation stated the change would enable the commissioner to deal with broad policy matters along with the three deputies. The deputies would assume the managerial role of coordinating the divisions reporting to them and, through executive sessions with the commissioner, coordinate the three functions of administration, personal health, and environmental health. As the commissioner noted: "The recommendation of the task force is, in effect, a recommendation to move toward a System 1–type organization and away from a System 4–type organization."

The commissioner received the report of the task force and was in agreement with its recommendation. He believed, however, that it was incomplete. He stated that the proposed structure would involve more than simple changes in the organization chart. It would involve changes in the ways employees had related to one another in the past—for example, division directors would no longer go directly to the commissioner but would, instead, report to the deputy commissioners. Moreover, the change indicated that division directors would have to become more assertive in the way they dealt with their own subordinates. These new behaviors would have to be learned, he reasoned, and the task force had not addressed these issues. With these thoughts in mind and expressed to the task force members, he directed them to reconvene and develop a plan which could be implemented along with the structural change and which would train the personnel of the department to act in those ways anticipated by the change.

Questions for Analysis:

1. What would be your plan for developing the new behavior required by the new structure.

2. Do you agree that the new structure tends to System 1 rather than System 4? What other evidence would you need to know fully?

3. Is there any basis for predicting whether the new structure will be more effective than its predecessor?

Practical Exercise II

Organizational Change in a Manufacturing Firm

In 1969, the Sanitary Surgical Bandage Company opened a manufacturing facility in a rural area of a southwestern state. The company had been organized in 1940 by its founder and present chief executive officer. Its products were sold nationwide and were recognized for their high quality. The company had grown from very modest beginnings to become a multimillion dollar organization. The opening of the facility in the Southwest was a strategic move to locate manufacturing facilities closer to the expanding market in that part of the United States.

The company's policies and practices reflected both the manner in which surgical bandages are manufactured and the founder's idiosyncrasies. For example, the company's manufacturing work force was predominantly women. This policy grew out of the historical practice of using women to make bandages by hand. Even though the company now used machinery which wrapped and packed the company's products, women were still employed as machine operators. In fact the chief executive selected the rural location because of the availability of women in the area's labor market. The chief executive had developed personnel policies based upon what he considered to be the special needs and circumstances of women factory employees. Among these was his insistence that supervisors and foremen be men selected from the immediate locale. He did not believe that women could supervise other women, at least in a factory setting.

The chief executive was ardently antiunion and believed that the best way to keep unions out of the plant was to keep the people happy. He insisted that all the company's plants be constructed with employees in mind. The plants were air conditioned, reasonably quiet, and clean. The company's fringe benefit package was unusually generous in terms of retirement, vacation time, and medical benefits. At the same time, he believed that the company should not establish a set of work rules. Such rules are usually found in manufacturing plants and they define procedures for granting pay raises, promotions, shift assignments, and other conditions of work. The chief executive insisted that such rules tie the hands of foremen and prevent them from responding to the special circumstances of each personnel decision.

The company's executive offices were located in Cleveland. Major policy directions in sales, personnel, production, finance, engineering, and legal affairs were developed by staff specialists and issued to all the company's manufacturing and sales facilities. Local plant superintendents and sales managers had little discretion in day-to-day operations. They were expected to follow policy, meet deadlines, keep the people happy, and avoid unionization.

Bob Ivory had just recently celebrated his fifth anniversary as superintendent of the southwestern manufacturing facility when he was confronted by a group of ten irate women employees. The spokeswoman of the group stated that they were representing all the women employees and that they had requested a meeting with Mr. Ivory to discuss company policy as related to the treatment of women. The spokeswoman, Sue Taft, said that unless Mr. Ivory made some drastic changes, the women of the plant were prepared to begin discussions with a union organizer. And while the women were reluctant to proceed with unionization, they were prepared to do so if management did not respond in good faith.

Mr. Ivory was alarmed. The forcefulness of Ms. Taft's argument and the aura of hostility within the group indicated to him that the women's concerns were genuinely felt. Moreover, he recognized that the threat of unionization could be carried out since women comprised 80 percent of the total work force. His alarm was compounded by the fact that this was the first instance of employee complaint to be brought to his attention since he had become plant superintendent. When he told the group of his surprise, Ms. Taft responded, "You should get out of your office and talk to the employees. You only hear what the shift supervisors want you to hear. For that matter, I am not sure that any of the women would have told you anything anyway. Until last week we were afraid to say anything because of what they would do to us."

"What do you mean? Who are 'they'? What would they do to you?" asked Mr. Ivory. "Mr. Ivory, you seem to be a nice guy, but you really are out of it! The shift supervisors and foremen have it all their own way. They can give overtime to whoever they want to. If you get in their way or cause them trouble they will put you on the night shift." One of the other women added, "Yeah, and once you get on their list, the only way to get off of it is to play house with them!" Mr. Ivory asked if any of them had ever personally experienced such treatment. "No," said Ms. Taft, "but we know plenty who have. My foreman is always telling dirty jokes and cursing around us. Some of the girls may like it, but I don't!"

After listening to the women for the better part of the morning, Mr. Ivory asked what it was that they wanted him to do. "I can't change company policy," he said. "I can't change what the boss in Cleveland sends down. There is no way to write work rules, and he would never let me hire women as foremen. And I sure can't fire all the foremen! What can I do?" "Well," said Ms. Taft, "you better get something started or we will be organizing for a union election by the end of the week."

Questions for Analysis:

1. How can Mr. Ivory determine whether a real problem exists?
2. Based upon what information is available above, what is your diagnosis?
3. What organizational change strategy should Mr. Ivory consider if the problem is primarily behavioral, rather than technological or structural?

part three

The Management Science School

Foundations of the Management
  Science School
Management Science Framework for
  Decisions
Break-Even and Inventory Control
  Models
Linear Programming Models
Network Models

12 Foundations of the Management Science School

INTRODUCTION

This section of the book shall examine the third major school of thought in management—the Management Science School. In the previous section we saw that a major goal of the behavioral science approach to management is to apply scientific methodology to solving the *human problems* facing management. The major goal of the management science approach is to apply scientific methodology to solving *large-scale management problems*. The idea of applying scientific methodology to large-scale management problems is not new. In fact, the central idea can be traced as far back as the 18th and 19th centuries. During that period, Eli Whitney, the inventor of the cotton gin, used a scientific approach to develop a mathematical model of manufacturing costs to enable more efficient use of the cotton gin. However, the recognized field of management science has only formally existed for approximately 25 years. It has been during this period that the individuals now associated with this field began to have a noticeable impact on the solution of complex military and business problems through the use of engineering and mathematical skills. During this period a new profession has come about: the "management scientist." Like the behavioral scientists these individuals have their own professional associations; the Operations Research Society of America (1952) and the Institute of Management Sciences (1953), in addition to their own scholarly journals, courses of study in business schools and engineering schools, and large numbers of jobs within all types of organizations.

The Purpose of This Section

While the models of the management scientist are mathematical and specialists in this field are trained in mathematics, the basic concepts of most models can be completely comprehended and appreciated with only an understanding of very basic mathematics and arithmetic. The purpose of this section of the book is to teach potential managers *about* selected management science models, not to teach them *to be* management scientists. There is no more reason for a manager to be a technically proficient management scientist than for a physician to be a bacteriologist. However, the manager must know what to expect of management science, its strengths and weaknesses and how to use mathematical models as *tools,* just as the physician must know what to expect of bacteriology and how it can serve as a diagnostic tool. The readers should keep this in mind as they read about management science.

BOUNDARIES OF THE MANAGEMENT SCIENCE SCHOOL

As is often the case with an emerging body of knowledge, there is much confusion over just what it includes. Since its early development is rarely a consciously planned effort, there may even be numerous approaches to studying the same phenomena which differ little except, perhaps, in name. This appears to have been the case with management science. Numerous synonyms for the term management science appear, such as managerial analysis, operations research, operational research, operations analysis, and systems analysis. They all share in common the desire to apply scientific analysis to large-scale managerial problems in all types of organizations.

The activities of management scientists have been characterized by an emphasis on the mathematical modeling of systems. Applications by operations research specialists, mostly confined to the production segment of business firms, began after World War II. During World War II, these individuals had successfully solved a number of military problems ranging from those of a logistical nature (equipment and troop movements) to developing strategy for submarine warfare.[1] As a result, after the war, operations research caught on quickly in some of the larger firms in the United States. Such companies as E. I. Dupont de Nemours and H. J. Heinz pioneered the use of early operations research applications. However, it was not until a few of these bolder firms had tried it with success that civilian operations research made any major headway in the United States.

While it is difficult to place clear boundary lines around the Manage-

---

[1] An excellent reference on this subject is E. S. Quade, ed., *Analysis for Military Decisions* (Chicago: Rand McNally & Co., 1964).

ment Science School, it is possible to distinguish certain characteristics of its approach. It is generally agreed that most management science applications possess the following characteristics:[2]

1. A Primary Focus on Decision Making. The principal end result of the analysis must have direct implications for management action.

2. An Appraisal Resting on Economic Effectiveness Criteria. A comparison of the various feasible actions must be based on measurable values that reflect the future well-being of the organization. Examples of such measured variables include costs, revenues, and rates of return on investment.

3. Reliance on a Formal Mathematical Model. These models are actually possible solutions to the problems, which are stated in mathematical form. The procedures for manipulating the data must be so explicit that another analyst can derive the same results from the same data. This *replicability* requirement is not new to the reader who saw in the previous section that this was also a major requirement of the behavioral science approach to management. In fact, replication is the keynote of scientific analysis.

4. Dependence on an Electronic Computer. This is actually a requirement necessitated by either the complexity of the mathematical model, the volume of data to be manipulated, or the magnitude of computations needed to implement the model.

The Role of the Computer in Management Science

Electronic computers have fostered most of the advances in the management science approach over the past two decades. In fact, it is not coincidental that computer technology developed in a parallel fashion with the field of management science. Undoubtedly there would be negligible interest right now in the field of management science (except perhaps for some applied mathematicians) if it were not for the vast data-generating capacity and computational ability of high-speed computers. The computer has gone through its own stages of development from a point where it could only process routine data to a point where it can now effectively assist in the conduct of management science studies. The increasing availability, understanding, and use of the computer have made it possible to turn heretofore theoretical mathematical models into everyday, here-and-now, practical decision aids.

Throughout this section of the book we shall examine, for illustrative purposes, simplified mathematical models in which all computations can be performed by hand. The reader will see that even repetitious use of

---

[2] Harvey M. Wagner, *Principles of Management Science* (Englewood Cliffs, N.J.: Prentice-Hall, Inc., 1970), p. 5.

these simplified models would be greatly aided by a computer, and real-world problems faced by managers in complex organizational settings are usually not amenable to hand solutions. Numerical solutions to these kinds of problems may require thousands of individual computations. A computer provides the solutions in a matter of minutes instead of weeks, with less possibility of error.

The Role of Mathematical Models in Management Science

Mathematical models are characteristics of the management science approach. However, before defining mathematical models let us examine two points. First, in the previous section of the book we saw that experimentation is an important part of the scientific approach. However, it is rare, if ever, that a manager can perform what would be considered a *bona fide* scientific experiment to test the feasibility of taking a particular action. The practicalities of the real world preclude any manager from doing this. In other words, a manager cannot usually experiment with inventory to determine which level minimizes carrying costs and ordering costs, or cannot experiment with the advertising budget to determine which combination of media (for example, radio, TV, magazines) produces the most favorable sales results. However, an accurately constructed mathematical model enables the decision maker to experiment with possible solutions without interrupting the ongoing system. If the model accurately represents the ongoing system, it will provide the decision maker with the results of proposed solutions. In other words, it will react as the real system would react; and, therefore, the decision maker can simulate the behavior of the real system. It is this experimental role of mathematical models which makes them useful to managers.

Second, while there are several different types of models, the emphasis on mathematical models in the Management Science School should be clear. In order to utilize scientific analysis, one must be "quantitatively oriented," since one of the major characteristics and prerequisites of scientific inquiry is quantitative measurement. Thus the models examined in this section of the book are quantitative or mathematical in nature.

Understanding the role of mathematical models in the Management Science School, we can now define exactly what a mathematical model is: *A mathematical model is a simplified representation of the relevant aspects of an actual system or process.*

At this point, the value of a simplified representation may be questioned. This is why the definition includes the two words "relevant aspects." It is obvious that the value of any model depends on how well it represents the system or process under consideration. A highly simplified model that accurately describes a system or process still provides a more clearly understood starting point than a vague conception which a manager mentally creates. Such a model forces the manager to consider systematically the variables in the problem and the relationships among the variables. Thus, forcing the manager to formalize thinking reduces the possibility of overlooking important factors or giving too much weight to minor factors.

In reality, readers are probably more familiar with models for decision making than they think. The accounting equation, $A = L + C$, is a mathematical model. In fact, it is the oldest decision-making model, since it dates back to the Renaissance. It is a mathematical model showing a simplified relationship between assets, liabilities, and capital. It does not resemble the actual system physically; but it does *behave as the real system behaves*. It is an abstraction of the financial condition of a particular enterprise at a given moment of time. On the other hand, the income statement is also a mathematical model that is an abstraction of the operations of a business over a period of time.

In conclusion, instead of studying the actual system, the managers can study a mathematical model or representation of the system. This enables them to manipulate variables in order to determine the effects such changes will have on the overall performance of the actual system. The managers can, therefore, experiment using the model and predict the effect such changes will have on the actual problem.

TYPES OF MATHEMATICAL MODELS

Before managers can understand, evaluate, and utilize mathematical models, they must be aware of the major types of these models. Mathematical models may be classified by the *purpose* of the model (descriptive or normative) and/or by the *types of variables* included in the model (deterministic or probabilistic).

Descriptive and Normative Models

A *descriptive model* is one which describes how a system works. That is, *it describes things as they are* and makes no value judgments about the particular phenomenon being studied. Many times a model is constructed solely to be a description of a real-world phenomenon in mathematical terms. This model can then be used to display the situation more clearly or to indicate how it can be changed. Descriptive models display the alternative choices available to the decision maker and, in some cases, help the decision maker determine the consequences or outcomes of each alternative. However, a descriptive model *does not* select the best alternative.

A *normative (or prescriptive) model* selects the best from among alternatives based on some previously determined criteria which are also included in the model. It tells *how the system should be* in order to achieve a particular objective. These models are also referred to as optimizing models and decision models since they seek the optimum from among all the possible solutions.

Deterministic and Probabilistic Models

A model is *deterministic* when the law of chance plays no role. In other words, the model contains no probabilistic considerations. For example the model, *Profit = Revenue* minus *Costs,* is a deterministic mathematical model. All of the factors taken into account in the model are exact or deterministic quantities, and the solution is determined by this set of exact relationships. In other words, in a deterministic model, we assume conditions of *certainty.*

Once chance or random variables are introduced, conditions of *uncertainty* exist and the model is said to be a *probabilistic* model. Probabilistic models are based on the mathematics of statistics. Conditions of

FIGURE 12–1

Types of Mathematical Models

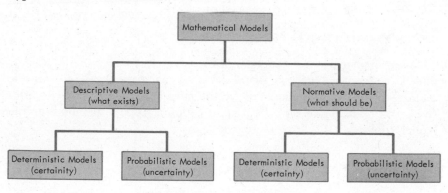

uncertainty introduced in the model are often based on observations of real-world events. For example, insurance companies make heavy use of actuarial tables that give the probability of death as a function of age. These tables can be considered probabilistic models.

Figure 12–1 summarizes our discussion to this point. It indicates that a mathematical model may be either descriptive or normative in purpose and contain either deterministic or probabilistic variables. At this time let us briefly examine some of the more popular mathematical models in the Management Science School. Several of these models will then be discussed in more detail in the remaining chapters of this section.

POPULAR MANAGEMENT SCIENCE MODELS

Decision Theory Models

In the last two decades, the systematic analysis of decision making has become known as "decision theory." Decision theory is firmly rooted in the fields of statistics and the behavioral sciences and has as its goal, to make decision making less of an art and more of a science. In the Management Science School it plays an important role since it is primarily concerned with assisting decision makers in organizations to improve their decision process under conditions of uncertainty. Decision theory focuses upon certain elements in decision making which are common to all decisions and provides a framework which enables a decision maker to better analyze a complex situation containing numerous alternatives and possible consequences. Decision theory models are normative in purpose and contain probabilistic variables.

Break-Even Models

One widely used mathematical model is known as the break-even model. While it did not originate specifically with the management science approach, it is included here because it is mathematical in nature. Its major function is to determine what will be the break-even point for the firm as a whole or any of its specific products or services. The break-even point is that particular level of operations where total revenue equals total cost and profit is zero. It can also be utilized to determine what level of profits or losses will be achieved at a particular level of output. The break-even model is descriptive in purpose and contains deterministic variables.

Inventory Models

In short, inventory models provide answers to two questions: "How much?" and "When?" Just as the firm is concerned with obtaining goods to be sold at the most favorable price, it must also be concerned with the point at which orders are placed for repeat goods and the quantity of each order. On one hand, enough inventory must be available at all times to insure that there are no lost sales or loss of customer goodwill due to stockouts; but on the other hand, frequent orders result in increased costs such as the storage costs from carrying an excessive inventory. The costs of ordering and carrying an inventory behave in such a way that one increases while the other decreases. Inventory models which are normative in purpose and contain deterministic variables enable the manager to determine the economic order quantity (EOQ) and the optimum reorder point.

Allocation Models

Allocation models are used in a variety of situations in which numerous activities are all competing for limited resources. These models enable the decision maker to allocate scarce resources to maximize some given objective. The resources may, in certain departments, be available time which the production manager must allocate to several different products in order to maximize the objective of profit. The resource may be an advertising budget which the marketing manager must allocate over several different advertising media in order to maximize the objective of the most exposure for the product(s). In each case, the manager wishes to find the optimum way to allocate the scarce resources, given certain objectives (profit, exposure) and certain constraints (available time, budget).

One of the most widely used allocation models is the linear programming model. Linear programming expresses the objective to be achieved in the form of a mathematical function, the value of which is to be maximized (for example, profits) or minimized (for example, costs). The constraints arc introduced which reduce the number of feasible alternatives. A powerful linear programming procedure known as the simplex method searches the feasible alternatives in order to find the particular one that maximizes or minimizes the value of the objective function. The linear programming model is normative in purpose and contains deterministic variables.

Network Models

Network models are extremely useful in planning and controlling both simple and complex projects. Actually, network models are as old as scientific management. The reader will recall the discussion of the Gantt chart as a contribution of Henry Gantt and the Classical Management School. While network models are more sophisticated, both are based on the same philosophy. The two basic and most common types of network models are PERT (Program Evaluation and Review Technique) and CPM (Critical Path Method). PERT is a method of planning and controlling nonrepetitive projects—projects that have not been done before and will not be done again in the same exact manner (for example, the Polaris missile). CPM is a planning and control technique used in projects for which some past cost data are available. Network models are normative in purpose and contain probabilistic variables.

Brand-Switching Models

One of the most important measuring devices used by marketing executives in determining the success or failure of their efforts is the share of the market secured by a product. Obviously, marketing managers constantly seek ways to increase their product's share of the market or to at least prevent the existing share of the market from declining. In order to do this, they must have some idea of the behavior of consumers, both in terms of their brand loyalty and their switching from one brand to another. Brand-switching models provide such information. Brand-switching models can be considered descriptive in purpose and contain probabilistic variables.

Waiting-Line Models

In the production department, workers waiting in line to requisition needed tools or raw materials cost money. Their managers would like to minimize idle time, but, on the other hand, they cannot afford to provide a great number of service facilities. Thus they must strike a balance between the costs of additional facilities and worker idle time. There are many other examples of processes which generate waiting lines. These lines are often referred to as queues. For examples, housewives often wait in long lines in a supermarket, while husbands may have to wait in line at a fuel pump in a service station. In many instances, customers become irritable when faced with long periods of waiting, and, if it becomes excessive, the business may lose customers. Waiting-line models, which are descriptive in purpose and contain probabilistic variables, enable managers to reach effective solutions.

Simulation Models

Simulation means to have the appearance or form of, without the reality. In many situations management problems are so complex that they cannot be depicted by a standard mathematical model. Simulation involves constructing a model which replicates some aspect of the organization's operation; then performing step-by-step computations with the model; thus duplicating the manner in which the actual system might perform. An individual simulation can be thought of as an experiment upon a model. Numerous trials or experiments are performed until a workable satisfactory solution, rather than an optimal solution, is reached. This experimental nature of simulation is an important advantage because the system can be studied under a wide variety of conditions which might be impossible using the actual real-world system. In this respect all mathematical models involve some degree of simulation. Simulation models are descriptive in purpose and contain probabilistic variables.

CONSTRUCTING MANAGEMENT SCIENCE MODELS

Behavioral scientists must use certain tools and methods (referred to as research designs) for obtaining information. In this section the steps that management scientists take to insure a logical approach for formulating and constructing mathematical models are examined. While several general approaches are available, the following series of steps is widely accepted:

1. Define and formulate problem.
2. Construct model.
3. Solve model.
4. Test solution.
5. Develop necessary controls for the solution.
6. Implement solution.

Define and Formulate Problem

This first step in the model-building process lays the foundation for all of the following steps. If a problem is ill-defined or loosely formulated, any model constructed on such a weak foundation will be of little or no value. A problem that is well defined and formulated is one in which all of the elements are clearly delineated. This includes determination of the objective(s) to be achieved, identification of alternative courses of action, and all known components of the particular problem.

The types of problems faced by managers will vary in complexity. For example, some will be relatively definable, with easily identifiable variables which are known to behave with a high degree of certainty. Others will contain a large number of variables which behave with a high degree of uncertainty. Thus, managers face problems which range from relatively simple and organized to complex and disorganized, with varying degrees of disorganization in between. Table 12–1 presents four types of problems faced by managers, the numbers and types of variables in the problem, and some popular management science techniques used to help solve each kind.[3] Let us briefly examine each type.

1. Simple and Organized. These kinds of management problems contain only a small number of variables which behave with a high degree of certainty. Some inventory problems are of this type where all variables are exact or deterministic quantities; the inventory model is extremely valuable in such situations.

---

[3] Adapted from: *Tentative Recommendations for the Undergraduate Mathematics Program of Students of the Biological, Management, and Social Sciences* (Berkeley, California: Committee on the Undergraduate Program in Mathematics, 1964), p. 12. Also see Max D. Richards and Paul S. Greenlaw, *Management: Decisions and Behavior* (Homewood, Ill.: Richard D. Irwin, Inc., 1972), chap. 20.

TABLE 12–1

Types of Problems Faced by Managers

Type of Problem	*Simple Organized*	*Simple Disorganized*	*Complex Organized*	*Complex Disorganized*
Number of variables..........	Few	Many	Few	Many
Type of variables..........	Deterministic (certainty)	Deterministic (certainty)	Probabilistic (uncertainty)	Probabilistic (uncertainty)
Example of useful management science technique..........	Inventory control model	Linear programming model	Decision theory	Network models

2. Simple and Disorganized. These kinds of management problems contain many variables, but all of the variables are deterministic (behave with certainty). The allocation-type problems would fall in this category. Linear programming models are useful in solving allocation problems.

3. Complex and Organized. Management problems of this type contain a small number of variables, but they are probabilistic (behave with uncertainty). A service station manager trying to decide at what levels to price gasoline faces this type of problem. Although not knowing what competitors will do, the manager does know that whatever it is, it is going to influence the outcome. Decision theory models are useful for problems of this type.

4. Complex and Disorganized. These kinds of management problems contain a great number of variables, and all of them behave with uncertainty. Examples of such problems are launching a new product, constructing a new hospital, and putting a man on the moon. The reader can imagine that constructing models for such problems is extremely difficult even with the aid of the electronic computer. Network models very can and have been used successfully for problems of this type.

Unfortunately for most managers, the majority of problems they face tend to be complex and disorganized, and very few normative models deal with this class of problem. What then does the management scientist do in order to gain the benefits of these types of models? The only alternative is to attempt to reformulate complex disorganized problems into less complex and more organized ones (that is, move from right to left in Table 12–1). If this can be done, then the problem becomes more definable and more easily adaptable to various management science models. Obviously, this task is not an easy one because the attempt to simplify a problem may eliminate one or more important variables and assume away the problem. Generally, there are three ways that management scientists break down complex problems into more definable ones:

a. Assume Certainty. In some situations, a management scientist may assume certainty in a problem, although some of the variables may be probabilistic in nature. For example, when facing an inventory problem, the management scientist often assumes that demand for the product is known when trying to arrive at the economic order quantity (EOQ) to replenish the inventory.

b. Simplify Relationships. Here the management scientist assumes that the relationship between variables is much simpler than it is in reality. For example, when utilizing the linear programming model it is assumed that the relationships among variables are linear, when in fact they probably are nonlinear.

c. Isolate Operations. Management scientists can attempt to isolate a particular operation or segment of the operation. They can seek to optimize the output from that segment and assume that the remaining parts are not adversely affected. For example, in a hospital, a management scientist might try to maximize space utilization while assuming that if this is achieved, other factors will not be adversely affected (for example, morale of hospital staff, patient care, etc.).

Construct Model

After the problem has been clearly formulated and defined, the model construction phase begins. This involves expressing the elements of the problem in mathematical form. Clearly, this is a vital phase. What is important here is that the model constructed responds in the same fashion as the real system. There are three basic elements of every mathematical model:[4]

1. Components. These are the parts of the model. They may be firms, households, warehouses, costs, media, and any other phenomena which is a part of the real system.

2. Variables. These relate in one way or another to the components of the model. They are often classified as *input variables* which arise outside the component and must be fed into it (for example, inventory, patients, students, raw materials); *status variables* which describe the state of a component (for example, salary, income, education, age);

---

[4] Guy Orcutt, "Simulation of Economic Systems," *The American Economic Review,* vol. 50 (December 1960), pp. 893–907.

and *output variables* which are anything generated by a component (for example, costs, demand).

3. *Relationships.* These specify how the values of different variables are related to each other. For example, inventory models specify the relationship between ordering costs and carrying costs.

The management scientist is faced with the task of determining all of the relevant components which affect the functioning of the system under study and arriving at measurable variables to represent these factors. Finally, the relationships among the variables must be determined and expressed in mathematical form.

Solve Model

Once the model has been constructed, the next step is to arrive at a solution to the model. For a normative model, this involves mathematical techniques for arriving at the best strategy or alternative. In the case of complex linear programming problems, this may involve numerous computations. In the case of a descriptive model where usually there is no solution, the model can be termed "solved" when it accurately describes the system under study. This is arrived at by manipulating the model until this point is reached.

Test Solution

Once the model is solved, the solution should be tested before it is applied to a large segment of the organization's operations. The reason for this should be clear: Testing the solution enables management to determine the effect of the model on a small scale, and, if any errors are discovered, the model can be altered accordingly and a new solution obtained. For example, the solution to an inventory problem could be tested on a small scale using perhaps one warehouse or store. In this way one can gain some insight into the value of the solution and adjust accordingly if changes are necessary. Then and only then should the solution be applied on a full-scale basis.

Develop Controls

Once the model is constructed and solved, there must be a provision for *concurrent* control. In other words, the model must be carefully and continually reexamined in order to insure that the variables and relationships have not changed. Whenever there is a change in any of the variables included in the model, it may be necessary to completely revise it. There are also many forces at work which affect management decisions but over which the manager has little or no control. Thus the need for tight *monitoring* of the model is vital. The reader can imagine, for example, the impact of the fuel shortage on the models used by oil companies for allocating fuel to service stations.

Implement Solution

After the model has been solved and tested, the solution should be implemented by or recommended to the manager, in cases where staff analysts have constructed the model. In any case, the manager must be aware of the objectives, assumptions, omissions, and limitations of the model. After this is done, further reformulation of the problem may result because of some previously overlooked factor which is deemed important. Before the solution is finally implemented, all personnel who will utilize the solution produced by the model should be made aware of the basic rationale behind the model and the advantages to be gained by implementing the solution. The manager must keep in mind at all times the behavioral ramifications involved in implementing change. These were discussed in Chapter 11. A well-constructed model may not provide its true benefit if individuals in the organization resist implementation or pay only token service to the solution provided by the model. Thus behavioral factors can vitally affect the success of management science solutions and must be considered by the manager.

CONTRIBUTIONS OF THE MANAGEMENT SCIENCE SCHOOL TO THE PRACTICE OF MANAGEMENT

Managers were faced with the problem of *planning, organizing, and controlling* their organization's operations long before the advent of the electronic computer and management science models; and they would still have to perform these functions if the field of management science did not exist today. In other words, it must be recognized that management science *is not* a substitute for management. Mathematical models can be especially useful as an *aid* to the manager performing the functions of *planning* and *controlling*. In order to justify its existence to the practicing manager, however, management science models must provide for more efficient and effective planning and controlling.

Finally, the reader should not construe our discussions in this section of the book as implying that mathematical models can provide the entire basis for *all* management decisions. This is inconceivable. We saw in the prior section (Behavioral School of Management) that there are many kinds of management decisions that should not or cannot rest solely on the manipulation of quantitative data. Many behavioral models are utilized in which all variables are not quantified. Also, successful implementation of a mathematical model must apply behavioral as well as mathematical science, because the resultant solution must be implemented by human beings.

SUMMARY

Thus far we have examined the Classical School of Management which was concerned, among other things, with the structure of formal organizations, the process of management, and the functions of a manager; and the Behavioral School, with its emphasis on human relations and the scientific approach to the study of human behavior in organizations. In this section the reader will be introduced to the third major block of material in the field of management, the Management Science School. In the following four chapters, selected management science models will be presented. While numerous models could be discussed, we have chosen those which describe generally the nature of the Management Science School.

DISCUSSION AND REVIEW QUESTIONS

1. What roles do mathematical models play in the management process of planning, organizing, and controlling?

2. Create a problem which a manager might realistically face. Now break the problem down into its subproblems.

3. Assume you are the athletic director at your school. You have been bombarded with complaints about the distribution of tickets to students for basketball games. Tickets are distributed beginning four hours before each game. This creates long lines at ticket windows and much discomfort on rainy days. In addition, crowds form in the lobby, which makes seating by game time very difficult. You have decided to try and improve this system. You decide first to construct a model of the system. What would be the components, variables, and relationships in your model? Develop some alternative solutions.

4. Assume that you drive to school each morning and more than one way exists to arrive at your destination (for example, freeway or through the city). You must decide which route to take. As you analyze this problem, the process of model building is actually taking place, although it is subjective in nature. What are some of the factors that would have to be considered in order to reach an effective decision?

5. After several semesters at your school, you are tired of becoming very irritated at registration time (long lines, closed courses, general havoc and bedlam). You have decided that something must be done. You contact the registrar's office and offer your services as a consultant. Since

they are desperate for any help they can receive, they accept your offer. You suggest that some kind of model needs to be developed. How would you go about developing this model? What would be some of the major considerations?

6. "Since a mathematical model cannot include every possible variable that affects a problem, it cannot be of much value as a decision aid." What is your opinion of this statement?

7. Are there any similarities between the Behavioral Science School and the Management Science School?

8. "The classical bureaucratic structure is a normative model for organizing a firm?" Comment.

ADDITIONAL REFERENCES

Bierman, H., Bonini, C., and Hausman, W.   *Quantitative Analysis for Business Decisions.* Homewood, Ill.: Richard D. Irwin, Inc., 1973.

Churchman, C. W., Ackoff, R. L., and Arnoff, E. L.   *Introduction to Operations Research.* New York: John Wiley and Sons, Inc., 1957.

Forrester, J. W.   *Industrial Dynamics.* Cambridge, Mass.: Massachusetts Institute of Technology Press, 1961.

Levin, R. I., and Kirkpatrick, C. A.   *Quantitative Approaches to Management.* New York: McGraw-Hill Book Co., 1975.

Miller, D. W., and Starr, M. K.   *Executive Decisions and Operations Research.* Englewood Cliffs, N.J.: Prentice-Hall, Inc., 1970.

Paik, C. M.   *Quantitative Methods for Managerial Decisions.* New York: McGraw-Hill Book Co., 1973.

Plane, D. R., and Kochenberger, G. A.   *Operations Research for Managerial Decisions.* Homewood, Ill.: Richard D. Irwin, Inc., 1972.

Rappaport, A.   *Information for Decision Making.* Englewood Cliffs, N.J.: Prentice-Hall, Inc., 1970.

Schoderbek, P. P.   *Management Systems.* New York: McGraw-Hill Book Co., 1967.

13 Management Science Framework for Decisions

INTRODUCTION

Management science stresses that the core of the manager's activities is making decisions. When planning for future expansion, when deciding to promote one of six subordinates, when deciding to place a particular price tag on a new product, a manager is involved in decision-making. The list of managerial decisions is endless.

Although the manager is engaged in other activities besides decision making, a main theme of the Management Science School is focusing upon the "how" of decisions. A *decision theory* framework is the cornerstone of the Management Science School.

Decision theory is subject to misunderstanding because of semantic conflicts and because it has been associated with sophisticated mathematical formulas and theories. Thus, many students of management believe that a background in advanced mathematics and statistics is necessary to comprehend fully the usefulness of decision theory. The discussion in this chapter indicates that the decision theory framework can be appreciated without an in-depth background in mathematics and statistics.

Objectives, Optimization, and Suboptimization

The manager today operates in an environment that is competitive, becoming more international, and scrutinized more closely by government, unions, and the public. Each of these environmental factors, and many others, influence the ability of the manager to achieve specific objectives. For example, the objective of a corporate manager cannot be neatly classified as profit maximization. Although profit is a necessary objective of business firms, it is only one of many. The decision-making activities of corporate managers are directed toward achieving such often stated objectives as: (1) improving market share; (2) developing human resources; (3) creating a favorable public image; (4) producing and marketing a quality product; and (5) generating profit.

In the everyday activities of decision making, managers often face situations where they cannot optimize two objectives simultaneously. If one is *optimized*, the other is *suboptimized*. For example: If output or production is optimized, employee morale may be suboptimized and vice versa. Another example would be a case in which the attainment of a short-run objective such as reducing maintenance expense may lead to the long-run consequence of increased production costs. In this case, the short-run goal was *optimized* at the cost of *suboptimizing* a long-run goal. Thus, the multiplicity of objectives complicates the real world of the decision maker.

The major goal of decision theory models in the Management Science School is to make decision making less of an art and more of a science. *Decision theory models*, then, focus on the elements in situations which are common to all decisions and provide managers with a framework which enables them to analyze a complex situation with numerous alternatives and possible consequences.

THE DECISION-MAKING PROCESS

The starting point in any analysis of decision making involves the determination of whether a decision needs to be made. If problems did not exist, then there would be no need for decisions. For example, suppose that the marketing director of a local bank, at the beginning of the planning period, establishes a specific marketing objective of increasing the number of personal checking account customers of the bank by 10 percent. Suppose that at the end of the planning period the objective has not been adequately accomplished. If this is the case, then the marketing director faces a problem, and some kind of decision will be required to solve this problem. However, before making a decision, the director would develop a number of feasible alternatives (actually these are potential solutions to the problem) and consider the potential payoffs and consequences of each possible solution. For example, two possible solutions might be to (1) lower the service charges on personal checking accounts or (2) eliminate all service charges on personal checking accounts ("free checking"). The marketing director would have to consider the payoffs and possible consequences of each alternative and make the decision.

The banker's decision-making process would be similar to that of most managers in various-organizational settings. The fact that managers at *all* hierarchical levels must make decisions distinguishes them from nonmanagers. Some of these decisions have a strong impact on the organization, while others will be important, but less crucial. The important point, however, is that *all* of the decisions made in an organization have some impact on the organization. As a result, they all have some effect (positive or negative, large or small) on the success of the organization. A basic flow diagram of the decision-making process outlined above is shown in Figure 13–1. As noted in Figure 13–1, all of the schools of management have studied various parts of the decision-making process. The management scientist, however, has placed a great deal of emphasis on constructing payoff tables and examining decision making under three distinct conditions: certainty, risk, and uncertainty. These are reflected in Figure 13–1.

FIGURE 13–1
The Decision-Making Process

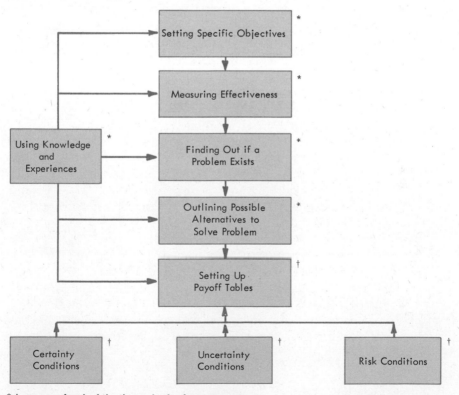

* A concern of each of the three schools of management.
† A specific concern of the Management Science School.

Decision-Making Variables

Managers operate within environments in which some variables are *controllable* and others *uncontrollable*. They can control what strategy will be selected. That is, they can initially establish a number of possible inventory levels for a given period. Then after considering such factors as available storage space, transportation possibilities, and costs of the inventory, the best inventory level can be selected. Thus, in a decision-making context, the one major variable that is controllable is the actual choice of a strategy.

Two variables which significantly influence the consequences of selecting a strategy are the states of nature and/or competitive actions. The term, *states of nature*, designates the possible events which may actually occur. The most uncontrollable state of nature facing mankind is death. For a business manager, what a competitor does is also uncontrollable. The term, *strategy*, in a decision theory context is used to designate the action selected by a manager to cope with the occurrence of possible states of nature and/or competitive actions. The uncontrollable factors (states of nature and/or competitive actions), plus the strategy selected, interact to yield a desirable or undesirable end-result.

States of nature are completely uncontrollable from the vantage point of the manager. For example, a manufacturer of children's toys knows that the accuracy of production forecasts will depend in large measure upon the state of the overall economy. Similarly, the executive of a tobacco corporation is faced with the problem of how much and what types of each of the firm's products should be produced, given the government campaign against certain tobacco products.

Typically, there are a large number of possible states of nature that can occur. It would be impossible to list them all and to determine the effects that each might have on outcomes. Normally, the manager would consider only those states of nature which are most likely to occur and would not become entangled in an endless list of uncontrollable variables which might occur.

In addition to the states of nature, another uncontrollable variable is the competitive action of market opponents. In a business environment, the total sales revenue received from the sale of a product, the return on capital investment, and the type of work force hired in a community will be affected by the actions of competitors. The actions and reactions of competitors are, of course, difficult to determine. Thus the activities of competitors in response to a particular strategy are uncontrollable.

Utility of Decision

Each decision made by a manager is designed to achieve some objective or set of objectives. The outcome of each decision reached yields some form of *utility* to the decision maker. The form which the utility of an outcome takes may be psychological or economic. It is possible to consider utility as a subjective measure of the worth of the payoff to the manager making a decision.

The main point to remember when discussing utility is that the reward received from each individual outcome is subjective. That is, each decision maker has a conception of what each outcome provides in the form of psychological gratification and/or economic benefits. To date, in the management science literature there exists no practical method which can compare in an orderly and systematic fashion the utilities of different managers. If, however, it were possible to accurately determine the utility derived by a manager for each outcome, the utility concept could then be expressed mathematically. The outcomes could be viewed as the "payoff" to the manager, which results from the interaction of strategies, states of nature, and competitive actions. This relationship in decision theory is often presented as

$$U = f(S,SN,CA)$$

which is read *U* is a function (*f*) of (depends on) *S*,*SN*,*CA*, where *U* designates utility, *S* designates the strategy, *SN* designates the state of nature, and *CA* designates competitive actions. The two important factors to consider are that the three major variables—namely the strategy, states of nature, and competitive actions—are highly interrelated, and the utility of the "payoff" as perceived by the individual manager is a subjective phenomenon. The opinions, attitudes, beliefs, experiences, and intuitions of human beings may result in different selections of strategies among managers because of their different perceptions and expectations of the utility of the payoff.

AN APPLICATION OF DECISION THEORY

The decision-making process illustrated in Figure 13–1 shows that the management scientist focuses attention on establishing payoff tables and proposing techniques for making decisions under conditions of certainty, risk, and uncertainty. The payoff table is used to study decision making under these three conditions.

The Payoff Table

In considering the decision-making process in general and the utility of payoffs in particular, the management scientist uses a payoff table. The table presents the payoff which can result from each strategy selected under each state of nature, or competitive action. The payoffs shown in the table can be expressed in dollars, apples, gallons of gasoline, satisfaction levels, or whatever category is appropriate for the decision being considered.

The payoff table *does not* eliminate the need to reach a decision. The manager must carefully scrutinize what it reflects, add personal experience and feelings, and then reach a decision. *The payoff table serves as a management science tool for organizing pertinent data.* An illustration of a payoff table is presented in Table 13–1.

The data presented in Table 13–1 deal with monetary payoffs to a

TABLE 13–1

Payoff Table for Exit Oil Company

Strategies Available to Management	State of Nature: Demand for Gasoline		
	Low	Moderate	High
Centralize the distribution of gasoline...........................	$3,000,000	$1,500,000	$2,000,000
Decentralize the distribution of gasoline...........................	1,000,000	1,500,000	3,700,000

decision maker in the Exit Oil Company. The decision maker has two distribution strategies and faces three possible states of nature. The decision involves selecting a strategy for centralizing or decentralizing the distribution of gasoline. The demand (state of nature) for gasoline is considered under three situations—low, moderate, and high. If the decision maker selects the strategy to decentralize and a low demand for gasoline occurs, the payoff would be $1 million. A decision to centralize the distribution in a market with moderate demand would result in a payoff of $1.5 million. The payoffs shown in Table 13–1 are considered *conditional values* because they are *conditioned* on the demand for gasoline in the marketplace. The distribution alternatives are controlled by the manager, and the states of nature (demand) are *uncontrollable*. The manager must select the alternative based on what the state of nature (demand) will be. In this particular problem competitive actions do not influence the strategy chosen.

Decision-Making Process: Certainty

When a manager knows exactly which state of nature or competitive action will occur, a circumstance of *certainty* exists. This would mean that the manager would be able to make perfectly accurate decisions, time after time. Of course, this type of decision-making environment is difficult, if not impossible, to find.

In reaching certainty decisions, the manager would only have to utilize a part of a payoff table and would have to examine a number of different strategies, but only the payoffs related to the one state of nature which will occur. Suppose that the decision maker at Exit Oil knew for sure that demand for gasoline was going to be high, and the objective is to generate the largest possible monetary payoff. Examination of Table 13–1 indicates that the best payoff under a condition of high demand would be achieved if distribution were decentralized. Thus, the lucky manager would select the decentralization strategy.

The manager is lucky because perfect information about demand is available. This may happen a few times in a manager's career, but it is the exception. In many situations the manager is completely ignorant of what state of nature and/or competitors' action will occur. The manager is forced to use *probabilities* when faced with a situation that requires making a decision under these types of conditions.

Decision-Making Process: Risk

In some decision situations the manager is able to develop an approximation of states of nature or competitive actions. The ability to estimate may be due to experience, incomplete but reliable information, or intelligence. In situations where estimates are made there is a *risk* involved, but there is not a complete lack of knowledge for reaching a decision. When risk is involved the situation requires the use of probability estimates.

Decision making under risk conditions, in addition to requiring probability estimates, also necessitates the use of *expected values*. The payoffs listed in Table 13–1 are conditional values because they will occur only if a specific state of nature occurs and a specific strategy is chosen. *An expected value is the conditional value multiplied by the probability of occurrence of the state of nature or competitive action.* Suppose that Exit Oil has knowledge that there is a 0.30 chance for high demand, a 0.50 chance for moderate demand, and a 0.20 chance for low demand. Management could proceed to use these probabilities in conjunction with the data shown in Table 13–1. Table 13–2 shows an expected value payoff table using the probability estimates.

TABLE 13–2

Expected Value Payoff Table for Exit Oil Company

Strategies Available to Management	State of Nature: Demand for Gasoline Probability of Demand			Total Expected Value
	Low 0.20	Moderate 0.50	High 0.30	
Centralize the distribution of gasoline....................	$600,000	$750,000	$ 600,000	$1,950,000
Decentralize the distribution of gasoline....................	$200,000	$750,000	$1,110,000	$2,060,000

The payoffs in Table 13–2 were calculated by taking the conditional payoffs in Table 13–1 and multiplying them by the probability of a particular level of demand occurring. The calculations for the centralization alternative are:

Total Expected Value = Low Demand Probability × Conditional
Value + Moderate Demand Probability
× Conditional Value + High Demand Probability
× Conditional Value.

or

Total Expected Value = 0.20 ($3,000,000) + 0.50 ($1,500,000)
+ 0.30 ($2,000,000)

or

Total Expected Value = $600,000 + $750,000 + $600,000
= $1,950,000

The total expected value for each strategy is equal to the sum of its expected values under each possible state of nature. The $1,950,000 figure represents an *average payoff* that would be received by Exit Oil if they decided to centralize on a great number of occasions under the same conditions.

In reviewing Table 13–2 it can be seen that the total expected value if the company centralizes its gasoline distribution is $1,950,000, while a decision to decentralize yields a total expected value of $2,060,000. Using only the dollar figures, it would be best to decentralize because of the greater expected value. The difference in the total expected values is $110,000. This means that the decision should be made with caution because of small differences in the two expected values. The note of caution is not intended to be an alarm but is instead a warning that the total expected value payoffs are similar and the manager has an interesting decision to make. Also remember that the probabilities are estimates that could be off target. This clearly indicates that the decision to centralize or decentralize is being reached under conditions of risk.

Decision-Making Process: Uncertainty

A number of individuals define decision theory as focusing primarily upon making decisions and improving the decision process under conditions of *uncertainty*.[1] The main thrust of this interpretation of decision

---

[1] The authors of this text, however, believe that decision theory also applies to certainty and risk decision making. However, for an excellent discussion of decision theory in an uncertainty context, see Harold Bierman, Charles P. Bonini, and Warren H. Hausman, *Quantitative Analysis for Business Decisions* (Homewood, Ill.: Richard D. Irwin, Inc., 1973).

theory is that the manager is faced with reaching a decision with no historical data concerning the probabilities of occurrence of states of nature or competitive actions.

A number of different decision criteria have been proposed as possible bases for decisions under uncertainty. These decision criteria include:

1. Maximizing the maximum possible payoff—the *maximax* criterion (optimistic).
2. Maximizing the minimum possible payoff—the *maximin* criterion (pessimistic).
3. Minimizing the maximum possible regret to the decision maker— the *minimax* criterion (regret).
4. Assuming equally likely probabilities for the occurrence of each possible state of nature or competitive action—the *insufficient reason* criterion.

The first step in making decisions under conditions of uncertainty is to construct a conditional value payoff table like that presented in Table 13–1. The next step would be the selection and application of one of the decision criteria.

Maximax Criterion. Hurwicz[2] suggested that some decision-makers think optimistically about the occurrence of events influencing a decision. If this philosophy is followed, the manager would select that strategy under which it is possible to receive the most favorable payoff. It is dangerous to employ this criterion because it ignores possible losses and the chances of making or not making a profit. A completely optimistic manager would examine the conditional value table and seek to maximize the maximum possible gain (maximax).

Returning to Table 13–1, the manager using the maximax criterion would list the most favorable payoff for each strategy as follows:

Centralize . . . $3,000,000
Decentralize . . . $3,700,000

If maximum monetary payoff is the objective, the decision maker would decentralize.

Maximin Criterion. There are managers who make decisions believing that only the worst possible outcome can occur. Wald proposed that this type of pessimism results in the selection of that strategy which maximizes the least favorable payoff.[3]

---

[2] Leonid Hurwicz, "Optimality Criteria for Decision Making under Ignorance," Cowles Commission Discussion Paper, Statistics, No. 370, 1951 (mimeographed); and R. Duncan Luce and Howard Raiffa, *Games and Decisions* (John Wiley & Sons, Inc., New York, 1957).

[3] A more complete discussion of the maximin criterion is presented in David W. Miller and Martin K. Starr, *The Structure of Human Decisions* (Englewood Cliffs, N.J.: Prentice-Hall, Inc., 1967), p. 116.

The pessimistic manager would examine Table 13–1 and look at the minimum payoffs for each strategy.

Centralize $1,500,000

Decentralize $1,000,000

These figures would result in the decision to centralize the distribution of gasoline. The decision maker has maximized the minimum payoff (maximin).

Minimax Criterion. If a manager selects a strategy, and if a state of nature or competitive action occurs that does not result in the most favorable payoff, regret occurs. The manager is regretful that the strategy selected did not lead to the best payoff. Savage introduced the minimax criterion to clarify the decision process which involves regret.[4]

Once the manager makes a choice and the state of nature or competitive action has occurred, the payoff is received. If the manager had known which of the various states of nature or competitive actions would occur, the strategy with no regret would have been selected. Thus, *managerial*

TABLE 13–3

Regret Table for Decision Maker at Exit Oil

Strategies Available to Management	States of Nature: Demand for Gasoline			Maximum Regret
	Low	Moderate	High	
Centralize the distribution of gasoline....................	0	0	$1,700,000	$1,700,000
Decentralize the distribution of gasoline....................	$2,000,000	0	0	$2,000,000

regret is defined as the payoff for each strategy under every state of nature of competitive action subtracted from the most favorable payoff that is possible with the occurrence of the particular event. For example, in Table 13–1, the most favorable payoff if the demand is high would be $3,700,000. If the manager decided to decentralize and the demand was high, he would have no regret ($3,700,000 − 3,700,000 = 0). However, assuming a decision to centralize, and high demand for gasoline exists, there would be a regret of $1,700,000 ($3,700,000 − 2,000,000 = $1,700,000).

The regret payoffs are presented in Table 13–3. The decision maker, in attempting to minimize regret, would decide to centralize. The payoff table indicates that a decision to centralize would mean that no matter

---

[4] L. J. Savage, "The Theory of Statistical Decision," *Journal of the American Statistical Association*, vol. 46 (March 1951), pp. 55–67.

what the demand for gasoline is the Exit Oil manager will never have a regret of more than $1,700,000. That is, centralization would minimize maximum regret (minimax).

Insufficient-Reason Criterion. The three preceding decision criteria assumed that without any previous experience, it is not worthwhile to assign probabilities to the states of nature or competitive actions. One well-known concept, however, is utilized in introducing probability into decision making under conditions of uncertainty. This is referred to as the *insufficient-reason criterion.* This criterion states that if managers do not know the probabilities of occurrence for the various states of nature and competitive actions, they should assume that all are equally likely to occur. In other words, managers should assign equal probabilities to each state of nature or competitive action.

Applying the insufficient reason criterion to the payoffs in Table 13–1 yields the following:

$$Centralize \text{ Expected Value} = \tfrac{1}{3} (\$3,000,000 + 1,500,000 + 2,000,000) = 2,166,667$$

and

$$Decentralize \text{ Expected Value} = \tfrac{1}{3} (\$1,000,000 + 1,500,000 + 3,700,000) = 2,066,667$$

The manager is faced with a close decision but would decide to centralize the distribution of gasoline.

A Review of Uncertainty Choices. The four decision criteria used for the Exit Oil decision illustrate that depending on the orientation of the manager, different strategies will be selected. The following decisions would be made:

1. *Optimist* would decentralize.
2. *Pessimist* would centralize.
3. *Regreter* would centralize.
4. *Insufficient Reasoner* would centralize.

This example employing only two alternative choices and three demand situations indicates that uncertainty decision making is difficult. The choice of a criterion is a personalistic phenomenon. Each decision maker at different times probably acts on each of these four criteria in making decisions.

SUMMARY

In the preceding discussion of decision-making criteria, it was easy to see that the decision theory framework can provide the manager with

---

[5] For another discussion of decision theory, see Stephen H. Archer, "The Structure of Management Decision Theory," *Academy of Management Journal,* vol. 7 (December 1964), pp. 269–87.

a systematic method for analyzing problems.[5] This is one of the practical advantages of decision theory. *It literally encourages the manager to discover and enumerate potential strategies, states of nature, and competitive actions.*

As noted in Chapter 12, decision theory models are useful for complex-organized types of problems. Recall that these problems contain a smaller number of variables, but they behave under conditions of uncertainty, that is, they are probabilistic. Placing them in a decision theory framework (by using conditional and expected value concepts) enables the manager to give "structure" to such problems. As such, the framework enables the manager to add some organization to a situation where none existed. Thus, while a manager may not actually construct payoff tables, the disciplined process of enumerating possible states of nature and competitive actions is itself a benefit of decision theory models.

The Management Science School uses as its central focal point the decision-making process. Decision theory enables us to study systematically how managers think about decision making. The framework is only a step in the direction of attempting to understand how decisions are made and how decision making can be improved.

DISCUSSION AND REVIEW QUESTIONS

1. The stock of the Payoff Corporation has paid dividends of $1.60 per share in 13 of the last 20 dividend periods. The other seven times, it has paid $1.40. What is the expected dividend?

2. Discuss what is meant by the statement that each decision situation and outcome has a specific utility for each manager.

3. Briefly describe the type of manager that would be most inclined to employ a maximax criterion—a maximin criterion.

4. The Ace Music Company is considering two strategies for promoting the records of a new recording artist. One strategy is to concentrate entirely on television advertising, the other is to concentrate entirely on newspaper advertising. In the past, the company's profits have been influenced by general economic conditions. The profit payoffs for each strategy depend upon future economic conditions as noted in the following table.

	States of Nature		
Strategies	*Downturn in the Economy*	*Stable Economy*	*Upturn in the Economy*
(S_1) Television advertising......	$ 4,000	$40,000	$60,000
(S_2) Newspaper advertising......	$10,000	$20,000	$30,000

  a.   What would the maximax choice be?
  b.   What would the minimax choice be?
  c.   What would the maximin choice be?
  d.   What would the insufficient reason choice be?

5.   A dairy store manager observes the daily sales of skim milk for a 100-day period and develops the table of sales presented below.

Skim Milk Sales

Quantities Purchased	Number of Days
40	20
50	15
70	15
100	30
120	20

The milk sells for $0.30 a quart and the cost to the store manager of securing the milk from the dairy is $0.20.
  a.   If 70 units are stocked every day, what will be the firm's expected profit per day over the long run?
  b.   Using the data presented in the table, what quantity (40, 50, 70, 100, or 120) should be purchased every day to maximize long-run profits?

6.   Why is it difficult to assume that many business decisions are made under conditions of certainty?

7.   What decision-making factors are not presented in payoff tables?

8.   An analysis and forecast of next year's sales results in the following probability distribution:

Total Demand	Probability
1000 units	0.20
1200 units	0.20
1400 units	0.40
1600 units	0.20

The price per unit is $58. The cost of the product is $38. If the product is not sold during the year, it is worthless.
  a.   Prepare a table of conditional values.
  b.   Prepare a table of expected values, and indicate the optimum choice if management is attempting to optimize profits.

9.   Why is it necessary and advisable to consider decision making in the domain of each of the three schools of management.

10.   Does the decision-making process involve the use of any principles of managing? Explain.

ADDITIONAL REFERENCES

Bross, I. D. F.　*Design for Decision.* New York: The Macmillan Company, 1953.

Halter, A. N., and Dean, G. W.　*Decisions under Uncertainty.* Cincinnati: South-Western Publishing Company, 1971.

Hein, L. W.　*The Quantitative Approach to Managerial Decisions.* Englewood Cliffs, N.J.: Prentice-Hall, Inc., 1967.

Kassorf, S.　*Normative Decision Making.* Englewood Cliffs, N.J.: Prentice-Hall, Inc., 1970.

Magee, J. F.　"Decision Trees for Decision Making," *Harvard Business Review* 42 (1964): 72–75.

Morgan, B. W.　*An Introduction to Bayesian Statistical Decision Processes.* Englewood Cliffs, N.J.: Prentice-Hall, 1968.

Raiffa, H.　*Decision Analysis.* Reading, Mass.: Addison-Wesley Publishing Co., Inc., 1968.

Schellenberger, R. E.　*Managerial Analysis.* Homewood, Ill.: Richard D. Irwin, Inc., 1969.

Schlaifer, R.　*Analysis of Decisions under Uncertainty.* New York: McGraw-Hill Book Co., Inc., 1967.

14 Break-Even and Inventory Control Models

INTRODUCTION

The managerial team of any institution is faced with many different kinds of cost problems that influence the daily operations of the organization; that is, the cost components must be studied, analyzed, and understood before goal-oriented decisions can be reached. Two specific management science models which are increasingly being used by managers are the *break-even model* and the *inventory model*. Both models and modifications of them deal with cost factors.

In this chapter the break-even model and the inventory control model will be examined. As is true in working with most of the quantitative models found in the Management Science School, both of the models have limitations. The primary objective of this chapter is to present the logic, assumptions, and limitations associated with the break-even and inventory control models.

THE ECONOMIC AND ACCOUNTING INFLUENCE

Economists and accountants have contributed many ideas, principles, and models to each of the three schools of management. In the area of cost-and-profit analysis, the economic influence is certainly obvious. Economists and accountants have clarified the meaning of such terms as fixed costs, variable costs, total revenue, marginal revenue, and marginal costs. This clarification has proved beneficial in developing and utilizing management science models to analyze various types of organizational problems. An understanding of the meaning of these terms is essential if the management science tools are to be employed effectively.

Fixed Costs

A group of costs remains fixed regardless of the level of sales generated and are aptly designated as *fixed costs*. The insurance on a warehouse must be paid regardless of whether the warehouse is being fully utilized. If a firm plans to utilize warehouse space, it has planned for this by purchasing a warehouse. Because of present production levels, it may not be completely utilized. Yet the warehouse is insured for a period of time (for example, one year) and the fixed insurance premium must be paid regardless.

As an organization grows in size, the amount of fixed costs incurred also increases. In addition, many fixed costs, although remaining fixed for normal variations in output, will vary if output is either exceedingly low or high. An example of such a situation would be hiring additional part-time salespeople during a peak demand season. These costs we can term "semifixed" costs. Thus, when we use the term "fixed" costs we are actually referring to the short run. In the long run, all costs are subject to some variations.

Variable Costs

Economists and accountants have identified costs that move in close proportion to changes in output as *variable costs*. In a manufacturing plant the amount of material used depends upon the number of units produced. This is also true with regard to the labor costs incurred in manufacturing the product—the more units of a product produced, the greater the total labor expenditure. Thus variable costs are related to the activity itself (for example, production of a product) rather than to creating capacity, as is the case with fixed costs.

Total Revenue

The anticipated or actually generated total revenue is calculated by using sales volume and price data. A manager forecasting total revenue would utilize the anticipated sales volume at each price level. If, however, total revenue is being determined after the product has been sold, the exact volume and price figures are used. In any case, the total revenue, price, and volume relationship can be expressed mathematically as

$$TR = Q \times P$$

where TR designates total revenue, Q designates anticipated or actual volume, and P designates anticipated or actual price.

Marginal Costs and Marginal Revenues

The term marginal cost is used to specify the additional costs incurred by producing one more unit of output. If costs and output are linearly related, marginal cost is constant per unit of output. It should also be apparent that the total variable cost (TVC) is determined by multiplying the constant marginal cost by the respective level of output. Of course, when costs are related nonlinearly to production levels, the marginal costs will vary at different levels of output.

Marginal revenue designates the additional revenue generated as a result of taking a particular course of action, such as selling one more unit. In an economic theory framework, when marginal revenue equals marginal cost the firm is achieving maximum profit. Thus, if the business manager is concentrating on generating profits as one of numerous goals, the marginal cost-marginal revenue relationship would be of concern. However, in utilizing the break-even and inventory models, the major focus is not upon the marginal concepts but upon the total cost and total revenue relationships. Without understanding the economists' concepts of cost and revenue, and the classification framework offered by the accountants, the assumptions and conclusions associated with the break-even and inventory models would have very little, if any, practical meaning to the operating manager.

THE BREAK-EVEN MODEL

At the end of an operating period a manager hopes that the revenue from the period's sales will be sufficient to cover production costs, marketing costs, administrative costs, and provide some amount of profit. However, if revenue for a particular period is sufficient only to cover the first three items, the seller has broken even or is operating at the break-even point.

In other words, if the firm had been able to increase its sales volume by only one item more than the break-even point, it would have shown a profit for the period. The break-even point is the particular level of operations where *total revenue equals total cost.*

The break-even model is a deterministic model used to study relationships between revenues, costs and profit. The model can answer such questions as: (1) What will be the break-even point in dollars, units, or capacity?; (2) What will be the profit or loss of producing and selling various quantities of a particular product?; and (3) What level of output and sales is needed to achieve a desired level of profit?

In order to utilize break-even analysis we must utilize the cost and revenue components discussed originally by economists and accountants and transposed into a quantitative framework by management scientists. Management scientists study the cost, revenue, and volume relationships by employing representative symbols. The following symbols are generally used:

$$BE = \text{break-even point,}$$
$$P = \text{selling price per unit,}$$
$$VC = \text{variable cost per unit,}$$
$$TFC = \text{total fixed costs, and}$$
$$Q = \text{number of units.}$$

The break-even point occurs when sales produce a margin above variable costs that equals the amount required for fixed costs. If a firm sells annually 80,000 units at $10 each, it would receive $800,000 in sales revenue. If the variable cost (VC) is $6 per unit, it obtains a marginal income of $4 per unit, or $320,000. If the total fixed costs for the firm are $320,000, the firm has broken even.

Using the symbols cited above allows us to derive the break-even formula. First we define the equation for total cost:

$$TC = VC \cdot Q + TFC.$$

Then we define total revenue:

$$TR = P \cdot Q.$$

At the break-even point the total cost equals the total revenue; therefore, equating these two equations yields:

$$P \cdot Q = VC \cdot Q + TFC$$

Solving for Q:

$$P \cdot Q - VC \cdot Q = TFC$$
$$(P - VC) \, Q = TFC$$
$$Q = \frac{TFC}{P - VC}$$

APPLICATIONS OF THE BREAK-EVEN MODEL

Sales Problem

Managers often use the break-even model to cope with many different types of business problems. For example, the manager of the Maxi Corporation may be concerned with the current state of the overall economy and is interested in ascertaining how much the sales of electric can openers could decline before operations resulted in a loss. Assume that all other cost components of the model remain unchanged. The Maxi revenue and cost data are presented as

$$Price = \$20.00 \text{ unit}$$
$$VC = \$12.00 \text{ unit}$$
$$TFC = \$80,000$$
$$Quantity \ Sold = 100,000.$$

We know that

$$BE = \frac{TFC}{P - VC}.$$

Thus,

$$BE = \frac{\$80,000}{\$20.00 - \$12.00};$$
$$BE = \frac{\$80,000}{\$8};$$
$$BE = 10,000 \text{ units.}$$

Since 100,000 can openers are being sold annually, and selling 10,000 can openers allows the firm to break even, it can sell 90,000 fewer can openers and still not lose money. However, if 90,001 fewer can openers are sold, it will incur an operating loss. Thus, if the company sells 100,000 units, the total revenue generated from sales would be $2,000,000. A reduction of $1,800,000 in revenue could occur before an operating loss is incurred. This, of course, constitutes a reduction in sales of 90,000 units ($1,-800,000/$20 = 90,000).

Distribution Problem

Managers are often faced with the problem of deciding how to distribute a particular product. For example, the Battel Pipe Company produces a stainless steel circular pipe rack which is distributed mostly through wholesalers to gift shops, tobacco shops, and variety stores. Originally the firm had planned to market the product as a novelty but then began to consider the product from a more practical viewpoint. After an extensive analysis of the potential market, the firm narrowed its distribution choice to two alternatives. The management of Battel is interested in determining what the break-even points are for Alternatives I and II. These alternatives are:

I. Market the rack to *wholesalers* who would then distribute the product to large department stores on a national basis.
II. Market the rack directly to *tobacco shops* on a national basis.

Cost data for the two alternatives are presented below:

Alternative I (*wholesalers*)		*Alternative II* (*tobacco shops*)	
Production costs (fixed)..................	$20,000.00	Production costs (fixed)..................	$20,000.00
Production costs (per unit variable).........	3.00	Production costs (per unit variable).........	3.00
Marketing costs and administrative costs (fixed).............	20,000.00	Marketing costs and administrative costs (fixed).............	40,000.00
Marketing costs and administrative costs (per unit variable)................	3.00	Marketing costs and administrative costs (per unit variable)................	1.00
Battel price charged wholesalers.......	8.00	Battel price charged stores............	6.00

By utilizing the break-even formula the following results are determined:

Alternative I

$$\text{Break-Even Point in Units} = \frac{\$40,000}{\$8.00 - \$6.00} = 20,000 \text{ units}$$

Alternative II

$$\text{Break-Even Point in Units} = \frac{\$60,000}{\$6.00 - \$4.00} = 30,000 \text{ units}$$

The above formulas have provided us with the break-even points for both of the alternative plans. Another way of examining the relationship of revenue, costs, and incomes for various volumes of sales is to employ the break-even chart.

It is common practice to graphically present break-even relationships. The relationships for Alternative I are presented in Figure 14–1. By use of the graphical analysis we verify the formulas. The break-even point is at 20,000 units or $160,000 sales revenue.

The total revenue line represents the relationship between price and volume. The area of fixed costs is marked off as a horizontal line which indicates the constant nature of the fixed expenditures. The total cost line begins at the same point as fixed costs and moves upward to the right for different output levels.

Figure 14–2 presents the revenue, cost, and income relationships for Alternative II. Once again, the break-even point determined graphically is identical to that found by using the break-even formulas.

The Break-Even Model and Decision Theory

The break-even model does not provide the manager with a complete understanding of the cost and revenue components. The manager, by

FIGURE 14–1

Break-Even Chart for Alternative I (wholesalers)

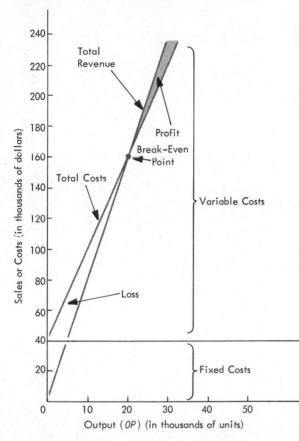

using the traditional break-even procedures discussed above, is not giving adequate consideration to the various levels of sales that are possible. In general, in coping with break-even problems the manager does not know exactly what levels of sales volume will be achieved. A method for dealing with the uncertainty of sales volume is to use a range of possibilities.

Let us assume that based on the assessment of the economy in general and the market for pipe racks in particular, the management of Battel estimates potential levels of sales for Alternatives I and II. In addition, the managerial team has estimated the probabilities of achieving the various levels of sales for both alternatives.

The range of sales and probabilities of occurrence for Alternatives I and II are as follows:

	Level of Pipe Rack Sales	Probability of Occurrence
Alternative I.....................	20,000	0.50
	30,000	0.30
	40,000	0.20
Alternative II.....................	20,000	0.40
	30,000	0.30
	40,000	0.20
	50,000	0.10

Using the sales data and the probability estimates will enable the Battel management group to determine the expected profit of each of the alternative plans. The reader will recall from the preceding Chapter 13 that the expected value of a particular event equals the value of the event if it should occur multiplied by the probability of the event occurring.

Using the cost data for the alternatives would enable the team to

FIGURE 14-2

Break-Even Chart for Alternative II (tobacco shops)

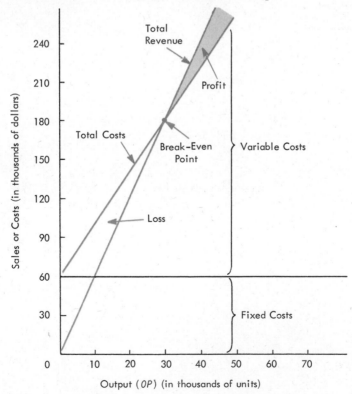

construct profit tables. Table 14–1 illustrates the sales level, revenue,

TABLE 14–1

Profit Levels of Alternative I

Level of Sales	Sales Revenue	Total Costs	Profit or Loss
20,000	$160,000	$160,000	$ –0–
30,000	240,000	220,000	20,000
40,000	320,000	280,000	40,000

cost, and profit relationships for Alternative I. The data for Alternative II are presented in Table 14–2.

By utilizing the probability estimates in conjunction with the data provided in the tables (14–1 and 14–2), the managers at Battel could deter-

TABLE 14–2

Profit Levels of Alternative II

Level of Sales	Sales Revenue	Total Costs	Profit or Loss
20,000	$120,000	$140,000	–$20,000
30,000	180,000	180,000	–0–
40,000	240,000	220,000	20,000
50,000	300,000	260,000	40,000

mine the expected profit of each of the alternative plans. Tables 14–3 and 14–4 present the expected profits for the two alternatives.

If the Battel managers have faith in the probability estimates, the cost data, and revenue data, and if profit is a significant criterion for decision

TABLE 14–3

Expected Profit for Alternative I

Level of Sales	Profit	×	Probability of Sales	=	Expected Profit
20,000	$ –0–	×	.50	=	$ –0–
30,000	20,000	×	.30	=	6,000
40,000	40,000	×	.20	=	8,000
		Expected Profit of Alternative I			$14,000

making, they would select Alternative I. The pipe racks would then be distributed through the wholesalers, since the expected profit for Alternative I is $14,000 as compared to an expected profit of zero dollars for Alternative II. The assumption is that if this type of choice were repeated many different times under the same conditions the profit achieved for

TABLE 14–4

Expected Profit for Alternative II

Level of Sales	Profit	×	Probability of Sales	=	Expected Profit
20,000.......	−$20,000	×	.40		−$8,000
30,000.......	−0−	×	.30		−0−
40,000.......	20,000	×	.20		4,000
50,000.......	40,000	×	.10		4,000
		Expected Profit of Alternative II			−0−

Alternative I would average $14,000. However, selecting Alternative II over the long run would yield an average profit of zero dollars.

LIMITATIONS OF THE BREAK-EVEN MODEL

In order for the break-even model to be properly applied to management problems, the decision maker should be aware of the following:

1. Break-even analysis is useful only over relatively short ranges of output. This is because it is assumed that there is a linear relationship among costs, output, and revenue. Thus, it is not a valuable long-range decision-making tool.

2. Since the break-even model is a deterministic model, it is a static tool. That is, the relationships are representative of only a point in time. Therefore it would be more valuable in relatively stable situations than in highly dynamic or volatile situations. It provides a simplified presentation of the relationships between cost, revenue, and output.

3. Utilizing probabilities and a range of sales volume injects a more realistic characteristic into the analysis. However, probabilities clearly indicate that the manager is operating under conditions of risk. The accuracy of the decision depends significantly on the accuracy of the probability estimates.

4. The break-even model should only be used to guide decision making. Its presentation provides a conceptual tool for understanding the relationships between costs, revenue, and output.

The important point to recognize is that utilization of the break-even model is an aid to the manager. It is definitely not a technique which can be used mechanistically without considering its limitations to reach important decisions.[1]

---

[1] For another discussion of break-even analysis as applied to distribution, see Frank J. Charvat and W. Tate Whitman, *Marketing Management: A Quantitative Approach* (New York: Simmons-Boardman Publishing Corp., 1964), chap. 10.

THE INVENTORY MODEL

Managers are often faced with the problem of maintaining an adequate inventory. The inventory could be dresses for the women's wear store manager; drugs for the manager of a hospital dispensary; iron ore for the manufacturer of steel; stainless steel for the producer of pipe racks. The adequate supply of raw materials, finished goods, or people is an integral part of the ongoing operations of these organizations. In this section we will examine a model that focuses upon controlling inventories so that costs are minimized. The examples cited will concentrate on finished goods, but the principles and concepts can be applied to raw material and human resource inventory control as well.

A basic reason for having finished goods in inventory is to separate manufacturing and distribution into independent, successive activities. The manager who must cope with inventory problems is usually concerned about inventory cost minimization. At times, decisions concerning the minimization of inventory costs and fulfilling customer demand are at cross-purposes. For example, a manager may be concerned about the cost of carrying large inventories but desires to satisfy the buyer's demand at the time of request. This is especially true in retail stores. The store owner only has a specified amount of storage space for food inventory and may fear that by not having a requested product on hand, the customer will become dissatisfied and not return in the future. The desirable course of action is to study systematically the cost components of inventory and the demand for the items so that customer service and goodwill are maintained at a high level.

The Inventory Decision

The seller or manufacturer of goods confronts two key inventory decisions if a complete and intelligent inventory program is to be developed. These mutually interrelated decisions are: (1) the size of each lot or batch of items to be purchased and (2) the time to order or request this quantity. By utilizing a basic technique (referred to as the economic order quantity model) which was developed by management scientists, the inventory decision process facing the manager can be made easier.

Cost Factors in Inventory Control

In resolving inventory control problems, the manager must initially identify the cost factors which affect the choices being considered. First, there are the *ordering costs* of getting a particular item into the firm's actual inventory. These costs are incurred each time an order is placed. They are clerical and administrative costs per order which also include the cost of receiving and placing into inventory the goods ordered.

Second, there are the *carrying costs*. These include the interest on money invested in inventory, storage space, rent, obsolescence, payment of taxes, and insurance on losses due to theft, fire, and deterioration, and protection. The carrying cost component is usually expressed as an annual figure and as a percentage of the average inventory.

To minimize inventory costs, managers attempt to minimize ordering and carrying costs. These two costs are related to each other in opposing directions as shown in Figure 14–3.

FIGURE 14–3

Ordering and Carrying Cost Relationship

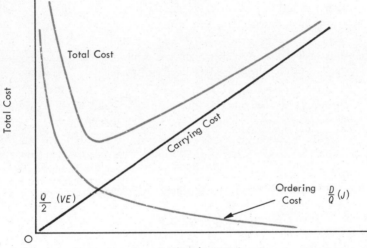

The number of orders for a given period of time is equal to demand (D) for the period divided by the size of each order quantity (Q). The total ordering cost per period (week, month, or year) is equal to the cost of placing each order (J) multiplied by the number of orders per period, $\dfrac{D}{Q}$, or $\dfrac{D}{Q}$ (J). It should be evident now that as the order size increases, fewer orders are required to meet the demand for a period, and consequently the ordering cost component will decrease. This is illustrated graphically by the downward sloping order cost curve in Figure 14–3.

The cost of carrying an item in inventory is calculated by multiplying the value of the item (V) by a percentage figure (E), which is management's estimate of taxes, insurance, etc., per period as a percentage of the value of inventory. The total carrying costs are equal to the cost of carrying one item (VE) multiplied by the average inventory $Q/2$. In the illustrative problem to follow, carrying cost is shown as a linear function. However, realistically the carrying cost factors should and would not be prorated as a constant percentage.

An example will illustrate why average inventory is assumed to be $Q/2$. Assume that the Battel company orders 500 pipe rack parts and uses 100 of them each week; at the midpoint of the first week it has on hand 450. Table 14–5 illustrates the number in inventory at the mid-

TABLE 14–5

Average Inventory Analysis

Week	Number in Inventory at Midpoint of Week
1...	450
2...	350
3...	250
4...	150
5...	50
	1,250

point of each week over a period of five weeks. Thus an average of 250 (1250 ÷ 5) parts were on hand over the five week period. The average (250) can also be found by utilizing the $Q/2$ formula, that is, 500/2.

Trial-and-Error Methodology

A manager can use trial and error procedures to determine what size of order to place. However, in attempting to select the optimal size of inventory from a cost standpoint, a number of assumptions are usually made.

1. The demand for the item over the period is known with certainty. Thus, we are developing the economic order quantity model (EOQ) under conditions of certainty.

2. The rate at which the inventory of the item is depleted is constant. Figure 14–4 below illustrates depletion at a constant rate. The average inventory is found under conditions of constant usage (for example, selling same amount monthly for the year).

3. The time necessary for acquiring an order of items after the order is placed is exactly known (that is, the lead time).

These assumptions are not completely realistic, but they allow us to study in an uncomplicated manner the development of the economic

FIGURE 14–4

Constant Depletion

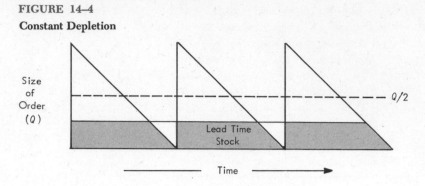

order quantity model. Further sophistication of the basic model can occur only if the simplified form is clearly understood.[2]

Let us assume that a steel mill is attempting to solve a lot-size problem involving iron ingots. The yearly demand, which is constant, for the ingots is established as 1,000. The administrative and clerical cost of placing an order is $40. The manager estimates insurance and taxes to be 10 percent per year. The value of a single ingot is $20. Thus, the components involved are:

$$D = 1,000$$
$$J = \$40$$
$$E = 10 \text{ percent}$$
$$V = \$20$$

The manager could utilize a tabular format to reach an inventory ordering decision that would minimize the total inventory costs. The size of inventory order and cost relationships are shown in Table 14–6.

A review of the total cost data in Table 14–6 indicates that placing four

TABLE 14–6

Trial-and-Error Method

Number of Ingot Orders	Size of Order Q	Order Cost D/Q (J)	+	Carrying Cost $Q/2$ (VE)	=	Total Cost
1.........	1000	$ 40	+	$1000	=	$1040
2.........	500	80	+	500	=	580
4.........	250	160	+	250	=	410
10........	100	400	+	100	=	500
20........	50	800	+	50	=	850

[2] For examples, see Richard B. Chase and Nicholas J. Aquilano, *Production and Operations Management* (Homewood, Ill.: Richard D. Irwin, Inc., 1973), chaps. 8 and 9.

orders of 250 each yields the lowest cost. However, note that the trial-and-error method could be tedious. To eliminate the tedious nature of the trial-and-error approach, management scientists have developed a specific order quantity model.

The EOQ Model

The trial-and-error method involves experimentation and manipulation of costs before the decision maker arrives at the minimum cost. Referring to Figure 14–3, we see that the minimum total inventory cost is at the point directly above the intersection of carrying cost and ordering cost. Thus, the EOQ formula may be derived by using this relationship between total carrying and ordering costs. It should also be noted that for simplicity the relationship shown is linear. The first step in algebraic derivation is to set carrying and ordering costs equal to each other.

$$\frac{Q}{2}(VE) = \frac{D}{Q}(J)$$

Solving for Q yields:

$$Q(VE) = \frac{2DJ}{Q}$$

$$Q^2(VE) = 2DJ$$

$$Q^2 = \frac{2DJ}{(VE)}$$

$$Q = \sqrt{\frac{2DJ}{(VE)}}$$

The final equation is commonly referred to as the economic order quantity formula, and can be used to solve the type of inventory order size problem facing the management of the steel mill. Using the data in our problem we can determine the economic order size, $D = 1,000$, $J = \$40$, $E = 10$ percent, and $V = \$20$.

$$Q = \sqrt{\frac{2(1000)(\$40)}{(\$20)(.10)}}$$

$$Q = \sqrt{\frac{\$80,000}{\$2.00}}$$

$$Q = \sqrt{40,000}$$
$$Q = 200$$

Reviewing the trial-and-error method shows that the least costly inventory strategy is to place four orders to satisfy the overall demand of

1,000. However, utilization of the more exact *EOQ* formula suggests that placing five orders of 200 each will be least costly. Since the five-order strategy was not considered in the trial-and-error procedures, the manager was not able to really minimize inventory costs.

The *EOQ* model can also be used to take into consideration changes in demand for a product. Let us assume that the demand is 1,000 for the first ten months of the year, and 2,000 for the last two months of the year. For the January–October period, the *EOQ* calculations would be as follows: $D = 1,000$; $J = \$40$; $E = 10$ percent; and $V = \$20$.

Thus,

$$EOQ = \sqrt{\frac{2(1,000)(\$40)}{(\$20)(.20)(10/12)}}$$

$$EOQ \cong \sqrt{48,000}$$
$$EOQ \cong 219 \text{ units.}$$

The November–December inventory strategy would be determined as follows: $D = 2,000$; $J = \$40$; $E = 10$ percent; and $V = \$20$.

Thus,

$$EOQ = \sqrt{\frac{2(2,000)(\$40)}{(\$20)(.10)(2/12)}}$$

$$EOQ = \sqrt{484,848}$$
$$EOQ \cong 696$$

The *EOQ* during the November–December peak period is approximately 696. This means that the manager must enter the decision process by determining whether two or three orders are appropriate. The human element is essential since $2 \times 696 = 1,392$ and $3 \times 696 = 2,088$, and the exact demand is 2,000. The *EOQ* decision for January–December was relatively clear-cut in that the demand of 1,000 could be satisfied with five orders of 200 each. The above example was used to show that despite the use of mathematical formulas, human judgment is still an important factor in many inventory control decisions.

LIMITATIONS OF INVENTORY CONTROL MODELS

The most obvious limitation of employing inventory control models as presented is that conditions of certainty rarely exist in the real world. In our problem, we have assumed that the correct time to order is known. Many times transportation problems, order requisition difficulties, and other related problems make the lead time (time between placement of an order and actual delivery of the order) a highly unpredictable phenomenon.

The estimation of demand is another problem area. Throughout our discussion, demand was stated as a specific amount. The demand for any item can at best only be roughly estimated. There are so many variables, such as competitors' prices, economic conditions, social conditions, and substitutable items, that can influence demand that stating definitely that it is 1,000 units annually or 2,000 units for two months is difficult.

The cost components and estimates such as ordering cost per unit and carrying cost are only subjectively based figures. Historical cost data, of course, improve the validity of the figures, but these data may not be accurate for the future.

Despite these limitations, the analytical approaches presented can aid the manager in reaching more effective judgments. The reader should recognize that the methods discussed are analytical approaches which attempt to yield optimal decisions. The emphasis, of course, is on the word "attempt."

DISCUSSION AND REVIEW QUESTIONS

1. Under what situations would the material costs for a product not be completely variable? That is, when would material costs be semivariable?
2. Is the *EOQ* model able to adjust to changes in demand over a period of time? Why?
3. How can decision theory and break-even analysis be simultaneously used in analyzing cost–profit problems?
4. A student of management science is presented with the following sets of data.

Set 1	*Set 2*
BE units = 40,000	*BE* dollars = 300,000
Price = $10	Price = $15
VC/unit = $ 8	*VC*/unit = $12

    If a complete break-even analysis is to be conducted on Set 1 and Set 2, what piece of information is needed in each case? Show all work.
5. If you knew at what point on a graph ordering costs and carrying costs intersect, what would you also know about the economic lot size?
6. Assume that the Battel Pipe Company probability estimates are as follows:

	Level *Pipe Rack Sales*	*Probability* *of Occurrence*
Alternative I....................	20,000	0.80
	30,000	0.10
	40,000	0.10
Alternative II..................	20,000	0.20
	30,000	0.20
	40,000	0.40
	50,000	0.20

If the cost information in the chapter remains as presented for both alternatives, which distribution method would be selected? Show all work in reaching a solution.

7. The Slag Valley Construction Corporation uses 5,000 pressure valves annually. The cost accountants ascertain that the ordering cost for securing the valves from suppliers is $60.00. Each valve costs $10.00. The carrying charge for the valves is estimated to be 20 percent per year of the value of the average inventory.

   a. Utilize the trial-and-error method to derive the economic order quantity for the following possibilities:
      Number of Valves in Order: 500, 1000, 2500, 5000
   b. Utilize the *EOQ* formula to determine the economic order size.

8. How are the following concepts related to each other?
   a. Marginal Cost .... Total Variable Cost
   b. Ordering Cost .... Carrying Cost
   c. Price .... Volume of Products Sold

---

ADDITIONAL REFERENCES

Baumol, W. J.   *Economic Theory and Operations Analysis.* Englewood Cliffs, N.J.: Prentice-Hall, Inc., 1965.

Bock, R. H., and Holstein, W. K.   *Production Planning and Control.* Columbus, Ohio: Charles E. Merrill Books, Inc., 1963.

Buffa, E. S.   *Production-Inventory Systems: Planning and Control.* Homewood, Ill.: Richard D. Irwin, Inc., 1968.

Hadley, G., and Whitin, T. M.   *Analysis of Inventory Systems.* Englewood Cliffs, N.J.: Prentice-Hall, Inc., 1963.

Starr, M. K., and Miller, D. W.   *Inventory Control: Theory and Practice.* Englewood Cliffs, N.J.: Prentice-Hall, Inc., 1962.

15 Linear Programming Models

INTRODUCTION

Linear programming models are among the most widely used types of allocation models. However, the use of linear programming for management decision making is relatively new. In fact, its origin dates back to the years just following World War II. The person credited with developing linear programming was George B. Dantzig, who at the time worked for the United States Air Force as a civilian.[1] He was a mathematician and was assigned to work on logistics problems. While working on these problems, he found that many of them could be formulated into a mathematical procedure and entitled it the simplex method.

Since World War II, linear programming models have been used increasingly to solve management problems. With the growth of the Management Science School and the simultaneous growth of the electronic computer, complex linear programming models are now being utilized on a wide scale.

What is a Linear Programming Model?

A linear programming model is an extremely useful device that *has the purpose of maximizing some objective such as profits or minimizing*

---

[1] See G. B. Dantzig, "Maximization of a Linear Function of Variables Subject to Linear Inequalities," in T. C. Koopmans, ed., *Activity Analysis of Production and Allocation* (New York: John Wiley and Sons, Inc., 1951).

some objective such as costs by determining what the future values of certain variables affecting the outcome should be in order to achieve the objective. The variables are ones over which the manager has some control.

The model is called linear because the mathematical equations employed to describe the particular system under study, as well as the objective to be achieved, are in the form of linear relations between the variables. A linear relationship between two or more variables is one which is directly and precisely proportional. Linear programming models are used in a variety of situations where numerous activities are all competing for limited resources. The manager must find the optimum way to allocate the limited resources given an objective and any relevant constraints.

MANAGEMENT'S USE OF LINEAR PROGRAMMING

There are numerous allocation problems which managers in all types of organizations must face. In many organizations managers have made effective use of linear programming in solving these problems.

For example, oil companies throughout the world probably have the best overall record of successfully employing linear programming models. This is because they face a large number of allocation-type problems. Most oil companies are fully integrated, which basically means that they are involved with the product through all the various stages right up to the final user. That is, they produce oil, refine it, market it, and move it through each stage to the user. As a result, the reader can imagine that oil company operations are highly complex and geographically dispersed. Accordingly, managers in oil companies must make allocation decisions involving such problems as:

1. The alternative areas from which they can derive crude oil.
2. The alternative areas from which they can transport crude oil.
3. The alternative methods of transportation (for example, pipeline, trucks).
4. The alternative locations where crude oil can be refined.
5. The alternative methods of refining crude oil.
6. "Cracking" crude oil into several alternative "blending stocks."
7. Combining various blending stocks into several dozen potential products (for example, fuel oil, gasoline, kerosene).
8. Combining various blending stocks for alternative quality levels for certain products (for example, computing the right mixture of octane components in the blending of different gasolines).
9. Shipping the manufactured products from refineries into market areas.

In each of the above situations managers must allocate some scarce resource among several competing alternatives with the objective of either maximizing profits or minimizing costs. For this reason oil companies employ management scientists to construct linear programming models in order to aid line managers in planning and controlling.

The Value of Linear Programming

Properly constructed linear programming models provide managers with three specific benefits:

Improved Planning.   Where applicable, linear programming models improve managers' planning skills because they expand their analytical ability. They enable managers to consider and evaluate a far wider range of possible allocation plans than would be humanly possible without their use.

For example, in the second section of this chapter we shall see that conventional graphical and algebraic paper-and-pencil computations can be applied in principle to very simple allocation problems involving two or three variables. However, in a real-world problem such as those noted above, such methods would be of little value. The simplex method of linear programming referred to earlier can, with the aid of an electronic computer, solve a problem containing over 500 equations and 1,000 variables in just a few hours. This is what is meant when we say that linear programming can expand the analytic ability, and therefore the planning ability, of a manager. It permits an exhaustive search of numerous alternative solutions and systematically searches for the optimum one. Previously, time constraints might have permitted examination of only a few possible alternative solutions when numerous potential solutions actually existed.

Improved Decisions.   Linear programming models can result in improved management decisions. Once a linear programming model is constructed there is no room for management judgment since the computer performs the computations and manipulations and provides a solution which maximizes or minimizes the stated objective within the given constraints. However, before the model is ready to be solved and after it is solved, human judgment and creativity can be used. For example, once a solution has been selected, the manager may alter or add a constraint or change the objective. The computer can then provide a new solution under the revised set of conditions. Only a manager, however, can determine which of the two solutions is best. In some cases the differences in the choices will be so slight that the manager may face an extremely difficult decision.

Improved Understanding of Problems.   Since linear programming models are highly efficient ways of analyzing very complex problems, they also improve a manager's comprehension and appreciation of these complex problems and, by structuring the problem, enable the manager to comprehend more easily the effects of alternative assumptions. They not only provide a solution but also enable the manager to understand the problem.

Some Specific Areas of Application

In this section we shall review briefly some of the specific areas in which linear programming has found wide use.

Product-Mix Problems.   In product-mix selection, a manager must determine the levels for a number of production activities for the planning period. For example, if a firm manufactures two products, both of which must go through the same three production processes, the manager faces a problem of this nature. The two products both compete for time in the three production processes, and the task of the linear programming model in this case would be to "allocate" the limited resources (available time in the three processes) in such a way as to produce that number of each product which will maximize the firm's profits.

Feed-Mix Problems.   Large farming organizations may purchase and mix together several types of grains for different purposes. Each grain may contain different amounts of several nutritional elements. For one situation, the production manager must blend the different grains for the purpose of producing a mixture for feeding livestock. The mixture must meet minimal nutritional requirements at the lowest cost. Linear programming can be used to "allocate" the various grains (each containing different amounts of the nutritional elements) in such a way that the resulting mixture will meet nutritional and diet specifications at the minimum cost.

Fluid-Blending Problems.   This is a variation of the feed-mix problem. In this case, the manager seeks to blend fluids such as molten metals, chemicals, and crude oil into a finished product. Steel, chemical, and oil companies make wide use of linear programming models for problems of this type. Computing the right mixture of octane requirements in the blending of different gasolines is an example of such a problem in the oil industry.

Transportation Problems.   Many manufacturers and large retail chains face the following problem: Given a number of sources of supply (for example, warehouses) and destinations (for example, customers), and the cost of shipping a product from the source to each destination, select those routes that will minimize total shipping costs. The reader can imagine the complexity of the problem if the firm has many warehouses in different parts of the country and thousands of customers also geographically dispersed. Linear programming provides a means for arriving at the optimum shipping program.

Advertising Media-Mix Problems. In most organizations, a manager must sooner or later face a media-mix problem: Given an advertising budget, how can the budgeted funds be allocated over the various advertising media in order to achieve maximum exposure of the product or service. This type of problem lends itself to the use of linear programming. There are a number of competing media (for example, five magazines) all competing for limited resources (the advertising budget). Linear programming is widely used in many advertising agencies for problems of this type.

While the above problems are probably the most popular areas of application, there are a multitude of other practical problems in which linear programming has proven its worth. For example:

1. Allocation of materials to machines in order to minimize production time.
2. Allocation of cargoes to ships and aircraft.
3. Allocation of coal to power stations to minimize shipping costs.
4. Production scheduling.
5. Personnel assignment.

There is no doubt that linear programming models improve the planning skills of managers. Linear programming models cannot, however, develop new ways of running the organization or consider possible alternatives not provided to them. Only the manager can do this. Linear programming models are tools that managers can use, nothing more.

AN APPLICATION OF LINEAR PROGRAMMING: A PRODUCT-MIX PROBLEM

Assume that the production manager of the Apex Corporation has the choice of producing two different products (A and B). Furthermore, both products must go through three departments (X, Y, and Z) to be completed. Assume that Department X is production, Department Y is assembling, and Department Z is packaging. Both products require the same amount of time in Department X, but, because of special features, Product B requires twice as much time in Department Y but less time in Department Z. Product A contributes $10 per unit to profits, and Product B contributes $12 per unit. The problem the production manager faces is to determine a production "program" for the two products.

In this particular problem, the products (A and B) are the competing users and the available time in the three processes (production, assembling, and packaging) represents the limited resources. If profit is the objective, then the production manager hopes to design a program that will maximize profits. In linear programming this is formulated into a mathematical expression known as an *objective function,* the value of which can be computed when the values of all the variables are determined. Finally, the capacity of the resources is limited. That is, there is only so much time per day available in each of the three departments. If we assume that no expansion plans are called for, then this limitation is expressed as a set of constraints which restricts the values that can be assigned to the competing products.

Thus, the task of the linear programming model in this case is to "allocate" the limited resources (available time in production, assembling, and packaging) among the competing users (Products A and B) in such a way as to maximize profit. To review, then, it should be clear that the linear programming model is *normative* in purpose since it selects the best alternative to optimize some objective (profit in this case) and contains *deterministic* variables since all variables are assumed to be known with certainty. Note also that in order to utilize the linear programming model it is necessary to *assume certainty* (all factors are exact or deterministic quantities) and *simplify relationships* (assume linear relationships among variables) in the problem. Let us summarize the above problem by introducing numerical values in Table 15–1.

TABLE 15–1

Apex Corporation Resources

Department	Minutes Required per Unit		Capacity per Day in Minutes
	Product A	Product B	
X (production)................	6	6	300
Y (assembling)................	4	8	320
Z (packaging)................	5	3	310
Profit contribution per unit...................	$10	$12	

A final key element of linear programming is the use of inequalities to express relationships. Equations are specific mathematical statements which are represented by an equals sign ($=$). For example, if profit is our sole objective in the above problem, we can express this in the following equation:

$$\text{Profit} = \$10 \text{ (number of Product A sold)} + \$12 \text{ (number of Product B sold)}$$

However, most problems cannot be expressed in equations such as our objective function. More often the problem may require only that minimum or maximum requirements be met. For example, in Table 15–1 it is stated that the time needed in Department X for one Product A (6 minutes) times the number of Product A's produced, plus the time required for one Product B (6 minutes) times the number of Product B's produced, must be equal to or less than the 300 minutes of available time per day in Department X. In this case, we must utilize inequalities to express the constraints. The above constraint is expressed as follows:

$$6A + 6B \leq 300$$

Any amount of time utilized which is equal to or less than 300 minutes per day would satisfy the inequality. When formulating inequalities, the sign ($\leq$) stands for "less than or equal to"; and the sign ($\geq$) stands for "greater than or equal to."

In order to develop an understanding of a typical linear programming problem we will work through this problem and solve it by the *graphical method*. We will also discuss the *algebraic method* and the *simplex method*. Of the three methods, the simplex method is the most general and powerful method. However, knowledge of the graphical method will provide a foundation for understanding the concepts and rationale of the simplex method. In addition, problems which have three or less competing candidates can be more easily solved by the first two methods.

THE GRAPHICAL METHOD

Since it is not possible to present graphically more than three variables, only problems with three or less competing candidates can be solved by this method. Since our product-mix problem presented in Table 15–1 has only two competing candidates (Products A and B) can be solved by the graphical method.

To begin solving the problem we must restate it in mathematical form. Since the goal is to maximize profit (*P*) the objective function is:

$$\text{Objective Function} = P = \$10A + \$12B$$

This equation is read: Profit equals $10 multiplied by the number of Product A produced, plus $12 multiplied by the number of Product B produced. Assuming we produced and sold 20 of each, then profit would equal $10 (20) + $12 (20) or $440.

The next step is to express constraints in mathematical form. The time used in the three departments cannot exceed the total time available per day in each of the departments. For example, the time needed to produce one Product A times the number produced, plus the time needed to produce one Product B times the number produced, must be equal to or less than the 300 minutes available each day in the production department (Department X). The constraints for all three departments can be expressed as follows:

$6A + 6B \leq 300$ minutes in Department X (production)
$4A + 8B \leq 320$ minutes in Department Y (assembling)
$5A + 3B \leq 310$ minutes in Department Z (packaging)

Finally, every linear programming problem has a set of *nonnegativity* constraints. These are imposed to insure that any values for A and B arrived at are positive. This is obvious, since there can be no such thing as negative production (we cannot produce a minus quantity of a product). Thus, the optimal solution must have nonnegative values for A and B or: $A \geq 0$ and $B \geq 0$.

Summarizing the problem in mathematical form yields:

Maximize Profit $P = \$10A + \$12B$

Subject to the following constraints

$$6A + 6B \leq 300$$
$$4A + 8B \leq 320$$
$$5A + 3B \leq 310$$

and

$$A \geq 0$$
$$B \geq 0$$

The next step is to designate, on a two-dimensional graph, Product A on the horizontal axis and Product B on the vertical axis and plot each of the three contraint equations. Each inequality is plotted by assuming that all the available time in the particular department is devoted to one of the products. For example, in Department X, if we did not produce any of Product B, we could produce 50 units of Product A. Similarly, if we produced no Product A we would be able to produce 50 units of Product B. The calculations for each department are as follows:

In Department X (production) let $B = 0$; then

$$6A + 6B \leq 300$$
$$6A + 6(0) \leq 300$$
$$A \leq 50 \text{ units of Product A}$$
when no Product B
is produced.

In Department X let $A = 0$; then

$$6A + 6B \leq 300$$
$$6(0) + 6B \leq 300$$
$$B \leq 50 \text{ units of Product B}$$
when no Product A
is produced.

In Department Y (assembling) let $B = 0$; then

$$4A + 8B \leq 320$$
$$4A + 8(0) \leq 320$$
$$4A \leq 320$$
$$A \leq 80 \text{ units of Product A}$$

when no Product B
is assembled.

In Department Y let $A = 0$; then

$$4A + 8B \leq 320$$
$$4(0) + 8B \leq 320$$
$$8B \leq 320$$
$$B \leq 40 \text{ units of Product B}$$

when no Product A
is assembled.

In Department Z (packaging) let $B = 0$; then

$$5A + 3B \leq 310$$
$$5A + 3(0) \leq 310$$
$$5A \leq 310$$
$$A \leq 62 \text{ units of Product A}$$

when no Product B
is packaged.

In Department Z let $A = 0$; then

$$5A + 3B \leq 310$$
$$5(0) + 3B \leq 310$$
$$3B \leq 310$$
$$B \leq 103 \text{ units of Product B}$$

when no Product A
is packaged.

The inequalities are illustrated on separate graphs in Figure 15–1 for each department and all together on one graph. The arrow associated with each line shows the direction indicated by the inequality signs (less than or equal to) in the constraint equations. This means that any combination of Products A and B which lie in that area can be produced, assembled, or packaged without exceeding the available time in the particular department. Finally, note that the nonnegativity constraints $A \geq 0$, $B \geq 0$ restrict us to zero or more units of Products A and B.

All values for Product A and B satisfying all three constraints are shown in the shaded region in Figure 15–1. Note that any pair of values for Products A and B that satisfies the constraints in Department X and Y also satisfies Department Z. To complete one unit of Product A or B, work must be done in all three departments. Therefore, the best com-

FIGURE 15-1

Constraint Equations

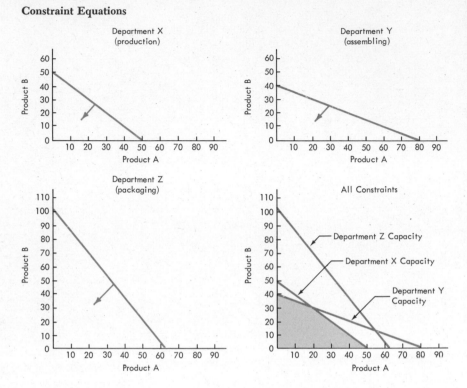

bination of Products A and B must fall within the shaded area in Figure 15–1. Any combination in this *feasibility space* will not exceed the maximum time in either Department X, Y, or Z.

The construction of Figure 15–1 is the first step in solving the problem by the graphical method. The goal is to locate at least one point from the shaded area in Figure 15–1 which will maximize the objective function.

Finding the Optimal Solution

The optimal solution must be guided by the objective function. If it were possible to plot the objective function in Figure 15–1 and determine the direction of maximum increase, we could then continue to move it in this direction until we reached the farthest point on the boundary of the shaded area in Figure 15–1. We would then have the optimum solution.

The problem can be solved by selecting any arbitrary profit figure and determining how many units of Product A alone or Product B alone would be needed to earn such a profit. Any profit figure will suffice, but common sense tells us to select a point within the feasibility space in

Figure 15–1. Let us assume a profit figure of $300. Since Product A con-
tributes $10 we would need 30 units in order to earn a profit of $300. If
we manufacture only Product B, we would need 25 units in order to earn
a $300 profit since Product B contributes a profit of $12. If we locate these
two points in the feasibility space and join them we obtain what is known
as a $300 equal-profit line which is nothing more than the locus of all
points (all combinations of Products A and B) which will yield a profit
of $300. This is illustrated in Figure 15–2 as a dotted line.

FIGURE 15–2

Equal-Profit Lines

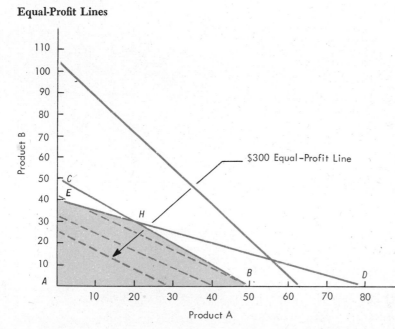

We could continue to construct these lines for higher and higher profit
figures as long as we remain within the feasibility space. This is also
illustrated in Figure 15–2 by dotted lines. We would be forced to stop
when we reached a boundary line or corner point of the feasibility space.
The highest combination still having a point in the feasibility space provides the optimal value of the objective function. When this occurs, we
have found the optimum solution.

The equal-profit line farthest from the origin and still within the feasibility space would be at point *H* in Figure 15–2. This occurs at the intersection of the Department X and Department Y constraints. Although
there are an infinite number of solutions within the feasibility space,
point *H* provides the optimum solution.

The coordinates of the point *H* can be read directly from the graph if it is constructed perfectly, but they are usually found by solving simultaneously the equations of the two lines which intersect to form point H, which is the only point common to both equations. The equations to be solved are:

$$\text{Line } BC \qquad 6A + 6B = 300$$
$$\text{Line } DE \qquad 4A + 8B = 320$$

To solve these equations simultaneously we
a. Multiply the first equation by 4.
b. Multiply the second equation by -3.
c. Add the results.

$$
\begin{array}{rrrrr}
4(6A + 6B = 300) = & 24A + & 24B & = & 1200 \\
-3(4A + 8B = 320) = & -12A + & (-24B) & = & -960 \\
\hline
& 12A & & = & 240 \\
& A & & = & 20
\end{array}
$$

d. Substitute 20 for A in the second equation.

$$4A + 8B = 320 = 4(20) + 8B = 320$$
$$80 + 8B = 320$$
$$8B = 240$$
$$B = 30$$

e. Point H is, therefore, $(20, 30)$.

We can now test the four points that delineate the feasibility space in order to determine the highest dollar profit.

$$
\begin{array}{llll}
\text{Point } A & (0,0) = & 10(0) + & 12(0) = \$0 \\
\text{Point } B & (50,0) = & 10(50) + & 12(0) = \$500 \\
\text{Point } E & (0,40) = & 10(0) + & 12(40) = \$480 \\
\text{Point } H & (20,30) = & 10(20) + & 12(30) = \$560
\end{array}
$$

The point that provides the most profit is point H where we manufacture 20 units of Product A and 30 units of Product B for a profit of $560.

This product-mix problem was provided only as an illustration of a linear programming model. Real applications of linear programming usually involve hundreds of constraints and sometimes thousands of variables. Obviously for such problems an electronic computer is a necessity. As we have noted previously, the graphical method cannot be used when there are more than three competing candidates. However, regardless of the number of competing candidates and constraints, the nature of linear programming is the same as was illustrated in the product-mix problem.

THE ALGEBRAIC METHOD

Where a linear programming problem has less than three competing candidates, a solution can also be more easily developed algebraically than through the use of the simplex method. The product-mix problem was stated as follows:

Maximize:

$$P = \$10A + \$12B$$

Subject to:

$$6A + 6B \leq 300 \text{ (Department X)}$$
$$4A + 8B \leq 320 \text{ (Department Y)}$$
$$5A + 3B \leq 310 \text{ (Department Z)}$$

The problem cannot be solved algebraically since we do not have equations because of the inequalities. We must first convert the inequations into equations. The above inequations can be transformed into equations by the addition of nonnegative variables known as slack variables (S) since they "take up the slack" and serve to form equations from the inequations of a linear programming problem. It is possible, because of the nature of the inequalities being of the "less-than-or-equal-to" type, that the optimum combination of Products A and B will not utilize all of the available time in each department. Therefore, we add to each inequation a variable which will take up the time not used in each department. Thus, we now have:

$$6A + 6B + S_x = 300 \text{ (Department X)}$$
$$4A + 8B + S_y = 320 \text{ (Department Y)}$$
$$5A + 3B + S_z = 310 \text{ (Department Z)}$$

S_x is equal to the total time available in Department X less the time used there to produce both products. S_y is equal to the total available time in Department Y less the time used there to assemble both products, and S_z equals the total available time used in Department Z less the time used to package both products. Thus, by adding slack variables we have converted the constraint inequations into equations. The slack variables will take on whatever value is needed to make the equation hold. For example:

Assume that ten units of each product are manufactured

Department X:

$$S_x = 300 - 6(10) - 6(10)$$
$$S_x = 180 \text{ minutes unused time in Department X}$$

Department Y:

$$S_y = 320 - 4(10) - 8(10)$$
$$S_y = 200 \text{ minutes of unused time in Department Y}$$

Department Z:

$$S_z = 310 - 5(10) - 3(10)$$
$$S_z = 230 \text{ minutes of unused time in Department Z}$$

Since idle time in any of the three departments can have no profit or loss, the slack variables have no money value and can be included in the objective function with zero profit contributions. Thus, the problem is ready for algebraic solution as follows:

$$P = \$10A + \$12B + \$0S_x + \$0S_y + \$0S_z$$
$$6A + 6B + S_x = 300$$
$$4A + 8B + S_y = 320$$
$$5A + 3B + S_z = 310$$

We will not devote the space needed to solve this problem algebraically since this is not the purpose of this chapter. The reader skilled in algebra may wish to do so. The solution, of course, will be the same as that achieved by the graphical method. It indicates 20 units of Product A and 30 units of Product B should be manufactured, which will provide a profit of $560 and 120 minutes of unused time in Department Z. If the reader refers to Figure 15–1 it will be seen that the constraint line for Department Z is the furthest from the origin since less time was needed to package the products than assemble or produce them. In fact, the feasibility space was formed only by the constraint lines for Department X and Y. Thus, it is not surprising that Department Z has slack time.

THE SIMPLEX METHOD

The simplex method is the most widely applicable and powerful of the linear programming techniques. Both the graphical and algebraic methods are special cases of the general simplex method. The major advantage of the simplex method is that it is capable of handling any number of variables. Because of this, it usually requires a very lengthy and involved computational procedure. For our purposes it is necessary only to outline the general characteristics of the simplex method.

The simplex method is similar to the graphical and algebraic methods in that conditions of certainty and linear relationships among variables are necessary in order for it to be used. Like the algebraic method, it requires that the problem be formulated in explicit mathematical terms, stating both the objective function and the constraints. Then an initial solution is developed which satisfies all of the constraints. Modifications in the initial solution are examined and the most favorable, in terms of the objective function, is incorporated into the second solution. This is repeated until no further improvements are possible. This computational routine of the simplex method is what is known as an *iterative process*. To iterate is to repeat mechanical and mathematical operations. Each *iteration* brings us closer to an optimal solution because each new solution yields a larger profit or lower cost than the previous solution.

The reader can imagine the value of the simplex method in many of the real-world problems which may contain hundreds of variables. It permits an exhaustive search of the possible solutions and systematically searches for the optimum one. However, the reader should see that the basic nature is the same as that which was illustrated in this chapter in the product-mix problem.

SUMMARY

In this chapter, linear programming has been discussed as a powerful planning tool for the manager. It has made possible the solution of many types of allocation problems which heretofore could only be dealt with (if at all) by trial-and-error methods. In addition, however, it has forced managers to more clearly delineate the variables and relationships affecting a problem. Thus forcing managers to formalize their thinking on specific problems enables them to visualize the key variables in a problem which brings organization and structure to a problem situation where little or none existed before.

The reader should not infer, however, that linear programming represents a remedy for the solution of all allocation decision problems. The employment of linear programming necessitates formulation of the decision problem in mathematical terms. This means in many cases the gathering of data and extensive calculations. In such a situation, the costs incurred in using linear programming may exceed any possible gains or savings that might be obtained from its use.

Linear programming can only be used for problems in which it can be assumed that the relationships between variables are linear. Many allocation problems may be such that linear programming approaches are not applicable. In addition, other important allocation problems involve such a degree of complexity that their solution is not possible via linear programming.

Finally, we noted that the linear programming model is a deterministic model. This means that all variables are assumed to be known with certainty. While this is clearly a simplifying assumption, there will be many problems where such an assumption cannot be made, or if made, the solution obtained through the use of linear programming will be of little or no value.

In conclusion, it is important for the manager to understand not only how linear programming is used, but also the conditions under which its use is feasible. This is not to deter from the value of the tool but rather to strengthen the conditions under which it is used.

DISCUSSION AND REVIEW QUESTIONS

1. The Lisa Ann Company makes two products. Product A contributes $20 profit and Product B contributes $12 profit. Each product must go through two manufacturing processes in order to be completed. Product A requires 12 hours in Department X and 4 hours in Department Y. Product B requires 4 hours in Department X and 8 hours in Department Y. There is a total of 60 hours available in Department X and 40 in Department Y. Find the optimum combination of the two products which would maximize total profit. Use the graphical method.

2. The Helene Manufacturers, Inc. produces two different models of professional hair dryers. Dryer A contributes $20 profit and Dryer B contributes $10. In order to be completed, each dryer must go through three manufacturing processes as follows:

	Dryer A (hours)	Dryer B (hours)	Available Time in Each Department (hours)
Department X	4	9	180
Department Y	5	6	150
Department Z	5	14	175

Using the graphical method find the optimum combination of the products which would maximize total profit. Suppose the company could concentrate all its efforts on one model. Would this change the solution?

3. It is said that linear programming is an excellent planning tool for the manager. Referring to what you have read about planning, answer the question, "What specifically can linear programming do in the planning function?"

4. In a very complete paragraph, describe exactly what is meant by linear programming.

5. What two conditions must a problem exhibit in order to enable the use of linear programming?

6. Can you think of an allocation problem other than those discussed in the chapter where linear programming might possibly be of some help? Describe it in a short paragraph indicating the objective and the various constraints.

7. Discuss the following statement: "Since conditions of certainty must exist in order for linear programming to be used, it is of little value to managers because conditions of certainty rarely, if ever, exist in the real world."

ADDITIONAL REFERENCES

Gass, S. I. *Linear Programming: Methods and Applications,* 2d ed. New York: McGraw-Hill Book Co., 1966.

Kwak, N. K. *Mathematical Programming with Business Applications.* New York: McGraw-Hill Book Co., 1973.

Levin, R. I., and Lamone, R. P. *Linear Programming for Management Decisions.* Homewood, Ill.: Richard D. Irwin, Inc., 1969.

Levin, R. I., and Kirkpatrick, C. A. *Quantitative Approaches to Management.* New York: McGraw-Hill Book Co., 1975.

Loomba, N. P. *Linear Programming: An Introductory Analysis.* New York: McGraw-Hill Book Co., 1964.

Naylor, T. H., and Byrne, E. T. *Linear Programming.* Belmont, California: Wadsworth Publishing Co., 1963.

Smythe, W. R., and Johnson, L. A. *Introduction to Linear Programming, with Applications.* Englewood Cliffs, N.J.: Prentice-Hall, Inc., 1966.

16 Network Models

INTRODUCTION

Certain techniques which may be used to combine resources or to control activities in order to see that plans are carried out as stated can be described under the general heading of *Network Models*. Such models are especially suited for projects which are not of a routine or repetitive nature and which will be conducted only once or a few times. In such projects there is a great need for some type of coordination to insure that certain tasks that must be completed prior to another task are actually completed. Some idea is also needed of approximately how long the entire project will take. In summary, some method is needed to avoid unnecessary conflicts and delays by keeping track of all events and activities—and their interrelationships—on a specific project. Network models provide the means to achieve these goals. As such, they are valuable aids in managerial *planning* and *controlling*.

NETWORK MODELS (PERT)

PERT stands for Program Evaluation and Review Technique. Developed through the cooperation of the U.S. Navy and the management consulting firm of Booz, Allen, and Hamilton, it can probably be considered the most popular network model. What exactly is PERT? It is a method by which conflicts, delays, and interruptions in a project are minimized by coordinating the various parts of the overall job in order

366

to complete the project on schedule. It does not solve a manager's problems, but it does help identify what the problems are and what solutions are realistic, as well as aiding in anticipating problems.

PERT is especially useful to management in nonrepetitive problem areas—ones which the manager has not previously encountered and is not likely to encounter again. The problem really is "How can the manager learn to manage work that is done only once?" This kind of problem must be faced in most one-of-a-kind development programs. Such programs have two major characteristics. First, they are extremely complex in that hundreds or thousands of interdependent tasks must be accomplished; and, second, most of the tasks are single-occurrence tasks that are not likely to be repeated. These are in contrast with repetitive processes such as the mass production of a product or the periodic re-orders of inventory for which management has past experience, standards, and costs. However, each task in a one-of-a-kind program must be performed on time and be of the necessary quality, just as with repetitive work. In other words, management must still *plan* and *control* nonrepetitive operations. PERT is extremely helpful in such situations because it enables a manager to think through a project in its entirety and to identify possible delays. As such, it usually results in a more optimum utilization of resources.

Fundamentals of PERT

There are two fundamentals of PERT and other network models: (1) constructing the network and (2) estimating activity time requirements.

Constructing The Network. PERT networks are developed around two key concepts: activities and events. An *activity* is the work necessary to complete a particular event. An *event* is an accomplishment at a particular point in time and consumes no time. In PERT diagrams or networks, an event is designated with a circle and an activity as an arrow connecting the two circles. This is shown in Figure 16–1.

In Figure 16–1 there are two events which are assigned numbers connected by one activity, designated with an arrow. Each of the two events occur at a specific point in time. Event 1 could represent the specific point in time "project begun" and event 2 could represent the specific point in time "project completed." The arrow connecting the two events

FIGURE 16–1

Two Events and One Activity

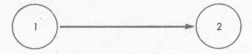

represents the activity—the actual work done—and the time necessary to complete the work. Thus, the two events in Figure 16–1 designate the beginning and end of the activity. The activity is what requires time, not the events.

The term *network* is used when several events and activities are combined in a diagram. Figure 16–1 is a very simple PERT network involving two events and one activity. A more complex PERT network is presented in Figure 16–2.

FIGURE 16–2

Pert Network

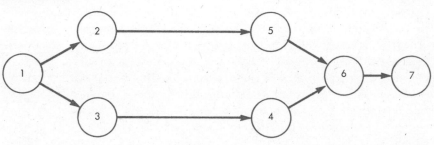

Examination of Figure 16–2 indicates that event 1 is the network beginning event since there are no activities leading to it, and event 7 is the network ending event since there are no activities leading away from it. Note also that event 1 is the beginning event for two activities, and event 6 is the ending event for two activities, as well as the beginning event for one activity.

In constructing the network, emphasis is on identifying events and activities with enough precision so that it is possible to monitor accomplishment as the project proceeds. There are four basic phases in constructing a PERT network.

1. Define each activity that must be done.
2. Estimate how long each activity will take.
3. Construct the network.
4. Find the critical path—that is, the longest path, in time, from the beginning event to the ending event.

All events and activities must be sequenced in the network under a strict set of logical rules (for example, no event can be considered complete until all predecessor events have been completed) which allows for the determination of the critical path.[1]

---

[1] For complex projects, networking is a difficult task better left to trained individuals. The reader interested in networking principles should consult Louis R. Shaffer, J. B. Ritter, and W. L. Meyer, *Critical Path Method* (New York: McGraw-Hill Book Co., 1965); or Jerome D. Wiest and Ferdinand K. Levy, *A Management Guide to PERT/CPM* (Englewood Cliffs, N.J.: Prentice-Hall, Inc., 1969).

The paramount variable in a PERT network is time—the basic measure of how long a project will take. Estimating how long each activity will take is extremely difficult since the manager has no experience to rely on in most cases.

Estimating Activity Time Requirements

Since PERT projects are usually unique, they are subject to a great deal of uncertainty. PERT is designed to deal specifically with this problem of uncertainty in determining the time estimates.

For example, assume you are trying to estimate how long it will take to complete a term project for your management class. You know that one activity will be to collect certain information. If all goes well and you do not encounter any obstacles, you believe that you could complete this one activity in eight weeks. However, if a situation occurred where you encountered numerous obstacles (dates, parties, illness, materials not available in the library, etc.), the chances would be greater that this one activity would take much longer to complete. Thus you could estimate a variety of possible completion times for this part of your term project.

Specifically, for PERT projects, *three time estimates are required for each activity.* The individual or group chosen to make each time estimate should be that individual or group who is most closely connected with, and responsible for, the particular activity under consideration. The three time estimates needed are:

Optimistic Time (*a*). This is the time the activity can be completed in if everything goes exceptionally well and no obstacles or problems are encountered.

Most Likely Time (*m*). This is the most realistic estimate of how long an activity might take. This is the time to be expected most often if the activity was repeated numerous times.

Pessimistic Time (*b*). This is the time that would be required if everything went wrong and numerous obstacles and problems are encountered.

Obviously, it would be extremely difficult to deal simultaneously with the optimistic time, the most likely time, and the pessimistic time. Fortunately, a way has been developed to arrive at one time estimate. It has been determined that an *expected time* (t_e), can be estimated satisfactorily for each activity by using the following formula:

$$\text{Expected time } (t_e) = \frac{a + 4m + b}{6}$$

Let us examine this methodology in relation to the term project mentioned above. Assume that you estimate that eight weeks is the most likely completion time (*m*) for the activity of collecting information.

However, you feel that there is a small chance (perhaps one time in ten) that the term project might be completed in two weeks. Therefore, the optimistic time (a) is 2. Finally, you feel there is also a slight chance things could go wrong and it would take ten weeks to collect the information. Therefore, the pessimistic time (b) is 10.

The reader can see that there is a greater chance that collecting the information will take eight weeks than any other time. In order to compute the expected time (t_e) from the three time estimates that have been provided we must determine at what time there is a 50–50 chance of completing the activity. This is what the expected time indicates, and the formula just mentioned provides that figure. Returning to the term project, the time estimates were as follows for the one activity of collecting information:

$$\text{Optimistic Time } (a) \quad = \quad 2 \text{ weeks}$$
$$\text{Most Likely Time } (m) \quad = \quad 8 \text{ weeks}$$
$$\text{Pessimistic Time } (b) \quad = \quad 10 \text{ weeks}$$

Substituting these time estimates into the formula yields:

$$\text{Expected Time } (t_e) = \frac{2 + 4(8) + 10}{6}$$

$$= \frac{44}{6}$$

$$t_e = 7.33$$

Thus, there is a 50–50 chance that the information will be collected in 7.33 weeks. Note that in the formula for computing the expected time (t_e), the weight that is given to the most likely time (m) is much greater than the weight given to the optimistic and pessimistic times, since each of them has only a small chance of occurring. Also, note that the optimistic and pessimistic time each receive the same weight.

It should be clear that the expected time (t_e) may be either greater or less than the most likely time (m), depending on the three time estimates. To illustrate an expected time (t_e) greater than the most likely time (m), assume the following three time estimates for collecting information for the term project:

$$\text{Optimistic time } (a) \quad = \quad 6 \text{ weeks}$$
$$\text{Most Likely Time } (m) \quad = \quad 8 \text{ weeks}$$
$$\text{Pessimistic Time } (b) \quad = \quad 16 \text{ weeks}$$

Substituting these values into the formula yields:

$$\text{Expected time } (t_e) = \frac{a + 4(m) + b}{6}$$

$$= \frac{6 + 4(8) + 16}{6}$$

$$t_e = 9$$

In this case the expected time (t_e) of 9 weeks is greater than the most likely time (m) of 8 weeks.

When there is a great amount of uncertainty in a project, this three-way time estimate is an important advantage of PERT. While it does introduce a complicating feature, it recognizes the realities which can cause problems in planning for the future. The three-way time estimate usually results in a greater degree of honesty and accuracy in forecasting time. If nothing else, it provides the manager with the opportunity to be aware of and to evaluate the degree of uncertainty involved, especially along the critical path. Estimating the time activity requirements is very crucial since they also serve as the basis for calculating the earliest expected date as well as the latest allowable date for the completion of the project. These ideas will be illustrated later in the chapter.

Some Applications of PERT

PERT (and variations of it) is probably one of the most widely used management science models. After it was introduced by the Special Projects Office of the U.S. Navy in 1958 on the Polaris missile project, PERT was widely credited with helping to reduce by two years the time originally estimated for the completion of the engineering and development programs for the missile. By identifying the longest paths through all of the tasks necessary to complete the project it enabled the program managers to concentrate efforts on those tasks that vitally affected the total project time. During the last two decades, PERT has spread rapidly throughout the defense and space industries. Today almost every major government military agency involved in the Space Program utilizes PERT. In fact, many government agencies require contractors to use PERT and other network models in planning and controlling their work on government contracts.

While the aerospace business faces peculiar problems, one-of-a-kind development work is also an important element in many other kinds of organizations and industries. In addition to developing space vehicles and putting a man on the moon, PERT has also been utilized successfully in:

1. Constructing new plants, buildings, and hospitals.
2. Designing new automobiles.
3. Coordinating the numerous activities (production, marketing, etc.) involved in introducing a new product.
4. Planning a sales campaign.
5. Planning logistic and distribution systems.
6. Coordinating the installation of large-scale computer systems.
7. Coordinating ship construction and aircraft repairs.

In addition to engineering oriented applications, it has also been utilized successfully in coordinating the numerous activities necessary to complete mergers between large organizations, for economic planning in underdeveloped countries, and even for smaller specific applications such as coordinating and planning all the tasks necessary for large-scale conventions and meetings.

The Value of Network Models

Properly constructed, PERT and other network models provide direct aid to managers in two important areas:

Improved Planning.   Network models enable managers to plan the optimum use of resources within overall time constraints. They help managers handle the uncertainties involved in projects where no standard cost and time data are available. Because it provides the manager with the interconnections of tasks and the estimated times, PERT increases the manager's ability to plan an optimum schedule before starting work. In other words, management can take a number of steps to reduce the total time needed to complete a project while the project is still in the planning stage. Time reductions can be brought about in a number of ways:[2]

1. By reducing the expected time on the longest path through the network (the critical path) by applying new resources or additional funds which are obtained from those activities that can afford it since they do not take as long to complete.
2. By eliminating some part of the project that previously might have been considered desirable but not necessary.
3. By transferring resources from slack to more critical paths.
4. By adding more resources—men or machines.
5. By purchasing a component if the time required to produce the component is too long.
6. By changing some work to parallel activities when they had previously been planned in a series.

Better Control.   A major advantage of PERT and other network models is that the tremendous planning involved in constructing the network contributes significantly to the definition and ultimate *concurrent control* of the project. We noted in the linear programming chapter that improved understanding of the problem is often a benefit of most management science models. In the case of PERT, the construction of the network is a very demanding task which forces the planner to visualize the number, different kinds, and sequence of all the necessary ac-

---

[2] Based on Harry Evarts, *Introduction to PERT* (Boston: Allyn and Bacon, Inc., 1964).

tivities. This kind of thinking in most cases cannot help but be a benefit in and of itself.

Effectively used, PERT can be valuable as both an internal and external control device. For internal control, it provides time schedules for each activity and networks can, therefore, be revised if unforeseen difficulties arise. Resources can be shifted and activities can be rescheduled with a minimum of delay on the outcome of the project.

For external control, in projects where subcontractors are used, the necessity for meeting scheduled dates can be stressed by showing the subcontractor the negative effects a delay will have on the entire project. When subcontractors are involved, it is vital that these firms meet their scheduled delivery dates. For example, the Polaris project involved some 250 prime contractors and almost 10,000 subcontractors. The failure of any one of these subcontractors to deliver a piece of hardware on schedule could have stalled the entire project.

PERT and People

While PERT has proven to be a valuable aid for management planning and control, there have been problems which some firms have encountered with it. However, the majority of the problems have not been with PERT itself, but with management's application of it.[3]

1. Acceptance. In some firms, line managers and technical personnel lack a full appreciation of PERT's benefits and limitations. This is due mainly to the failure of top management to support the implementation of it. Acceptance should clearly not be a problem. In fact, one of the major benefits of PERT is its common language which can be understood in all parts of the organization (or outside the organization) and enables all parties to see how their efforts relate to the total project. The network diagram can enable a foreman to understand the sequencing of various jobs and the importance of concentrating on critical ones. It can also help middle managers keep track of day-to-day operations and take necessary corrective action while helping top management concentrate on crucial problems in the overall project.

2. PERT Misuse. Unfortunately, PERT has at times been misused. Because of its value as a planning and control device, some overzealous managers have extended its application in some areas where it should not have been used.

3. Resistance to Change. The Behavioral School identified resistance to change as a common phenomenon. As such, it often stands in the way

---

[3] See Peter P. Schoderbek, "PERT—Its Promises and Performance," *Michigan Business Review*, vol. 17 (January 1965), pp. 25–32. Also see H. S. Phelps, "What Your People Should Know About PERT," *Management Review*, vol. 5 (October 1962), pp. 44–51.

of the initial adoption of PERT. When the introduction of PERT results in alterations in work procedures, it is bound to be met with resistance unless management has undertaken the necessary preparations. Approaches to implementing change in organizations were discussed in Chapter 11.

Other Popular Network Models (CPM and PERT/Cost)

At approximately the same time the U.S. Navy was developing PERT, the DuPont company was extremely concerned with the high costs and long time periods required to bring new products from the research and development stage to the production stage. Because of this they undertook a study which resulted in the development of a network model known as CPM (Critical Path Method). CPM is quite similar to PERT and, next to PERT, is probably the most widely used network model. It, too, has spread widely since its development and is particularly concentrated in the construction industry.

CPM departs from PERT in that CPM brings into the planning and control functions the concept of cost. However, this is not to say that PERT completely omits the cost concept. In PERT models, cost varies directly with time for all the activities of the project. In other words, when a reduction in time has been achieved, a reduction in cost is assumed to have been achieved.[4]

Another area of departure between PERT and CPM is that CPM uses a single time estimate for each activity; whereas PERT uses three. The user of CPM is assumed to have a more solid basis when estimating the time required for each activity.

Whether PERT or CPM is used will be determined by the needs of the program or the type of project. When time can be estimated accurately and costs can be determined in advance, CPM is probably the better of the two network methods. A good example of this type of project is a construction project where material and labor costs can be determined fairly accurately and in advance. However, when there is a high degree of uncertainty and/or the need for control over time outweighs control over costs, PERT is probably the better choice of the two.

Development of a CPM network follows the same principles as a PERT network so there is no need to repeat them. The real difference lies in estimating the times for each activity.

In their original forms, both PERT and CPM were time-oriented network models, in that as planning tools they enabled managers to estimate the time necessary to complete a project. Early users of both models

----

[4] When PERT was originally developed, it did not consider the direct relationship between cost and time. However, the latest versions of PERT present highly sophisticated cost analysis procedures.

recognized the need for an extension of the network techniques into the area of cost control. The argument was simply that managers are concerned with costs as well as time. In fact, some argued that costs in some cases are more important than time. The introduction of costs into PERT and CPM seemed to be not only a logical but desired extension of these network models. One of the more recent versions of PERT has been named PERT/Cost. Like PERT it was developed by the armed services and some industrial organizations for use in weapon systems development projects. Basically, it adds the costs of resources to the schedule developed by the traditional PERT networking procedures.

AN APPLICATION OF PERT: PRODUCT DEVELOPMENT

Assume you are the production manager for Fly-Hi Aircraft Company. The government has requested that your firm develop a prototype model of an aircraft engine which can be used in special purpose airplanes.

FIGURE 16–3
PERT Network

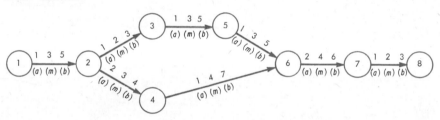

Since the government is always in a hurry, you would like to have the model developed as quickly as possible. The first step is to define each task that must be done. After consulting with the production and engineering departments, you conclude that the project consists of eight activities.

1. Develop engineering specification for the engines.
2. Obtain test models of the engines.
3. Locate suppliers for component parts that will be needed for subassembly 2.
4. Develop production plans.
5. Begin subassembly 1.
6. Place orders for component parts and wait for receipt of component parts needed for subassembly 2.
7. Begin subassembly 2.
8. Begin final assembly.

TABLE 16–1

Description of Activities and Events in Figure 16–3

Activity	Description	Prerequisite Activities	Event Description
1–2......	Develop engineering specifications		2—Specifications completed
2–3......	Obtain test models	1–2	3—Test models obtained
2–4......	Locate suppliers of component parts	1–2	4—Suppliers located
3–5......	Develop production plans	2–3	5—Plans completed
5–6.....	Begin subassembly 1	3–5	Subassembly 1 completed
4–6......	Place orders for component parts and await receipt	2–4	6—Component parts received
6–7......	Begin subassembly 2	5–6 and 4–6	7—Subassembly 2 completed
7–8......	Begin final assembly	6–7	8—Engine completed

The network for the project is shown in Figure 16–3 with the estimates of the optimistic (a), most likely (m), and pessimistic (b) times. Note that events 3 and 4 are branched. This is because activities 2–3 and 2–4 can be performed simultaneously. A detailed description of the activities and events in the network is provided in Table 16–1.

Our first task is to calculate the expected time for each activity in the network. In Table 16–2 the three time estimates are given and the expected time (t_e) is calculated using the formula

$$t_e = \frac{a + 4m + b}{6}$$

Figure 16–4 shows the PERT network with the expected time (t_e) values for each activity.

TABLE 16–2

Calculation of t_e Values for Network

Activity	Optimistic Time (a)	Most Likely Time (m)	Pessimistic Time (b)	t_e (in weeks)
1–2.......................	1	3	5	3.0
2–3.......................	1	2	3	2.0
2–4.......................	2	3	4	3.0
3–5.......................	1	3	5	3.0
4–6.......................	1	4	7	4.0
5–6.......................	1	3	5	3.0
6–7.......................	2	4	6	4.0
7–8.......................	1	2	3	2.0

FIGURE 16-4

Expected Time (t_e) for Each Activity

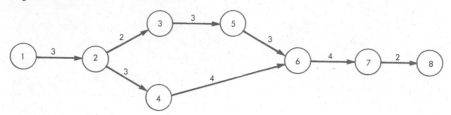

Calculation of Earliest Expected Date

Once the PERT network has been constructed and the expected time (t_e) has been calculated for each activity we can turn our attention to calculating the *earliest expected date* (T_E) in which the project can be completed. *The earliest expected date of an event is found by calculating the longest path from the network beginning event to the particular event in question, whether it is the network ending event or some other event.*

Examination of the network reveals there are two paths through the network, path 1, 2, 3, 5, 6, 7, 8 which takes a total of 17 weeks; and path 1, 2, 4, 6, 7, 8 which takes a total of 16 weeks. Thus, if we begin at once, completion of the network can be expected no sooner than 17 weeks.

Let us suppose that the manager wants to determine the time to complete a particular event which is not the network ending event. For example, when will event 5 be completed? To determine this we do exactly as we did previously; sum the paths from the network beginning event to the particular event in question and choose the longest path if there is more than one path. Thus, the (T_E) for event 5 is (path 1, 2, 3, 5) 8 weeks.

We can calculate the earliest expected date (T_E) for each event in the network by utilizing the same rule, by taking the longest path from the network beginning event to each of the other events in the network. This is shown in Figure 16–5.

FIGURE 16-5

Earliest Expected Date for Each Event in Network

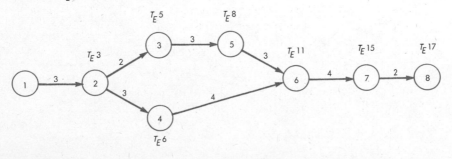

The importance of the *earliest expected date* (T_E) is that *it provides us with the dates on which certain work will be completed*. If the computed dates are unsatisfactory operations can be adjusted.

Before leaving the calculation of (T_E) let us examine event 6. It is somewhat different since it has two paths leading to it, path 1, 2, 3, 5, 6 which requires 11 weeks, and path 1, 2, 4, 6 which requires 10 weeks. Therefore, the (T_E) of event 6 is 11 weeks because (T_E) is the longest path from the network beginning event to the particular event in question.

The Critical Path

We have just seen that the longest path through the network determines the earliest expected date of the network ending event. This longest path is more commonly referred to as the *critical path*. Thus, *the critical path is the most time-consuming path of activities from the network beginning event to the network ending event*. In the above network it is path 1, 2, 3, 5, 6, 7, 8.

Latest Allowable Date

The *latest allowable date* (T_L) *is the latest date on which an event can occur without creating a delay in the scheduled completion of the project*. In Figure 16–5 we determined the longest path through the network by utilizing the earliest expected dates for each of the events. To calculate the $(T_L$'s) we subtract from the network ending event back to the event in question. (T_L) for an ending event is equal to the date directed by management for completion of the project. Assume that management directs the project to be completed within 20 weeks. However, if a directed date was not specified, then $T_L = T_E$ for the network ending event. The (T_L) values for the entire network are shown in Figure 16–6.

By now the reader should note that when we calculated the $(T_E$'s) we

FIGURE 16–6

Latest Allowable Date for Each Event in Network

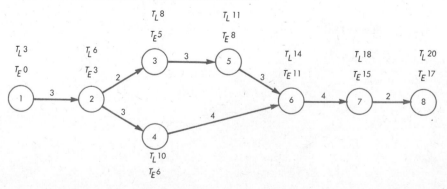

found (by addition) the longest path from the network beginning event to the particular event in question. When calculating the $(T_L\text{'s})$ we subtract in order to find the longest path from the network ending event back to the particular event in question.

In Figure 16–6 the (T_L) of an event is found by subtracting the expected time (t_e) for the activity from the previous (T_L). For example, the (T_L) for event 3 is found by subtracting the (t_e) of activity 3–5 from the (T_L) of event 5, or $11 - 3 = 8$.

Examine event 2. Note that when two or more paths yield different values we always choose the smaller when calculating the (T_L) of an event. Remember, in calculating the (T_E) of an event we always choose the larger value. Calculating the (T_L) of event 2 we get:

$$\text{Path 2–3} = \ \ 8 - 2 = 6$$
$$\text{Path 2–4} = 10 - 3 = 7$$

Since we choose the smaller value the (T_L) for event 2 is 6. This is because path 2, 3, 5, 6, 7, 8, involves 14 weeks and path 2, 4, 6, 7, 8, involves 13 weeks, and if we expect to complete the network in 20 weeks, event 2 must be completed within 6 weeks after the network beginning event in order to allow 14 additional weeks for the completion of the project.

Slack Time

Slack time is *time to spare in the completion of an event.* In Figure 16–6 we can see that event 6 does not have to occur until 14 weeks after the start of the network. However, event 4 is expected to be done in 6 weeks after the beginning of the network. Since activity 4–6 takes 4 weeks event 4 does not have to be achieved in 6 weeks. We could actually take 10 weeks to complete it and still meet our directed date of 20 weeks. Thus, there is slack on path 1, 2, 4, 6, 7, 8 and if we fall slightly behind we do not have to worry. Slack time is calculated by using the following formula:

$$\text{Slack Time } (S) = T_L - T_E.$$

The calculations of slack time are shown in Table 16–3.

Figure 16–6 and Table 16–3 show slack time on the critical path. Can such a situation exist? The answer is "yes" because the target of 20 weeks is three more than needed. However, note that the critical path has less slack (three weeks) than path 1, 2, 4, 6, 7, 8, which has four weeks. From a practical standpoint this indicates that we could fall three weeks behind somewhere on the critical path and still not jeopardize the completion date. It also means that we can shift resources, if possible, to the critical path, thereby perhaps shortening the time of the entire project. This is an important use of the slack time computation.

TABLE 16–3

Calculation of Slack Time for Events in Network

Event	T_L	—	T_E	= Slack Time
1	3	—	0	= 3
2	6	—	3	= 3
3	8	—	5	= 3
4	10	—	6	= 4
5	11	—	8	= 3
6	14	—	11	= 3
7	18	—	15	= 3
8	20	—	17	= 3

Before leaving this discussion we should mention that it is also possible to have a network in which the (T_L) of the network ending event is less than the (T_E) for the same event. This would occur when we have allowed the project less time than it is expected to take us to complete the project. In such cases, which are atypical, the network has negative slack, which would mean it is behind schedule before it begins. A case could also arise where $T_L = T_E$. This would be the case previously mentioned where there is no specified date for completion.

PERT and Uncertainty

The reader will recall that when we began our discussion of PERT it was pointed out that there was uncertainty involved in the time estimates. The reason for this is that the entire PERT network is based upon estimates of time. Specifically, there were three estimates of time, each with some degree of uncertainty attached to them. Even the expected time (t_e) value, while statistically sound, is uncertain because it was calculated using the three time estimates. However, probability theory provides a means of reducing some of this uncertainty. Specifically, there are methods for dealing with these uncertainties with the objective of estimating the probability that a project will be completed by (T_L). It is not necessary to devote time and space to this topic at this point. However, the interested reader will find this topic covered completely in the Appendix to the book.

SUMMARY

Network models are widely used in both business and government organizations and have an excellent record of successes. They are especially suited for nonrepetitive types of projects and as such are widely used in development projects. In the application section of the chapter we examined how one network model, PERT, could be used as a planning and control device in a product development project. While network models are extremely valuable aids in planning and control, the reader should remember that as with all management science models, they are only aids to the manager. How effective they are depends on how the manager utilizes them.

DISCUSSION AND REVIEW QUESTIONS

1. Why can PERT be used for effective *concurrent* control?
2. Cite some nonrepetitive problems for which *PERT* would be useful as a planning and control tool. Cite others than those discussed in the chapter. Use your personal experiences if necessary.
3. Assume that you have been assigned a term project in one of your management courses. Data for the report will come from both library sources and personal interviews with local businessmen. It is your task to collect both types of data. You have a total of ten weeks in which to complete the assignment. List the activities and their optimistic, most likely, and pessimistic times; and construct a PERT network for the project.
4. Place the following activities in the form of a PERT network.

a.	Remove carburetor	*o.*	Clean and replace air filter
b.	Rotate tires	*f.*	Test drive car
c.	Put on snow tires	*g.*	Remove air filter
d.	Tune motor	*h.*	Complete tune-up

5. Answer in detail the following brief questions:

   a. Can there be slack time on the critical path?
   b. Can there be slack time on a noncritical path?
   c. Can there be any such thing as negative slack?
   d. Of what value are the slack time calculations?

6. Assume that you have just received word to begin production on a special device that your company will produce for the government. You have developed the PERT network for the project along with the time estimates for each activity. These are shown below. Assume you must complete the project in 35 weeks. Determine the expected time, earliest

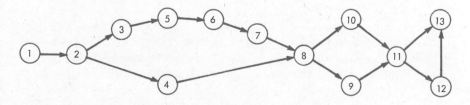

| | Time Estimates (weeks) | | |
Activity	Optimistic Time	Most Likely Time	Pessimistic Time
1–2	1	2	3
2–3	2	4	6
2–4	2	4	6
3–5	1	3	5
4–8	2	4	6
5–6	4	7	10
6–7	1	2	3
7–8	1	2	3
8–9	1	2	3
8–10	1	2	3
9–11	2	3	4
10–11	3	4	5
11–12	1	2	3
11–13	4	6	8
12–13	1	1	1

expected date, and latest allowable date for each activity and identify the critical path.

ADDITIONAL REFERENCES

Baker, B. N., and Eris, R. L.   *An Introduction to PERT-CPM.* Homewood, Ill.: Richard D. Irwin, Inc., 1964.

Hein, L. W.   *The Quantitative Approach to Managerial Decisions.* Englewood Cliffs, N.J.: Prentice-Hall, Inc., 1967.

Levin, R. I., and Kirkpatrick, C. A.   *Planning and Control with PERT/CPM.* New York: McGraw-Hill Book Co., 1966.

Lockyer, K. G.   *An Introduction to Critical Path Analysis.* New York: Pitman Publishing Corporation, 1964.

Martino, R. L.   *Finding the Critical Path.* New York: American Management Association, 1964.

Miller, R. W.   "How to Plan and Control with PERT," *Harvard Business Review* 40 (1962): 93–104.

———.   *Schedule, Cost and Profit Control with PERT.* New York: McGraw-Hill Book Co., 1963.

Olsen, R. A.   *Manufacturing Management: A Quantitative Approach.* Scranton, Pa.: International Textbook Co., 1968.

Page, J. C., and Stolle, J. F.   "Space Age Technique to Launch New Products (PERT Program)," *Sales Management* 93 (1964): 22–27.

part four

Contemporary Management

**Contemporary Management in a
Dynamic Environment**

17 Contemporary Management in a Dynamic Environment

INTRODUCTION

At the beginning of this book we asked the question, "What can be done in the present to prepare future managers for the future?" The result has been a book organized around the idea that tomorrow's manager should know about the management process and the managerial functions of planning, organizing, and controlling; about group and individual behavior; about organizational structure; and about various behavioral and quantitative techniques that managers utilize as they perform the managerial functions.

The evolving field of management is forcing each individual manager to examine, utilize, experiment, and discard various ideas in all of the three schools. What this means is that there is no one best way to manage. Instead, there are a variety of ways to manage appropriately. In the first section of this final chapter we shall present a framework which seeks to bring together the three major approaches to the study of management and provide a foundation for the manager of the future to formulate a reality-centered conception of the managerial process. This chapter will also examine our changing social environment, information technology, and the international environment and the dynamic influences of these developments on contemporary management. The separate and combined effects of these developments reinforces the necessity for reality-centered management.

REALITY-CENTERED MANAGING

The manager who is competent to use approaches from each of the three schools of management is what we term reality-centered. The following statement aptly describes the manager of the future:

> . . . the future executive is going to have to possess a greater breadth and intensity of knowledge than did managers past and present. The complexity of future organizations, and the confusion of society, will require that managers have a considerable knowledge of the techniques of economics and the behavioral sciences, perhaps some grasp of engineering and the physical sciences, and certainly a good conception of quantitative methodology and computer technology. More than being a mere "tool user," however, the future manager is going to have to be a humanist as well as a technocrat. He will have to have the ability to understand people and to appraise situations and to make judicious decisions that will be followed.[1]

If the manager recognizes that useful concepts, techniques, and models exist in the three schools of management, this is a step in the direction of reality centeredness. This is not to say that experience and/or wisdom will be totally useless in the modern era of management. Instead, the need for a balance of classical, behavioral, management science approaches, and experience is more realistic and contemporary. Sole reliance on classical principles, or behavioral suggestions such as participative management, or management science models is as sterile and stagnant as relying solely on past experience. An appreciation of the schools of management and experience is what the reality-centered manager should attempt to accomplish. This kind of thinking will go far in making a manager more effective in contemporary organizations.

INTEGRATING THE THREE SCHOOLS OF MANAGEMENT

One of the major problems that must be overcome if managers are to adopt a reality-centered approach is that they must be able to visualize what various concepts, techniques, and models can do to improve their organizations. The ideas suggested by such people as Taylor, Fayol, Urwick, Maslow, Herzberg, Bales, Fiedler, Hurwicz, and Savage must be placed into an integrated framework. It has been suggested that each of the concepts, techniques, and models can be placed into one of two categories.[2]

---

[1] Joseph W. McGuire, ed., *Contemporary Management: Issues and Viewpoints* (Englewood Cliffs, N.J.: Prentice-Hall, Inc., 1974), p. 651.

[2] This classification scheme was developed by Paul R. Lawrence and Jay W. Lorsch, *Organization and Environment* (Homewood, Ill.: Richard D. Irwin, Inc. 1969). It is appropriate for integrating the three schools of management.

The first category includes factors that focus upon greater order, systematization, routinization, and predictability. This category will be referred to as the *closed system* (*CS*) factors. The second category includes factors that are primarily designed to develop greater openness, sharing, creativity, and individual initiative. This category will be designated as the *open system* (*OS*) factors.

Both the (*CS*) and (*OS*) factors are valuable for the reality-centered manager. Neither set is all right or all wrong for every management problem situation. It is best to perceive them as the extremes of a continuum along which the concepts discussed in this book can be placed.

A Graphical Representation

In order to acquire a clearer understanding of the blending of various techniques and models from the three schools, a diagram will be utilized. The factors specified in the diagram are not a complete referencing of every possible approach or technique. However, the diagram does provide a guiding framework for the future manager.

Figure 17–1 indicates that at the core of the management process are the functions of planning, organizing, and controlling. Behind the application of any of the techniques and models displayed in Figure 17–1 are these core functions. Thus, they are clearly represented as the basic foundations of the field of management.

In Figure 17–1 the specific discipline that has influenced the evolution of each school is also presented. For example, it is the statistics and mathematical areas that have had a pronounced and obvious influence on the Management Science School. On the other hand industrial engineering, economics, and specific management experience have significantly affected the development of the Classical School of Management.

Selected approaches from each of the three schools of management are also specified in Figure 17–1. These approaches are associated with one of the two orientations. For example, authority can be used to exercise control over a job task. This use would demand compliance and would be inflexible. However, a manager may use authority to allow subordinates to make autonomous decisions. Subordinates might be allowed to plan their own work schedules or to establish their own budgets. Therefore, authority can be interpreted as both a closed system (*CS*) and an open system (*OS*) factor, depending upon the manager and the situation.

If management by objectives (*MBO*) is examined closely it becomes apparent that the main objectives is to have subordinates participate in the setting of goals. Theoretically, the (*MBO*) program will allow them to develop and grow on the job. They will be able to display greater initiative and creativity. Thus, (*MBO*) leans toward the (*OS*) side of the continuum.

FIGURE 17–1

Integrating the Three Schools

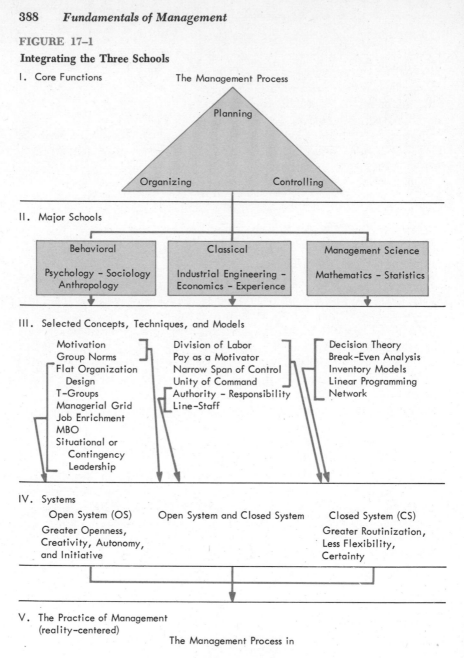

I. Core Functions — The Management Process

Planning

Organizing   Controlling

II. Major Schools

Behavioral	Classical	Management Science
Psychology – Sociology Anthropology	Industrial Engineering – Economics – Experience	Mathematics – Statistics

III. Selected Concepts, Techniques, and Models

Motivation
Group Norms
Flat Organization
  Design
T–Groups
Managerial Grid
Job Enrichment
MBO
Situational or
  Contingency
  Leadership

Division of Labor
Pay as a Motivator
Narrow Span of Control
Unity of Command
Authority – Responsibility
Line–Staff

Decision Theory
Break–Even Analysis
Inventory Models
Linear Programming
Network

IV. Systems

Open System (OS)   Open System and Closed System   Closed System (CS)

Greater Openness,
Creativity, Autonomy,
and Initiative

Greater Routinization,
Less Flexibility,
Certainty

V. The Practice of Management
   (reality-centered)

The Management Process in

Business Organizations
Educational Institutions
Government Agencies
Health–Care Organizations
Military

Examination of linear programming models suggests that they are designed to aid the manager in developing a program for the optimum allocation of resources. The utilization of linear programming focuses upon predicting the most optimum use of equipment or warehouses or personnel. Thus, this model meets the criteria of a closed system factor.

The two major categories (CS and OS) provide a framework for classifying the numerous concepts of the three management schools. The advantage of having this type of framework is that instead of arguing about which managerial school is most accurate, the student of management focuses upon what each concept can accomplish most effectively. For example, a narrow span of control generally yields a routine orientation, while a wide span of control encourages a more open and creative orientation. There are certainly many gray areas when utilizing this classification system. That is, would a span of control of eight subordinates be considered a narrow or a wide span? The framework cannot deal with such debates. Its primary purpose is to offer a starting point for blending the concepts and techniques found in the three schools of management.

The Contemporary Manager

The increasing number of concepts and techniques offered by the schools of management and the rapid pace of change require that a more sophisticated managerial cadre be called upon to make organizational decisions. An understanding of the boundaries established by classical scholars in presenting the functions of planning, organizing, and controlling is essential. Managers in contemporary organizations will need greater technical skills, conceptual skills, diagnostic skills, awareness of social and ethical issues, and a deep concern for human resources.

The skills and abilities required to perform effectively in a contemporary management position will be derived from a number of sources such as: (1) educational preparation, (2) professional training and development, and (3) actual experiences on the job and in society. The education, development, and experience of managers will be a continuing process.

The specifics of the exact type of educational background, developmental process, and experience are beyond the scope of this chapter. It is anticipated, however, that knowledge of economics, the functional areas of business (for example, accounting, marketing, and production), quantitative methods, computers, and the behavioral sciences will be invaluable. This is not to say that any manager can master each of these broad areas. It is, however, feasible to assume that managers in organizations can maintain a working knowledge of the more relevant and pertinent concepts associated with each of the areas. The required comprehension is possible if the educational programs of universities and colleges, management development programs, and daily organizational activities encourage the preparation of reality-centered managers.

MANAGEMENT AND THE CHANGING SOCIAL ENVIRONMENT

It is common today to read articles or hear speeches calling for more "people consciousness" or "social responsibility" on the part of managers in every type of organization. In considering the meaning of these demands, it is important to note that this movement is only one part of a much broader and more pervasive change in the values of people in our society. It is no coincidence that demands for more social awareness among the managers of large organizations, the concerns of the younger generation, minority group protests, the consumerism movement, women's rights, discontent on the nation's assembly lines, concern about ecology, and problems in the nation's prisons have all occurred almost simultaneously. The last few years have been characterized by such phrases as "the meaning of work," "the quality of life," "the environment," "power to the people," and numerous others. The common ingredient of each of these so-called movements is *people*, and each of them will profoundly influence every type of organization—public and private—in our society during the next decade.

The demands for more social awareness and responsibility from the nation's managers is only one part of the overall attempt on the part of our society to make all institutions—business, government, educational, hospitals—more responsive to human needs. The managers in these organizations will be called upon to react to these demands. Earlier in the book we indicated the necessity of monitoring the organizations' external environment for important inputs to the management process. As society's values and needs change, they must influence the management process. These needs and changing values must be reflected in the alternatives considered and the priorities assigned by managers.

For example, within many organizations there has been increasing discontent and protest over the depersonalization or dehumanizing aspects of many jobs, (that is, the quality of life at work). The middle section of this book concentrated entirely on the Behavioral School, with the recognition that contemporary management thought and practice are incomplete without a basic understanding of human behavior. The ideas and techniques discussed in that section are not exclusive to the management classroom. They are becoming an important part of the knowledge of contemporary managers and are having an impact on current approaches to management. Examine for a moment some important changes occurring in one of the nation's largest manufacturing firms:[3]

1. The firm is actively encouraging decision sharing with workers through a series of programs in its plants and offices.
2. The backgrounds of entering executives are changing under a concentrated program. In 1972, one-half of the college graduates hired were black or women.
3. An index is being developed to measure worker attitudes and relate it to cost and productivity. In the future it is expected that company executives will be judged not only on a financial balance sheet, but on a human resources balance sheet as well.
4. First-line supervisors are put through leadership courses that concentrate on encouraging a more open attitude in their dealings with subordinates.

These kinds of changes are not isolated examples. They are taking place in all types of organizations both public and private, large and small. Table 17–1 summarizes some expected changes in managerial practices in business organizations in the foreseeable future. Examination of the table reveals that most of the expected changes reflect the ferment within our society and our evolving "people-oriented" values. While Table 17–1 is concerned specifically with business organizations, most of the changes are pervasive, reflecting changes in societal values, and will extend far beyond business managers to those in every type of organization in our society. It is also interesting to note that many of the forecasted changes reflect a more open-system orientation.

Business Organizations and Social Responsibility

During the last decade society has been placing increased demands on large business organizations for greater social responsibility—that is, business involvement in solving both social and ecological problems. Some executives have replied, "Why us?" while others have agreed. Some firms commit resources to social action programs; others agree they should but, as yet, have not; and still others believe that they meet their social responsibilities by being profitable, providing employment, and paying taxes. The problem is a very real and complex one with which business organizations and our society will be forced to come to grips during the next decade.

In early history the wealthy and the powerful have often assumed responsibility for the welfare of those less fortunate around them. It is

---

[3] "GM Zeroes In on Employee Discontent," *Business Week,* May 12, 1973, pp. 140–44.

TABLE 17–1

Past versus Future Managerial Practices*

Past	*Future*
Assumption that a business manager's sole responsibility is to optimize stockholder wealth	Profit still dominant but modified by the assumption that a business manager has other social responsibilities
Business performance measured only by economic standards	Application of both an economic and social measure of performance
Emphasis on quantity of production	Emphasis on quantity *and* quality
Authoritarian management	Permissive/democratic management
Short-term intuitive planning	Long-range comprehensive structured planning
Entrepreneur	Renaissance manager
Control	Creativity
People subordinate	People dominant
Financial accounting	Human resources accounting
Caveat emptor ("let the buyer beware")	Ombudsman
Centralized decision making	Decentralized and small-group decision making
Concentration on internal functioning	Concentration on external ingredients for company success
Dominance of economic forecasts in decision making	Major use of social, technical, and political forecasts as well as economic forecasts
Business viewed as a single system	Business viewed as a system within a larger social system
Business ideology calls for aloofness from government	Business-government cooperation and convergence of planning
Business has little concern for social costs of production	Increasing concern for internalizing social costs of production

* George Steiner, presidential address before the American Academy of Management (Minneapolis, August 15, 1972).

probably the lingering survival of this paternalistic belief that today demands from the large business organization the kind of social responsibility that has throughout history been expected of wealth and power. In the context of present times these expectations fall in such areas as educating the young, policing the streets, cleaning up polluted air and water, teaching disadvantaged citizens how to earn a living, rebuilding ghettos and providing management expertise for city governments.[4]

As problems such as these continue to mount, business managers of

[4] See Hazel Henderson, "Should Business Tackle Society's Problems?" *Harvard Business Review,* vol. 46 (July–August 1968), p. 77.

the future will be more than ever faced with reconciling their responsibilities to two groups of people, stockholders and society in general. In addition to the belief that power implies responsibility, there are other reasons why the modern corporation will be looked toward for help in solving society's problems. For example, more and more citizens are realizing that in addition to having the power, the modern business corporation also has the technical know-how to aid in solving the nation's problems. The federal government itself holds a similar viewpoint and has begun actively to solicit the aid of the large corporation. For example, in the late 1960s the federal government announced a plan whereby private industry would be given the responsibility for hiring and training the majority of the nation's hard-core unemployed. Industry, in turn, would receive a measure of government subsidy.[5]

While there are strong arguments *for* social responsibility by business organizations, there are also some powerful arguments *against* it. For example, there are those who maintain that the large corporation administers a wealth that it does not own and, therefore, should not be forced to develop a social awareness over the use of assets that are owned ultimately by private citizens. There are others who seriously question whether it is proper to place public problems on the shoulders of corporate managers. They point out that persons who are highly skilled in business matters may not be so in matters of politics, the humanities, and the social sciences. They also note that such persons are in no way accountable to the voters for their decisions and could, in determining what is best for society, turn into paternalistic rulers. Finally, many people believe that business may suffer serious consequences by accepting too heavy a burden of social responsibility since capital and managerial talent may be drained by other activities which are alien to the profit motive.

One of the major problems surrounding the entire issue appears to be clearly defining what social responsibility is as well as deciding what society should reasonably expect from the business firm in this area. Notwithstanding these problems as well as the debates pro and con, it appears that demands for socially responsible business behavior will continue and probably increase. While the direction and extent of these demands cannot be known at this time, many business organizations are responding to the present challenges. Following are some specific instances where business has taken on responsibilities which can be considered social in nature:

1. The city of New York called in McKinsey and Company to analyze the city's air pollution problems, and the Traffic Commission invited

---

[5] Ibid., p. 78.

Sperry Rand, and later IBM, to help solve the city's growing traffic headache.[6]

2. The governors of Alabama, California, Nebraska, and other states have borrowed business executives, whose salaries continue to be paid by their respective companies, as consultants in seeking ways to trim the costs of state government.[7]

3. A large western bank has, since 1971, sponsored a tennis program (using professional instructors and company employees) for disadvantaged youth.

4. A supermarket chain in the West has, since 1970, conducted a continuing, multifaceted program for encouraging and aiding food consumers in becoming more ecologically effective as individuals, as well as altering certain internal practices of the firm in the interest of ecology.

5. A large eastern firm, newly located on the shores of a heavily polluted lake, instituted an ongoing program of research studies and seminars as well as internal operational changes with the goal of reaching workable solutions to the critical pollution problem. (Note: The sponsoring firm was not a polluter.)

The Manager's Dilemma

Thus, managers may find themselves on the horns of a dilemma. When they attempt to become involved in society's problems they may be faced with a group of very angry stockholders who maintain that companies have no legal right to retain earnings for such uses, and that the stockholders should decide how the money is spent, since the stockholders are the rightful owners. On the other hand, when managers attempt to maximize profit for the stockholders they may be faced with the wrath of other citizens who claim that corporate managers have no respect for the needs of society as a whole and are failing to safeguard the environmental conditions that provide for the survival and growth of the business organization.

The root cause of the conflict over social responsibility appears to lie in the irreconcilability of two theories of the corporation[8]—the theory of the *traditional corporation* on the one hand, and the theory of the *metrocorporation* on the other. Both theories express extreme viewpoints.

The *traditional corporation* is an instrument of a single group—the shareholders—and has one clear-cut purpose: conducting business for profit. The prior claim of the stockholders on earnings after taxes is unquestioned, and management has to do no "balancing" of interests in

---

[6] Ibid., p. 78.

[7] Ibid., p. 79.

[8] This discussion is based upon Richard Eells and Clarence Walton, *Conceptual Foundations of Business* (Homewood, Ill.: Richard D. Irwin, Inc., 1961), pp. 468–76.

distributing the earnings. This traditional view recognizes no social responsibilities except for legal ones and leaves the public interests to the care of the state. As we noted previously, the view has been attacked as being shortsighted and ultimately self-destructive.

The opposite model of the traditional corporation is the *metrocorporation,* which assumes limitless social responsibility. In this type of corporation, managers accept an accountability to many different segments of society. This type of corporation is a major social institution with comprehensive aims, and it is far removed from the strict, limited objective of the traditional corporation: profit for the stockholders. The metrocorporation emphasizes its rights and duties as a "citizen" in its relationships with the various groups in its environment. The dangers of this model were also previously pointed out: undue power for managers and the danger of them becoming paternalistic rulers; incompetence in areas such as humanities and politics; and the suboptimization of corporate economic goals and functions.

Obviously, the above descriptions represent two opposite extremes. The business manager of the future will undoubtedly find a middle ground between these positions. The following statement should aid in establishing this position.

> The large business corporation is here to stay. It is an indispensible instrument for getting done some of the things that people want done. It is neither the exclusive instrument of one class of interests nor an indiscriminate roster of "social" interests. Like other large organizations, the corporation has to be tempered to the times; and as a viable instrument it must adapt to the changing requirements of our free, complex, and interdependent society.[9]

Thus, it is necessary to find a position somewhere between the extremes of the traditional corporation and the metrocorporation which will take into account public expectations and not be in conflict with management's responsibilities to the stockholder. This model has been referred to as the *well-tempered corporation.*[10] This viewpoint holds that the claims of stockholders and creditors will more likely be met if a firm develops a position as a socially responsible company. This can only be done if management integrates the factors of production with respect to the primary interests of the owners and the prevailing norms and values of society. Since the values of our society are changing rapidly, so is the definition of a socially responsible firm. The following statement reflects a realistic response to the difficult questions of "What is a socially responsible firm?"

---

[9] Ibid., p. 474.
[10] Ibid.

The answer to this question will change and eventually must be answered by society itself. It may be best to define the socially responsible firm as one that anticipates what the public will expect from it and attempts to meet these demands before the public focuses its criticism upon it. In a nutshell, the socially responsible firm is one that is responsive to (even anticipates) the demands of society, not only economic ones, but social and environmental ones as well.[11]

This will be a major task facing the managers of the future.

The Future

Issues of social responsibility, ecology, the meaning of work, the quality of life, minority employment, sex discrimination, etc. have very important "value" implications for management. Contemporary managers will be forced to weave these value changes into their own concept of what a manager should do and be. This process cannot be learned through reading a textbook since it extends far beyond the classroom.

It is inconceivable to imagine that a society can be confronted with critical shortages, insufficient natural resources, and ecological pollution without experiencing a change in values. During the past several decades managers operated for the most part in an environment characterized by abundance and a societal commitment to growth. If the next decade is characterized by shortages and a societal commitment to conservation, then conflicts will undoubtedly arise with which managers will be forced to deal. In fact, some individuals see our society shifting from a "things first–people second" orientation to one of "people first and things second."

Such a reorientation of our societal values will have a profound impact on future management practice in every type of organization. What it will mean is that the manager of the future will not be able to act as an isolationist with respect to society (and other societies as well) because the measure of an effective manager in the future will likely be more than efficient performance alone.

INFORMATION TECHNOLOGY AND ORGANIZATION DESIGN

A number of management scholars have predicted the impact of information technology on organizational design. This relatively new technology is composed of several related components. First, the high-speed computer is a major element that managers must cope with on an ever increasing scale. Second, statistical and mathematical methods of man-

---

[11] R. Joseph Monsen, *Business and the Changing Environment* (New York: McGraw-Hill Book Co., 1973), p. 121.

agement scientists are compatible with the new technology. The utilization of these models in conjunction with high-speed computers is emerging as an important application of information technology.

It has been postulated that information technology will have a significant impact on the middle and top management of organizations. Whisler and Leavitt have predicted that in many instances the information technology thrust will lead to just the opposite conclusions from those proposed by naive individuals advocating "participative" management approaches.[12]

The main ingredients of the Whisler and Leavitt forecast are as follows:

1. Information technology should push upward in the organization structure the boundary between planning and performance. A significant portion of the planning currently being done by middle level managers will be given to such specialists as organizational analysts and management scientists. These specialists will be located at the top managerial levels. In effect, the middle manager's job would become more structured, routine, and predictable. The middle manager would be operating within what we have referred to as a closed system.

2. The availability of high speed computers in conjunction with new mathematical and statistical techniques will enable large corporations to move to recentralization of the planning, organizing, and controlling functions. This recentralization trend will allow the top level managers to take on activities that call for more creativeness, innovation, and openness.

3. The new technology and the movement toward recentralization will necessitate a reorganization of the middle management level. A number of middle manager jobs will be downgraded. That is, those managers will have less organizational status and receive less remuneration. Other middle management positions will be upgraded and be considered within the revised organizational design as top management positions.

4. The line separating top and middle management will be drawn more clearly. Managers who are innovators and coordinators will be found at the top echelons.

These four major ingredients have led Whisler and Leavitt to predict that the organizational structure of the future would resemble a football balanced on the top of a bell. This form of structure is illustrated in Figure 17–2.

Anshen has viewed the new information technology as enriching rather

---

[12] Harold J. Leavitt and Thomas L. Whisler, "Management in the 1980s," *Harvard Business Review*, vol. 36 (November–December 1958), pp. 41–48; and Thomas L. Whisler, *Information Technology and Organizational Change* (Belmont, Calif.: Wadsworth Publishing Co., 1970), pp. 63–66.

FIGURE 17–2

Whisler and Leavitt Predicted Structure

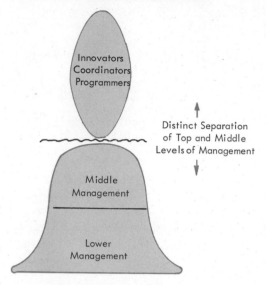

than shrinking the role of managers at the middle level.[13] The major points of difference between Whisler and Leavitt and Anshen concern the task of middle management and the role of the professional experts (top management).

It is Anshen's contention that because of the increased concern in the modern organization with problem identification, decision implementation, and new opportunities to find solutions, middle managers will be top managers in miniature. It is also Anshen's belief that the innovators or the professional experts in the Whisler and Leavitt framework will occupy positions of growing stature, responsibility, and influence in organizations. They will not, however, assume fundamental responsibilities of top-level managers. Professional experts are perceived by Anshen as having limited perspectives that are often not suited for the pace of dynamic decision making that is so essential in contemporary organizations.

It seems clear that the effects of information technology and advances in technology in general will result in a number of different organizational designs. Instead of predicting that organizations will follow a football-bell shape or any other specific design, it would be more realistic to propose that designs will differ. The viable organizations of the future will fall somewhere on a continuum ranging from highly routine pro-

---

[13] M. Anshen, "The Manager and the Black Box," *Harvard Business Review*, vol. 38 (November–December 1960), pp. 85–92.

duction work to the creative work performed by trained scientists and professionals.[14] In fact, some organizations will perform tasks that range from routine to highly creative. Thus, it is possible that different designs may be appropriate for different divisions or units or departments of the same company. Some organizations will have dual hierarchies or as many as three, four, or five hierarchies. Perhaps one hierarchy would be for technical personnel, one hierarchy for support personnel, and one for those concerned with public image and environmental control.

The essential point is that the simple bureaucratic or nonbureaucratic dichotomy is not relevant in changing society. It is best to consider the environment, the technology, the task, and the personnel of an organization as being closely linked to the design strategy pertaining to an organization. Thus, mixed and diverse designs will characterize contemporary organizations.[15]

MANAGEMENT AND THE INTERNATIONAL ENVIRONMENT

A major concern of management in the future will be the continued growth of the *multinational firm*—a firm with branches, divisions, and subsidiaries in foreign countries. Since the end of World War II, a growing number of U.S. corporations are investing private capital in overseas divisions, branches, and subsidiaries at an accelerated rate. It is estimated that approximately 5,000 American corporations currently operate in foreign countries.

U.S. corporations have invested in foreign countries for the same basic reasons they have invested capital in the domestic United States. These reasons vary from firm to firm, but most fall under the three interrelated goals of: (1) increasing long-term growth and profit prospects, (2) maximizing total sales revenue, and (3) improving overall market positions. Whatever the reasons, there is little doubt that the multinational firm will be commonplace in the near future. The complexity of the problem facing the management of a multinational firm is summarized in the following statement:

> We must recognize that firms like IBM, World Trade, Royal Dutch/ Shell are very complex, geographically decentralized systems embedded frequently in as many as a hundred different countries, in advanced, developing, in market-oriented, and command economies. They must be

---

[14] For an excellent classification framework for studying organizations, consult the ongoing research and work of Andrew Grimes, Stuart Klein, and Fremont Shull, "Matrix Model: An Empirical Test," *Proceedings for the Midwest Academy of Management,* 1970.

[15] For a number of insightful viewpoints of organizational design, refer to James D. Thompson, ed., *Approaches to Organizational Design* (Pittsburgh: University of Pittsburgh Press, 1966).

organized to serve billions of potential customers. AT&T has 679,100 employees and operates in the framework of the U.S. market with a 200 million population. General Motors has a somewhat higher number of employees and operates in as many countries as states with populations of more than a million. The management skills in General Motors . . . are rather different I would maintain.[16]

It is not difficult to see some of the problems a firm faces when it crosses national boundaries. One of the more obvious would be when it attempts to market its product or service in a foreign country. Depending on the cultural environment, different approaches would be necessary in advertising, pricing, and selecting channels of distribution for the firm's product. These types of problems are currently being examined in an emerging field of study known as *comparative management*. Because, of the importance of the multinational firm in the future growth and expansion of American industry, the reader should become familiar with the basic purposes of comparative management.

Comparative Management

Comparative management deals with problems of management and managerial efficiency in various countries. It seeks to detect, identify, classify, measure, and interpret similarities and differences. Essentially, the comparative method "focuses on how thing *are*, rather than on how things *could be* (as in policy making) or on how they *should be* (the 'principles' approach)."[17]

The scholars engaged in comparative management research believe that the tasks facing a manager in the domestic environment differ greatly from those faced in a foreign environment. This belief is exemplified in the following statement:

> The subsidiary manager in Brazil may be a U.S. expatriate[18] who will have to learn Portugese, understand Brazilian politics, the economics of rapid inflation, and the difficulties of being considered a good citizen of Brazil. He will have to train local managers and learn to trust them, as well as his compatriots. This is a rather challenging task—not wholly different conceptually from the Pennsylvania manager—but different

[16] Howard V. Perlmutter, "Some Management Problems in Spaceship Earth: The Megafirm and the Global Industrial State," *Proceedings of the Academy of Management,* August 1969, p. 76.

[17] J. Boddewyn, *Comparative Management and Marketing* (Glenview, Ill.: Scott, Foresman and Company), 1969, p. 3.

[18] The term *expatriate* is used to refer to those U.S. executives who have permanent assignments outside the geographic boundaries of the United States. The reader should also be aware that many U.S. firms attempt to employ local nationals whenever possible to manage overseas operations.

enough to make it possible for a manager to be a great success in Pennsylvania and a disaster in Brazil.[19]

Comparative management scholars also believe that existing management knowledge has some drawbacks in terms of orientation and application in two different types of cultures and economies. They contend that most existing studies of management have taken place within a framework where there has been little concern for the external environment in which the firm must operate. As long as the external environment is the same for all firms (for example, all firms operating in the United States), this approach is valid. However, in the situations where the external environment differs, they believe that present management knowledge is inadequate. In such cases where environments do vary, as is often the case between nations, they believe it is necessary to study the external pressures and constraints upon internal management. They contend that a manager may perform adequately in the internal management of the firm, but is also substantially influenced by external factors in the particular country which directly influences management effectiveness.[20]

Introducing the External Environment

Several scholars have attempted to develop models for the analysis of management, taking into account the influence of external environments. These individuals have recognized that external cultural environments affect the practice of management.

One promising approach is the model developed by Professors Farmer and Richman. Their model attempts to identify the effect of cultural factors on the various management functions. An adaptation of the model is shown in Figure 17–3.

As noted in Figure 17–3, Farmer and Richman divide external and environmental constraints into four classes: educational, sociological-cultural, legal-political, and economic.

1. Educational constraints include such things as literacy level, the availability of specialized vocational and technical training, the prevailing attitude toward education, and the extent to which education matches requirements for skills and abilities. These educational factors may support or limit effective management.

2. Sociological-cultural constraints include a great number of factors. Some of the most important are the general attitude of the society toward managers, the dominant views of authority and subordinates, the extent

[19] Perlmutter, "Spaceship Earth," p. 76.

[20] Richard N. Farmer and Barry M. Richman, "A Model for Research in Comparative Management," *California Management Review*, vol. 7 (Winter 1964), p. 56.

FIGURE 17–3

Farmer-Richman Model for Analyzing Comparative Management

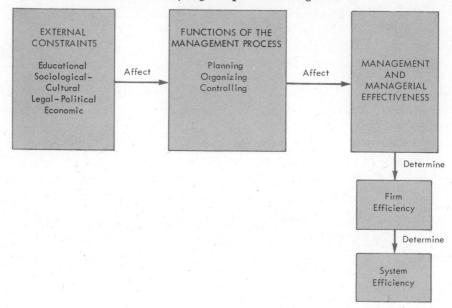

of union-management cooperation, and the dominant view of wealth and material gain.

3. Legal-political constraints include such things as defense policy and national security, foreign policy, political stability, and the flexibility of law and legal changes.

4. Economic constraints would include such factors as the basic economic system in the country, whether private or public ownership prevails, whether it is a competitive economy based on sound money, and the extent to which the government controls economic activities.

From their identification of the various management functions and of a manager's external environment, Farmer and Richman constructed their model. While it is undoubtedly subject to revision in the future, the model does distinguish the managerial functions from the environment in which the managing occurs. Probably their major contribution is narrowing the concept of management to the managerial functions and separating from it consideration of external environmental factors which can influence actual practice in specific instances. In so doing, the model appears to be a useful means for evaluating management and for presenting the variables that may make effective management differ between cultures.

While the field of comparative management is new and will undoubtedly undergo many changes as it progresses, the approach taken by Farmer and Richman has a great deal of usefulness. An additional advantage of their approach is that it can be a useful practical aid for firms operating in differing cultural environments. By specifying the areas of external constraints which may exist and identifying the elements within each area, they provide management in multinational firms with an orderly framework within which to perform the managerial functions of planning, organizing, and controlling in varying environments.

SUMMARY

In a relatively short span of history our society has evolved from small family and work units into one made up of complex organizations, the responsibility for the function of which rests upon their managers. Thus the importance of the manager to the effective functioning and well-being of our society cannot be overestimated.

Presently available evidence suggests that the manager's job will become even more complex and difficult in the future. This book has attempted to provide (given the present state of knowledge) future managers with those concepts and tools that will be useful to them. It is our belief that the concepts, techniques, and models emerging from the three schools of management thought offer future managers much of what they will need.

Contemporary managers who develop the ability to cope with rapid change will undoubtedly find the future rewarding. Thus, although the challenges of the future are frightening in many respects, the opportunities available for the manager with proper training are unlimited.

DISCUSSION AND REVIEW QUESTIONS

1. If you were asked to describe the field of management in a one-page essay, what would you say?
2. It is generally assumed that computer experts still do not have much influence on the policy makers in organizations. Do you believe that their status and power within the organization will change in the future? Why?
3. Many management scholars believe that new functions will be found in the organization chart of the future. These functions will be additions to the traditional functions such as finance, marketing, public relations,

and production. Do you foresee any new areas on the organization chart of tomorrow? What will be some of the responsibilities of the executives heading up these new areas?

4. Develop a figure which will enlarge upon and extend the schools of management and the concepts presented in Figure 17–1.

5. Assume that you have been working for the XYZ Corporation for six years in its Chicago office. You have been offered and have accepted a promotion to division head in your field. However, the job opening is in the company's branch in Malaya. Upon arriving at your new assignment, would you approach the job any differently than if you had been given the same job in the firm's plant in Buffalo, New York?

6. Choose any foreign country with which you are familiar. Outline the major elements of its culture that in your judgment would influence the type of management you would expect in a typical firm.

7. Choose any management technique or approach (for example, budgeting, participative management) and divide it into management fundamentals and those aspects which you feel would be influenced by cultural variables.

8. Assume that all corporations take on added social responsibilities. Whom do you feel will bear the additional costs—stockholders, employees? Or will prices increase?

9. A man calls at your home and represents himself as conducting an educational survey. When you admit him to your home, he proceeds to ask a few questions about the children in school and then begins a sales talk about encyclopedias. Does this and other types of activities by business firms have any relationship to social responsibility?

10. A corporation in your city has just announced that it will contribute $25,000 to the Department of Marketing at your school to be used to study consumer buying habits in your state. How do you view this act? Is it altruistic? Is it motivated by a desire for profit?

ADDITIONAL REFERENCES

Anshen, M., and Bach, G. L., eds. *Management and Corporations, 1985.* New York: McGraw-Hill Book Company, 1960.

Davis, K., and Blomstrom, R. L. *Business, Society, and Environment: Social Power and Social Response.* New York: McGraw-Hill Book Company, 1971.

Luthans, F., and Hodgetts, R. M. *Social Issues in Business.* New York: The Macmillan Company, 1972.

Massie, J. L., and Luytjes, J. B. *Management in an International Context.* New York: Harper and Row, Publishers, 1972.

McGuire, J. W. *Contemporary Management: Issues and Viewpoints.* Englewood Cliffs, N.J.: Prentice-Hall, Inc., 1974.

Negandi, A. R., and Estafen, B. D. "A Research Model to Determine the Applicability of American Management Know-How in Differing Cultures and/or Environments," *Academy of Management Journal* 8 (1965): 309–18.

Sethi, S. P. *Up Against the Corporate Wall: Modern Corporations and Social Issues of the Seventies.* Englewood Cliffs, N.J.: Prentice-Hall Inc., 1974.

Sethi, S. P., ed. *The Unstable Ground: Corporate Social Policy in a Dynamic Society.* Los Angeles: Melville Publishing Company, 1974.

Steiner, G. A., ed. *Issues in Business and Society.* New York: Random House Inc., 1972.

Walton, C. C. *Ethos and the Executive.* Englewood Cliffs, N.J.: Prentice-Hall, Inc., 1969.

Appendix: Computing the Probability of Achieving the Completion Date in a PERT Network

In Chapter 16 a formula was provided which has been shown to estimate satisfactorily the expected time (t_e) for each activity in a PERT network. An additional formula not discussed in Chapter 16 can be used to estimate satisfactorily the standard deviation (σ) for each activity. The formula is:

$$\sigma = \frac{b - a}{6}$$

The reader should recall from an elementary statistics course that the standard deviation is a statistical measure which indicates the tendency for data to disperse around the mean. In PERT projects, it will aid us in calculating the probability of achieving the completion date of the project. In order to illustrate how this is done, let us examine the simplified PERT network in Figure 1.

The optimistic time, most likely time, and pessimistic time estimates are listed for each activity. First, we shall compute the estimated time (t_e) and the standard deviation for each individual activity. Finally, we shall compute the standard deviation for the network ending event.

FIGURE 1

PERT Network

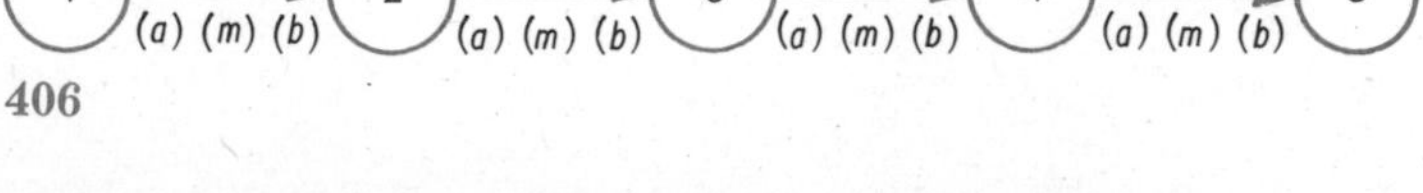

406

Our first step is to calculate the expected time (t_e) for each of the activities and determine the earliest expected date (T_E) for the network ending event. This is shown in Table 1. Our next step is to calculate the standard deviations for each individual activity. This is shown in Table 2.

TABLE 1

Expected Times for PERT Network in Figure 1

Activity	Optimistic Time (a)	Most Likely Time (m)	Pessimistic Time (b)	$\dfrac{a + 4m + b}{6} = t_e$
1–2	4	6	8	$\dfrac{4 + 24 + 8}{6} = 6.0$
2–3	4	10	16	$\dfrac{4 + 40 + 16}{6} = 10.0$
3–4	6	12	16	$\dfrac{6 + 48 + 16}{6} = 11.7$
4–5	4	12	20	$\dfrac{4 + 48 + 20}{6} = 12.0$

T_E (network ending event 5) $= 6.0 + 10.0 + 11.7 + 12.0$
$$T_E = 39.7 \text{ weeks}$$

Now that we have the standard deviations for each of the individual activities we would like to obtain some probability measure that will indicate the chances of finishing on time. In order to obtain this we must calculate the standard deviation for the network ending event (σT_E). To calculate the standard deviation for the ending event in a series, we take the square root of the sum of the individual activity standard deviations squared. This is expressed mathematically as:

$$\begin{aligned} \sigma T_E &= \sqrt{\Sigma(\sigma)^2} \\ &= \sqrt{(0.67)^2 + (2.0)^2 + (1.67)^2 + (2.67)^2} \\ &= \sqrt{0.449 + 4.0 + 2.79 + 7.13} \\ &= \sqrt{14.37} \\ \sigma T_E &= 3.8 \text{ weeks (rounded).} \end{aligned}$$

We now have two specific measures for this network:

1. The earliest expected date (T_E) for the network ending event (39.7) weeks, and
2. The standard deviation (σT_E) of the network ending event (3.8) weeks.

We are interested in the likelihood of meeting the scheduled completion date of the project (T_L). We would also prefer to have that likelihood expressed quantitatively in terms of probability. PERT procedures can provide this information.

TABLE 2

Standard Deviations for PERT Network

Activity	Optimistic Time (a)	Pessimistic Time (b)	$\dfrac{b-a}{6}$	Standard Deviation (σ)
1–2	4	8	$\frac{4}{6}$	.67
2–3	4	16	$1\frac{2}{6}$	2.00
3–4	6	16	$1\frac{0}{6}$	1.67
4–5	4	20	$1\frac{6}{6}$	2.67

The difference between the earliest expected completion date (T_E) and the latest allowable date (T_L) is divided by (σT_E) in order to express the difference in standard deviations (σT_E's) which has traditionally been denoted by the letter Z. Thus we have

$$Z = \frac{T_L - T_E}{\sigma T_E}.$$

Since the earliest expected date (T_E) is the sum of a series of means of probability distributions, (T_E) will tend to be distributed according to the normal probability distribution, and the Z value which we compute can be evaluated by using the Table of Areas under the Normal Curve shown at the end of this Appendix.

Assume that the network in Figure 1 must be completed in 44 weeks. We illustrate the (T_E) and (T_L) of the network ending event in Figure 2 below.

In order to determine the number of standard deviations Z we are from the mean, we subtract the (T_E) value from the (T_L) value. This is actually slack time on this particular critical path. We then divide the

FIGURE 2

Probability Distribution of Network Ending Event

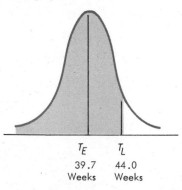

T_E	T_L
39.7 Weeks	44.0 Weeks

FIGURE 3

Probability Distribution ($T_E = T_L$)

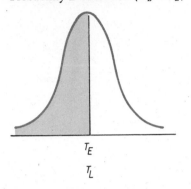

T_E

T_L

slack time by the standard deviation of the network ending event in order to get the number of standard deviations the slack time represents. This is shown as follows:

$$Z = \frac{T_L - T_E}{\sigma T_E}$$

$$Z = \frac{44 - 39.7}{3.8}$$

$$Z = \frac{4.3}{3.8}$$

$$Z = 1.13$$

In order to determine what percentage of the curve is contained within 1.13 standard deviations from the mean we must consult the Table of Areas under the Normal Curve. We find that 1.13 standard deviations from the mean encompasses 37.08 percent of the curve from the mean. We know that 50 percent of the area under the curve lies to the left of the mean. Thus, our chances of finishing before the latest allowable date (T_L) is approximately 87 percent. The remaining difference (13 percent) is the probability that we will finish after the latest allowable date.[1]

Before proceeding, let us examine Figures 3 and 4. Figure 3 illustrates the existence of zero slack on the critical path. In this case, Z would equal zero and the probability of meeting the latest allowable date (T_L) equals 0.50. Figure 4 illustrates a case where the (T_L) value lies to the left of the (T_E) value; that is, where we have negative slack on the critical path. In this case we know from the beginning that we have less time available to complete the job than we know we shall need. The shaded area in Figure 4 indicates the probability of finishing on time.

---

[1] This calculation assumes that the task times along any path are independent.

FIGURE 4

Probability Distribution $(T_L < T_E)$

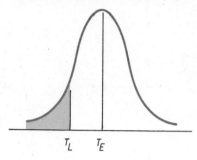

Here, Z will be negative and the probability value is equal to 0.50 minus the value in the table. In this case the probability of meeting the latest allowable date will be less than 0.50. The unshaded area in Figure 4 indicates the probability of being late which in this case is greater than 0.50.

Now let us return to the problem discussed in Chapter 16 and calculate the probability of achieving the completion date. First, we must calculate the standard deviations for each individual activity on the critical path. This is shown in Table 3.

TABLE 3

Standard Deviations for Critical Path Activities

Activity	Optimistic Time (a)	Pessimistic Time (b)	$\dfrac{b - a}{6}$	Standard Deviation (σ)
1–2	1	5	$\frac{4}{6}$	0.67
2–3	1	3	$\frac{2}{6}$	0.33
3–5	1	5	$\frac{4}{6}$	0.67
5–6	1	5	$\frac{4}{6}$	0.67
6–7	2	6	$\frac{4}{6}$	0.67
7–8	1	3	$\frac{2}{6}$	0.33

Now that we have the standard deviation for each activity on the critical path we can calculate the standard deviation for the network ending event.

$$\sigma T_E = \sqrt{\Sigma \sigma^2}$$
$$= \sqrt{(0.67)^2 + (0.33)^2 + (0.67)^2 + (0.67)^2 + (0.67)^2 + (0.33)^2}$$
$$= \sqrt{2.0}$$
$$\sigma T_E = 1.4 \text{ weeks}$$

Our next step is to compute the slack time on the critical path. We divide the slack time by the standard deviation of the network ending event (σT_E) in order to get the number of standard deviations Z the slack time represents. This is computed as follows:

$$Z = \frac{T_L - T_E}{\sigma T_E}$$

$$= \frac{20 - 17}{1.4}$$

$$Z = 2.14$$

Examining the Table of Areas under the Normal Curve reveals that a Z value of 2.14 encompasses 48.38 percent of the curve from the mean of a normal distribution. We know that 50 percent of the area under the curve lies to the left of the mean of a normal distribution. Our chances of finishing before the latest allowable date (T_L) of 20 weeks is about 98 percent, shown as the shaded area under the curve in Figure 5.

FIGURE 5

**Probability Distribution of
Network Ending Event**

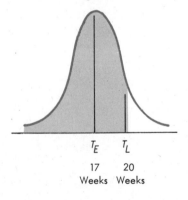

T_E T_L

17   20
Weeks   Weeks

Table of Areas under the Normal Curve

z	.00	.01	.02	.03	.04	.05	.06	.07	.08	.09
0.0	.0000	.0040	.0080	.0120	.0160	.0199	.0239	.0279	.0319	.0359
0.1	.0398	.0438	.0478	.0517	.0557	.0596	.0636	.0675	.0714	.0753
0.2	.0793	.0832	.0871	.0910	.0948	.0987	.1026	.1064	.1103	.1141
0.3	.1179	.1217	.1255	.1293	.1331	.1368	.1406	.1443	.1480	.1517
0.4	.1554	.1591	.1628	.1664	.1700	.1736	.1772	.1808	.1844	.1879
0.5	.1915	.1950	.1985	.2019	.2054	.2088	.2123	.2157	.2190	.2224
0.6	.2257	.2291	.2324	.2357	.2389	.2422	.2454	.2486	.2517	.2549
0.7	.2580	.2611	.2642	.2673	.2704	.2734	.2764	.2794	.2823	.2852
0.8	.2881	.2910	.2939	.2967	.2995	.3023	.3051	.3078	.3106	.3133
0.9	.3159	.3186	.3212	.3238	.3264	.3289	.3315	.3340	.3365	.3389
1.0	.3413	.3438	.3461	.3485	.3508	.3531	.3554	.3577	.3599	.3621
1.1	.3643	.3665	.3686	.3708	.3729	.3749	.3770	.3790	.3810	.3830
1.2	.3849	.3869	.3888	.3907	.3925	.3944	.3962	.3980	.3997	.4015
1.3	.4032	.4049	.4066	.4082	.4099	.4115	.4131	.4147	.4162	.4177
1.4	.4192	.4207	.4222	.4236	.4251	.4265	.4279	.4292	.4306	.4319
1.5	.4332	.4345	.4357	.4370	.4382	.4394	.4406	.4418	.4429	.4441
1.6	.4452	.4463	.4474	.4484	.4495	.4505	.4515	.4525	.4535	.4545
1.7	.4554	.4564	.4573	.4582	.4591	.4599	.4608	.4616	.4625	.4633
1.8	.4641	.4649	.4656	.4664	.4671	.4678	.4686	.4693	.4699	.4706
1.9	.4713	.4719	.4726	.4732	.4738	.4744	.4750	.4756	.4761	.4767
2.0	.4772	.4778	.4783	.4788	.4793	.4798	.4803	.4808	.4812	.4817
2.1	.4821	.4826	.4830	.4834	.4838	.4842	.4846	.4850	.4854	.4857
2.2	.4861	.4864	.4868	.4871	.4875	.4878	.4881	.4884	.4887	.4890
2.3	.4893	.4896	.4898	.4901	.4904	.4906	.4909	.4911	.4913	.4916
2.4	.4918	.4920	.4922	.4925	.4927	.4929	.4931	.4932	.4934	.4936
2.5	.4938	.4940	.4941	.4943	.4945	.4946	.4948	.4949	.4951	.4952
2.6	.4953	.4955	.4956	.4957	.4959	.4960	.4961	.4962	.4963	.4964
2.7	.4965	.4966	.4967	.4968	.4969	.4970	.4971	.4972	.4973	.4974
2.8	.4974	.4975	.4976	.4977	.4977	.4978	.4979	.4979	.4980	.4981
2.9	.4981	.4982	.4982	.4983	.4984	.4984	.4985	.4985	.4986	.4986
3.0	.4987	.4987	.4987	.4988	.4988	.4989	.4989	.4989	.4990	.4990

Glossary of Terms

Acceptance Theory of Authority A theory of authority which Barnard proposed according to which the ultimate source of authority is the decision of the subordinate to accept the superior's orders.

Accountability The process by which a subordinate reports the use of assigned resources to a designated superior.

Activity The work necessary to complete a particular event in a PERT network. It consumes time, which is the paramount variable in a PERT system. In PERT networks, three time estimates are used for each activity: an optimistic time, a pessimistic time, and a most likely time.

Administrative Duties The 16 guidelines which Fayol believed should direct the manager in carrying out the organizing function. There is considerable overlap between his 16 Administrative Duties and his 14 Management Principles.

Allocation Models This type of management science model is used in a situation where several possible candidates or activities are all competing for limited resources. It enables the user to allocate scarce resources in order to maximize some predetermined objective.

Anthropology Examines all the behaviors of man which have been learned. This includes social, technical, and family behaviors. It is often defined as the study of man and his works.

Authority The legitimate right to use assigned resources to accomplish a delegated task or objective. The right to give orders and to exact obedience. The legal bases for formal authority are private property, the state, or a Supreme Being.

Behavioral Change Planned change in the attitudes, skills, and knowledge of organizational personnel.

413

Behavioral Motivation Theory   The Behavioral School of Management advocates the pluralistic view of motivation which emphasizes that many different types of needs influence behavior, and that man is motivated by the desire to satisfy many needs.

Behavioral School of Management   A body of literature which is characterized by its concern for human behavior in the work environment. The school's primary means for acquiring knowledge is the scientific method with emphasis upon research. The School of Management thought which followed the Classical School. The first phase may be identified as "human relations" theory. This phase became popular in the 1940s and early 1950s. The second phase was the "behavioral science" approach which came into popular use in the early 1950s.

Behavioral Science Approach   This approach to the study of management can be thought of as the study of observable and verifiable human behavior in organizations, using scientific procedures. It draws especially from psychology, sociology, and anthropology.

Brand-Switching Models   This type of management science model provides the manager with some idea of the behavior of consumers in terms of their loyalty and their switching from one brand to another.

Bureaucracy   A form of organization which has many of the characteristics of the classical organization design, that is, it is highly structured and centralized, with narrow spans of control.

Carrying Costs   These are the costs incurred by carrying an inventory. They include such costs as the taxes and insurance on the goods in inventory, interest on money invested in inventory and storage space, and the costs incurred because of the obsolescence of the inventory.

Case Study   This type of research design attempts to examine numerous characteristics of a person or group over an extended period of time. Since the results achieved by a case study are usually based on a sample of one, the user cannot be certain as to their generality. Most case studies raise questions for future research.

Certainty Decisions   A decision is made in which the manager is certain about which state of nature or competitor action will occur. Thus, the probability that a particular event will occur is 1.00.

Classical Management Motivation Theory   The classical approach to motivation emphasized monetary incentives as prime means for motivating the individual. This approach was undoubtedly strongly influenced by the classical economists who emphasized man's rational pursuit of economic objectives.

Classical School of Management   A body of literature which represents the earliest attempts to define and describe the field of management. The school's main focus is on formally prescribed relationships. Its primary means for acquiring knowledge are personal observation and case studies.

Closed System (CS) Factors   Management concepts and techniques which focus upon greater order, systematization, routinization, and predictability. Most of the management science techniques and many classical concepts fall into this category.

Coercive Power   This is the power of a leader that is derived from fear on the part of the follower. The follower perceives the leader as a person who can punish deviant behavior and actions.

Command Group   The command group is specified by the formal organization chart. The group of subordinates who report to one particular supervisor constitutes the command group.

Comparative Management   This emerging field of study deals with problems of management and managerial effectiveness in various countries. It seeks to detect, identify, classify, measure, and interpret similarities and differences.

Components   These are the parts of a management science model. They may be firms, households, warehouses, costs, or any other factor which is part of the system or process being modeled.

Concurrent Control   Techniques and methods which focus on the actual, on-going activity of the organization.

Contingency Organizational Design   This is the view that the internal functioning of organizations must be consistent with the demands of the organization task, technology, and external environment, and the needs of its members if the organization is to be effective. Contingency design focuses on what is best for a particular organization.

Contributed Value   A measure of efficiency which relates value added to sales or profit.

Controlling Function   All managerial activity that is undertaken to assure that actual operations go according to plan.

Critical Path   This is the longest path in a PERT network, from the network beginning event to the network ending event.

Decentralization   This concept can be viewed as the pushing downward of the appropriate amount of decision-making authority. Each organization practices a certain degree of decentralization.

Decision Theory Models   Focus upon certain elements in decision making which are common to all decisions and provide means to enable a decision maker to better analyze a complex situation which contains numerous alternatives and possible consequences. Strongly rooted in the fields of statistics and the behavioral sciences.

Defense Mechanisms   When an individual is blocked in attempts to satisfy needs, one or more defense mechanisms may be evoked. Some of the most common are withdrawal, aggression, substitution, compensation, repression, regression, projection, and rationalization.

Departmentalization   The process of grouping jobs together on the basis of some common characteristic; typically, the basis is product, client, location, process, or function.

Descriptive Models   This type of model is one which describes how a system works. It describes things as they are and makes no value judgments about the particular thing being studied. It may display the alternative choices available to the decision maker, but it does not select the best alternative.

Determinants of Personality   The formation of the human personality is influenced by the mutual interaction of many factors. Four general classifications of factors must be considered: constitutional determinants, group-membership determinants, role determinants, and situational determinants.

Deterministic Models This refers to the type of variables included in the model. A model is deterministic when the law of chance plays no role. All the factors taken into account in the model are assumed to be exact or determinate quantities.

Dialectic Process of Change A concept which recognizes that any change which management implements in reaction to a particular problem will create new problems; the solution to a problem creates the environment within which new problems will emerge.

Direction A subfunction of control which refers to the manager's act of interpreting orders to a subordinate.

Discounted Rate of Return The rate of return which equates future cash proceeds and the initial cost of the investment.

Earliest Expected Date (T_E) This is found by calculating the *longest* path from the network beginning event to the particular event in question, whether it is the network ending event or some other event.

Econometric Analysis A technique which involves the specification of relationships among many variables and the verification of relationships through statistical techniques.

Emergent Leader The leader who emerges from within the group. This person is a personification of the group's attitudes, values, beliefs, and opinions.

EOQ Model This refers to the economic order quantity model. It is used to resolve size of order problems. A manager concerned with minimizing inventory costs could utilize the *EOQ* model to study the relationships between carrying costs, ordering costs, and demand.

Equal Profit Line Used in graphical solution, traces the path of the objective function across the feasibility space, for an arbitrary profit (cost) level. The level which passes through that point of the feasibility which is farthest to the right and upward is the profit at optimality.

Event An accomplishment at a particular point in time on a network. It consumes no time.

Expected Time (t_e) This is one time estimate for each activity in a PERT network calculated by using the formula:

$$t_e = \frac{a + 4m + b}{6},$$

Where:

a = optimistic time
m = most likely time
b = pessimistic time

Experiment This type of research design contains two key elements, namely, manipulation of some variable by the researcher and observation or measurement of the results.

Expert Power The power which individuals possess because followers perceive them to have a special skill or special knowledge or special expertise.

External and Environmental Constraints Scholars engaged in comparative management research have recognized that external cultural environments do affect the practice of management. Many of these scholars have attempted to identify the affect of cultural factors on the various management functions. They divide external and environmental constraints into four classes:

1. *Educational constraints.* These include such things as literacy level, the availability of specialized vocational and technical training, and the prevailing attitude toward education.
2. *Sociological-cultural constraints.* These include such factors as the general attitude of the society toward managers, dominant views of authority and subordinates, and the prevailing attitudes toward wealth and material gain.
3. *Legal-political constraints.* These include such factors as defense policy and national security, foreign policy, and political stability.
4. *Economic constraints.* These include such factors as the basic economic system in the country, whether private or public ownership prevails, and the extent to which the government controls economic activity.

Feasibility Space Only takes on meaning in a graphical solution, and then only in the two-dimensional case. Defines area which contains all combinations of all variables which satisfy the inequalities. Bounded by lines representing the structural constraints.

Feedback Control Techniques and methods which analyze historical data to correct future events.

First-Line Management The lowest level of a hierarchy; managers at this level coordinate the work of nonmanagers but report to a manager.

Fixed Costs These are costs that remain fixed regardless of the level of sales generated or the number of units produced. Costs such as property taxes, depreciation, and insurance premiums are considered fixed.

Flat Pyramid Structure An organization type that reduces the layers of management, widens the span of control of managers at various levels, and is often more decentralized with regard to decision-making autonomy.

Forecasting Projections of the future from which management derives budgets and plans.

Friendship Group A group that is established in the work place because of some common group characteristic (for example, the members like professional football), and that extends the interaction of members to include activities outside the work place.

Frustration This occurs when individuals are unable to satisfy their needs. Frustration may result in constructive problem-solving behavior or defensive behavior.

Functional Foremanship The application of division of labor at the foreman level, as suggested by F. W. Taylor. It involves splitting the task of the foreman into eight subtasks and assigning each subtask to a separate individual.

Goal Priority   The relative importance of goals, both in the short and long run.

Goal Structure   Refers to (1) the delegation of authority to pursue subgoals and (2) the relationship among multiple goals.

Graicunas' Law   A mathematical formulation of the relationship between the number of subordinates (N) and the number of potential superior–subordinate contacts (C), that is to say,

$$C = N \left(\frac{2^N}{2} + N - 1 \right).$$

Group Cohesiveness   The attraction of members to the group in terms of the desirability of group membership to the members. In a straightforward manner, this is the "stick-togetherness" of a group.

Hawthorne Studies   Provided the impetus for the human relations approach to management. The studies were conducted by a group of researchers from Harvard University at the Chicago Hawthorne Plant of Western Electric. The general progression of the research took place in four phases: (1) Experiments in Illumination, (2) Relay Assembly Test Room Experiment, (3) Interview Program, and (4) Bank Wiring Observation Room Experiment.

Hierarchy of Needs   A widely adopted pluralistic framework of motivation. Developed by psychologist A. H. Maslow, the theory stresses two ideas:

1. Only needs not yet satisfied can influence behavior.
2. Man's needs are arranged in a hierarchy of importance. When one level has been satisfied, a higher level need emerges and demands satisfaction.

Maslow also distinguishes five general classes of needs: physiological, safety, social, esteem, and self-actualization.

Horizontal Specialization of Management   The process by which the natural sequence of a task is broken down into specialized subgroups and a manager is assigned the authority and responsibility for coordinating the subgroups.

Human Relations Approach   Brought to the attention of management the important role that individuals play in determining the success or failure of an organization. It embarked on the critical task of compensating for some of the deficiencies in classical theory. Basically, it took the premises of the Classical School as given. However, it showed how these premises were modified as a result of individual behavior and the influence of the work group.

Incremental Influence   This concept refers to the influence of a leader over and above the influence base bestowed because of position in the organization.

Inequality   A functional relationship which allows latitude in variable values. Expresses either an upper or lower limit that combined variable values may take on.

Informal Group Norms   The agreement among group members to adhere to a level of production, a group attitude, or a group belief.

Insufficient-Reason Criterion   If a manager is operating under conditions of uncertainty, it is assumed that there is an equal probability that each of the possible states of nature or competitive actions may occur.

Interaction Analysis   The technique developed by R. F. Bales to study group interaction. Through the observation of groups working on solving a case, Bales determined that task and human relations specialists emerge. Based upon observing the group interactions and answers to questions as to what occurred within the group to solve the case, Bales developed an interaction profile.

Interest Group   A group that forms because of some special topic of interest. Generally, when the interest becomes weaker or a goal has been achieved, the group disbands.

Inventory Models   This type of management science model answers two questions relating to inventory management: "How much?" and "When?" It provides the manager with the point at which orders should be placed for repeat goods and the quantity of each order.

Investment Decisions   Decisions which commit present funds in exchange for potential future funds. These decisions are controlled through a capital budget.

Job Depth   The relative freedom that a job holder has in the performance of assigned duties.

Job Enlargement   This is a form of despecialization in that the number of tasks performed by the employee is increased. The increase in tasks theoretically makes the job more interesting and challenging and consequently work becomes more psychologically rewarding.

Job Enrichment   Suggested formally by Herzberg, this involves building into individual jobs greater scope for personal achievement, recognition, and responsibility. It is concerned with strengthening the motivational factors and is concerned only incidentally with maintenance.

Job Rotation   The procedure of moving a worker from one work station to another work station to minimize boredom.

Job Scope   The relative complexity of the assigned task as reflected by its cycle time.

Latest Allowable Date (T_L)   This is the latest date on which an event can occur without creating a delay in the scheduled completion of a PERT project. T_L for an ending event is equal to the date directed by management for completion of the project. If a directed date is not specified, then $T_L = T_E$ for the network ending event.

Leader-Member Relations   This is a dimension of leadership (Fiedler) that refers to the degree of confidence which followers have in their leader.

Leadership   A much defined, yet nebulous, term. In the context of the behavioral school the term refers to the ability of a person to influence the activities of followers in an organizational setting. The emphasis is on the fact that the leader must interact with his followers in order to be influential.

Legitimate Power   This refers to the power which a leader has in the managerial hierarchy because of rank. For example, the department manager who is ranked higher than the foreman in the managerial hierarchy, possesses more legitimate power.

Line Function   The activities of departments which contribute directly to the creation of the organization's output. In manufacturing, the line functions are manufacturing, marketing, and finance.

Maintenance Factors   Distinguished by Herzberg in his "two-factor" theory of motivation. Maintenance factors are those conditions of the job which operate primarily to dissatisfy employees when they are not present. However, their presence does not build strong motivation among employees. Herzberg distinguished 16 of these factors (for example, salary, job security, work conditions).

Management   The process of coordinating individual and group activity toward group goals.

Management by Objectives   A management technique which consists of the following major elements:

1. Superiors and subordinates meet to discuss goals and jointly establish attainable goals for the subordinate.
2. The superior and subordinate meet again after the initial goals have been set to evaluate the subordinate's performance in terms of the preestablished goals.

Management Functions   The activities which a manager must perform as a result of position in the firm. The text identifies planning, organizing, and controlling as the management functions.

Management Science   While it is difficult to place clear boundaries around this emerging discipline, we can say that most management science applications possess the following:

1. A primary focus on decision making.
2. An appraisal resting on economic effectiveness criteria.
3. Reliance on a formal mathematical model.
4. Dependence on an electronic computer.

Management Science School   A body of literature which is characterized by its use of mathematical and statistical techniques to build models for the solution of technical operational problems. The school's primary means for acquiring knowledge is mathematical deduction.

Marginal Costs   A cost concept popularized by economists. These are the costs incurred by producing one more unit.

Marginal Revenue   An economist-proposed concept that designates the additional revenue attained by selling one more unit.

Market Survey   A set of techniques which enables the manager to estimate the attitude of consumers toward aspects of a product or service.

Mathematical Model   A mathematical model is a simplified mathematical representation of the relevant aspects of an actual system or process.

Maximax Criterion   The optimistic manager believes that only the most favorable result will occur, and decides to maximize the maximum payoff.

Maximin Criterion The pessimistic manager believes that only the least favorable result will occur, and therefore decides to maximize the minimum payoff.

Metrocorporation This view is the extreme opposite of the *traditional corporation*. This view holds that the corporation has limitless social responsibilities and the managers hold themselves accountable to several groups in society.

Middle Management The middle level of an administrative hierarchy; managers at this level coordinate the work of managers and report to a manager.

Minimax Criterion The manager believes that once a decision is made and an outcome occurs, there will be some regret, and selects that strategy which results in the least regret.

Mooney's Theory of Organization A theoretical statement based upon Mooney's personal experience and his analysis of the forms which organizations have taken throughout history. According to Mooney, the underlying principle of all organizations is *coordination*, which is implemented through the *scalar* process. The result is a system of specialized tasks which Mooney terms the *functional* effect.

Motion Study The process of analyzing work in order to determine the preferred motions to be used in the completion of tasks. Motion study is a major contribution of scientific management, principally through the efforts of Taylor and Gilbreth.

Motivation This term is defined as the inner state that activates or moves. It can be described as all the inner striving conditions such as drives, desires, and motives.

Motivational Factors Distinguished by Herzberg in his "two-factor" theory of motivation. Motivational factors are those job conditions which, if present, operate to build high levels of motivation and job satisfaction. However, if they are not present, they do not prove highly dissatisfying. Herzberg distinguished six of these factors (for example, achievement, recognition, advancement).

Moving Budgeting A form of budgeting which involves periodic updating through time.

Multinational Firm A firm with branches, divisions, and subsidiaries in foreign countries. It is currently estimated that approximately 5,000 American firms operate in foreign nations.

Normative Model This type of model is specifically constructed to select from among alternatives the best alternative based on some previously determined criteria, which are also included in the model. It tells how the system should be in order to achieve a particular objective.

Objective Function Expression of the sole objective of the problem, maximize if profit, minimize if cost, made up of linear summation of the products of the quantity of each variable and the respective unit profit (cost).

Open System (OS) Factors Management concepts and techniques which focus upon developing greater openness, sharing, creativity, and individual initiative. Most of the behavioral concepts and many classical concepts fall into this category.

Ordering Costs   A major cost component that is considered in inventory control decisions. Each time the firm orders items for inventory, it must formally contact the supplier. This preparation usually includes some clerical and administrative work in placing the order and labor to put the items in inventory. The clerical, administrative, and labor costs make up the ordering cost element in inventory control models.

Organizational Change   The process of diagnosing and implementing changes in the structural, behavioral, or technological components of an organization.

Organizational Psychology   Studies man's behavior and attitudes within an organizational setting, including the effect of the organization upon the individual and the individual's effect upon the organization.

Organization Structure   The formally defined framework of task and authority relationships. It is analogous to the biological concept of the skeleton.

Organizing Function   All managerial activity which results in the design of a formal structure of tasks and authority.

Participative Approach   A technique advocated by behavioralists which stresses the idea that employees throughout the firm should be allowed to participate in decision-making.

Payback Period   The length of time that it takes for an investment to pay for itself out of future funds.

Payoff Table   A two-dimensional array of data which indicates in tabular form the payoffs for various strategy, state of nature, or competitive action combinations.

Personal-Behavioral Theories   This refers to a group of leadership theories that are based primarily on personal and behavioral characteristics of leaders. Included in this category are theories based on opinion and on extensive research in actual organizations.

Personality   The general sum of traits or characteristics of an individual. It is a very important determinant of individual behavior and motivation.

Planning Function   All managerial activities which lead to the definition of goals and to the determination of appropriate means to achieve those goals.

Preliminary Control   Consists of techniques and methods which attempt to maintain the quality and quantity of resources.

Principles of Management   In classical management theory, "principles of management" refers either to rules of conduct which should guide manager's behavior or to the underlying laws of nature which determine the structure of organizations.

Probabilistic Models   Models based on the mathematics of statistics. Conditions of uncertainty are introduced in the model often based on observations of real-world events.

Profitability Measures   Measurements of efficiency in the business firm; may be the ratio of net profit either to capital or to total assets or to sales.

Psychology   The study of human behavior. This behavioral science and many of its branches have provided many concepts and theories useful in the study of management.

Rate of Return   A general concept which refers to the ratio of annual returns to the initial cost of the investment.

Reality-Centered Management   A view of management which recognizes a need for a balance of classical, behavioral, and management science approaches, as well as experience. Reality-centered managers would seek to blend both experience and the schools of management and recognize that in order to be effective in the contemporary organization they cannot rely solely on one approach.

Referent Power   This refers to the power of a leader based on attractiveness. That is, the leader is admired because of some personal qualities and the follower identifies closely with these characteristics.

Reward Power   This refers to the power generated by the perception of followers that compliance with the wishes of leaders can lead to positive rewards (for example, promotion).

Risk Decisions   These are decision situations in which managers do not know for certain the probability of occurrence of the state of nature or competitive actions. However, they have some past experience and/or data upon which they can rely to develop probabilities. These probabilities are used with conditional values to determine expected values.

Sample Survey   In this type of research design, the collection of data is from a limited number of units which are assumed to be representative of the entire group.

Scalar Chain   The graded chain of authority through which all communications flow.

Sensitivity Training   A form of educational experience which stresses the process and emotional aspects of learning.

Simulation Models   Simulation involves constructing a model which replicates some aspect of the firm's operation and by performing step-by-step computations with the model, duplicates the manner in which the actual system might perform.

Situational Theory   The situational theory of leadership advocates an approach in which the leader understands behavior of self, the behavior of followers, and the situation at hand before adopting a particular style.

Slack Time   This is the time to spare in the completion of an event. It is found by using the formula:

$$\text{Slack Time } (S) = T_L - T_E$$

Slack Variable   Variable introduced into constraint inequalities in order to form equalities. Their unit profit (cost) is zero.

Social Psychology   This branch of psychology deals with the behavior of individuals as they relate to other individuals.

Social Responsibility   During the last decade, society has been placing increased demands on large business organizations for greater social responsibility—that is, business involvement in solving both social and ecological problems.

Sociogram   A diagram which illustrates the interpersonal relationships existing within a group. By use of the sociogram it is possible to trace communication patterns within a group.

Sociology   Attempts to isolate, define, and describe human behavior in groups. It strives to develop laws and generalizations about human nature, social interaction, culture, and social organization.

Sociometric Analysis   The use of self-reports to find personal preference and repulsion patterns of members of work groups.

Soldiering   A term which was used during the scientific management era to refer to the observed practice of output restriction. That is, workers were observed to be producing at a lower rate than what would ordinarily be expected.

Staff Functions   The activities of departments which contribute indirectly to the creation of the organization's output. Ordinarily, the staff personnel advise line personnel.

Status Consensus   The agreement of group members about the relative status of members of the group.

Status Hierarchy   The ranking of a group member within the group, that is, the prestige rank order of group members forms the status hierarchy.

Structural Change   Planned changes in the formally prescribed task and authority relationships.

Structure (in Group Context)   The term "structure" refers to relatively stable relationships among members of a work group. It is basically the group culture which influences the group's reward system—norms, among other things.

Suboptimization   The objectives which a manager is attempting to achieve are often dependent. Thus, the optimization of one can result in a lower degree of attainment for at least some of the multiple objectives. This lower degree of attainment is known as suboptimization.

Supervision   A subfunction of control which refers to the oversight of subordinate's work activity.

System-4 Organization   An organizational type which stresses open, supportive leadership and group methods for decision making and goal setting.

Tall Pyramid Structure   A structure which fosters narrow spans of control, a large number of management levels, and more centralized decision making.

Task Group   A formal group of individuals working as a unit to complete a task.

Task Structure   This refers to the degree of structure imposed on the follower's job. The job may be routine or non-routine. If the job were routine it would be spelled out in detail—an inspector on the assembly line. While the job of the research scientist has relatively little task structure.

Technological Change   Planned changes in the use of techniques and knowledge appropriate for the organization's purpose.

Theory X   A set of assumptions about the nature of man which, according to Douglas McGregor, underlies the classical management theory. The assumptions stress the indolent characteristics of man.

Theory Y   An approach to management which is based on assumptions which are exactly the opposite of Theory X. They are:

1. Workers do not inherently dislike work.
2. Workers do not want to be controlled and threatened.
3. Workers under proper working conditions seek out additional responsibility.
4. Workers desire to satisfy other needs besides those related to job security.

Time Series Analysis A statistical technique for analyzing the relationship between a specified variable and time.

Time Study The process of determining the appropriate elapsed time for the completion of a task or job. It was part of F. W. Taylor's effort to determine a fair day's work.

Top Management The top level of an administrative hierarchy; managers at this level coordinate the work of other managers, but do not report to a manager.

Traditional Corporation This concept of the corporation views it as an instrumentality of a single group—the shareholders—and has one clear-cut purpose: conducting business for their maximal profit. This view recognizes no public responsibilities except for legal ones and leaves the public interest to the care of the state.

Trait Theory The trait theory attempts to specify which personal characteristics (physical, personality, mental) are associated with leadership success. It relies on research that relates various traits to success criteria.

Uncertainty Decisions These are decision situations in which no past experience or historical data is available. Thus, any one of a number of criteria are employed depending upon the personality of the manager.

Unity of Command A management principle which states that each subordinate should report to only one superior.

Unity of Direction The process of grouping all related activities under one superior.

Unsatisfied Need An unsatisfied need is the starting point in the process of motivation. It is a deficiency of something within the individual that provides the spark which leads to behavior.

Variable Budgeting A form of budgeting which targets expected costs at various potential output levels.

Variable Costs These represent costs that vary closely with changes in production. For example, as the number of units produced increases, the amount of material used also increases. Thus, the cost of material used to produce a product would be an example of variable costs.

Vertical Specialization of Management The process by which the right to command is delegated downward so as to create a hierarchy of positions graded by degrees of assigned authority.

Vroom's Model One of the more recent models of motivation which expands upon those developed by Maslow and Herzberg. It views motivation as a process governing choices and explains how the *goals* of individuals influence their *effort*.

Waiting-Line Models Waiting-line models enable the manager to reach optimal decisions in facilities planning. They help in striking a balance between the cost of additional facilities and some other factor such as idle time or customer ill will.

Well-Tempered Corporation This view lies between the two extremes of the *traditional corporation* and the *metrocorporation*. This type of corporation takes into account public expectations, but also does not conflict with management's responsibilities to the stockholders. This viewpoint holds that the claims of stockholders and creditors will more likely be met if a firm develops a position as a socially responsible company.

Indexes

Name Index

Subject Index

This book has been set in 10 and 9 point Caledonia, leaded 2 points. Part numbers are 24 point Scotch Roman italic and chapter numbers are 36 point Scotch Roman italic. Part titles are 24 point Scotch Roman and chapter titles are 18 point Scotch Roman. The size of the type page is 27 x 45½ picas.

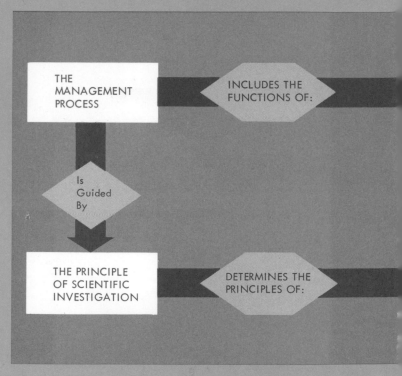